WALK
ON
GLASS

WALK ON GLASS

Lisa Robinson

 Newmarket Press *New York*

Copyright © 1982 by Lisa Robinson

Library of Congress Cataloging in Publication Data

Robinson, Lisa.
  Walk on glass.

  I. Title.
PS3568.03122W3   *813'.54*   *82-2254*
ISBN 0-937858-05-6   *AACR2*

FIRST EDITION

1 2 3 4 5 6 7 8 9 0   F/C

Manufactured in the United States of America

For my parents and for Richard

WALK ON GLASS

1

WINTER, 1974

Jeff couldn't believe Marty Paretta's office. A tank full of brightly colored tropical fish was built into the length of an entire wall. One corner of the huge room was taken up by an electronic bowling game and an Elton John pinball machine. Every available surface was covered with Marty's collections of art deco paperweights, antique clocks, bubble gum machines and chocolate-chip-shaped cookie jars. A large neon dollar sign flashed on and off, and a massive bronze gong loomed behind Marty's desk. Gold records—tokens of gratitude from musicians with whom Marty had worked—lined the walls.

Jeff saw all this and knew he was home.

Marty sat behind the huge, cluttered desk and cleaned his nails with a stretched-out paper clip. He was unnaturally tanned, dressed in an expensive beige leisure suit with the jacket unbuttoned almost to the waist, and pants that fit too snugly across his stocky thighs. His thinning, dyed black hair was slicked and shiny across his head. Gold rings adorned the fingers of both hands. His looks contrasted sharply with Jeff's; not only because Jeff was twenty years younger, and wore faded jeans and a T-shirt, but because Marty no longer looked hungry. As head of contemporary talent at the ACS Talent Agency, he had a percentage of the top rock acts he had brought there. He was Major.

"Look," said Marty, across the large fake marble desk. "Before you begin, let me tell you something. I won't go down there. I don't go below Fourteenth Street. You can't pee in those places."

"Marty," said Jeff, leaning on the desk across from him, "I want you to know, I was practically out the door of Brandy's, leaving, when I heard her start to sing. I walked all the way back inside. Lindel James is a fucking knockout. She's the new Janis."

Marty rolled his eyes and leaned back in his chair. "*Every* chick is the next Janis. *I* remember when every chick was the next Streisand. Meanwhile Janis, God rest her soul, was a big pain in the ass."

"I didn't mean she was *like* Janis," Jeff said quickly. "I assure you, Lindel doesn't touch a drug. But the energy, the voice, it's unbelievable. And she's gorgeous. Long, jet-black hair. The most amazing eyes you ever saw. They're so intense. And the body." Jeff shook his head. "You gotta see her, Marty." He paused. "Lindel James is *money*."

The phone rang. Marty looked at the intercom. One second later it buzzed, and with a look of relief, Marty picked up the phone.

"Yeah," he said, "put him on." After about ten seconds, he shouted into the phone, "Screw him! Let him *go* to Marino. We booked that little pisher when he was *nothing*."

He slammed down the receiver, looked at Jeff, and sighed. "Where was I?" He stared straight ahead for a few seconds, then said, "Listen, you know Charlie Schwarz? Probably not, he was before your time. He used to manage The Bums. Lead singer used to dress up in a chicken costume. No? Well, anyway, they had a few big hits in the late sixties."

Marty paused, as if trying to recall just which hits they were. He went on. "Anyway, he comes in to see me the other day. I ask him, 'Charlie, what can I do for you?' I figure, he has some act. For old times' sake, I'll talk to the guy. Comes in, I swear I'm not making this up, with a huge rubber band. I mean a *huge* rubber band, must have been four feet long, and six, eight inches wide. Maybe two inches thick."

Jeff started to speak but Marty held up a hand. "No, wait, listen," he said. "That guy had a group that had two top forties, and I think maybe even a gold album, for Christ's sake. I mean he was something, you know? Comes in here six years later with a goddamned *rubber band*."

"Marty, I don't see the point . . ."

Marty's eyes widened. "*Shmuck*. He comes in here and tells me that this rubber band is the *next big thing*. Bigger than The Beatles, he says. Tells me it's a toy, a hammock, kids can swing in it, he says. Wants me to help him market it. Get rock stars to endorse it. To *pose* in it. It'll make a fortune, he says."

"Marty, what the fuck does this have to do with my singer?"

"You don't get it?"

"Get what?"

Marty's shoulders dropped. He stared at Jeff.

"Listen," he tried again, "last week another asshole comes in here with some fluorescent blue jewelry he wants to peddle at rock concerts. Shines in the dark, he says, and he turns out the lights, and so it does. Probably also causes cancer."

"*What* is the connection here?"

"Jesus." Marty raised his voice. "You think that this chick is great, someone else comes in here and wastes my time with a rubber band or jewelry what glows in the dark. You know how many there are out there?"

"How many what? What are you talking about? This *is* a talent agency, right?"

"Shmuck, there are all kinds of definitions of talent."

Jeff stared with disbelief.

"Look," said Marty, "she has no record contract, right?"

Jeff waved his hands. He got up and started pacing in front of Marty's desk.

"You never heard a voice like this," Jeff said, excited now, talking with an almost evangelical zeal. "It's a cross between that cool kind of Laura Nyro thing, and, oh . . . just the hottest rock and roller. That's why I said Janis. But it's more than that. She's special. There are no comparisons. Could you compare Mick Jagger with anyone? Or Jimi Hendrix? Or Tina Turner?"

"Sit down," Marty commanded. "You're making me nervous."

Jeff sat down. He absentmindedly twisted a strand of his curly brown hair around his forefinger.

"Meanwhile, she has no record contract," Marty repeated. "And she's played in these Village dumps for how long?"

"Only a few months," Jeff mumbled.

"Then how come no one else has heard of her? What, you ran around town with a glass slipper?"

"Christ!" Jeff exploded. "I would think that you'd be glad I got to her first."

Marty sighed. He opened the top of the huge glass jar filled with Perugina chocolates and popped one in his mouth. He offered one to Jeff, who shook his head impatiently. "Look, sweetheart," Marty said, "I don't know how to tell you this, you being fresh out of the mailroom and so enthusiastic and all, but this business is just not as speculative as it once was. It's no longer the alternative culture or the goddamn Woodstock generation. The days of a Clive Davis shlepping to a San Francisco to sign anything that drew breath are finito."

"You'd have to have been deaf, dumb and blind not to have gone there then and done that," retorted Jeff. "That was hardly the radical step, and seven years later, he's still dining out on it."

"Well, how many others did it?" Marty said. "Anyway, things are different now. Without record company advertising and tour support, I can't afford to take a chance on a new act. It's as simple as that. When she gets a deal, *then* we'll talk." Tossing the paper clip he'd been playing with into the wastebasket, Marty looked at Jeff, and then, pointedly, at his own huge gold digital watch.

Without budging an inch from his chair, Jeff said quietly, "When she gets a fucking deal, I won't need you. I'm giving you a chance of getting in on the ground floor."

Marty's laugh was short and unpleasant. "You know something? I'm tired of getting in on the ground floor. We sign a Zeppelin, for example. We spend years building them, they get big, and then they go off and book their own tours to save the goddamn ten percent. That's what that phone call was about a few minutes ago. I won't even tell you the name of the act this time. It makes me sick."

Neither one of them said anything for a few seconds. Jeff reached into his jeans pocket for a stick of gum. Marty rearranged some papers on his desk. He muttered, "Today The Vipers' lawyer is coming to see me. Goddamn English groups are all a pain in the ass." He looked toward the window.

"Marty," Jeff said, "we're not through here. I don't have a demo to play you because I'm not going begging to the record companies. But by the time I get through, everyone's going to want her. See her at the Grotto, as a favor to me."

"Jeff," Marty said gently, "I don't go see new acts."

"You don't go see new acts?" Jeff was incredulous. "Then how the fuck does anyone get signed around here?"

"Acts come to me already established." Marty sounded impatient. "Or people tell me things. Sometimes I wish they wouldn't. Like these Vipers. We signed them because some secretary who's supposed to have great ears tells us she saw their picture in *Melody Maker* and they're big there. Big there, ha. The number of big British bands who can't get arrested in America . . ."

Marty's voice trailed off, and again he looked at his watch.

He continued, "Anyway, we take a chance on them, and now, for their first American tour, the goddamned lead singer has to *approve* everything. I never heard of such a thing. We get them a decent tour, headlining, even, in small but respectable halls—based on their goddamn English reputation and support from Acme who distribute their records here—and this lunatic says not enough coloreds."

"What?"

"Brian Davis," Marty said. "The lead singer. *He* has to decide who's opening for them. He's lucky he's not the opening act. He wants to remind the American kids where their music comes from. Can you imagine this?" Marty laughed and shook his head. He went on, "Who the hell does he think is coming to see his band? Kids, with long hair, who get stoned and drink beer and throw up or whatever it is that they do. They do *not* want to see some ancient shvoogola what sits on a stool playing the goddamn blues. They don't even want to see the shvartze groups with the dance routines and the turquoise suits. But this kid wants coloreds, so we have to round some up. I don't even know where to *find* any."

"Marty, please. Forget that for a minute." Jeff stood up again and walked behind Marty and then back in front of the desk. "I'm not some secretary with ears who reads *Melody Maker*. I'm telling you, Lindel James is worth checking out. If I didn't know this, would I be getting personally involved in this way?"

"Look, you're a decent kid." Marty leaned back in his chair and yawned. "You've been out of the mailroom now what, one month? I know you want to be an agent, but you can't begin by bringing us someone who's not even signed to a record company."

"That's ridiculous. People signed already have agents."

"That is often the case. You have a point. But, on the other hand, people change agents all the time. That's what you said you were going to do. Steal people. Get out there, in all those toilets you say you hang out in. Find out who's unhappy where, get them here. Not to try and unload some cockamamie unknown."

Jeff leaned down toward Marty, his hands on the desk. "All I'm asking you to do is come and see her when she's at the Grotto. Or, get some people from the record companies to come, stir up some interest. You know those people. I assure you, it wouldn't be an embarrassment for you to do this. Honestly, Marty, trust me on this one. My ass is on the line too. After all, I'm managing her. Would I steer you wrong?"

Marty never liked it when someone said "honestly." He knew that Jeff Stein, if given the opportunity, would steer him wrong in a minute. He hadn't meant it when he called him a decent kid. The little creep was a born killer.

He sighed. He doodled on a pad, the one that said "Calm Down." Why didn't the phone ring now, he wondered. He wasn't even sure why he had bothered at all with this kid. He just sensed there was something about Jeff Stein; he was fast. It would be better to keep him on his side for as long as he could.

"Look," said Marty, "I like you. But not that much. I'll call Tim Harrison over at Jacar. That fruit is always on the lookout for new stuff. But that's it. I'm not calling in any favors with the heavies on this one."

The phone rang. The meeting was over. Jeff started to thank Marty, but Marty was already talking into the receiver and waved Jeff out of the office. As he started to leave, Jeff looked at his watch. He had counted on five minutes for this exchange. He was mistaken by only twenty seconds.

Lindel James leaned down to tune her guitar and pushed her long, dark hair out of her eyes. In ten minutes she would go onstage and sing to this room full of strangers. Facing an audience, any audience, wasn't easy. To get on a stage was to climb over a very high invisible wall, one too high to go back over if she changed her mind. She was terrified to reveal herself in this way, but she had always known that she had no other choice.

The dressing room at Brandy's was tiny and bare except for two chairs, a large mirror on one wall, and a metal garbage can filled to the brim with empty beer bottles. The walls were dark gray—badly in need of a fresh coat of paint—and big chunks of plaster threatened to fall from the ceiling. Three nights ago, when Lindel had first met Jeff Stein, he had tried to convince her to forget about singing in Brandy's again but she needed the money, and she felt obligated to finish the five-night engagement. Tonight was the last night, and she wondered if Jeff would show up. He said he had to meet some record company people; he hinted that it had something to do with her. She wondered if he really meant all the things he had said when they met. For so long she had needed someone to tell her what he told her that night.

Now Jerry Paulsen, the bartender who also ran the stage lights, stuck his head into the dressing room.

"You're on in five minutes, okay?" he said. "And you'll never guess who's out there."

He paused dramatically.

Lindel looked at him.

"Who?" she said.

"Carla Martin." He let the name sink in.

Carla Martin—America's current folk rock princess. She had worked her way up from the streets of Greenwich Village to superstar status in Los Angeles, and now, even though her record sales were not what they once were, she had a huge concert following.

"What's *she* doing here?" Lindel said, feeling a stab of anxiety.

"She's with a whole crowd," said Jerry. "I guess she stops in every now and then for old times' sake. She got her start here, you know."

How could one not know, thought Lindel. There was a photo of Carla as large as a billboard in the front of the club. But all Lindel said was, "Don't tell me where she's sitting, I'll get too nervous."

Jerry raised an eyebrow. "I wouldn't have thought you'd care about Carla Martin," he said. "She's real brown rice and granola. Not your kind of music at all."

"I know . . ." muttered Lindel, getting up to check her face in the mirror. "Still . . ."

"Of course she doesn't seem to be like her image at all," Jerry hinted darkly, but before Lindel could ask him what he meant, he was gone.

Lindel looked into the mirror and automatically put some Vaseline on her lips and more kohl around her eyes. Somehow, knowing that Carla Martin was in the audience made tonight seem that much more special. Lindel tried to tell herself that it shouldn't make a difference, but nevertheless, it did. For six months Lindel had performed in these showcase clubs to half-empty rooms, to drunks, and to tourists who yelled out requests for old Dylan or Peter, Paul and Mary tunes. Obviously, Carla Martin had not come to see her; she was probably just making a nostalgia tour of her old stomping grounds or worse, slumming, but still ... you never knew. Lindel had heard all these stories about musicians who helped each other. Linda Ronstadt had helped three of her backup singers get recording contracts. Carly Simon wrote songs for her friend, Libby Titus. David Bowie had produced Iggy Stooge and Lou Reed. Elton John had signed singer Kiki Dee to his own record label. Such things happened all the time. Maybe Carla Martin would like her.

Lindel picked up her guitar and went to the door of the dressing room. She opened it, took a deep breath, and started to walk down the long, narrow hallway that led to the dark club with its small wooden stage. She felt the familiar nervousness begin, the adrenalin start to go. In a few minutes she'd be onstage. She was ready. She'd been ready for this for almost all of her twenty-four years.

As she walked onstage, Lindel immediately saw Carla Martin seated at the center of a large table right down front, surrounded by men, at least one of whom looked like a bodyguard. Carla Martin was a short, buxom girl with masses of long, red, curly hair. She was leaning across the table and talking in a loud voice to a very good-looking blond boy who could not have been much older than nineteen. There was a champagne bucket on the table with a bottle stuck in it and the club's owner, Tommy Slater, was fussing over Carla and her party like a mother hen.

Lindel tried not to look at the table. But, as she sat down, and waited in the semidarkness for her name to be announced, it was impossible not to look at Carla Martin. Carla appeared harder, somehow, than in her photographs. And she looked tired, drawn. Tommy was refilling all the glasses at the table and purposely ignoring the small glass vial of white powder that Carla had passed to the good-looking young blond boy. Everyone was aware of Carla—either fawning over her or trying to pretend that they weren't looking at her—but Carla wasn't smiling.

"Ladies and gentlemen," Jerry announced over the sound system, "Brandy's is proud to present . . . Lindel James."

There was some scattered applause, the talking in the room subsided a bit, and Lindel felt her heart beating so fast, so loud, that she was afraid she might faint.

She sat on a high stool at the center of the stage, and picked up her guitar. She started to sing, softly at first, then her eyes closed, and feeling the surge of power that always came with the music, she sang louder, stronger.

She could never explain the way she felt when she sang. Even with just the guitar, she heard so much more in her head. The music was something that she always felt she could count on. No matter what else happened, she had this. When she sang, she felt in control.

She was midway through the second song when she heard the crash. Someone had dropped a glass—or several glasses—on the floor. Lindel continued to sing, trying not to look in the direction of the commotion. The noise got louder, with chairs being pushed back from tables and suddenly a voice yelled out of the darkness, "Get the fuck off the stage!"

Lindel froze. Carla Martin stood up, eyes blazing, a bottle of champagne in her hand, and she headed for the stage. Two of the men and the young blond boy at her table tried to restrain her but she shook them off and stormed to the side of the stage and was up the few steps and standing next to Lindel before anyone realized what was happening.

Lindel just sat there, rooted to the chair, unable to think or to move.

"*Listen, you bitch,*" Carla Martin leaned over and hissed into Lindel's face, "*I* feel like singing now, okay? So you can just get the hell off, *now.*" And she aimed the open bottle of champagne in Lindel's direction and a full spray of the bubbly, stinging liquid went directly into Lindel's face.

It could not have been more than two seconds that Lindel sat there, stunned, staring at Carla, who was shaking, quite drunk, but it seemed like forever. *Help me,* Lindel was thinking, not knowing to whom she was directing the silent plea, not knowing what to do, where to go.

And then in an instant there were people all around them; pulling Carla off the stage, Tommy frantically whispering to Lindel, "Sing, goddammit, *sing!*" and Lindel, her eyes stinging from tears and champagne, shaking her head, getting up, whispering, "I . . . can't . . ." and running off the stage into the dressing room.

Twenty minutes later, Lindel still sat in the dressing room, staring into space. Her hair was wet, stringy, and smelled sour from the champagne. The mascara streaked down her face, and she silently smoked a cigarette. Jerry leaned against the wall, and looked at her with concern.

"Listen," he said, "let me at least put you in a cab, send you home, *something.*"

Lindel shook her head slowly. She didn't say anything. She felt numb.

Jerry stood up. "Look, you won't let me do anything for you?"

Lindel again shook her head no.

"Well, I'll go find Tommy. At least we can get you your bread and you can go home."

"I don't want to go out there," Lindel whispered.

"Honey, I told you, she's gone. They cleared her out and into the limo right away. Jesus, was she loaded! I'd been hearing rumors, but I didn't think it was that bad . . ."

"Why did she do it?" Lindel said softly, looking up at Jerry, who stood at the door. "I don't understand."

"Who knows?" Jerry said. "Jealousy, maybe. Could be that one of the guys at the table made a flattering remark about you and it pissed her off. In the state she's in, between the booze and the coke, her nerves are on edge, she's jagged. Probably hasn't slept for days. Under pressure. Stardom and all that." He gave a short laugh and left the room.

Lindel sat alone for a very long time. So many thoughts raced around in her head. Things she should have done, should have said. She should have kept on singing. She felt drained, humiliated.

After awhile, when Jerry did not return, she packed her guitar in its case and put on her coat and went inside to the bar. The lights were on, the room was empty, and the chairs were on the tables. It must have been close to four A.M. Jerry was behind the bar, counting money, closing up.

"Where's Tommy?" said Lindel, sitting on a barstool.

Jerry turned to face her. "Didn't he come in to see you?" he said.

"No, why?" Lindel said.

Jerry looked embarrassed. "Oh, Jesus. Look, I might as well tell you, he's obviously such a prick he's split for the night . . ."

"Tell me what?"

"He's not going to pay you for the last three nights."

"What?" Lindel raised her voice.

"He's pissed off you didn't finish the set. You were signed for five full nights, and since you didn't sing tonight . . ."

Lindel stared at him. "Are you serious?"

"Afraid so. Want a drink?"

"No, I do not want a drink," she said, visibly angry. "I want the money he owes me."

"Here," Jerry said, pouring a glass of wine and putting it in front of her. "You need it."

Lindel lit a cigarette. "I can't believe this. First Carla . . . Now he's not paying me? It wasn't my fault that I didn't finish the set."

"Doesn't matter," Jerry said, putting dollar bills in a pile. "You signed on for the whole engagement, and he gave you money for two nights up front. You technically didn't finish the full engagement, so he feels he doesn't have to pay you."

"How can he get away with it?" Lindel said.

"Oh, it happens a lot around here."

Lindel took a sip of wine. She stared helplessly at Jerry. "Isn't there anything I can do?"

"I'd suggest that you get yourself a good manager," Jerry said.

Lindel didn't answer. She knew she should go home, get some sleep. But she couldn't leave; she just sat there watching Jerry close up the bar, aware of the familiar smell of stale beer and wet dollar bills.

The night had been a disaster. And she had started out so full of hope.

She knew that the time had come; she had to do something to change her life.

Lindel walked into her bedroom, lay down on the bed, and lit a cigarette. The sun was starting to come up and the sky was a dark, royal blue velvet. A gentle wind caused the white organdy curtains to flap softly against the open window. She loved those curtains; they had been in her bedroom in her Livingston, New Jersey home ever since she could remember, and even though this apartment was bare—except for the bed and in the living room, a piano and record cabinet—these curtains she had brought with her from home gave her a sense of stability, of permanence. And while her sense of home, of having to belong somewhere, had always been important, it was the music that came first, and because of it Lindel had always known she was different.

For as long as she could remember, there had been music in her house. Her mother played the piano, there was a large classical music record collection, and Lindel loved to sing. And when people asked her what she wanted to be when she grew up, she would answer without a moment's hesitation that she was going to be a singer. They probably would have laughed at her had she said what she really felt—that she was a singer already.

Even as a young girl her voice was not the standard pretty one; it was unusual—throaty, sensual, not a child's voice at all. In school she would keep her voice down low during the national anthem, not wanting to be singled out. Sometimes she was aware of the strange looks that passed between her parents when they heard her sing. Lindel possessed something she did not totally understand, and it made her feel like a freak.

Except for the music, Lindel's home was quiet. The telephone rarely rang. Her parents—shy, solitary people—had little social life and they did not encourage their only child to bring friends home. It was as if they thought that the closeness of their small family could somehow protect them all from the outside world.

As Lindel got older, she wrote little songs, figuring out the melodies on the piano, writing down the words and keeping them in secret journals. She couldn't read music but didn't need to; she never forgot one note of any song she ever wrote. It was all in her head; it was hers alone.

She'd lie in bed late at night and hear the train whistle and the crickets outside the window. She'd wait for her parents to go to bed; she'd lie absolutely still until she heard them shut their door. Even then, it wasn't completely safe—not until she heard the faint sounds of her father's snoring.

Then, almost like a secret ritual she'd pull the covers up over her head and turn on the small transistor radio and listen to the New York stations, devouring the music. Turning the dials until she heard jazz—feeling as if her heart would break at the wondrous piano of Thelonius Monk, feeling sophisticated, listening to the cool saxophone of Sonny Rollins. The disc jockeys, with their smooth, knowing voices, talked directly and personally to her. She'd find a gospel station, and she'd shut her eyes tight and imagine herself in the middle of a large choir, wearing a long red robe, clapping her hands, carried away with the emotional sound of this music that was so unlike anything she'd ever heard. It was like listening to the highest poets; and she knew that she was indirectly in the presence of something great, of people who could *command* a room. These musicians were more than inspiration; they were her friends.

But most of all, there was the rock and roll. Elvis Presley, Chuck Berry, and later on, The Rolling Stones and the music from Motown—all of it dark, almost forbidden, yet, instant recognition. She had to be alone with this music, only then was she able to imagine.

To imagine what it would be like when she got onstage. How she would be able to get out all those things she had been keeping inside. No one knew, not yet. But they would one day.

Sometimes when she was alone in the house in the afternoons, before her mother came home from work at the bookstore and her father from the office, she'd play her records, the records she went to New York City to buy. She was glad she had no brothers and sisters, no one to have to worry about hearing her as she sang along, in front of the mirror, watching herself. She had no real sense of what she might look like to others; foolish, possibly, or too big, probably, but inside, she felt wild.

It had been well over a year and a half since she had come to New York to try and sing in public for the first time. And then there had been David, and she had been sidetracked.

In the six months since the breakup with David, Lindel once again became obsessed with her music. But it was hard to write songs when she had to worry about the details of a career. She wondered if Jeff Stein was really going to help. Certainly when she met him, three nights ago, she could almost hear the pieces of her life fall into place. What she liked most about him was that he didn't seem scared of anything. She wondered what he would have done tonight.

Now she just wanted to go to sleep. To blot out this terrible night. And to wake up tomorrow morning and let Jeff Stein take care of everything for her. He said he could set up a showcase at the Grotto next week. Maybe he would be able to make it all work, to make everything all right.

Carefully, methodically, Tim Harrison laid out four lines of cocaine on a small mirror while Ronnie Marren flipped through the pages of the latest issue of *Rock Scene*. The two of them were alone, in Ronnie's office in the Blue Grotto, and it was ten-thirty. Way too early for the backroom crowd. Tim liked these private times; there were few distractions, and he could get more than his usual share of Ronnie's attention.

"What do you hear about the Electric Toys?" said Tim, passing the mirror across the desk to Ronnie. Ronnie leaned down and, holding a finger against one nostril, did two lines with a plastic straw.

"They're still looking for a manager, and a record deal," said Ronnie. "They don't want that much, maybe twenty thousand dollars to sign, which, of course, will be applied toward their recording budget. And they'll settle for an eight percent royalty rate. It looked like Atlantic was interested, but Bobby told me that no one there returns his calls."

"The *singer* shouldn't be making the calls. Why don't they just get a good lawyer?"

"Probably can't afford it." Ronnie picked up the phone and pressed the intercom button. "Send in a waitress," he said into the phone and hung up. He leaned back in his chair and, picking up a pair of mirrored sunglasses from the desk, he stared at his reflection. Tim watched with fascination. Ronnie never seemed to tire of looking at his own large, expressive face that was—by his own definition—"like sculpture." Huge blue eyes stared out from solid bone structure, all framed by black curly hair that fell below his ears.

Ronnie's dark good looks were duly appreciated by the seemingly endless parade of young, eager girls who flocked to his club. It wasn't often that he left the Grotto at four in the morning without one or two of these girls in tow. His conquests were legendary and that, plus a fanatical devotion to his club, combined to make him overly intense. Where did Ronnie get the energy, Tim wondered. Even the coke didn't help *him* all that much these days.

Ronnie continued talking about the Electric Toys. "Even if I book them in here and give them half the door, we can only fit about five hundred people. At six bucks a head, that's three thousand, so fifteen hundred goes to the band, and they can only work here once every few months. I have too many bands who want to play here. Divide that by the four guys in the band—it's barely enough for them to eat and pay their rent. Our room's too small, but they can't get a bigger booking until they have a record company. There aren't enough places for new bands to play. I feel like I'm running a crusade here."

Ronnie paused for a moment, then went on, "I remember when I let Patti Smith play here the first time. She was scared to death. Now I hear that Clive is after her. Remember when Bob Marley did that surprise set? And when Springsteen was here?" Ronnie sighed.

"If only you'd recorded those nights," said Tim.

"Nah," Ronnie shook his head. "That's not my style. I just loved to be able to do it, you know? Just to know that somewhere in the midst of all of this there is a little oasis, and that I had something to do with helping present *talent*." He said the word with reverence. "Even if they forget, and they do, or they don't give credit, and they don't, or they don't come back, which most of them do not, I know that I helped and they know it too, and the important thing is that it happened. And that's *that*."

"What do you hear about a Stones tour?"

"Same thing you do. Keith wants to do it, Bill and Charlie are off in France, and Jagger hasn't made up his mind. Same old story."

There was a knock on the door and a waitress came into the room, carrying a Coca-Cola with a piece of lime for Ronnie, and a glass of white wine for Tim.

Ronnie and Tim stopped talking while the waitress handed them the drinks. Tim leaned back in his chair and stretched his long legs out in front of him. He wore tight black corduroy jeans, cowboy boots, and a faded blue work shirt under a black leather jacket. His only concession to the bitter winter temperature was a navy blue wool scarf around his neck. Even though he was exhausted and unshaven, there was something attractive about Tim Harrison. Tall and slim, with sandy-colored hair, Tim had a casually elegant face and bright brown eyes that didn't miss much.

After the waitress left, Tim said, "So who is this Lindel James?"

"A knockout," said Ronnie. "Really, a big, sexy, ballsy chick. Gorgeous, you know, with a certain soulful look. Reminds me of someone . . . I'm not sure who. She only came in here once with Jeff Stein. I never even heard her sing."

"How come you gave her the gig?"

"Look, she's a dynamite-looking lady. And he told me she has an unusual voice. Unusual, he said. No bullshit, he said. And no band yet, so no hassles with amps and roadies and sound checks. Anyway, he's struggling, this Jeff Stein. We're all struggling, no? We hope, we plan, we dream. You can see it in the kid's eyes. He's hungry. He reminds me of me when I first started the club. I really cared so much about the acts I put on. I still do, but you know . . . anyway, we all have to help each other, we're all part of the same struggle. Besides, she's doing it for free. And that's *that*."

Tim was used to Ronnie and his raps. How could one not find him amusing when he cared so passionately about all of this. It couldn't be sweeter. Whereas he, Tim, was finding it harder each day to retain any of his original enthusiasm.

"I can't get anyone in the company to consider looking at any of the cute, sexy new bands around," Tim complained.

"Well, it isn't the sixties anymore," said Ronnie, lighting a joint. "Things just aren't the same for you house hippies."

"Ain't it the truth," Tim sighed. "Those were the days. When I could whisper in the ear of record company presidents and tell them who to sign. Quarter of a million dollar contracts for the groups. Limousines around the clock. Those mansions in Beverly Hills . . . " Tim's voice trailed off.

There had been more, he remembered. When he had worked at Acme Records, before they signed all those dreadful blues bands, there had been the trips to Europe, the unlimited expense account, the dope, the boys.

Tim's musical taste—which leaned strongly to threatening, hard-edged rock—was superb. He had managed to keep one foot in with the Village folkies, like Dylan and Neuwirth, while he maintained close ties to the dark, drug-ridden late night world of the heavy rock groups like the Velvet Underground, the Jefferson Airplane, and Led Zeppelin. He knew all the visiting drag queens from London and San Francisco as well as anyone who counted in the Warhol set, the underground theater or the art world. He had known everyone and everyone knew Tim Harrison. It had been a time of great promise.

"Things couldn't be duller now," Tim said. "They're starting to give me that 'commercial potential' rap."

"What did you expect?" said Ronnie. "It's all corporate now, like selling shoes. I thought, though, that the old man liked you."

Tim didn't say anything. It was true that Marc Garnier, the president of Jacar Records, had once considered Tim his protege. But that was two years ago, after Tim left Acme. These were different times. Everyone he signed to Jacar got great press, but none of his acts had had a real mainstream hit. Tim knew that he had to come up with something soon, or this whole number would be over.

The intercom buzzed and Ronnie picked up the phone. Tim tried to look as though he wasn't listening, but after a few minutes, when he still couldn't tell who was on the other end of the line, he lost interest and got up to leave. Mouthing the words "See you inside," he went into the back room.

Tim's usual table was off to the side, but with a good view of the stage. He preferred this small table so that only a few select people could join him. His tab at the Grotto was, by now, a joke, and even though Jacar usually paid it without too much trouble, he had to be careful. The accounting department was still not pleased about his Washington, D.C. hotel bill from last year's peace rally.

As he watched people come in, he thought the whole thing with Lindel James was a puzzle. First he had received a phone call from Marty Paretta, someone he hardly knew. Paretta had mumbled something about a favor for Jeff Stein, but that was all that Tim could get out of him. Then Ronnie called and said that Lindel was singing tonight. Tim wasn't sure why they had bothered to call him; she didn't sound like his kind of act.

But just in case, he would check her out. And to be really safe, he had mentioned her to a few other people. He still had a personal stake in everyone thinking that he was the first to know about anything new.

The room started to fill up a little after eleven. Waitresses rushed by, taking drink orders. Tim thought he saw Jeff Stein scurrying around the back of the stage, but he couldn't be sure. He ordered a carafe of white wine, put on his dark glasses, leaned back in his seat, and looked around. There was a buzz of anticipation in the air. Tim recognized the usual faces.

Within fifteen minutes, the three other chairs at Tim's table were taken: one by his friend Lillian Rosten, who was the only rock columnist who mattered, the others by two cute boys he had met the night before in the Ninth Circle.

"Has she done any other gigs in the Village?" Tim asked Lillian. "Have you seen her yet?"

"No, darling," said Lillian, as she adjusted an embroidered shawl around her shoulders. "But she'd better be good. I got out of my sickbed to be here because you said she was supposed to be phenomenal."

"She's the wave of the future," Tim said solemnly, as the lights dimmed.

With no introduction, Lindel James walked onstage. She wore a loose, flowing black blouse over shiny, skintight black trousers and black stiletto ankle boots. She smiled nervously at the audience, then, holding an acoustic guitar, she sat down on a high stool and started to sing. Softly at first, then, gaining more confidence, her voice came through clear and strong.

Within seconds, even the most jaded in this crowd stopped talking and paid attention.

With only the glow of a small candle on the table for illumination, Tim and Lillian exchanged significant looks. Lindel's voice was like nothing Tim had ever heard before, yet there was something strangely familiar about it. He gave up trying to place it, and for the next half hour completely turned himself over to Lindel James.

At the end of the second encore—unheard of for an unknown in this place—Lillian murmured, "Lovely," and rushed off backstage. Tim just sat there, ignoring the babble of the boys at the table, concentrating on what he'd just seen, trying to figure this out.

It wasn't just her looks. Carly was good-looking, so was Joni, if you liked that pale type. And it wasn't just the voice, either. After all, no one could touch Baez's pure, high soprano, and there was Ronstadt . . . and the rockers, Janis, Patti Smith . . . It was something else, something altogether unique. She didn't owe a thing to anyone, her voice was completely her own. And it was totally uncompromising. She sang with passion, as if she knew she had no other choice. And her eyes . . . her eyes got to him. Although he was sure it wasn't so, she seemed to be looking directly at him during her entire set. If she could make everyone in the audience think that . . . Obviously, Jeff Stein was no fool.

The girl was magic.

Lindel James was no ordinary singer.

Lindel James was money.

2

Lindel turned the radio off. There was nothing she wanted to hear on the radio these days. It was all predictable Muzak fit for supermarkets and elevators. None of it had anything to do with the music that had changed her life.

She leaned back against the pillows on her bed and lit a cigarette. The light from the bedside lamp cast shadows on the dark wooden floor. She watched the smoke from her cigarette curl slowly toward the ceiling. She needed time to think. So much had happened in the month since she had first met Jeff Stein at Brandy's, three weeks since her performance at the Grotto. Life had taken on a fast forward quality.

The night Lindel met Jeff, he had been waiting by the dressing room door, and, as she was putting her guitar away he had introduced himself and asked to take her for a drink. It was raining, and he held his brown leather jacket over her head as they raced into the bar next door to Brandy's. She had ordered a glass of white wine, and he had a ginger ale. The new Roxy Music single was on the jukebox. Jeff's fingers rapped against his glass of ginger ale, he popped several pieces of gum into his mouth at one time, and he had a habit of curling one strand of his curly brown hair around his forefinger. He wasn't still for a minute.

He had said, "Look, if you like me, and you're willing to give me a chance, why don't we try this: you give me three months, pay me nothing, even if I get showcase gigs for you. Consider it good faith, an investment, whatever. Then, you pay me a reasonable commission, something like twenty-five percent, when I get you a record deal, which is a sure thing as soon as I get Clive or Ahmet or Marc to see you."

"Who are they?" she had asked.

His eyes widened. "What? Clive Davis, the president of Arista Records, Ahmet Ertegun at Atlantic, Marc Garnier at Jacar? What rock have you been hiding under?"

"I've only been singing in these clubs for a few months," she mumbled, pushing her hair back from her face. "I don't know much about the business."

He nodded approvingly. "Well, that's what you'd have me for. I'd like to be your manager, but first, I'll prove to you that I can deliver."

She had looked at him. "I never heard of such an offer. You believe in me that much?"

"In you, yes. And in myself, too."

She didn't speak for a few minutes and he said, "Look, we could both go and get lawyers, and draw up a contract, but that's expensive. First, we'd have to get a fucking letter of agreement that we're negotiating a management deal, and the whole thing could take months. You know how lawyers are."

She didn't, but still had said nothing.

"And," he continued, "both our lawyers will feel that neither one of us is getting enough. I see this all the time with our artists. The alternative is to shake on it, trust each other, and save ourselves a lot of time and aggravation. That's what Geffen did with Joni Mitchell. Carly told me last week that she and Arlyne Rothberg don't have a contract. Steve Paul still doesn't have paper on Johnny and Edgar Winter."

"Well," she said, sipping the wine, "I'm not sure."

"Lindel," he looked at her, "I've learned in this business that something either feels right or it doesn't. This feels right to me, and I have pretty good instincts. What about yours?"

"I don't know. I never had to decide anything this important before."

"Well, maybe you want to talk it over with someone? Parents?"

"No," she said. "My parents moved to Arizona a year ago

because of my father's health. I love them, but we don't talk more than a couple of times a month."

She took a sip of her drink and added, "Besides, they've never even seen me sing in public. They would just tell me that I could make my own decision. And," she smiled, "they never discouraged my singing, but I think they still want to know why the music has to be so loud."

"Maybe you have a boyfriend you want to discuss it with," he suggested.

She hesitated, wondering if she should tell him about David. She decided to say nothing.

He looked into her eyes. He seemed very serious. "Let me ask you something," he said. "I don't know that much about you yet, but aren't you tired of shlepping from one fucking dump to another? Wouldn't you rather have someone take care of all this for you? The hardest thing is for the artist to convince someone else how great she or he is. That's where I come in. You just make the music. I go in and negotiate your royalty rate and recording budget, advances. The more money I get them to commit to you, the more they'll have to promote and advertise so they make their money back. If I get you a contract, and you're happy with the terms, then we formalize. What do you have to lose? I know how to orchestrate this, how to get the press to pay attention, who we need on our side to get your records on the radio. Lindel, I can *make* this happen for you."

She hadn't answered right away. He had refilled her wine glass, and poured some into his empty glass. He seemed more in touch than any of the other would-be, sleazy managers she'd run into on this scene. He was younger; he seemed to *get* her. She couldn't be forever afraid of taking this step.

Finally, she had said, "Well . . . okay. But I have to tell you, I'm nervous. I feel as though we're starting out on a very long, blind date."

"Don't worry. Leave all the sordid business details to me. From here on," he had said, "half of everything you make is yours." And they had both laughed.

Now the ring of the telephone interrupted her thoughts. It was Jeff, in a phone booth around the corner, wanting to stop by. She looked at the clock, remembered that Tim would be there within the hour, and told Jeff to come on up.

Five minutes later Jeff was at her door, with a copy of *Billboard* and a brown paper bag in his hand.

"Chinese," he said in response to her questioning look. "I always like to have the serious talks with Chinese food. It helps me think."

"Well, Tim is picking me up soon to go have dinner," she said, "so I don't want any. What serious talk?"

"Tim's coming?" He hesitated for a moment, then continued to walk into the living room. "Well, we can go over some things before he gets here."

He sat down on the bare floor, in front of the small empty fireplace, and proceeded to open cartons of food.

"Let me bring you some utensils, at least," she said. "Your eating habits are really primitive."

She returned from the kitchen with a fork, napkin, two glasses, and a bottle of wine.

Jeff was staring at a double page pullout ad in *Billboard*. "Can you believe this Mike Branson album?" he said. "It's a fucking *monster*. It just proves what shlepping across the country for all those years can do."

"I think he's so boring," she said. "I just don't get it."

"Well, of course he's boring," Jeff said quickly. "But that's the point. He's cute. And he sells."

"I suppose so. Still, I don't get it."

"It won't last, of course. Most of these one-shot successes end up pumping gas in two years. Although maybe Branson's different, maybe his manager invested well for him."

Lindel sat down on the floor next to Jeff and peered into one of the cartons of food.

"Want some?" he said, handing the carton to her.

She shook her head no.

He looked around the nearly empty room. "I wish you'd get a table and something to sit down on in here."

"I don't have any money. My parents gave me some when I came here but I've gone through most of it. And I never made much from playing those coffee houses. Anyway, I like it this way. It makes me feel like I haven't started my real life yet. Besides, I hate clutter."

"Clutter is one thing. A chair is another. I swear, the first money we get I'm going to get you some furniture. This is ridiculous."

They sat in silence for a few minutes. Jeff was busy eating; Lindel flipped through *Billboard*. She didn't see anything to hold her interest and put it down.

"I don't get why you live here," Jeff said between mouthfuls.

"Where should I live?"

"Every musician I know lives in the Village, or in one of those lofts in Soho."

Lindel made a face. "You'd have to drag me by the hair, screaming, to get me to live in Soho. It looks like East Berlin. I like this neighborhood."

"The fashionable West Twenties?" He smiled.

"It's quiet at night," she said. "It's perfect for working on my songs. I have no idea who the neighbors are and I like it that way."

She filled their wine glasses. Jeff continued to eat. She was constantly amazed at his appetite. He always seemed to be eating, yet he never gained any weight. He probably burned off all the calories by talking.

Lindel got up and went into the bedroom. Tim was supposed to be here in a half hour, but he was always late. She looked in the mirror and decided to put on some eye makeup. No need to worry about Jeff alone in the living room. Give him some Chinese food and a copy of *Billboard* and he could play by himself for hours.

She changed from her white terrycloth robe into a pair of jeans, a black cotton blouse and black leather boots, opened a fresh package of cigarettes, and walked back inside to join Jeff. He was leaning against the wall.

"So," he looked up at her, "I think everything's going according to plan with Jacar."

"What do you mean? Tim said that Garnier's still on vacation and won't be back until next month."

"I know, but it's all over the street that we're talking."

"How could it be a secret when you've encouraged me to go everywhere with Tim for the past few weeks?"

"I said a party here and there. The Grotto." He sounded annoyed. "I didn't say you practically had to have him move in. I don't see what it is you like about him so much anyway."

She lit a cigarette. "There's something about him that just gets to you. He's funny. And he's plugged into a whole scene that I don't know about. You can talk to him for five minutes and feel that you've been filled in on everything that's happened, without having to even go anywhere."

[24]

"As long as he talks you up to Garnier and it sweetens the deal. Has he mentioned anything to you yet about a band?"

"No. Why?"

"Well, what are your thoughts?"

She didn't answer for a minute. Then she shook her head. "I don't know. It's hard for me to talk about the way I feel when I sing, but . . . well, I know that when I sing with the guitar, I wish I could move around more. I hear so much more in my head. And . . ." She stopped.

"Go on," he said, looking at her.

"It's just something I feel I can count on. No matter what else out there goes wrong, I've got this. It makes me feel in control. It's hard to describe. Sometimes I feel it just has to get . . . out. In a bigger way."

"Of course," he said. He was excited now, standing up, pacing. "You need a band. It's exactly what I said to Tim. It will help fill out the sound . . ."

"No, that's not what I mean," she interrupted. "Although I'm sure the addition of other instruments would sound good. After all, I'm a singer, not a guitarist. But it's the music that makes me feel strong, and this is something that's inside me. It's so clean, and I have a feeling of where I want to go with it. I've almost gotten there one or two times, it's like a kind of rush . . . Something takes over and I feel as though I'm in danger of stepping over that edge, and maybe not coming back. Oh, I can't explain it."

"No, I understand completely," he said smoothly. "Look, you know I think you're extraordinary, and capable of something quite special indeed. We have to take this step by step. And I think a band is the next step."

"You seemed to like me when you heard me sing alone."

"Of course, honey, who wouldn't like you?" He walked to the window and turned to face her. "Like you—I *love* you. We have no argument here. I just think that for the purposes of a record, for a tour, a band is a necessity."

"But there's no money."

"There will be when we sign a deal."

"How can you be so sure that we're signing so fast?"

"Lindel, this is Jeff. Please." He stopped pacing, stood still, and dramatically pointed one finger to his chest. "You think I can't carry it off? You're looking at the guy who worked in the mailroom at ACS and the Universal Employment Agency at the same time. And when I saw an ad about to be placed in *Cash Box* for an agent to sign rock acts at ACS, I phoned and gave myself the job. Of course," he added quickly, "that was some time ago."

Lindel laughed. "What happened when they found out?"

"Who found out? Maybe Marcia realized about the job thing, but she thought it was funny. My point is, you've got nothing to worry about. There's no way I won't get you a contract."

"When am I going to meet Marcia?"

"Soon, soon. I guess I should set up a lunch or something."

"Or I could stop by your office. I don't know why I just can't come in and meet the people you work with. Meet your secretary, at least. Marcia must think it's strange that I've never come in."

"No, she doesn't," he said quickly. "It's all part of your mystique. Trust me. The next time you perform, they'll all come."

"When am I going to sing again? I mean for an audience of more than just you and Tim? I want to sing."

"Soon, soon. The buzz is still so good from the Grotto that I want to keep you under wraps a little while longer. Let's get the record deal done first. And I've got to set up a company for your publishing and have a management contract drawn up for us. And . . ."

"Stop," she said. "All this business talk just confuses me and makes me nervous." She took the empty food containers into the kitchen.

He followed her inside. "I know, honey, I know. You don't have to worry about this stuff. That's what I'm here for. You're the artist. You just have to continue to write wonderful songs and sing."

The downstairs buzzer rang and she went to answer it. "It's Tim," she said, surprised. "For once, he's early."

Jeff walked into the living room, over to the window, and looked down into the street. He let out a long, low whistle. "He's got a silver limo down there the size of a city block," he said. "Does he always travel in such style?"

"Sometimes he has groups coming and going from the airport and he keeps the car."

"Where are you going?"

"I don't know. Probably just someplace in the Village for dinner." She hesitated. "Want to come?"

"No." He shook his head. "Thanks, but you two go and gossip and have a good time. I've got a few stops to make. I'll call you in the morning."

"I keep telling you—I'm not up in the morning. Besides, why can't I call you?"

"Oh, honey, I'm always out of the office. Or in with Paretta. It's easier this way. Anyway, I'm off now."

Jeff smiled and leaned over to give her a good-bye kiss. At the front door, he said hello to Tim who was out of breath from climbing the three flights of stairs, and then Jeff was gone.

"I thought he'd never leave," said Tim, walking into Lindel's bedroom and collapsing onto the bed.

Lindel stood in the doorway, looking at him.

"Why don't you like him?" she said.

"Jeff?" Tim feigned innocence. "I adore him. What do you mean?"

Tim sat up on the bed and reached into his jacket pocket for a cigarette.

"Since when do you smoke?" Lindel was surprised.

"Oh, every once in a while." He shrugged. "Want one?" He handed her the pack.

"Lucky Strike? No, thanks. I'll stick to my Merits. As it is, I'm smoking too much."

"There is no such thing," Tim said, offering her a light. "It'll make your voice sound sexier."

He looked at her. "You look so great in black," he said. "It gives you that really gaunt look."

"Mmmm," she said. "Nervous, you mean. Maybe I should wear something a little brighter . . ." She looked at the clothes hanging in her open closet.

"Don't be silly," said Tim. "You look terrific. You could just use a touch more blush-on. But your hair is fabulous. Don't ever straighten it."

He got up from the bed, walked to the window, and poked his head outside.

"It's insane out there tonight," he said. "Full moon. Fat people on the street laughing harder than usual. Anyway, I'm really hungry. Are you ready to go eat?"

"Sure," she said. "Where?"

"I thought that little Mexican place you loved so much."

"I loved?" She laughed. "Obviously, you have your heart set on it. Let's go."

They walked down the stairs and got into the long, silver stretch limousine. The windows were tinted for privacy; from the street no one could see who was inside the car. Extra seats provided room for five in the back, and there was a small bar, with eight heavy crystal glasses and two matching decanters filled with brandy and scotch. Small Perrier bottles and chilled splits of champagne were lined up neatly and underneath there was a complete stereo setup and a small color TV.

Lindel collapsed with laughter against the plush maroon seats.

"We're only going three blocks," she said. "We hardly need to take this ridiculous car."

"What?" Tim sounded horrified. "Why else be involved in show business if not for the steady diet of luxury?"

Within minutes they pulled up in front of the tiny Mexican restaurant, and Lindel was embarrassed when the limousine driver jumped out to open the door.

She and Tim walked inside and immediately went to the table in the corner. Lindel sat down with her back against the wall.

"I still don't see what it is you like about this place," she said.

"It's so adorable. Very California."

"A real plus," she said, lighting a cigarette.

"You'll see. You'll love it when you move there."

"Never."

"Wait," he said. "Wait until you're rich and you won't want to deal with the winters here. You'll wake up every day to flowers and sunshine . . ."

"I hate the music they make there," she said.

"The Doors? The Byrds?"

"That's all finished and you know it. Now it's all session musicians, churning out music for young adults."

"You'll see. You'll go there. You'll love it."

The waiter came to take their order. Lindel asked for a margarita and some guacamole dip. Tim ordered the same, plus a nachos and three beef tacos with beans and rice. Lindel stared at him.

"What have you been smoking?"

"I know," he said. "I'm starved. The kid I was with this afternoon brought in some great dope from San Francisco."

"*Was* some great dope from San Francisco?" she teased.

"That too," he nodded.

They sat in silence for a moment. She smoked her cigarette. Tim cleaned his sunglasses with a paper napkin.

The waiter brought the drinks and the guacamole. Lindel thought about how in such a short time she had grown so accustomed to Jeff and Tim. They were now a major part of her life. Jeff was her biggest fan, calling daily, listening to her songs, bolstering her spirit, managing her dreams. And Tim with his entertaining gossip and his flattery. She knew she should be careful about the flattery. Flattery never did you any favors.

It had been a while since she'd shared her life with anyone, but she didn't want another romance right now. Jeff and Tim, both of them totally platonic and completely on her side, were like an invasion, but she welcomed the noise. She hadn't realized how lonely she'd been.

Tim was talking. "Did I tell you about the singer in Detroit who's jumping off the stage into the audience? He's with Cyclops, that old band from the Village. I think the drummer used to be a trick of mine in the sixties. I can't believe their new incarnation. None of them wear shirts and at their age they're lucky that not a one of them has a hair on his chest. Nothing could be more hideous than chest hair except a redhead with chest hair."

He continued. "Jimmy, the lead singer, has silver hair sticking out all over his head in points. Anyone who makes real hair look like nylon is a star. I'm going out there next week to check them out. Want to come?"

"How can I?"

"I can write it off on my expenses. It's called wooing the artiste."

"Don't be silly. I shouldn't be hanging out with you so much."

"Are you kidding? Jeff loves it. He knows that it can only help you."

"Why isn't he talking to other record companies?"

Tim rolled his eyes. They had been through this before.

"Who should he talk to?" he said. "Acme is obsessed with the British—you'd be lost there. Polydor doesn't exist in this country. So far, Casablanca is a one-act label. CBS is too corporate, Royal is all black, and Warners and A & M are West Coast. You're stuck with us."

"Somehow I can't believe that this is the best way to do it," Lindel muttered. "To wait for one company, to ask Lillian to hold up that article about me . . ."

"You don't want to waste publicity now, there aren't any records in the stores. And Jacar is the best company."

"Well, anyway, I can't come to Detroit. There's no reason for it."

"You could check out musicians for your band."

"What band?"

"Oh, didn't Jeff tell you? Let's see, how did he put it? He said he'd put the entire fucking Mormon Tabernacle Choir behind you if it would help you get a record deal."

Lindel shook her head. "He has such a way with words."

She had been thinking more and more about a band. A guitarist, drummer and bass player. She could put an ad in the *Village Voice,* hold some auditions . . .

Tim had already begun some new tale. " . . . and then the three of them were all kicked out of the hotel at four in the morning because she was yelling to the kid, 'Fuck my husband! Fuck my husband!' I think she's a cow," Tim continued. "She's not even a fag hag. Anyone who fucks seventeen-year-old boys is a faggot."

He lit a cigarette and signaled the waiter. "I'm getting another drink. You've hardly eaten a thing," he said. "Want something else?"

She shook her head no.

Tim took the pale green American Express card out of his jacket pocket.

"Let's go," he said. "I want to stop at the Grotto and then I'm going to the new leather bar on Canal Street. They have fabulous fist fucking right onstage. Want to come?"

She made a face. "No, thank you."

"You don't know what you're missing," he said, and without looking at the bill, signed it.

"I think I'd rather sit at home, stare at the walls, anything."

"How can you expect to write songs unless you expose yourself to everything?" he pouted.

She got up to leave. "That's what I like about you," she said. "You have my best interests at heart."

"I'm serious," he insisted. "You really should see what's going on everywhere."

"I write songs about love and hope," she said. "I can live without your walks on the wild side."

"Now there's a good song title," he smiled, and together they walked out of the restaurant.

3

The Academy of Music was packed. The opening act was on their third encore when Jeff and Lindel walked through the backstage door into the hot, noisy concert hall.

Jeff immediately ushered her to the rear of the orchestra. He always said he wouldn't be caught dead sitting in a seat, and Lindel didn't want to sit in the office with the usual music business faces. Some of those people would do anything to avoid seeing the act.

The two of them stood behind the shoulder-high partition that sealed off the last row of the orchestra. Tim appeared out of nowhere to stand next to them. As he and Jeff talked, Lindel looked around.

It was a particularly rough crowd tonight. The British groups always got the real hardcore fans who careened around in the aisles and the back of the hall, stoned on cheap wine and downs.

A boy in front of Lindel had passed out, his head hanging over the arm of his chair. He remained oblivious to the burly ushers who knocked into him as they went about their usual business of pushing people back to their seats. In the orchestra, a group of twenty people were standing, turning and pointing up toward the mezzanine. Somebody was probably threatening to jump.

A girl who couldn't have been more than sixteen was vomiting all over the stairway, and Tim said, "When you can hear them throwing up, it's a sure sign that the band isn't loud enough."

The theater must have been beautiful at one time. It had been one of those grand movie palaces, with huge chandeliers, carved, ornate ceilings, and Lindel heard that there used to be velvet curtains on the stage. Now gum was stuck underneath the seats, burns from marijuana joints had ruined the chairs, and once you went upstairs, out of the orchestra, the place smelled like cat urine. The rock audiences had turned it into a dump.

And yet . . . the first ten rows of people were standing up, fists raised, dancing and jumping in time to the music of the opening act. On a good night, there was a joyous feeling in the Academy. And Lindel was sure that it all looked quite different from the stage. You could get completely enveloped by the sound, by the rush of performance. She always felt the same way when she went to the Academy; she wanted to be up *there*.

Jeff turned to her and said, "After this and the set change, we've got at least a half hour to kill before The Vipers. They're really running late."

"That's what I hate about this place," Tim complained. "There's not even a decent bar in the neighborhood. Whoever thought we'd miss the Fillmore and Ratners?"

"Let's go into the office," said Jeff, leading the way.

A tall black man whom everyone in the music business loved and called Big George stood outside the door to the office. Tim flashed his permanent backstage pass and Big George nodded and let the three of them inside.

In the tiny office, promoter Howard Stein played backgammon as he leaned against the paisley patterned pillows. These days, he seemed to run all the concerts from this room.

The office was crowded; The Vipers were a big draw. Sally Paretta, Marty's wife, sat next to Howard, and talked nonstop to Carl Willis, the president of Acme Records.

" . . . ninety percent of the gross after expenses, but you should have *seen* what he called expenses. And the next thing we heard, the maids went in the morning after and found two naked fourteen-year-old girls, sobbing, tied to each other and the bed, with fish dangling out of their cunts. It's amazing he's not dead. After he shot up his usual dose of smack, he snorted about ten lines of charley, took two Quaaludes, a tab of acid—who takes acid anymore?—then drank an entire bottle of Jack Daniels . . .''

Marty Paretta was talking about The Vipers in too loud a voice.

"I feel like a goddamn caterer," he said. "At least this group didn't demand Dom Perignon."

"You mean rockstar's mouthwash?" Howard said, looking up from the backgammon game. "They're not at that stage yet. Wait."

"Well," said Marty, pouring himself a glass of the Mouton Cadet, "their dressing room food requests were bizarre. Egg salad for the bass player, M & M's for the drummer. They refused to ride in limos, said it was too 'elitist,' so I had to get station wagons for twenty-five people. The whole thing has been a major pain in the ass."

"But when was the last time a British group sold out all across the country within hours on their first tour like this?" said Carl Willis. "The Stones? The Who? In 1966?"

Lindel watched Jeff. He was so eager to be a part of all of this. Ahmet Ertegun popped his head in the door and waved to Earl McGrath, who laughed madly at something said to him by Linda Ronstadt. David Bowie sat in a corner accompanied by a black woman with short blonde hair. Andy Warhol snapped photos of Steve Paul, David Johansen and Danny Fields. Lindel didn't know anyone well enough to talk to except Tim, and he and Ronnie Marren were in a corner, their heads bent down as if they were taking cocaine. But Lindel knew better. Even in this world of easy drugs, people were piggish about sharing their cocaine in public. They'd rather sneak off to the bathroom, something which never failed to amuse Lindel, who thought the whole ritual was sleazy and depressing.

She got up and went out the door and around backstage to find a mirror so she could tie her hair back off her face. The bathroom next to the small kitchen was occupied, so she started to go upstairs.

"Sorry, honey," the bearded guard said, "I can't let anyone up to the dressing rooms without a laminated backstage pass until the end of the show."

"I'm just going to the ladies' room."

"Yeah, I know," he smiled. "Sorry. No one in the dressing rooms without the laminated pass."

She debated whether or not to go and get Howard, then decided not to bother.

So, The Vipers had an attitude. She'd heard about their entourage, their friends, roadies, even their own disc jockey who came with them to play records before their act. Laminated tour passes. Their first time in America and they were acting like stars.

She was amused, then annoyed. Who did this Brian Davis think he was? She turned around and went back into the office.

Jeff was talking to Jane Rose, who worked for The Rolling Stones, and to Frank Barsalona, the only rock booking agent who could give Marty competition. The tiny room was smoky and Lindel coughed.

Jeff looked at her quickly and said, "Okay, let's get out of here."

Once they were back inside the hall Jeff said, "I don't understand how it is that you smoke so much, and yet you start coughing the minute we're around people who smoke."

"It's not that," she said. "I just feel claustrophobic. Besides, I don't have any reason to be there."

He looked at her sharply. "Where did you go?"

"Nowhere. Come on, we might as well see what these Vipers are all about."

On the steps the roadies were piling huge Marshall amps on top of one another, testing the microphones, and hammering the drum kit onto its platform.

There was a buzz of anticipation in the air.

Old R & B records, Jimi Hendrix, and reggae dub songs blasted over the sound system. Lindel had to admit that The Vipers had good taste.

"Jesus," Jeff muttered, looking at his fake Cartier tank watch, "they really are taking their sweet time. If they play for one second more than fifty-five minutes, they'll go into overtime and Howard will have a fit."

The house lights started to dim, and a very tall, voluptuous girl with bright yellow hair walked to the microphone. With a pronounced upper-class English accent, she shouted, "Here they are, New York—you've been waiting for them—The Vipers!"

The audience was instantly on its feet.

Three banks of white lights streamed onto the stage. Tiny red dots lit up the amps. The musicians were in shadows. Then a sound, so loud, so deafening, erupted from these five musicians who stalked the stage.

Even without the hot, white spot that hit the center of the stage, Lindel would have known where to look. It was impossible, in fact, for her to keep her eyes off Brian Davis.

Tall and thin, with well-defined muscles, he wore no shirt. His chest looked like marble. His hair was short, cut very close to his head and revealing a most amazing face. High, prominent cheekbones, a full, sensual mouth. But it was his eyes—even from the back of the hall, Lindel could feel the power of his gaze.

His voice was like a drill, hammering away one minute, snarling and seductive the next. The music was nonstop energy, an assault on the senses. This was music to dance to, to shake you out of apathy. It could not be ignored.

Brian Davis grinned at the audience, he charmed them, then he sneered. He seemed dangerous, purposely perverse. He was, perhaps, a poseur; a good actor, a performer in the tradition of Mick Jagger. But while Jagger was slightly camp, Brian Davis was menacing.

She watched him as he hit the side of his face with the microphone. As he flung himself into the audience and then raced back onstage and crawled on top of the amplifiers and just sat there, singing, leering at the crowd. She felt as though she was eavesdropping, watching someone truly crazed, someone on the edge of madness.

She could barely make out the lyrics of the songs, but it didn't matter. She knew that he meant every word he sang.

The music continued with its crashing, pulsating energy. The band had obviously been influenced by rhythm and blues, but this was no white act covering a black sound. This was rock and roll at its most threatening, its most exciting.

Brian Davis had a true sense of theater. And sex. His entire performance was pure sex.

She glanced at Jeff. He, too, seemed transfixed. They said nothing to each other. She wouldn't have known what to say. She had no words for the turmoil going on inside her. She was awestruck and uneasy at the same time.

Brian Davis was outrageous, not because what he did was so

shocking; after all, there was little left that could really shock. It was his attitude. It was something that could not be explained to strangers. It was what made the difference between just pop entertainment and truly great rock and roll; its ability to set you free, to block everything out, to make you feel *alive*.

Lindel watched in stunned fascination. Instantly she knew that he did what she wanted to do. He took what she did so much further. He made what she did seem so tame.

Tim came over and stood next to Lindel. She didn't want him there, didn't want Jeff there, she didn't want to be under such scrutiny. She'd give anything to be alone now with her thoughts.

To her right, Tim said, "He's such a beauty."

"I don't believe what they all look like," Jeff shouted into her left ear.

Lindel looked at the rest of the band.

Seeing pictures of them in the English music papers and those advance pieces in *Rolling Stone* and the *Village Voice* was not at all the same as seeing them in the flesh. Usually people looked smaller onstage than in their photos, but The Vipers seemed larger than life.

Each man's hair was short, cut close to his skull. They all wore dark colored T-shirts, tight black leather jeans, and shoes without high heels. Everyone was his own height. This, when so many groups still clung to platform shoes and satin, pop-star clothes. Instantly, they made all other bands look dated.

The guitarist snapped the cord on his guitar against the stage like a whip, and the audience went crazy. The nearly three thousand people in the place were all standing up on their seats, and Lindel, Tim and Jeff could no longer see the stage.

"Let's go around to the side, by the office," suggested Jeff. "We can see there."

Lindel wanted to say that she'd seen enough, but she felt powerless to say or do anything except stare, dumbstruck, at this performance. She followed Jeff as if in a dream, ignoring the kids who bumped into her, the crowd along the side of the wall. All she could think of was Brian Davis.

For one minute she took her eyes off him to watch the audience. Eyes closed, fists raised, standing, jumping, swaying in time to the music. Passing joints back and forth. It was hot, sweaty. The entire place smelled like sex. Her heart was pounding.

She had seen great rock and roll before, but this was different. Her mind had been filled lately with Jeff's talk of Marc Garnier and royalties and studios and publishing and contracts, and here came Brian Davis.

It was as if they met, recognized each other, and he had slapped her in the face and walked away without a word.

Hours later, alone in bed, Lindel leaned over to look at the large red numbers lit up on the clock. It was five in the morning, and she still couldn't stop thinking about Brian Davis.

The cool cotton sheets were smooth against her naked body. Lighting a cigarette, she leaned back on the pillows, turned out the light, and watched the glow of the cigarette ash in the dark.

She had not wanted to meet him tonight. She pleaded a headache to get away from Jeff and Tim, who couldn't wait to go backstage. She put her cigarette out in the ashtray next to her bed and turned out the light. She closed her eyes, sank even farther down into the pillows, and thought about Brian. It had been such a long time since anyone had affected her in this way.

She wondered what he would be like. Her hand, under the thin blanket, had been resting against her breasts, and it was almost unconsciously that she now moved it—down along her stomach, then down farther . . .

It would be raining when they met, and Lindel would be aware, at first, of only the smell and the sound of the rain. They would go somewhere special; a large, ornate hotel suite, with the heavy satin curtains closed so tight that the room would be pitch black. Only the light from the crack under the door would reflect on them so they would just barely be able to make out the expressions on each other's faces.

She would look at him. His head to one side, his hair slightly tousled, his arms smooth in a black shirt. A tight excitement would take over, Lindel would not be able to say a word. She'd be lying down, the same way she was now, leaning against the back of the bed, and he'd be sitting on the edge of the bed, looking at her.

She could see Brian perfectly. His face, each feature, was clear. It was a face she had known all her life, perhaps, or the face she saw when she looked into the mirror. His mouth, prominent and sensual, curled just a bit into that slightly cruel grin. His eyes: sharp, clever, looking right into her.

Lindel heard her breath coming faster now, her hand moving, touching, eyes closed tight.

"It's been so long," she would whisper, and he would smile.

He'd be naked now, leaning over and kissing her mouth, running his tongue slowly over her lips, softly at first, making them wetter; then harder, more insistent, softly touching her neck, her breasts. He would touch her harder, and taking her in his arms, kiss her, bite her smooth flesh, softly at first . . . then harder . . . entering her . . . inside her . . . covering her mouth with one hand as she cried out.

Lindel slowly opened her eyes. She lay perfectly still and stared into the night. Her eyes could make out the objects in the room; her clothes, where she had tossed them, over a chair in the corner. The bookcase next to the window. She reached for a cigarette.

She thought about how he looked onstage. How sure of himself he was. How arrogant, completely in control. His performance was an inspiration. She wanted to feel like that—to feel that rush coming from her, at her. To almost lose herself. To come back, of course, but to get out there, and feel the power that the audience would give her in return for her voice, her performance.

And she knew, as she lay there, that there was something she wanted from Brian Davis. Something only he could give her, and that she wanted more than anything she had ever wanted in her life.

4

Jeff felt oddly uncomfortable waiting alone for Marc Garnier in the big corner office suite. With the large room and the adjoining executive dining room and kitchen, Garnier's office was designed to intimidate. A bar was hidden behind white Formica cabinets, there was an expensive and elaborate built-in electronic system, and the single humorous touch—a dart board with a photograph of Acme President Carl Willis—was affixed to one wall.

The soft leather chairs and couches reflected a traditional, conservative taste. Instead of the usual corporate beige or gray carpeting, oriental rugs of blues and burgundies covered a highly polished, dark wood floor. From his green leather chair behind the somber mahogany desk, Garnier had access to a battery of phones, intercom system, and buttons that regulated the complicated video and stereo system on the opposite wall.

Medals and plaques were framed on the wall as testimony to Garnier's philanthropic nature. Jeff wanted to go and look inside the private bathroom—he thought he saw a bed against one wall—but he was afraid that Marc would come in, and he didn't want to be caught snooping. He realized that even though Marc Garnier had produced ten gold records and was the only record executive to be named to the National Academy of Recording Arts and Sciences Hall of Fame, there were no self-congratulatory gold discs framed on his walls. This was class. It was a far cry from Marty Paretta's flashy office. Jeff made a mental note that when he got them, he'd put his gold records in the bathroom.

Jeff was impressed with the Jacar Building. It had obviously been designed with maximum efficiency in mind. Even the light switches on the walls of Garnier's twelfth-floor office were the same octagonal shape as the elevator buttons in the lobby. The overall color scheme was a soothing and monotonous pale gray, with an occasional touch of black. The effect was businesslike, austere.

Jeff had heard that the floors that housed the record company were only slightly more lively than the rest of the building. Posters, tour books, mobiles, and other rock and roll paraphernalia covered the office walls. Otherwise, it was typical corporation decor. Tim had explained it: the more plants you had in your office, the more power at your command. Secretaries had no plants at all, while assistant directors of departments had two. Department heads could have three; vice-presidents, six. This was laughed at, but adhered to, by everyone.

He wished Tim would get here. He could use the moral support. His confidence, not easily diminished, was jostled just a bit, the longer he had to wait. Soon the door opened and Jeff turned around to see Tim come into the room.

"I'm not early, am I?" said Jeff.

"No," said Tim. "He's usually late."

Tim sat down on one of the two dark green leather couches behind Jeff.

"How do you think we should handle this?" said Jeff. "Should I talk first, or you?"

"Don't be silly," said Tim, rolling a joint. "The man has run this company since 1960 and before that he had that rhythm and blues label. He's signed a few people in his time. You don't choreograph a meeting with Marc Garnier."

Jeff felt foolish and said nothing. For the two months leading up to this meeting he had tried to play it cool, waiting for the Garniers to return from their extended vacation in the Caribbean. He wouldn't admit it to anyone, but he had his heart set on Jacar. They had the best distribution, the best promotion, and he was sure that Tim would be a powerful ally. He wanted the best for Lindel, and he was determined to do it in an unprecedented way.

No demo tapes, no series of demanding try-out performances, no in-office auditions like that asshole from Royal had suggested. That much he could spare Lindel. So now he sat, waiting for the one man who could help him make it all happen, who would take him to the next step.

Jeff turned his attention back to Tim, who was talking. "And so he invited all the press to show up, and when they got there, it was a vacant parking lot littered with wine bottles and bums he had driven uptown from the Bowery."

"Garnier? What was this for?" laughed Jeff.

"Oh, one of the big English groups. I can't remember if it was Zeppelin or Yes. I know it was the day after he had rented the entire Beverly Hills Hotel to celebrate his fifteenth year in the business."

"I think I read about that in one of the columns," said Jeff. "He and his wife—what's her name?"

"Alexis," offered Tim.

"Right. They never seem to spend much time in New York."

Tim took a drag on the joint and started to offer it to Jeff, who waved it away.

"He has a house in London, an apartment in Paris, a house in Beverly Hills and a place in the Hamptons," Tim counted on his fingers. "Oh, and the townhouse here in New York. The man doesn't exactly have to rough it."

"Have you ever been on the plane?" asked Jeff.

"Yeah, a couple of times. To London and L.A. It's a cute plane. Not too big, seats about thirteen. Mainly it's a pleasure not to have to wait for baggage."

The door opened and Marc Garnier walked into the room. Silver-haired, of medium height and well built, he wore a dark gray tweed suit that Jeff thought was the most beautiful suit he had ever seen. A pink silk shirt, burgundy twill tie, and glove leather black shoes completed his outfit. Jeff had purposely not dressed up for the meeting—he hadn't wanted to appear too anxious—but now, confronted with Marc Garnier's impeccable taste, Jeff, in jeans, Adidas sneakers, and a Thor Heyerdahl T-shirt under a velvet sports jacket, felt like a slob.

Jeff stood up. Marc smiled, they shook hands, and Marc waved Jeff back into the chair. Jeff watched Garnier walk to the bar and pour some Perrier water into a glass.

Although at least twenty years older than either Jeff or Tim,

Marc Garnier radiated a youthful energy and vitality that instantly took over the room. He turned to Jeff with a sudden, disarming smile.

"I'm sorry," he said in just a trace of an elegant French accent. "What will you have?"

"A Perrier, too, I guess."

Marc nodded with approval. "I'm not a morning drinker, either."

Marc handed Jeff the glass of bubbly water and turned to Tim. He laughed out loud when he saw that Tim was lighting a joint.

"I cannot believe that you insist on smoking that stuff," he said, smiling. "I would think that now that it's accepted even in these corridors, you would have given it up."

Jeff joined in the laughter and said, "It's really such a middle-class drug now. You can't go to a movie theater on the upper East Side and not be surrounded by marijuana smoke."

"Next year it'll be like that with cocaine," said Tim.

Marc walked behind his desk and settled into the dark green reclining leather chair. Jeff thought that perhaps in no other business could two men with two such radically dissimilar styles sit across a desk, about to bargain with one another.

At first, the talk was general. Marc and Tim discussed the charts. One never knew anymore; Zeppelin could disappear for two years and then come back with something that would enter the charts at Number One. And what was one to think of Kiss? They really were just Grand Funk with makeup, said Tim. Everyone agreed that Sol Greenberg's latest claim that he had commitments from three out of four Beatles for a reunion was pathetic.

Then Marc looked directly at Jeff. There seemed to be a twinkle in his eye. Amazing, thought Jeff. After all these years, he still enjoys this.

"Well, Jeff," Marc said softly, "Tim tells me your girl is something special."

"I think so," said Jeff, and waited.

Tim said nothing. The smell of marijuana drifted over to Jeff. The morning sun streamed through the huge windows, creating a pattern of geometric shapes across Marc's desk.

Jeff said, "She hasn't played that many places yet. But I'm sure Tim told you how she went over at the Grotto."

"I'm sorry I missed it," said Marc. "I like that place; Ronnie's done a really good job."

Marc ran his fingers through his hair. He turned his chair around to look out the window. Then he turned back and looked intently at Jeff.

"Tim says you haven't talked to anyone else?"

"Well, there have been offers . . . but I haven't seriously talked to anyone, no. I think it's obvious that you're the best, and we've grown so fond of Tim . . ." His voice trailed off.

Marc stood and walked to the window directly behind his desk. He turned his back to Tim and Jeff and stared outside the window, as if he was looking for something.

"I forgot how beautiful this city can be," Marc said. "Crisp. So calm from up here."

He paused for a second, then continued.

"Well, Jeff, I think we are the best," he said. "We certainly can get more records in the stores than anybody else."

He leaned over the back of his chair and faced Jeff.

"But also," Marc continued, "I like to think that we care about our artists. We build careers here. When we signed Davey Jones, for example, we committed ourselves to an advertising and promotional budget. We brought him over to talk to the press and radio stations before his record was released. It built up the excitement."

"Remember when he came here that first time wearing a dress?" said Tim.

Marc continued. "And, from the minute his signing photo appeared in the trades, he had his own product manager who coordinated the marketing campaign with our publicity department, our radio promotion staff, the art department for the album cover, ads, and so on. We also sent him on a personal little promotional tour of the branch offices around the country, so he'd meet the men who have to actually get the record on the radio stations in each city, as well as the distributors who get it in the stores."

Marc took a sip from his glass of Perrier. He sat down and leaned across the desk, his hands clasped lightly together in front of him. He smiled at Jeff, who had been listening with rapt attention.

"I'm very interested in Lindel James," said Marc, as Jeff's heart began to beat just a bit faster.

"Very interested," Marc admitted. "And I'd like to be able to say that I will come and see her perform. But . . ." He paused, and with that Jeff's heart lurched. "I'm afraid that our sales conferences will take up the next two weeks, and then I have to go to Los Angeles for those foolish Grammy Awards. I understand you've been waiting for me to return, and I really don't want to hang you up any longer."

Jeff's heart began to sink. He had not expected this. Why had Garnier called the meeting if he was going to turn him down? He didn't dare turn around to look at Tim, who still remained silent. His heart was pounding; his palms were wet. It seemed like an eternity before Marc spoke again.

"So, if it's all right with you, I'd like to make a verbal agreement now."

Relief spread through Jeff's body.

"Well, uh, yes, of course," said Jeff. "But there are probably a few things we should discuss first . . ."

Marc waved his hand impatiently. "Details," he said. "You can have your lawyer get in touch with our business affairs department."

"Well," said Jeff, "there is one thing we really should agree on first."

"What's that?" said Marc.

Jeff hesitated, then blurted out, "Lindel will be signed to my production company, and I'll provide her services to you."

Marc looked at Tim, then back at Jeff. "I assume that Lindel has agreed to this?" he asked.

"Oh," Tim broke in, "they're thick as thieves."

"An unfortunate analogy." Marc smiled. "Well, Jeff, I suppose it's all right, although she is an unproven artist, but I don't foresee a problem. After all, we want her, and as long as she signs the standard artist's inducement letter, which states that she is willingly providing her services to us through you, then it can all be worked out rather quickly. I don't want to wait too long. As I said, you'll have your lawyer get in touch with Mike Kahn in business affairs . . ."

"Actually," Jeff interrupted, "I was planning on negotiating this myself."

"Jeff, you're nuts," Tim spoke up. "You've got to get a lawyer. These guys in business affairs are killer sharks."

Marc looked amused. "As you can see, Jeff, Tim is no company yes man. Sometimes I wonder who he's working for."

"I know what I'm doing," Jeff said.

Marc looked at Jeff, then at Tim, then back to Jeff and said, "I'm sure you do, Jeff, I'm sure you do. But I cannot, in good conscience, allow you to make a serious mistake. It's to protect us, too, of course, from any future . . . ah, claim, you understand." He sighed. "These days, the lawyers are running the business."

Feeling on much surer ground now, Jeff said, "What kind of deal are we talking about?"

"Standard production deal. Probably around a fifty thousand dollar advance against her eventual royalties, a reasonable budget for recording, escalating clauses based on how well the album sells. And that promotional budget I've mentioned to you. Does that strike you as fair?"

"Seventy-five thousand advance," Jeff said boldly. "Fifteen percent royalty. And tour support. Enough to take her across the country with a band for five weeks."

"Jeff," Marc said gently, "I usually don't hammer out these things."

Tim broke in. "Jeff, if Marc puts his approval on this, you'll get pretty much what you want."

Marc swiveled his chair around again to look out the window. He said nothing. He tapped a pencil against his finger. Jeff wondered if the meeting was over. Perhaps he'd been too brash, gone too far, offended the man.

Then Marc turned around to him and said, "Jeff, this might interest you. I'm thinking of starting something new here. Creating smaller, independent labels. I hear the Stones want one. I believe that Ahmet is planning to give one to Zeppelin at Atlantic. Streisand, they say, wants her own production deal."

Marc went on. "It's a three billion dollar industry now, and we're such a big company I've come to realize that with musicians there is no such thing as too much personal attention."

Jeff waited. What did this have to do with him?

"Our superstars want to bring in their own people," said Marc. "For example, say the Stones have their own team working within the Jacar complex. We're just down the hall from knowing instantly what Jagger wants."

Jeff suddenly realized that for the whole time he'd been in Marc's office, the phone had not buzzed once. He was flattered. Marc had even done it without making the usual big show of telling his secretary to "hold all calls." The man had style.

"Now, I have another idea," Marc went on. "Not only do I want to establish these labels for our top acts, I'm thinking of forming independent units, self-contained little production teams, if you will, based around the talents of a particular person whom, we feel, has potential. For example, do you know Artie Weinstock?"

Jeff had heard of him. He managed three groups of former L.A. session musicians who had made it big. He was supposed to be an obnoxious loudmouth.

"I've asked him to consider bringing his bands here when their current contracts elsewhere are up," said Marc. "It would be his own deal, his own company, with an option to bring us new acts as well."

Jeff's mind started racing. The man was obviously putting out some kind of feeler. He decided to take a chance.

"Marc," he said, "are you suggesting that I . . ."

"Well," Marc smiled, "I'm not saying anything. Yet. But think about this. Tim tells me that you have found one of the really special singers. Now I've done some research, and I'm aware that she had only been in folk clubs a few months when you saw her. Why you?"

He paused, ran his fingers through his hair, and continued. "I mean, Jeff, let's be honest. You and I know that it takes a special kind of talent to recognize talent. A special vision, to be able to instantly appreciate an artist's potential, especially when you see her in a minimal setting, without benefit of band, proper sound or lights . . ."

Jeff nodded in agreement.

"And so," Marc said, "I think we should consider the possibility that you might be very useful to us, and we to you."

Jeff hesitated. "I'm not sure I understand."

"Well," Marc said, "let's see what happens with Lindel. But if she's a success, don't think that we wouldn't be aware of your part in it. You strike me as a very . . . enthusiastic young man. So it might not be out of the question to consider giving you a budget to sign other acts. Nothing too grand, of course, and I'm just throwing out this idea as a possibility. But you could get royalties on their albums, too. And we might be able to find office space for you right here at Jacar. You could bring in an assistant. Just think about it."

Well, thought Jeff, his heart pounding, why not? Why the fuck not? After all, he was out there, he had found Lindel, and he could find others. Just last week he had heard about that new band from New Jersey, the one whose lead singer wore those ripped T-shirts and shouted insults at the audience. Sounded gimmicky, but interesting. They didn't have a manager, either. He was certain that the possibilities were endless.

Marc Garnier tossed the pencil he had been holding into a tray on his desk. Jeff stood up. The meeting was over. Lindel would record for Jacar Records. No, Lindel would record for Jeff Stein's production company, and Jacar would distribute the records. And he, Jeff Stein, got more than he bargained for.

He'd have the chance to develop his own label. He'd leave ACS, and take Marcia away from Marty Paretta to work for him. With her contacts, her ability to find out all that useful information, she'd be invaluable to him.

As he left the office, he could barely keep from running, skipping, down the long hallway to the elevator.

He had taken the big chance, acting as though the deal was set, telling people it was only a matter of dollars. Asking for—no—informing Marc of the production deal. Taking a chance that Marc wouldn't turn him down.

He couldn't believe it. It had almost been too easy. But he would make it work. And now he couldn't wait to call Lindel and tell her the good news.

He'd be able to sign other acts, have an expense account, travel. He'd move out of that one-room dump on the fifth floor of a crumbling brownstone next door to a welfare hotel on West Seventy-third Street and get a decent apartment.

He'd *be* somebody in this goddamn business.

He was home free.

A few seconds after Jeff had closed the door behind him, Tim let out a low whistle and said, "What was that?"

"You know," said Marc, tapping the cigarette against the edge of a large onyx ashtray, "there's not a manager alive who doesn't fancy himself the next Albert Grossman. Or Brian Epstein. And even The Beatles weren't enough for Brian. What am I risking?

Say I did give Jeff Stein fifty thousand dollars to find new acts, and we tossed a couple of empty offices into the deal. He might come up with something."

"I actually think Jeff is okay," said Tim. "I think he knows what's shit and what will sell."

"These days . . ." Marc smiled, "who can tell the difference?"

Marcia Weissman hung up the phone shortly after midnight and felt as though she might burst into tears. Damn that little Elise Goodman. She just couldn't wait to get to a phone to break the news.

"Jeff and Lindel," Elise had said. "Having dinner at the Four Seasons. How can he afford it?"

"What were you doing there?" Marcia had said.

"Steve had some clients in from out of town and they needed some girls to go with them to dinner."

"That's so tacky."

"A girl's gotta eat." Elise had been cheerful. "I don't care, I've never been there and I wanted to see what it was like. I didn't have to *fuck* anyone."

Marcia had waited for the details.

"So there they were," Elise continued, "at some table in the back. We were by the pool. And their heads were close together. I'll bet anything they're doing it."

"Elise, please. I don't think Jeff 'does it,' as you put it, with anybody. Besides, I don't care about his private life."

"Oh? Since when? Anyway, she has this amazing long black hair . . . "

"So I've heard."

" . . . and she kept brushing it away from her face. I swear the waiters must have panicked that it would catch fire in the candle. You should have seen the way the help was hovering. Jeff had this . . . expression on his face, like he was so proud, as if he thought they were so attentive because she's beautiful. But I'm telling you, it was the hair. I'll bet they thought there was going to be a fire . . ."

Marcia tuned her out, and finally managed to get off the phone. She walked into her bathroom and opened the door to the medicine cabinet. She broke a yellow Valium in half and swallowed it down with a glass of water. She walked back into the only other room in the apartment, pulled the flowered print studio couch open, took off her maroon velour robe, and lay back against the lavender pillows.

She wished she had some chocolate, right now. Maybe she should put a coat over her nightgown, put on some boots and just run out to the all-night delicatessen. A Mounds bar, that's what she needed, or maybe a jelly doughnut. The really gluey kind, with lots of powdered white sugar on the top and not enough raspberry jelly oozing inside.

She had completely misjudged Jeff. Just because he wasn't married, or gay, she thought that there could be something between them. Even though he'd never really made a pass at her, it had seemed to Marcia that because of all the time they spent together, all those talks they'd had, that they were getting close. She knew his ambitions, and she was sure she could help. They could be a team.

So even though she worked for Marty Paretta she had done all these little extra things to assist Jeff's cause: taking copies of the trade magazines from other people's wastepaper baskets to give to him, finding out all she could about deals, passing the information along to Jeff. She took management and record company contracts to the Xerox machine, studied the copies at home at night, and put them on Jeff's desk in his new, tiny office, with clauses underlined that she thought would be particularly helpful to him in his future negotiations.

But now, all he cared about was Lindel James, and she, Marcia, felt like a fool.

She reached for the remote control on the small table next to the sofa bed, and turned on the television. Pressing buttons until she found an old black and white movie on Channel Five, she turned the sound way up; maybe it would block out her thoughts. On the screen, Barbara Stanwyck was dressed in a shiny, long gown, smoking a cigarette, sipping what appeared to be a martini and playing roulette. *That's what I should be like,* Marcia thought. Getting all done up in sexy, silver dresses and leading a glamorous, independent life.

Pushing the lilac and white-striped covered down quilt aside, she got out of bed and went into the tiny kitchenette. She took a glass from the cabinet above the sink and opened the refrigerator to take out the half bottle of wine. Pouring the wine into the glass she caught her reflection in the round, red-framed mirror that hung on the wall above the sink. She looked awful. There were deep circles under her eyes, and that extra five pounds was beginning to show in her face. Maybe she should cut her hair in a new way. Or change the color again.

She closed the refrigerator door, and, taking the glass of wine with her, went back to bed. She should have gone out with that radio promotion man from Acme tonight. They would have had a good dinner, maybe seen a movie, and probably had some decent sex. It had been weeks since she'd been to bed with anyone. She needed a man to hold her, to make love to her. It didn't even matter if he was married and had to leave in the middle of the night; anything was better than moping around her apartment, having to deal with Elise's news about Jeff and Lindel.

Marcia hadn't even met Lindel yet; for some reason Jeff seemed determined to keep them apart, which was fine with Marcia. She was in no mad rush to meet this girl whom Jeff had described in such nauseatingly glowing terms. What could she possibly have in common with a beautiful, probably arrogant, singer? Marcia had no desire to be friendly with musicians. They were all the same. They lived in their own little worlds.

She remembered when she first saw Jeff Stein. It had been almost two years ago, at Max's, just before it was no longer fashionable to go there. Marcia, who went there nearly every night, was always at the center of a large, lively table in the back room. She had only just started working as a receptionist at ACS, but was already on familiar ground in the world of agents, promotion men, and record company employees who, six years after Warhol had turned Max's into a hangout, still frequented the place. She noticed Jeff—she noticed every man who came into the place—and there was something about him that made her look twice. He was short, and fairly ordinary looking, but he sent out a wave of crackling energy; he worked the room with his eyes and seemed to take in everything that was happening around him, and Marcia liked that. He always came in, and left, alone. A few months after she saw him for the first time, he introduced himself, and mumbled something about working for a law firm. He never said what it was that he did, but when he asked her three months later if there was an opening in the ACS mailroom, Marcia suspected that he had been a messenger for that law firm, and that quite possibly, he had been fired. It was obvious that he wanted to get into the music business, and Marcia figured it would be fun to have him around. She helped to get him the mailroom job, and, when she moved up to work as secretary to Marty Paretta a year later, she encouraged Jeff to get out of the mailroom and try to get some clients of his own. She hadn't counted on Lindel James.

Now, she leaned over and turned off the lamp next to the bed. She lay back against the pillows—arranging them in the order she liked: the two big pillows against the back of the sofa, with the small neck pillow along the top, and the two round ones on each side. It made her feel better to have all these pillows propped up around her, with pretty lavender and purple colors and tiny floral prints. The studio apartment was tiny, but Marcia had tried hard to make it cozy, romantic. She liked to surround herself with frilly things—from the pink satin lingerie cases that lined the drawer of her only bureau to the wicker basket full of lacy pillows. The ruffled curtains that matched the green and coral print of the sofa bed and the silk flowers arranged in a green vase on the table all helped to create a sense of order that was often a welcome relief after a disappointing day in the office.

She turned the TV sound down, and stared at the screen. The combination of the Valium and the wine was beginning to make her feel drowsy. Still, she thought about Jeff. She had been so sure that for once she'd been on the right track. Maybe her mother had been right, perhaps she was too aggressive. Her mother should know; her own aggressive demands had pushed her father right out the door when Marcia was seventeen. Marcia was still close to her father, a man who lit up a room just by entering it. Her father—who had told her when she was twelve that she shouldn't be a lawyer, like he was, because, as he had smiled at her with affection, "women lawyers are too hard." Remembering that now, she had to laugh. Too hard. No chance of that. Perhaps if she'd been just a little bit more "too hard" she wouldn't be lying here in a studio apartment, in the heart of the stewardess district at the age of twenty-seven, alone, going to work each day for Marty Paretta, whose ego was so huge he thought he singlehandedly invented the music business.

She stared at the TV screen, silently pleading with it to hypnotize her into a deep, untroubled sleep. She didn't want to think about Jeff Stein anymore tonight; her feelings toward him were becoming all too disturbingly familiar, and caused her to remember things she wanted to forget . . .

Marcia was a regular at Arthur that summer of 1966 and Robin, the doorman, had given her a big smile.

"Hi, honey," he said. "You look adorable. There's a seat for you at Sybil's table."

Marcia practically floated inside, her eyes grew accustomed to the darkness and she looked at her reflection in the smoky mirror that lined the inside wall of the main room. She looked like every other eighteen-year-old girl in the room: short, dark Sassoon styled hair with bangs that reached her three pairs of false mink eyelashes. She wore an orange and white checked Rudi Gernreich knit mini dress and white Courreges boots cut above the ankle. There had been the big problem with the bra; after hours of attempting to safety pin the straps in the back of the dress so they wouldn't show out of the deeply cut armholes, she gave up. The hell with it, she figured, she wouldn't wear a bra. Her tits were okay, although she'd have to think about starting to exercise her legs, particularly if dresses stayed at this length.

She looked at the crowded dance floor and recognized a few celebrities. Judy Garland, Jackie Kennedy, Nureyev. Onstage, the house band, The Wild Ones, was playing, with lead singer Jordan Christopher singing directly to his lady, Arthur's owner, Sybil Burton. Marcia looked for Billy, saw his head leaning back with his eyes closed as he thrashed on the drums, and she walked over to the prestigious corner table against the wall and sat down on the small cushioned stool. Sybil gave her a wink, poured her a glass of champagne, and leaned over to whisper, "They'll be through after this number." Marcia nodded and smiled. She'd been sleeping with Billy Rhodes for a few weeks, and she loved the status it gave her at this most famous of the several discotheques that had popped up in the past few years in the city. She had been living a fast, somewhat schizophrenic life this year after high school graduation. Each morning she left her mother's West Side apartment and went downtown to New York University where she half-heartedly took just enough courses to pretend she was getting a college education. She'd come home at four-thirty, fall asleep for a few hours, and wake up in time for a quiet dinner and then she'd hit the clubs.

First there had been Ondine, the trendy disco right under the Fifty-ninth Street bridge, with its clientele of models, fashion designers, and English rock bands. Then came the fancier discos: L'Interdit, Il Mio and Le Club. She only went to those with a date. She'd stagger home at three in the morning, rip off her false eyelashes, and get four hours of sleep until she had to get up and face the subway again.

The minute Arthur opened, it was *the* place to be. A glittery little jewel box of a disco, with mirrors lining the walls that made it perfect for everyone on the dance floor who couldn't take their eyes off themselves. The recorded music was loud and very current: Bob Dylan's "Like a Rolling Stone," Manfred Mann's "Little Black Book," The Rolling Stones' "Satisfaction," Aretha Franklin's "Respect." It was here that Marcia started to become aware of the music that was changing her generation.

Of course, Marcia really went to the clubs more for the men than for the music. She really scored the first time she left Arthur with Billy Rhodes. She couldn't sleep all night at his apartment, she had to still make the appearance at her mother's. But something had clicked with Billy, and she'd been back to the club, and later, in his bed, every night since.

Now, the band finished their set and Billy came down off the stage and walked over to her. He sat down, and she smiled at him, handing him her glass of champagne.

"No . . . thanks," he said, looking around uneasily.

"Want to dance?" she said.

"No."

"Sorry, I forgot. You must be bushed. It was a great set. Did you see Judy Garland dancing?"

Billy didn't say anything.

"What's wrong?" she said.

"Uh, listen," he started, and she felt an awful clutching around her heart.

He stopped, looked at her, and then, avoiding her eyes, he said, "Look, I really think things have been getting a little too heavy with us, you know what I mean?"

"I thought we were having fun." She tried to sound calm.

"Yeah, you're a good chick," he said, "but you know, I can't be so tied down. It's like . . . well, I just like to do my gig here, then whatever happens . . . uh . . . happens."

She looked at his dark brown eyes, his long, curly brown hair. She had been thinking about his face all day. She saw his eyes follow this year's skinny blonde model. She could have murdered him right on the spot.

"So," he continued, "let's just be friends, okay?"

Just like that, she thought, but said only, "Sure." She swallowed down the rest of the champagne, gave him a blinding smile, and, murmuring something—she wasn't sure what—she got up and headed for the ladies' room.

She tried to blot her eyelashes with a tissue before the tears came, but it was too late. The eyelashes, all gummy, were already half off. And all that business of worrying about the bra. She felt humiliated.

These rejections had started to happen with alarming frequency in the past year. She couldn't seem to hold on to a boyfriend for more than two weeks. She knew she got clutchy sometimes, and although she couldn't seem to help it, it frightened her. She didn't want to end up alone. Here she was, not even married yet, and already like her mother. At times like this she thought that she had to do something to change the pattern of her life.

Damn, she had forgotten to close the curtains, and the morning sun was streaming through the windows. Half asleep, Marcia reached for her small alarm clock and groaned when she saw it was only six forty-five. The television was still on, cartoons flickered on the screen. The half full glass of wine had created a sour smell, and Marcia, in a stupor, got up to close the curtains and take the wine glass into the kitchen before trying to go back to sleep.

Twenty minutes later she was just falling into a deep second sleep when the phone rang. Who the hell was calling at this hour? It had to be her mother, or Marty . . . Marcia was instantly awake, and picked up the phone.

It was Jeff.

"I didn't wake you, did I?" His voice boomed into the phone.

"Oh, it's you." She was glad to hear his voice, and then remembered Elise's call last night and was immediately annoyed. "Of course you didn't wake me," she said. "I always get up about four hours before I have to go to work. It gives me a chance to brush my teeth, have coffee . . ."

"Listen," Jeff cut her off. "I've got fabulous news. Garnier's going to sign Lindel."

Marcia's heart sank. "That's great, Jeff." She tried to sound pleased.

"Yeah, isn't it? But listen, you haven't heard all of it—"

"Jeff," she broke in, "can you hold on a second? I've got an awful headache. I have to take an aspirin."

He laughed. "Late night, huh? Yeah, I'll hold on, but hurry up."

She got out of bed and took her time going into the bathroom to get an aspirin from the medicine cabinet. She swallowed one aspirin with a glass of water, and then, on second thought, took the bottle and another glass of water back to the table next to her bed.

She got back into bed, arranging the pillows behind her head and covering herself with the quilt.

"Hi," she said into the phone.

"Jesus," he muttered, "what the fuck took you so long? Anyway, so Garnier seems really hot for her, he offered me a fabulous deal, but that's not all." He stopped, and waited.

She didn't say anything. She was determined not to make this easy.

"Get this," he couldn't control himself, "she's going to be signed to my production company."

"Your what?"

"You heard me," he said, laughing proudly.

"But you don't have a production company," she said. *You barely have a job,* she wanted to add.

"I have one now," he said. "Valhalla."

"What?"

"That's what I'm calling it. Valhalla Records . . ."

"Wait a minute," she broke in. "What do you mean Valhalla Records?"

"Garnier told me he's thinking of setting up independent labels. He so much as told me that if Lindel makes it—and she's going to make it if I have to personally take her fucking record to every station across the country—he'd like to give me my own label."

"Are you on some kind of weird drug?" she asked.

Jeff laughed. "You know I don't take weird drugs," he said. "Marsh, baby, this is the *emmis.* Believe me, it's all true."

"But why would Garnier give you a label?"

"Thanks for the confidence," he said dryly. "You seemed to think I had a good shot at getting ahead up to now."

Don't remind me, she thought, but she said, quickly, "But I know you. Garnier doesn't know you, he's never even heard Lindel sing."

"Well, Tim told him about Lindel. And all I can say is that the old man has some fucking good instincts. So, Lindel will record for my production company, which, if I'm lucky, will end up being my own record company." He stopped.

Marcia couldn't have been more depressed. It was at moments like these that she wished she had a cigarette. She didn't smoke, but she wished she had a cigarette just the same. She needed something to hold on to.

"She's going to be the biggest fucking star," Jeff crowed. "Records. Movies. Television. Everything. And I'll be her agent, her manager, the head of her record company, the whole shebang. And, as Ronnie Marren would say, that's *that.*"

Marcia didn't answer. Jeff sounded so pleased with himself. And not once had he mentioned a word of thanks for her help.

"Well," he demanded, "aren't you going to congratulate me?"

"Congratulations," she said. Her voice, she knew, was spiritless, but she couldn't help it.

"Now," he continued briskly, "the reason I called you . . ."

Marcia was stunned. Could he possibly be waking her up at seven in the morning to ask a favor?

" . . . and so I couldn't wait to tell you and see what you thought about it."

Marcia realized she hadn't heard what he had said.

"What I thought about what?" she said.

"About coming with me," he said impatiently.

"Where?"

"Aren't you listening to me? I said, to Jacar."

"To Jacar?"

"What is this, a fucking echo? Listen, Marsh, I know it's seven in the morning but—oh, wait a minute, is someone there?"

Marcia wanted to laugh. Only Jeff Stein would think that if someone was with her in bed she'd still be talking to him on the phone. "No, I'm alone."

"Anyway, I said that I think Garnier will give me some office space there, and obviously I'll need a secre- —an assistant—so it's perfect, don't you think?"

In an instant she understood it all. Jeff was asking, no, telling her to come with him. She'd be his assistant. Well, she heard his slip of the tongue, but essentially she'd be his assistant. At his production company. Working for him. No, with him, working for Lindel James. And whoever else he signed, for she had no doubt that with his chutzpah he would be able to parlay this into something major.

"Marsh, are you there?" He sounded irritated.

"I'm here. I'm just thinking," she said quickly. She reached over to the glass of water and swallowed another aspirin.

"Thinking?" his voice roared into the phone. "About what? Don't tell me you'd rather work for that fucking Marty Paretta than me. Jesus, I'm talking here about getting in on the ground floor of something." He softened his voice. "We'd be a team. It's perfect."

Marcia wished her headache would go away. She couldn't think straight. "Well," she said, hesitating, "why don't we talk about it later? I'm sure there's no rush . . ."

"No." Jeff was firm. "I want to be able to walk into that office for the last time today and know that you'll walk out of there with me. If you're worried about money there's no problem. Garnier guaranteed me advances, a promotional budget, escalation clauses—there's more than enough to cover salaries for both of us for a start. And later, well obviously we would talk about percentages of the acts, and so forth." He stopped for a minute to let this sink in, then he said quietly, "Marsh, I need you."

There. He had said it.

Oh, he probably didn't mean it the way she had hoped, or maybe he didn't mean it at all. Faced with the choice of working in the dead-end job of Marty Paretta's secretary or taking a chance on building something new with Jeff Stein, she knew what her answer would have to be. But she didn't want him to know how easy it was for her to make this decision. She was getting tired of being so available all the time.

"Well," she said slowly, "this is all a bit too much for me to digest all at once."

"Don't give me that crap," Jeff snapped. "Yes or no?"

He was trying to act with his usual bravado, she decided, but deep down he was nervous. He needed her and he wouldn't let her see how nervous he was. He probably didn't call to tell her this last night because he thought she was out on a date. That must have been it, otherwise why would he have called now, at the crack of dawn, and ask her if someone was there with her? She didn't think he was jealous—but he was possessive, and she realized that she didn't mind that at all.

The thing was, from a purely objective business viewpoint, it was a great opportunity. And there wasn't a long line of people breaking down her door to rescue her from ACS and give her this chance.

"Well?" he demanded.

"You have to give me some time to think about it," she said, determined not to give in too quickly. Not this time.

"How much time do you need? I'll be at the office at eleven. You can let me know then."

"Jeff," she started to speak but was stopped by the click as he hung up the phone.

She slowly replaced the receiver, leaned back against the pillows and closed her eyes. She was exhausted, and slightly hung over from the wine and the Valium from the night before. The aspirin hadn't helped get rid of her headache, but her mind could not be still. An office at Jacar Records. With Jeff. She'd make more money, she could get some decent clothes. There would be no avoiding meeting Lindel, but she'd worry about that later. For now, she was content to focus on Jeff Stein and Valhalla Records—not a bad name, actually—and what they could do together.

She stretched her arms above her head and looked at the clock. It was only seven-thirty but she knew she would never be able to go back to sleep. It was just as well; she should get to the office early, before Marty got there, so she could start xeroxing his Rolodex.

6

Jeff sat in his new office at Jacar Records and reached across the desk to open the May 15 issue of *Billboard*. His offices were two small rooms behind the package room on the same floor as the publicity department. It was obviously some kind of storage space that they turned over to Jeff after he and Marcia came to Jacar, but he didn't mind. All he really needed was a phone and a desk; what did he care if he didn't have plants, or a window; he knew he wasn't going to be in this tiny room—with Marcia next door—for very long. Marcia, of course, had defiantly brought in her own plants for her desk, and some Warhol flower prints for the wall in an attempt to pretty up her office, but Jeff wouldn't go to that trouble. As long as his two phone lines, and intercom connecting his phone to Marcia's, worked. As long as she picked up the phone and could say "Valhalla Records," Jeff was content. For the moment.

He looked through *Billboard* until he found Lindel's signing photo. The photo was the usual trade shot; Lindel looked great and he looked like he belonged in a police lineup. He would have to remember to shave for future photographs.

He read the caption:

New folk rock sensation Lindel James has signed a long-term recording contract with Valhalla Records, to be distributed by

Jacar Records. Pictured at the signing are (left to right), Jacar Records President, Marc Garnier; Vice-President in Charge of Marketing, Larry Katz; Tim Harrison of Jacar's A & R Department; Miss James and her manager, President of Valhalla Records, Jeff Stein.

Jeff cringed at that "folk rock" bit; otherwise, he was pleased. Unless the artist was a major star, it was unusual for Marc Garnier to be included in a signing photo for a new act. He had done it as a favor to Jeff, who knew that Lindel's reputation at Jacar would be enhanced by an association with the president. It certainly wouldn't hurt Jeff's prestige at the company, either.

After the original deal for Lindel to record with Jacar had been set, Jeff agreed to put her back into the Blue Grotto. Just for one show, he reasoned, as a sort of celebration, and a way of letting some of Jacar's people come to see her sing. Tim had managed to get Marc Garnier to show up, even though he and his wife, Alexis, arrived with some of their friends midway through the set. Ronnie Marren had made a big fuss over the Garniers, sending over several bottles of champagne, and Jeff had been a nervous wreck. Afterward, in the dressing room, the Garniers had been charming, effusive with praise for Lindel, and Marc had pulled Jeff aside to tell him to start thinking of setting up Valhalla Records.

Now, pushing the magazine away, Jeff started to go through the morning mail. Two invitations to music business testimonial dinners went right into the wastebasket. On second thought, Jeff picked them out of the garbage. Those Jew of the Year dinners were important. Lots of deals went down at those things. He remembered when he'd first been at ACS and had rented a cheap tux to go some charity dinner at the Waldorf where he had mingled with the rest of the crowd for the cocktails and the free hors d'oeuvres. He was sure that no one even noticed his absence at the five hundred dollars a plate dinner which followed in the main ballroom. Things would be different now.

The phone buzzed, and he pressed the intercom button.

"Larry Katz is on the line," Marcia said. "He wants you upstairs to go over Lindel's bio and publicity campaign."

"I'll call him back."

Jeff fished around the papers on the desk until he found the bio sent to him two days ago by the publicity department. He crossed out lines like "spirited imagination" and "expressing her generation's joys and sorrows." Dammit, he had told them to make it simple, keep it short, and include none of this ancient flower child bullshit. If he didn't do everything himself, the results were impossibly corny.

When Jeff made the modest deal for Jacar to distribute Valhalla Records, he got a fifty thousand dollar advance for Lindel, a thirty thousand dollar budget toward his initial operating costs, and—within reasonable limits and subject to Jacar's approval—expenses to assist him in signing new acts. Royalty escalation clauses, and tour support for his acts were all written into the thirty-five-page contract. Word got around quickly that Jeff, who had no finished product, or any kind of track record, was Marc Garnier's new pet project. That alone was enough to cause everyone in the company to view him with nervous suspicion.

But with musicians it was an entirely different matter. It was as if an alarm had gone off in that community, as if someone had opened the sewers and a plague of rats came scurrying out. A day did not go by when he did not receive at least five demo tapes and fifteen phone calls. Where did all these unsigned bands come from? He had a hunch that Tim, whose own office was just down the hall, was sneaking his old, unsolicited and unlistened-to tapes onto Jeff's desk, but he couldn't be sure. His desk was now piled high with such tapes, with accompanying notes like:

Dear Jeff Stein,
    You're our only hope. No one knows we exist.
        Sincerely,
        The Vinyl Solution

When Jeff got the money from Jacar, he immediately moved into a three-room apartment on Gramercy Park East. It didn't bother him at all that he paid his rent with money that was supposed to go toward advances for new groups. He knew that he would make the money back. He needed to keep up appearances, he had to have some place to entertain musicians. A place where they could hang out, get stoned, and play their songs for him. Offices were too impersonal, he wanted the right atmosphere in which to woo these groups.

A king-size bed on a platform and complicated stereo system

dominated the bedroom. He arranged to have the TV speakers hooked up to the stereo sound and connected a new Sony videotape machine to his television set. His telephone had three lines and was permanently attached to a phone plug and tape recorder so he could record all his conversations.

The sunken living room was two steps down from a tiny hallway that led out of the bedroom, and was decorated with two large couches, a round oak table with four matching chairs, and a reproduction of a hanging Tiffany lamp. The walls were lined with framed, old Fillmore posters that Jeff claimed were given to him by Bill Graham. The overall effect looked expensive, especially to starving musicians.

He cultivated the rock press, convinced that no one took this bunch of parasites as seriously, or entertained them as lavishly, as he did. A small scene grew up around him, probably because no one before had bothered to take the time.

At first, Lindel had been confused by Valhalla. Over the course of a few days, Jeff had patiently outlined it all to her: he would be her manager and, for the time being, act as her agent in setting up her first tour. He explained that she would be recording for his company—Valhalla—but that it fell within the Jacar umbrella and Jacar would distribute the records to the stores. He gave her the artist's inducement letter to sign that guaranteed to Jacar that she was willing to record for Valhalla. He went through his management contract with her and showed her how he got twenty-five percent of her income and pointed with care to the parts that spelled out what he was committed to do for her. He flipped through his own thirty-five-page contract with Jacar and pointed out clauses he felt would interest her. They were in her apartment and it was three A.M. and finally she pushed the papers aside.

"I'm exhausted," she said, leaning back against the wall next to the fireplace. "I can't take it anymore. None of these contracts are written in English. What does it mean when it says 'shall include but not be limited to'? I'm a musician, not a lawyer. The only thing I understand is that you're calling it Valhalla Records, which isn't bad, and that I get five percent of something. But do you realize that nowhere in these contracts is there a mention of *music?*"

"No?" Jeff said. "Remind me to put it in for the future to impress other artists."

"Seriously, Jeff, I hate all this stuff."

"Of course you do," Jeff said soothingly. "I just wanted you to understand what you're signing. But don't worry about it. I'll have a lawyer look over all of it for us, and then you can sign it."

"I don't understand why you have to look for other acts," she said. "We haven't even done my record yet. Why would they give that to you anyway? Tim said that Garnier just likes to gamble."

Jeff laughed out loud. "Lindel, honey, don't pout. First of all, it'll probably be ages before I even have time to think of another act. I did it so I'd have more power up there for you."

"How?"

"If they think I'm going to come in there screaming about several bands, they're more likely to give me what I want. This will only strengthen my position at Jacar. Trust me on this one."

Once he had convinced Marcia to move with him to Jacar, she had been indispensable: helping to set up their offices, even shopping for towels and sheets for his new apartment. She embraced the beginning of Valhalla Records as if it was a joyous adventure. With her he often played the role of music mogul to the hilt, and would tell her, "I'm not a musician, I don't have that talent. But I've got good ears, and if I see something I believe in, then it's a total gas for me to be able to present it to the public. *I'm* the one who has to get it across. I'm the one who got Lindel the contract, who'll have to hire the band, get the money to put her on the road, book the tour, pay the bills. What I do is an underrated art."

With Lindel he would switch to the more humble, "You're the artist, I'm just the Jewish manager" routine.

But his confidence seemed to know no limit, and his energy was boundless.

Now he slammed Lindel's bio down on his desk, then took it, tore it in half, and dialed Marc Garnier's extension.

Within seconds, the president came on the line.

"Jeff," he sounded pleased to hear from him, "what can I do for you?"

"Look," Jeff said, clearly angry, "the publicity department is supposed to write a bio, occasionally send out press releases and photos, plant items in the columns, send out copies of the tour itineraries, arrange interviews, and pay for the press parties, right? Well, I'm going over this bio these idiots in your publicity department did for Lindel and it sucks. So, now I'm starting to worry about the ad campaign. In our contract it clearly states that everything about Lindel is to be subject to my reasonable approval, but this lousy bio is already on the letterhead and I'm pissed off. Marc, that was not a formality, I meant it. And the same goes for the print ads, the radio ads."

Marc was silent. Obviously, he was not used to dealing with such trivia. But his availability had been part of their deal.

"Why don't you talk to Larry Katz about it?" Marc suggested. "Those people all work for him. I'll tell him to expect your call."

"Never mind. He just called me a little while ago. I'll go up there now."

"Now? Oh, I don't think he'll still be in now," Marc said. "It's twelve-thirty, he's probably on his way to lunch. But don't get too upset about this, Jeff. It can all be worked out. And remember, when you talk to Larry, he's a nice guy, but he is a bit stiff. I'm sure that you realize in a company as big as ours, you have to be able to deal with all kinds of people to get what you want."

In the month Jeff had been at Jacar he noticed that these jokers came into work at eleven, went to lunch at twelve-thirty, didn't come back to the office until three-thirty in the afternoon, and then went to some press party at five. He heard that in the winter, if there was the slightest sign of a snowflake, the commuters didn't even try to make it into town. And when they did, they spent half their time rounding up concert tickets for their children.

Jeff figured out that on the average, the middle-level executives put in a work day of maybe three hours. The only ones who seemed to do any real work were the heads of departments, the president, and the secretaries. It was a wonder that any records at all got on the radio or into the hands of the buying public.

Twelve-thirty. He had a few hours to kill before he could see Larry Katz. He had nothing to do, and he wasn't hungry. Maybe he'd go over to Goody's and see if there were any decent in-store marketing ideas he could use for Lindel's album.

Three hours later, Larry Katz stared at Jeff from across his desk.

"Jeff, you're kidding. You can't possibly release thousands of birds in Times Square the day the album is released. I don't care if the song is called 'White Bird.' Can you imagine the mess it'll create with the traffic?"

"I want to do it," Jeff insisted.

"Jeff," Larry sounded patient, "we'll never get a permit, so this is a pointless discussion. It's such an obvious publicity stunt, and we don't do things that way at Jacar. Within the industry, or at a convention, it's another story. There's a time and place for this kind of a gimmick."

Jeff was bored with Larry Katz. The man had been head of marketing for too many years. His major coup had been getting the promotion men to dress up in colorful costumes when they pushed the new record releases at the radio stations. One year he had sent in a naked girl with the Christmas releases, and it caused an uproar, been the talk of the industry for weeks. The man had the imagination of an underwear salesman.

"Look," said Jeff, raising his voice, "I don't care how you're used to doing things here. My agreement with Marc was that we do things my way with my acts. We'll get the TV crews there, and even if the birds just sit there, crapping, and tie up traffic, it's worth a fortune in publicity. Everyone will remember Lindel's name. And if they fly away, so, that'll be a gorgeous sight."

"Think about this for a minute," said Larry. "If you rent the birds, and they fly away, what about that?"

Jeff waved his hand. "Those are details. I'm sure we could probably buy the fucking things. Or they're trained not to fly away. Or we could round some pigeons up in the park and spray them white. I don't care. It'll work. Remember last month, Led Zeppelin wanted to make some antiwar statement and they let all those doves loose at an outdoor concert in England? Most of the birds just stood on the goddamned stage, they even got caught in the wind machine. So what? People still talk about it."

Larry was exasperated. "Listen, Mike Todd. All you'll need is one bird crushed by a taxi in Times Square and we'll have the ASPCA on our backs so fast we won't know what hit us. We absolutely cannot, *will* not, do it."

Jeff wouldn't even bother to call Marc back on this one. He knew that Larry would complain, Marc would sigh, they'd roll their eyes at each other and mutter about how irresponsible Jeff Stein was. And then they'd end up doing it his way. They were too afraid not to; too afraid that maybe he really did know something that they didn't.

Lindel looked at the sheet music and the pages of song lyrics spread all around her on the floor in her apartment. She looked at Hank Cromwell, who sat next to her, and she smiled.

"I can't thank you enough," she said. "You've really pulled all these songs together."

Hank smiled back at her. "My pleasure. Besides, it was all there in your head, anyway. I just helped you finalize it for yourself."

"I didn't realize when I got you for my bass guitarist that I had found such a brilliant arranger as well."

Hank's grin got wider. "Aw shucks, ma'am. It was nothing."

"No," Lindel insisted, "it is not nothing. These songs sound so good now. They sound so close to what I hear in my head."

She got up and walked over to the window. She looked outside onto the street for a few minutes, and then turned to face Hank.

"Want to call it a night?" she said. "Or should we work more?"

Hank shrugged. "It's up to you. I could put in another hour or so."

The phone rang, and Lindel went into the bedroom to answer it. She came back into the living room and said, "It's Tim. He's at the Grotto. Do we want to meet him?"

"Do you?" Hank said.

"Umm . . . not really," Lindel said. "I think I'd rather try to do one more song. Unless you want to go out?"

Hank shook his head no. "I'd rather make music anytime than sit in some bar. Tell him thanks anyway."

"Who?" Lindel was on her way into the kitchen. "Oh, Tim. I already hung up."

A minute later she returned with a bottle of beer and a glass of white wine. She handed the beer to Hank and sat down on the floor again, facing him.

Hank wore a pale blue button-down shirt with the sleeves rolled up, and faded blue jeans. He was well over six feet, and thin, with short black hair as dark as Lindel's, and he wore small wire-rimmed glasses.

It had only taken her two weeks to put her band together. When she saw Hank Cromwell, jamming at Max's Kansas City one night with some ex-members of The New York Dolls, she knew she had found the perfect bass player. He was sweet, gentle, and he knew more about old rhythm and blues songs than anyone she'd ever met. It was Hank who had brought her Eddie Rosen—the easygoing, solid drummer who had put in time with four unsigned Long Island bands and was thrilled to finally join up with someone who actually had a recording contract. And after weeks of auditioning all the wrong kinds of guitarists who answered Lindel's ad in the *Village Voice,* Hank showed up with Tony Valeska, whom he managed to woo away from studio session work. Lindel thought that Tony's satin trousers and velvet jackets would have to go, but his face was delicate, fine-boned, and his guitar playing was inspirational.

Jeff and Tim seemed to take the new band for granted when they played together for the first time at the SIR rehearsal studios, but to Lindel it was at first a shock, then a relief, to hear her songs played by someone other than herself. It was tangible, audible proof of what she had suspected was there all along.

She looked at Hank and felt a surge of affection. She was lucky to have found him. He was just the type she had occasionally wished she'd had for a brother.

Lindel lit a cigarette, started to say something, and then stopped.

Hank raised an eyebrow. "What were you going to say?" he asked.

"Oh ... nothing." Then she got up and walked over to the record player. She looked through the small stack of records until she found what she was looking for. She pulled the album out of the shelf and held it up for Hank to see. "Have you heard this?" she said.

"The Vipers' new import? Of course. It's fantastic, isn't it? I saw them a few months ago at the Academy of Music ..."

"Me too ..." she said.

" ... Brian Davis is fantastic," Hank said. "I couldn't stop thinking about that performance for weeks."

"Me neither," she murmured, wondering just how much she should say: if she should tell him how since that time she had seen Brian Davis onstage, she had made it a point to get his album and how she listened to it nearly every day. Listening to his voice, to the words he'd written, trying to get some clue as to what he was really like.

"I'd like for us to really get across that feeling," Hank said. "You know, that . . . hard edge. Direct. Totally uncompromising. Like The Vipers do."

"Exactly," Lindel said. Thank god he understood. But it was even more than that. To her, Brian's music and Brian himself were all mixed together in this . . . expectation that she couldn't quite define.

"What do you know about him?" she asked, sitting down.

"Not much. Really just what I've read in the English papers. He's supposed to be smarter than John Lennon or Peter Townshend, as cunning as Jagger, and with the musical soul of Keith Richards. Impossible to believe any such creature exists."

Lindel didn't respond for a minute, then she said, "Why doesn't he tour here more?"

"Claims he doesn't care about 'breaking America.' He's joked about being quite content with this 'cult' audience, with playing for their real fans, the ones who have followed them for the past four years. Of course, he's much more than a cult singer. He's a superstar all over Europe."

"You don't know anyone who knows him?" Lindel said.

Hank shook his head no. "I think he's a bit of a recluse."

She wanted to ask more but was afraid to show so much interest. Brian Davis provoked a disturbing response in her and it was not something she cared to reveal to anyone.

So all she said was, "Well, if he's a recluse, he more than makes up for it when he's on a stage. Anyway, do you want another beer?"

"Sure," Hank said. "I'll get it."

When he returned to the living room he sat down and said, "Do you mind if I ask you a personal question?"

"No. I mean, I don't think I do." She smiled. "What is it?"

"Well," he seemed uncomfortable, shifting his long legs around into a yoga-like position, "I've known you for about six weeks, and we've been working nearly every night. You're easily one of the most gorgeous women I've ever seen in my life and yet . . ." He stopped.

"Go on," she said softly.

"Well, I know it's none of my business, and stop me if I'm out of line, but I'm really curious. You don't have a boyfriend, do you?"

Lindel shook her head slowly. "No," she said softly, "I don't. And you can ask me anything you like. Really. I feel . . . very close to you."

She hesitated. She lit a cigarette, and stared at her hands for a few minutes, saying nothing.

"I broke up with someone about ten months ago," she finally said. "I'm not sure I've fully recovered."

"Who was he?" Hank said.

"Oh . . . his name was David. You wouldn't know him. He was a bartender at the Old Tavern in the Village. I don't think he's there anymore, though. He was a drunk, I guess, but it was like that old joke—I never knew he was drunk until I saw him sober." She tried to laugh.

Hank just looked at her.

"Actually," she went on, "it wasn't very funny. I had been living with him for four months when it happened. He didn't come home one night, and when I woke up at six A.M. and he wasn't lying in the bed next to me, I felt an unexplainable sense of panic. He usually closed up the bar at four, four-thirty, and was back at the apartment by five."

"This apartment?" Hank broke in.

She nodded yes, and continued. "I was instantly awake, turning on the lights, checking the clock and calling the bar. There was no answer. I tried to calm down, telling myself that he probably just went with some of his friends to eat, or to an after-hours place. But that wasn't like him at all, really. Not only did he usually rush home to me each night, he telephoned at least three times during the evening to see that I was all right, to tell me that he loved me."

She stopped talking for a minute, then she said, "You know, after college I came to New York to sing. I never really was interested in anything else. But I met him in the Village right away, and just started spending all my time with him. He seemed so sophisticated, we had so much to talk about. He wasn't like any of the boys I'd ever gone out with. I never was that social anyway, I guess, and he was the first real boyfriend I'd ever had."

"Really?" Hank interrupted. "I don't understand it. Why?"

Lindel smiled. "I just wasn't interested, I guess. Or maybe I was afraid. I don't know, I just always found the music so much more . . . compelling than suburban teenage social life."

"I know what you mean," Hank said.

"Anyway," she continued, "I was in love with him, and it was a brand-new, scary but wonderful feeling. I was sure, too, that it would help my music." She ground out the cigarette and immediately lit another. Hank just sat there, listening, not saying a word.

"We spent days in bed," she continued, "and we took long walks, went to the movies. Sometimes at night I'd go meet him at the bar and wait for him to close up and we'd go eat spaghetti at that all-night Italian place on East Fifty-second Street. The night he didn't come home, I figured maybe that's where he was, maybe I should call him there. But something stopped me. I didn't want to look like I was checking up on him. His hours were so crazy anyway, that it didn't occur to me to be really scared. I was sure he'd be home soon."

She went on. "But at the sound of every car that stopped on the street, I raced to that window," her head nodded toward the window, "looking down to the street to see if he was getting out of a cab. He didn't return that morning, or the next day, and when I called the bar that night I was told that he had been in, but was taking the night off. He hadn't said where he could be reached. I got crazed, I was frantic, calling all the bars where I knew he went. But the answer was always the same. He had been in, but he left. I got into a cab and went downtown, to the Village, to Bleecker Street and to MacDougal and went from one bar to another looking for him. Finally, I saw him in the Kettle of Fish. With a blonde. He was very drunk, or stoned, or both, and abusive, and the girl with him had a hateful smirk on her face."

Hank broke in. "Lindel, you don't have to tell me this."

"I want to," she said quietly. "Anyway, I was shocked, humiliated. I ran out of there—god knows how I got home—and I cried for hours. And still, I expected that he'd run after me, that every car that stopped in the street was a cab with him in it, that any minute I'd hear his key in the door."

She drank some wine, and said, in a flat voice, "When he came back two days later, he was full of remorse. He begged my forgiveness, he didn't know what had happened to make him act so badly, he just had these terrible ... moods. And I was actually glad, relieved, to see him, to have him back, and determined that things between us would be better than before. But you know, I never really trusted him again. And nearly every night that I waited here for him, I would look at the clock and around four A.M. I would start to feel that terrible anxiety. Every night for months."

She stopped talking, and after a few seconds of silence, Hank asked gently, "So, what happened?"

"Almost a year later, he didn't come home one night, and he stayed away for a week. I packed up his clothes in three shopping bags, called a taxi to take them to the bar, changed my phone number and the locks on the door." She gave a short, almost strangled laugh. "I needn't have bothered, he didn't even try to get through. And then I realized, with a combination of anger and a kind of strange relief, that it was over. Just like that. After all that time. As long as he was with someone, it didn't really matter to him who it was. What had been between us just hadn't meant the same thing to him as it had to me."

Lindel and Hank sat, saying nothing, for a long time. Finally, he said, "You don't really miss him, do you?"

Lindel looked thoughtful. "No, I don't miss him. I guess sometimes I miss the intimacy. I get lonely. But I'm glad to have my own life back. And to be able to make this record. Speaking of which," she leaned over to look at Hank's watch, "it's three A.M. and we have to go into the studio tomorrow. I'd better let you get some sleep."

Hank laughed and stood up. "You have such a tactful way of throwing me out," he said, looking around for his jacket.

"I guess I am tired." Lindel smiled. "All that chewing your ear off."

"Anytime ..." Hank said, as they walked to the front door.

"Well," Lindel said, giving him a quick kiss, "good night. Thanks for listening."

Hank looked directly into her eyes. "I said anytime, and I mean it. You're very special to me. After all, you're making it possible for me to do what I've dreamed of all my life. I think you understand what that means."

He opened the door, leaned over to kiss her on the top of her head, and then he was gone.

Lindel sat on a high stool inside Studio A of the Sound Factory, wearing headphones and partially surrounded by a screen. In the hallway outside the studio, Hank and Tony tuned their guitars. In the control room, the engineers were setting up for the first take of "White Bird," while the producer, Richie Viner, walked back behind the elaborate mixing console and sat down. He wore his trademark little taxi driver's cap, and had the ever-present cigarette in his hand as he began to set the dials.

"Where's Hank?" Lindel called into the control room.

Richie pressed the talkback button. "He's just outside in the hallway. You need him?"

Hank appeared behind the console and looked questioningly at Lindel through the glass. Tony had followed him into the control room, and he went right to the lumpy brown leather couch, where he lay down.

"Oh, there you are," Lindel said. "Where's Eddie?"

"He's not here yet," Hank said. "I think he said something about stopping at Manny's to get some new cymbals. Why, what's wrong? Aren't you just doing a rough vocal now?"

"Yes. I just wondered . . ." Lindel's voice trailed off.

"Can she hear us?" Tony leaned up from the couch and turned to Richie, who shook his head no. "What's the matter with her? She's just doing the rough vocal. We don't have to do our overdubs until tomorrow, right?"

"She just likes having us all here, I guess," said Hank. "You know, if she wants an opinion or something."

"Next she'll be asking opinions of the kid who brings in the coffee," muttered Tony from the couch.

Hank's eyes quickly flashed to the talkback button to make sure it was off.

Richie laughed. "Hey, Tony, *I* used to be the kid who brought in the coffee."

"What's the matter with you?" Hank went over to Tony and sat down next to him on the couch. "You seem edgy."

Tony sat up, pulled a joint from the pocket of his black leather jacket, and said, "Oh, it's Susie. She pisses me off."

"What now?" said Hank, who was silently glad once again that he had no steady girl.

"Well," Tony looked around and lowered his voice, "she keeps bugging me about singing on the record."

"Who singing on what record?" Hank took the joint Tony passed to him.

"She sings. Actually, she's not too bad. She wants to sing backup vocals on this record."

Hank smiled. "I assume you haven't mentioned this to Lindel."

"No, not yet."

"I wouldn't, if I were you," said Hank. "I'm sure she's planning on doing all the harmonies herself."

"Well," Tony said, "I don't know. Maybe I could just sneak her in one day when Lindel's not here. Just to pacify the bitch. I'll ask Jeff."

"Ask Jeff what?" said Jeff, as he came in with Tim and a short, pretty blonde girl Hank thought he recognized from the Grotto.

"Oh . . . nothing." Tony looked sheepish.

"Where's Eddie?" said Jeff, looking around.

"Buying cymbals," said Hank. "Manny's is open late."

"Cymbals?" said Tim, darkly. "I *haaate* cymbals."

Jeff sat down on the couch next to Hank, and Tim took the remaining empty chair. The girl who came in with Tim stood quietly against the wall. From the corner of his eye Hank noticed that she wasn't his type—not thin enough—but she had the kind of wide green eyes and helpless good looks that contrasted with the overt sexuality of her tight blue jeans, silk blouse unbuttoned to reveal high, pointy breasts, and a thin strand of gleaming pearls. Tim made no move to introduce her, and Hank felt sorry for her, standing there, all alone, so he stood up and put out his hand.

"I'm Hank Cromwell," he said, as she grasped his hand gratefully.

"Lucy Walker," she responded.

"Oh, I *am* sorry darling," said Tim. "I just assumed you knew everyone. Tony . . . Richie . . . this is Lucy."

"What's going on in there?" Lindel shouted from inside the studio.

Richie pressed the talk button so she could hear him through the glass. "Nothing. Ready? Let's do it, okay?" he said.

The tape started to run. Lindel closed her eyes, listened to Tony's backing track through the headphones, and started to sing.

In the control room Jeff passed a joint to Tim and quickly looked up. "What's she doing?" he muttered. "I've never heard her do it like this before."

Lindel was singing, then half talking, then shouting the lyrics to the ballad "White Bird" in a kind of improvisational chant. She sang the chorus, then whispered some words; Jeff couldn't be sure of what she was saying, but it had a rhythmic, hypnotic effect. It sounded like poetry, then, just as quickly, it was a joyous, lush love song.

"This is fucking great," said Jeff. "It's gonna be a smash."

"You don't think it's too . . . 'political'?" said Tim.

"Nah, it's a great gimmick," said Jeff. "I know she didn't do it purposely, but the lyrics might make people think it's anti-war, or something, but they could also think she's singing about herself. Kids can identify with all that ambiguous shit about freedom, wanting to fly. It's perfect."

Lindel's eyes were closed; she didn't see Jeff and Tim talking. No one could touch her when she sang, when she felt she was getting it right. She felt so good, she probably would have done it for free.

As the echoes of the last line faded over the speakers, Richie's voice came through her headphones. "Incredible," he said. "Want to come in and listen?"

"No, I think I want to do it again. I can get the last line better."

"Baby, it was a great take," Richie said. "Maybe you should just try the last line?"

Jeff glared at him. "If she wants to sing the whole goddamn song ten times to get the last line right, let her. We don't have to be so fucking chintzy."

"Hey man, you were the one who told me to try to keep the cost down. Suit yourself," Richie said. "I just thought it was a great take."

Lindel yelled, "Hey, you guys, what are you doing in there, are we doing this again or not?"

"Sure, baby." Richie's voice was soothing. "Ready?"

7

It was one-thirty in the morning, and Tim Harrison and Lucy Walker tried to hail a taxi in front of the tiny CBGB club on Bleecker Street and the Bowery. Two yellow Checker cabs with brightly lit "On Radio Call" signs passed them by.

"It's no wonder," muttered Lucy, "in this neighborhood."

"Darling, this neighborhood couldn't be more fabulous," said Tim. "Anyway, you wanted to come here. I couldn't have kept you away."

"Well, I'd been hearing so much about all these new bands," Lucy said. "I wanted to check it out. But I should have brought the car." Tim stood in the middle of the empty street and looked both ways. Not a cab in sight. Broken beer bottles and overflowing garbage cans littered the street, and two men slept in the doorway of the flophouse that was next to CBGB's.

"My ears are still ringing from that group," Lucy said, pulling her sweater tighter around her small frame. "What's their name?"

"Task Force," said Tim, still concentrating on finding a cab. "They're from Akron, Ohio."

Tim hailed the cab, and as they got in he said to Lucy, "The Grotto?"

"Of course." She smiled. "The night's still young."

The back room in the Blue Grotto was fairly empty, and Tim and Lucy automatically went to Tim's regular table. The waitress came over right away, and after she took their drink order, Tim said to her, "Ronnie around?"

"I haven't seen him for a few hours. I don't think he's in the office, either, but I'll go look."

When she was gone, Tim looked at Lucy. Her short blonde hair was cut like a man's but somehow it only accentuated what was a fragile face. She was tan most of the year, Tim knew, but this was not one of those times, and the paleness of her skin and hair made her seem almost angelic. At that thought, Tim had to smile.

"What's funny?" Lucy said.

"Oh ... nothing," Tim said, then added, "Have you lost weight?"

"No," she grinned, "this sweater is two sizes too big."

"What a great idea," Tim said. "You should buy *all* your clothes two sizes too big. It makes you seem so ... frail."

"I didn't buy it two sizes too big." She sounded annoyed. "It's not my sweater."

Tim knew she wanted him to ask whose sweater it was, and he purposely remained silent. If she was going to name-drop again, it would be without encouragement from him. The waitress brought their drinks, and Tim leaned back in his chair and surveyed the room.

"Amazing, isn't it?" he said. "Only two o'clock and it's dead already."

"It's Monday night," said Lucy, sipping brandy. "Mondays are always dead."

"Mmm, maybe. But CBGB was packed. I have to tell Ronnie. He should know that he's got some competition."

Lucy raised her eyebrows. "Are you kidding? That place? Don't be silly. Who's going to go there?"

"Wait and see. There were almost a hundred people in there tonight. To see a totally unknown band from Akron, of all places. God knows what they're putting in the water in Akron these days."

"They were weird, weren't they?" Lucy agreed.

"I thought they were adorable," Tim said.

"What, with those songs about bank accounts and nuclear energy? The lead singer looks loony."

"I know him," said Tim. "He's mad as a hatter. But there's something about them that's special. I wish I could sign them, but I'd never be able to get them in the door at Jacar."

Lucy looked around the room. "There really is no one here tonight," she said. "I heard that Rod Stewart was in town . . ."

"Wishful thinking," said Tim. "Rod hasn't been this far downtown in years."

Lucy took a tiny bottle of white powder out of her pocketbook and unscrewed the top.

"Here?" Tim said. "Out of respect for Ronnie, we should at least do your drugs in the bathroom."

"Oh, what's the difference," said Lucy, digging one long fingernail into the bottle then quickly pressing her finger against one nostril as she inhaled. "So tell me," she said, "what's Lindel really like?"

Tim thought a minute, then said, "You know, I honestly don't know."

"What do you mean? You've spent months getting to know her, you signed her, I thought you two were best friends."

Tim finished his glass of wine and signaled the waitress for another round of drinks.

"Well, we do spend a lot of time together," he said. "I guess I'm one of her best friends . . . I don't know. She doesn't seem to have any real friends."

"No boyfriend?" Lucy pressed.

Tim shook his head. "I've never heard her mention one. She did mention some guy she used to go with, but I think they broke up almost a year ago."

"She's not having a thing with Jeff, is she?"

Tim laughed out loud. "Jeff Stein? You don't know how funny that is."

"Well, I don't know." Lucy seemed put out. "He couldn't keep his eyes off her at that session. I don't think it's so crazy."

"Lucy, you've been around enough managers and artists to know what that's about."

"Well, anyway, I thought she was terrific. I'm sorry we didn't get more of a chance to talk."

Tim looked at her sharply, but Lucy's face remained impassive as she continued talking.

"Why don't you bring her here one night after the session?"

[80]

"She likes to go home after the session," said Tim. "She hasn't been out in weeks."

"Well, why don't you try?" Lucy was more insistent now. "Maybe she'd like to come with us to see a band. As you said, she could probably use some friends . . ."

"I didn't say that," Tim cut in.

"Well, you know what I mean."

"Yes," Tim said slowly, with a strange little half-smile, "I think I do."

Tim liked to hang out with Lucy Walker. She really couldn't be considered just a groupie, because she had all that family money. She had credit cards and an expensive Greenwich Village co-op apartment paid for by her parents, who paid, too, for her small sports car and large wardrobe.

Her parents disapproved of what they perceived as her playgirl life, but as long as she continued to take acting and dancing classes in New York City, and seemed to have some goals, they agreed to continue to support her.

When The Rolling Stones had come to San Francisco in 1969, Lucy was sixteen, and ran away from her family's home on Russian Hill to sneak into Brian Jones's hotel suite. He kicked her out after only one night, but she dined out on it for the next five years. Being around a band as famous as that seemed incredibly glamorous and Lucy was hooked. She became a familiar face backstage at the Fillmore West, and for the next few years there wasn't a major musician who passed through the city who didn't get to know Lucy Walker.

She came to New York from San Francisco on a private jet with Led Zeppelin in 1972, and never went back. She actually did register for acting classes with Stella Adler, but after a year she was bored, and, since the classes were held at night, and she was missing too many great concerts, she stopped going, although she neglected to tell her parents. She still did go to the dancing class three afternoons a week; after all, she needed to stay in shape.

She and Tim became fast friends that year she came to New York. He knew everyone, and was a great source of information. When things were slow, and there were no bands in town, he was fun to spend time with, and they usually talked on the phone at least once a day. For the past few months, Tim had been talking nonstop about Lindel James, and Lucy had finally been able to get him to take her to one of Lindel's sessions.

Now Lucy had another plan. But she'd have to be careful; Tim didn't miss much. She'd have to try and work it so that Tim thought it was all his own idea.

It was two A.M. when Lindel left the studio. Jeff and Tim had gone to Ahmet Ertegun's party for Manhattan Transfer at the Carlyle Hotel, and she was alone.

She walked to Sixth Avenue, sidestepping the occasional drunk, and turned downtown. The city was so still at this time, and while Jeff would have yelled at her for walking alone, she always felt safer, more at home in that dark night than she did in a bright, busy afternoon.

On nights like this, when she could escape from everyone at the end of a session, she felt free. Jeff had been hassling her, something about the publishing of her songs, and taxes, and finally she just told him that whatever he did was fine with her—she was busy making music. Now she could walk for hours, looking in shop windows, feeling the silent rhythms of the city. Sometimes, when she got in this mood, she'd walk way uptown to the upper East Side and look at the linens in the stores on Madison Avenue, the empty bakeries, the elegant bookshops. It was all a source of unexplained inspiration. Even though she'd grown up in the suburbs, her teenage years had never been filled with wild car rides in the middle of the night. This kind of walk, alone, was perhaps the most reckless thing she ever did. It gave her a certain satisfaction, as if she had a secret soul that she would share with no one else. Lately, it had gotten crowded around her. She needed time to breathe.

Now she was tired, but she knew that the twelve more blocks until she got home presented no problem. She looked forward to being in her apartment, taking off her clothes, and getting into a soothing hot bath. Damn, she forgot to buy food, and she was hungry. She had envisioned a cozy little scene for herself. Maybe even take that small color television set—the one Marc Garnier had given to her when she'd signed the contract—into the bathroom and watch a late night movie while she soaked in the tub and sipped some wine. Except there wasn't any wine. She never had any time these days to take care of such things. But something would be open all night; she could get some fruit, or ice cream, at least. It was surprising to her how small things like that could give her so much pleasure, how they could relieve the tension of the work. Of course, tomorrow the whole thing would begin all over again: the studio, the arguments with the band or Richie or both about one track or another, the continued debate about the title for the album. But for now, she could unwind, be by herself, and not feel the need for anyone, or anything else in the world. It was a special time, part of the waiting time. Waiting for her other life, her real life, to begin.

As all the plans accelerated, Lindel felt a combination of excitement and dread. She grew increasingly nervous, particularly around Jeff.

"Do you realize I haven't looked at a newspaper, read a book, gone to a movie, seen another band, or even had an evening out in nearly three months?" she said to Jeff. "Everything has totally revolved around this record. I haven't even seen anyone except you, Richie and the band."

They were in the control room, Lindel, Jeff and Richie, listening to three different versions of vocals for "Roll On," which Jeff had decided should be the follow-up single to "White Bird." Jeff was wearing a plaid shirt that Lindel particularly disliked and he was making some notes in the small looseleaf notebook he carried with him everywhere these days. Richie finished rolling a joint, lit it, and passed it to Lindel.

She shook her head, refusing the joint, and said, "Jeff—are you listening to me? I'm taking off for a little while. I've just got to get out of here, take a break."

Jeff closed the notebook and said, "Where are you going? I'll go with you."

"No," she said, quickly. Then seeing his hurt look, she said, "I just feel like being alone for awhile. Maybe I'll go home and clean my apartment. Or I'll get my laundry ready to take in. Everything is such a mess. I don't seem to have time to get organized."

"I told you." Jeff took the joint from Richie. "Marcia can arrange all that stuff for you."

Lindel reached back behind her neck and stretched her arms in the air. She pulled her hair back off her face and, picking a rubber band off the console, tied her hair into a ponytail. "Marcia runs the office," Lindel said. "She can't organize my life. From what I saw up there, it looked like you've got her really overworked as it is."

Jeff eyed her suspiciously. "Did she tell you that?"

"When would she have told me that? I only met her at the office and had that one lunch with the two of you at the Tea Room last month. And you were so busy talking she and I could barely get a word in edgewise."

Lindel got up to go, and gave Richie and Jeff kisses good-bye.

Maybe she would stop by the Grotto after all, she thought, as she looked for a taxi on Seventh Avenue. Tim had mentioned he'd be there, and she hadn't been in the place in a long time.

She could use some casual conversation and a few glasses of wine. It would help her relax, and maybe even help her, eventually, to be able to get to sleep.

"Lindel, you met Lucy Walker, didn't you?" Tim introduced the short blonde girl who sat at his table in the Blue Grotto.

"I think so," Lindel said as she sat down. "You were at the studio a few weeks ago, weren't you?"

"Yes." Lucy smiled.

Lindel was disappointed not to find Tim alone. Even though she had complained about it to Jeff, she had found it increasingly difficult to have to make small talk with civilians, anyone who wasn't an integral part of helping to make her album.

Without asking, Tim poured a glass of white wine for Lindel and said, "How'd it go tonight?"

"Okay, I guess," said Lindel. "But my neck hurts so much I can barely turn my head."

"It's tension," said Tim. "Come here." He put his hands on Lindel's shoulders and began to massage around the back of her neck.

"Ahh," Lindel sighed, smiling. "I can't believe how great that feels. Where on earth did you learn how to do that?"

"I've had a lot of practice." Tim grinned, massaging harder. "Ssh, don't talk, just relax."

No one said anything for a few minutes. Lindel looked around the room. She didn't recognize anyone. This probably wasn't a good idea. She should be home, in bed.

"I saw the proofs of your album cover today," said Tim.

Lindel turned around and looked at him. "And?" she said.

"Oh, it's fabulous," Tim said. "Lucy, wasn't I saying before how gorgeous the photo was?"

"He did," nodded Lucy. "He said that you looked gorgeous. I can't wait to see it."

"Jeff wanted it to be glamorous," said Lindel. "But I was afraid I looked too haughty . . . too high fashion."

Tim shook his head. "No," he said. "You look mysterious. It's perfect."

"I'll have to ask Marcia to get me a copy," Lindel said.

"Oh, that's right," smiled Tim. "I heard you finally met the Cosmopolitan Girl."

"I liked her," Lindel said, annoyed.

"Have you ever seen her ridiculous apartment?" Tim said.

"No . . . our friendship hasn't gone that far. Mostly, she just calls and relays messages from Jeff, wakes me up, that sort of thing."

"Does she still have a crush on Jeff?"

"Jeff?" Lindel was surprised. "Does she? I have no idea." She thought about leaving. Tim was in one of those moods and he was getting on her nerves. But Lucy seemed sweet. Lindel didn't want to leave after only fifteen minutes. It would be too rude.

Lindel turned to Lucy. "What do you do?" she asked.

"Oh . . . not much." Lucy smiled wryly. "I was taking acting lessons, but I'm not sure I've got the discipline to really work at a career."

"Lucy's waiting for someone to discover her at a soda fountain," said Tim.

"*Tim* . . ." Lindel said. Lucy looked hurt and Lindel immediately felt sorry for the girl. Tim was just impossible sometimes.

"I really like the whole music scene," Lucy said quietly, "but I can't see myself sitting in an office all day. I do have so much free time though, it seems as though there should be something I could do."

Her sentence hung in the air as Lindel sipped the wine and Tim yawned. Lucy, not sure if he was making fun of her, shot him a furious look.

"I didn't know you were looking for a *job*," said Tim. "When did all this come about, and why?"

"I'm bored," Lucy said. "I have a lot of time on my hands. I'd like to feel useful. I don't know . . . sorry I brought it up."

For some reason Lindel felt herself responding to the girl. Actually, they were probably about the same age, but there was something about Lucy that made her seem fragile. It wasn't just her soft blonde looks, or her huge green eyes. She seemed . . . likable, refreshing.

Just then Tim raised his hand and a big smile appeared on his face.

"I've got it," he said.

"You look like a light bulb just went off over your head," Lindel said.

"I've got the *best* idea," he said.

Lucy and Lindel just looked at him.

"Why doesn't Lucy work for you?" he said to Lindel.

"Doing what?" Lindel said.

"Oh, you know, things. Taking care of the details."

"Details?" Lindel said.

"Laundry, shopping, making appointments, getting drugs. You know."

Lindel laughed. "That's ridiculous. I don't take drugs. And Marcia makes all the business appointments. Why would Lucy want to do all that other stuff? I hardly see her as a shlepper."

Lucy said nothing.

Tim continued. "Lucy loves the business, and she loves your music," he counted on his fingers. "She's bored, and she's organized. Believe me, you're going to need a personal assistant, and she has money so you wouldn't even have to pay her much."

"Tim!" Lindel was outraged. "You're talking about her as if she wasn't here."

"Oh, I'm used to him." Lucy smiled, then added softly, "Tim, I don't think this is such a good idea."

"I think it's a fabulous idea," Tim insisted. "Every big rock star has an assistant."

Lindel made a face. "I'm not a big rock star."

Lindel turned to her. "Do you think this is a good idea?"

Before she could answer, Tim said, "You could pay her when you started to make money. I know Jeff would go for the idea."

"Look, Tim," Lucy broke in, "you're embarrassing me. We've just met. I think we should drop this."

"Well, at least I think you should think about it," Tim said.

The three of them sat in silence for a minute. The J. Geils Band's new single was on the jukebox, and Lindel thought about how great Peter Wolf's voice sounded. She wondered if she should add some echo to her voice on one of the songs. Lucy drank her wine and nibbled on the few remaining peanuts in the small white bowl on the table. Lindel lit a cigarette. She thought about Tim's bizarre but intriguing idea about Lucy. How would it work? She couldn't imagine having someone around her apartment. But it might be a relief to be rid of all those annoying daily chores. And to have a friend to talk to. It was something to think about.

"I'm exhausted," Lindel said suddenly. "I've got to go to sleep."

"I'll drop you off on my way uptown," said Tim.

"Uptown?"

"He found a new bar," Lucy said.

"I don't know how you find the strength," said Lindel. "To say nothing of the continued interest. It's after two in the morning."

"That's the best time," Tim said. "Anyway what about my Lucy idea?"

"I'll think about it," Lindel said. "I really will. And talk to Jeff. That is," she turned to Lucy, "if you're interested?"

"Oh . . . yes, I'd be interested," said Lucy, who stared directly at Lindel, ignoring the wink that Tim gave her behind Lindel's back.

Lindel had been trying to get out of bed for an hour. Today, she was in no rush to get to the studio. They were having trouble with her final vocal for "Roll On"—hadn't gotten it right in twenty takes last night—and she wasn't looking forward to starting all over again.

She hadn't slept well; she couldn't sleep with the air conditioner on; it was bad for her voice. The air in her bedroom was muggy, stifling.

She heard the key turn in the front door.

"Lindel, you up?" Lucy shouted from the hallway.

"Mmm," she said. "Come on in."

Lucy walked into the bedroom and sat down on the edge of the bed. She wore a green sundress and large, dark sunglasses. Lindel sat up in bed, pulled the sheet around her and reached for a cigarette.

"Give me one too," Lucy said in a husky voice. "Then I'll go make some coffee. Lord knows, I need it."

"What's the matter?" Lindel said.

"I haven't been to sleep yet. I ended up with Tim and these musicians I used to know from San Francisco. We staggered out of the Grotto at four, then stopped by Ronnie Marren's. It was one of those nights."

Lindel didn't say anything. She recalled that Lucy had said yesterday that she'd been up all night the night before, too.

Lucy went to turn on the air conditioner and started picking up clothing that Lindel had scattered on the floor.

"Don't bother doing that," Lindel said. "I just dropped everything on the floor when I got back from the studio, I was so exhausted. I'll pick it up." Lucy had been working for her for three weeks, but it still embarrassed Lindel when Lucy cleaned up after her.

"Don't be silly," Lucy mumbled, as she walked out of the bedroom into the kitchen.

Lindel remained in bed for a few minutes and listened to Lucy puttering around the kitchen. It was amazing how someone she'd only known for a month had managed to make herself become so essential.

When Lucy had offered to help out and asked only for expense money until Lindel could pay more, Jeff reluctantly agreed. Even Lindel was surprised at all the things Lucy found to do. Lucy liked to say that she relieved Lindel of all the silly chores so Lindel didn't have to do anything except make music, and Lindel had to admit that it made things easier and most of the time, Lucy was fun to have around.

Getting out of bed to go into the shower, Lindel heard the sounds of water running in the kitchen sink, drawers opening and closing, and Lucy singing. Lindel stopped, and listened to Lucy singing "White Bird." Lucy's voice was nothing special, but she had a good memory. It had taken Lindel a month to get her own song right, and Lucy only heard the final version of that a week ago in the studio.

She walked into the kitchen.

"How come you remember all the words?" she said to Lucy, who quickly put something that looked like a small mirror into her dress pocket.

"Oh," Lucy smiled, still wearing the sunglasses, "it's so catchy. I just loved hearing it the first few nights in the studio, that's all. So I borrowed the lead sheets."

Lindel frowned. "Lead sheets. Where'd you get those?"

"From Richie." Then she added, "I'm positive that song is going to be a hit."

"Well," said Lindel, "thanks. But I'd rather you didn't take those things out of the studio. I'm not sure Jeff's done the copyrights on them yet."

"I'm sorry." Lucy looked upset. "I only took them for one day."

"Oh, forget it," Lindel said. "I guess I'm just touchy, with this record almost done and all."

Lucy gave her a relieved smile, and went into the bedroom. She came back out and said, "I'm going to drop off this laundry. See you later at the studio."

"Okay. Thanks."

"And don't forget. Those horn players are coming back in again at three to see if you want them on 'Roll On.' "

"I did forget," Lindel said. "Did Richie tell the guys?"

"I'm sure he did, but I'll see Eddie and Hank so I'll warn them."

"You'll see them?" Lindel was surprised.

"I stop by their place to wake them before the studio. It's on the way."

After Lucy left, Lindel sat at the table for a long time. The apartment was so quiet, so still.

She didn't know what to make of Lucy. Sometimes Lucy would look at her in a way that Lindel found unsettling. Even though it was a luxury to have all her errands done for her, Lucy was too solicitous, and it made Lindel uncomfortable. And she suspected that Lucy took too many drugs.

Lindel took a container of orange juice out of the refrigerator. All she had ever wanted was to be a good singer. No, a great singer. And now there were all these other things, and all these people around, each with a particular job to do based on her. It was like a well-oiled little machine.

She seemed within range of having it all happen the way she had wanted it to, and now she was scared. Scared to see her life begin to mesh with what had, at one time, been a dream.

8

When Lindel heard the finished album on the studio's giant speakers, all she could think of was that she wanted to do it over again. Just one word, she thought, placed in the middle of a particular song, would give the song more power; she was embarrassed that her voice seemed so loud, and she wasn't sure about the sequencing of the songs. Jeff told her that it was always this way with a finished album, she retorted that he couldn't possibly know, and he shrugged and made notes in his little book about his plans for the album's release.

The only remaining problem was the title.

Lindel and Hank had been in the studio with Richie, mixing the final tracks, until eight in the morning, and then Jeff had called this summit meeting at ten o'clock that night to decide the title. Lindel had told Lucy just to tell Hank about the meeting; she didn't want anyone else from the band there. Now she turned around and looked to Hank for help. He smiled at her.

"Don't worry," he said, "we'll come up with something."

"But we've been here for two hours," Lindel said.

No one said anything for a minute. Then Jeff got up and started pacing.

"Okay," Jeff said to Lindel. "You don't want any of the song titles: 'Roll On'? 'White Bird'?"

Lindel made a face. "Don't get me started on the song titles. I'm not even sure I like *them* . . ."

"Okay," said Jeff. "What about 'Moonbeam'?"

"*Moonbeam?*" Lindel and Hank cried in unison.

"Look, I'm just trying to come up with some ideas, is all," Jeff said with annoyance. "You want to run a contest?"

"Why not just 'Lindel James'?" Lucy suggested.

"I like it," Lindel laughed. "It has a nice ring to it."

"No, that's out," said Jeff, sitting down on the edge of the console. "We need a great selling title here. Something . . ."

" . . . accessible," Lindel muttered.

"Oh look darlin'," Jeff said, "don't start. When you want to make records and tack them onto fucking trees to be appreciated by the artistic few, then you can make these cracks. Meanwhile, think of a title." He looked at his watch. "And think of it within a half hour, because I'm going to bed and I want to get moving with Jacar in the morning."

"Maybe Tim should be in on this," Lucy suggested.

"No thanks," said Lindel. "I've already heard his ideas. All of them depicting some sort of horrible death."

Lindel took a cigarette out of her pocketbook and looked around for a match. Jeff pulled a lighter out of his brown leather bomber jacket and leaned over to give her a light. She sat back against the couch and immediately started to cough.

"*What* is that?" Jeff said.

"Nothing," Lindel said. "I'm just tired."

"You've been coughing like that for weeks," Lucy said.

"Well, you'd better cut out the cigarettes before the tour," Jeff snapped. "I won't have you hacking your way across the goddamn country. You've got six weeks and thirty cities to do coming up and we were lucky to get them. At this rate, your voice won't hold up."

"I'll be fine," Lindel said. "I told you, I'm just tired. Now can we please think of something?"

"How about 'Walk on Glass'?" Hank said quietly.

Lindel turned around to look at him.

"Who's used that?" Jeff said.

"No one," Hank said. "I just remember that it was something Peter Townshend once said. About how being involved with rock and roll was like trying to walk on glass . . . I don't know, forget it, I guess."

"No," said Lindel, still looking at him. "I like it. What do you think?" She turned to Jeff.

"It's great," he said. "Isn't it, Lucy?"

"Great," she echoed.

" 'Walk on Glass' . . . Hank, that's really good." Lindel smiled.

"Okay, we all agree? Then that's it," said Jeff, grabbing his jacket from the couch.

"Wait a minute," said Lindel. "Can we use that? I mean there's no song by that name on the album."

"Who cares?" said Jeff. "I like the title and it doesn't matter if there's no song by that name. I can sell anything," he said, and he ducked as Lindel hurled the nearest thing she could find—a copy of Kal Rudman's radio tip sheet—at his head.

The next morning, Jeff threw himself into what he considered nothing short of war between himself and Jacar Records. The art department claimed that it would take six weeks for the album cover to be ready, he told them to get it done in three. The publicity department urged Jeff to do a major mailing of advance pressings, with personal letters to each journalist—many of whom were, by now, his friends—but he knew better.

"Let them wait," he had said to Susan Blond, Jacar's publicity chief, "and ask for it themselves rather than we try to shove it down their throats."

He argued with the advertising department. They no longer believed in taking big ads in any magazines other than *Rolling Stone*. Jeff wanted half-pages, at least, in everything including the *Rock Scene* and *Trouser Press*. He called Marc Garnier about tour support, about radio ads; he wanted TV spots in key cities, and, because as far as he was concerned, the money was free, he used the month of August to spend lavishly on equipment for the band, including their own sound system—virtually unheard of for a new group; on clothes for Lindel; better quality paper for the album's inner sleeve; more phone lines for his office, and charged it all to Jacar.

The week that the advance pressings of the album were due, Lindel was filled with a sense of dread. An *album* . . . of her own. She looked at the proofsheets of the artwork—which she taped around a Stones album to see how it would look when finished. How had she ever let Jeff talk her into that art deco typeface? And she was nervous about the photo; it was almost too sensual.

She had waited for this for so long, planned for it, worked hard at it, and now that it was almost here, it seemed something alien, foreign, unwieldy. It no longer belonged just to her.

When the magnum of Dom Perignon was delivered to her apartment she figured this was The Day. When the Chinese food came, she was sure of it. At eight o'clock her doorbell rang and there stood Jeff, holding a dozen of her favorite Sonia roses in one hand and a manila envelope in the other.

"Trying to soften the blow?" she said.

He laughed, and walked past her into the apartment.

"Is that *it?*" She eyed the package suspiciously.

"This is it, honey. It's a big day for us."

"Oh my god." She sat down on the couch.

"Come on," he said, "this is an occasion." And he walked over to the turntable, and started to remove the test pressing from its envelope.

"No, wait," she said. "I think this isn't such a good idea. Maybe I should hear it alone first . . ."

He turned and looked at her.

"Well," he said, clearly choosing his words carefully, "if you like. But Lindel, it isn't as if we haven't heard it already. And this is as exciting for me as it is for you."

"Oh, don't pout, for Christ's sake. Put the damn thing on."

She definitely would have rather heard it alone. Jeff—always there, always watching her, gauging her reaction, waiting to see how he should respond, afraid to say the wrong thing. Sometimes she thought she would suffocate. But then, he had been there with her, and this was as much of a triumph—if it was to be considered that—for him, as for her. She couldn't shut him out now.

The first strains of the band came through the medium-sized speakers, and she knew in exactly how many seconds she would hear her voice. She was glad that they had chosen "Roll On" for the first track, it was upbeat, and had a good hook to get people to listen to the rest of the album. There it was, her voice . . . it still sounded funny to her. She could appraise it better if it was someone else's, but it was hard to feel that connection between what was coming out over the speakers—to remember those words she wrote, and her voice. She still thought of that voice coming from somewhere else; as if it was some other "her" singing. The ballad followed, the one everyone thought would be a hit. She wasn't so sure, but she knew that "White Bird" did sound strong. It was beyond pretty; she sounded as if she was in command. The band sounded good, Tony's guitar lines were never obtrusive, and the rhythm tracks were solid and sexy. She began to relax.

She actually liked this record. She probably would have liked it more if it hadn't been hers. She would never know what it would be like to hear it, as a stranger would, for the first time, and it wasn't exactly the album that she had envisioned she would make, but she felt good about it.

When they had listened to both sides, Jeff leaned over and took the needle off the record. He turned and looked at her, eyes lit up, very wide, and smiled.

"Fuckin' dynamite," he said.

She said nothing.

"Come on," he said, "say something, dammit."

She wished she didn't have to say anything. But she owed him this.

"I love it," she said quietly.

Jeff jumped up and grabbed her in his arms. He tried to dance around with her, whooping and hollering until, out of breath and collapsing with laughter, they both fell onto the couch he had insisted she buy.

"Whew," he said. "That's over. Now we can eat."

She tuned out his chatter, thinking that right now she felt an odd combination of sadness and anticipation. It was, after all, only one record and she would make others. It was just so permanent, and there were just a few things that she wished she could fix . . .

Jeff sat down and started to eat. Lindel pushed the food around on her plate. After five minutes Jeff realized that she hadn't touched a thing, and without skipping a beat, he started in on her food.

"Don't worry, honey," he said, his mouth full of chicken with garlic. "It can't miss."

"Don't say that." She raised her voice. "I've told you not to say that."

"Lindel, you know I wouldn't let you release it if it wasn't good. You just told me you love it. Pass the rice."

She gave him a sullen look. He leaned across the table and took the bowl of rice.

"I never said I loved it," she muttered.

"*Love,* you said, I heard you. I have total recall. You said love."

"Oh look, you'd better get used to it. I'm going to go through a million changes before the thing is out. I'm just scared, that's all. Nothing major."

"Scared," he said, "of what?"

"Of where I fit. The same thing I'm always scared of. That no one will want to hear me sing. That they won't like it . . . And you keep telling me how hard it is to get airplay, how important publicity is . . ."

"Stop it." He was firm. "I shouldn't have told you about all of that. From now on I promise I'll try not to fill your head with the business shit. They'll write about you, don't worry. And who cares what they say, as long as they spell the name right."

"Jeff, that line went out with the twenties."

Jeff put his fork down, wiped his mouth with his sleeve, and seemed to be through with his meal. He looked at her, long and hard. She knew that on the way was a Major Statement. She waited.

"Do you want to do the album over?" he said.

"Probably. Yes. In reality? No. I'm sure it would come out more or less the same."

"Okay, so we've established that this is the best record you can make at this time. I might add, it's better than anything anyone else is doing too. Now, let's go on. Do you want me to buy it back from Jacar? Or refuse to put it out? To say, as head of your record company, that it doesn't meet a commercially acceptable standard?"

"Can you do that?"

"Read your contract. Yes, I can. Of course, I wouldn't. Unless you want me to."

"Don't be silly," she mumbled. "You're purposely trying to make me look foolish. I get it; humor me, explore all the impossible options, and make me realize just how lucky I am."

She sat there, thinking about what he had said, waiting for the rest. He didn't disappoint her.

"Okay," he said, staring directly into her eyes. "You're right, you know. You don't fit and Janis didn't fit and Hendrix didn't fit and the Stones don't fit and Morrison didn't fit. And I, for one, am not going to let you forget it, or drive yourself crazy like this. You've got an amazing, fucking unbelievable voice and the world has always listened, paid attention, stopped whatever it was doing, for a special voice. I'm so sure of this, Lindel . . . I just know I'm right."

She let out a long, low whistle. "Where did you learn how to say all the right things?"

He looked offended. "I meant every word."

"Well," she said, taking the dishes to the sink, "I certainly hope so. And that's good. You've got enough balls for the two of us. You're going to need it."

Lindel sat along the wall at the middle of a large oblong table in Patsy's Restaurant. All around her were various Jacar Record executives, and Jeff and Tim. She hadn't wanted this dinner, had complained about it to Jeff, but he had put his foot down.

"How many of them do I have to fuck?" she had said.

"Lindel, for god's sake," Jeff had been exasperated, "they'll work harder on the album if they feel they have more of a personal relationship with you."

"It's their job to work on my album," Lindel said.

"Yeah, yeah, I know," Jeff said. "Still, trust me on this one."

Tim had agreed to come along, but not until after he had told her, "You'll adore this bunch. They all wear polyester shirts with the long pointed collars outside the jackets and practically down to the waist."

"I don't care about that," Lindel had said. "What are they like?"

"As people, you mean? Let's just say they're the ones who get paid well enough to have to nod their heads in time to the music at concerts."

So here they were, assembled in Lindel's favorite Italian restaurant and Jeff was well into his current tap dance—as Marcia would put it—about the tour.

"She," Jeff nodded in Lindel's direction, "wanted me to book her in small clubs in just a few northeastern cities to try things out."

He smiled at Artie Johnson, Bill Carson, Denny Carillo, Stan Rubenstein and Paul Dickinson. They all turned to smile at Lindel and then back to Jeff.

"I haven't really worked with the band in front of an audience yet," Lindel said softly.

"Sweetheart," said Jeff, "I told you that three weeks of rehearsals would straighten everything out, and it has. She's fucking dynamite. Isn't she, Tim?"

All eyes turned to Tim.

"Fucking dynamite," Tim agreed.

"Listen," Artie Johnson broke in, "you wanna order, or what?"

"Sure, let's order," said Jeff, looking for the waiter.

"The veal is out of this world here," said Denny Carillo.

"The veal marsala or the veal parmigiana?" said Paul Dickinson. "Which veal?"

"Any veal," said Denny Carillo. "Trust me. You can't go wrong with the veal."

"Order me the veal marsala," said Bill Carson, standing up. "I've got to go to the little boys' room." He gave them a wink.

"I didn't know you were looking for little boys," said Paul Dickinson and everyone broke up laughing except Lindel and Tim.

"Oh, brother," Tim muttered to himself.

The waiter appeared and took their order, and Jeff continued to talk.

"So," he said, "I've been telling the lady that in order to sell a debut album by a total unknown, of course, we have to get her on the radio, but it's terrifically important that she be seen by as many people as possible. Isn't that right, Denny?"

Everyone turned to Denny Carillo, who was head of radio album promotion.

Denny nodded his head. "Look," he said, "these fucking kids at FM radio think they own the world. They're too hip to take a gift. Well, some of the jocks in the Midwest won't turn down good blow, but you can't count on them to play the record. At least the shvartzes understand what radio is about."

Turning to Lindel, he said, "Babe, I think you're the greatest. My twelve-year-old loves your record and he's got ears. He picks only hits."

Jeff broke in, "Lin, honey, this man influences more radio people than anyone else. I don't know how he does it."

"He has some heavy shit on them, that's why," said Artie Johnson, and everyone laughed except Lindel and Tim.

"No, honestly," Jeff pressed. "I'm telling you, I heard him on the phone yesterday. Within ten minutes he had a record on the radio. Just one phone call, and half of it in Jewish. Can you believe it? This, from a good Italian boy like Carillo." Jeff shook his head and smiled. "You'll be president of your own company one day, Denny, you'll see. Anyway, Denny knows I'm right about this tour."

"Hey," said Stan Rubenstein, who was the head of advertising, "I think you've done a phenomenal job, Jeff. To get her into so many five-hundred-seat clubs, and in several cities as opening act in those three-thousand seaters? Of course, the fact that we're giving you tour support—paying for a lot of the hotels and the transportation and ads in each city—well, it helps."

Bill Carson returned to the table and said to Lindel, "You going to Cleveland? Great hotel in Cleveland, called Swingo's. Lives up to its name. Of course in the old days it was all dumps. I'll never forget when I fixed up Jim Morrison with these black hookers in Cleveland. Boy, did they put on a show . . ."

Jeff cut in, "Bill is in charge of A & R."

"What exactly does A & R mean?" said Lindel.

"To tell you the truth," Bill smiled, "I don't know what it means either. It used to mean artist and repertoire . . ."

"No," Artie Johnson broke in, "it's artist relations."

"No," said Paul Dickinson, who was in sales, "that's A.R. . . ."

"Isn't it arrange and record?" said Denny Carillo. "I think that's what it meant in the fifties."

"Whatever," said Tim, sounding annoyed. "It means getting the drugs and meeting the acts at the airport."

No one said anything for a few seconds, and then several of the men started to talk at once. Lindel tuned it out. She would be pleasant, do as she was told for tonight. But her mind was far away. Let them all talk about how this tour was to sell the record. She was determined that this tour be an adventure. She'd heard about the mile after mile of orange shag rugs, airport lounges, and bloody marys in plastic cups. The musicians she knew had all told her how, if you could get a decent pizza in Fort Wayne you would remember it for weeks. She didn't care. She couldn't wait.

The day after the dinner in Patsy's Jeff called Lindel and said, "It went well, don't you think?"

"Which did you like better?" she said. "When Bill Carson came back from the bathroom with his nose practically dripping and talked about the hookers in Cleveland or when Paul Dickinson ate a scab off his own elbow?"

"What? I didn't see that."

"He ate a scab off his elbow. Ask Tim. And what does Artie Johnson do?"

"No one knows," Jeff admitted. "But he's close to Garnier."

"Jeff, he didn't know the release date of the album."

"He knew vaguely when the album was coming out," Jeff argued. "He just wasn't sure of the *exact* release date. Look, you'd better get it into your head that this is a business made up of garment center rejects. Artie is one of the more cultivated ones."

"He had monogrammed joints," Lindel said, her voice full of wonder.

"What?"

"Monogrammed joints. Didn't you see when he passed them around? His initials had been printed on the rolling paper."

Within two days she met six heads of departments, and while one or two of them seemed like decent people who probably were good at their jobs, the rest did, indeed, fall into the caricature category. She had yet to meet Teddy Sommer, who was in charge of tour publicity. Only twenty-three years old, Teddy had made a name for himself when he had been fired from Acme's publicity department for telling the editor of *Circus* that Acme's top folk artist was, as Teddy put it, "in and out of the bins." When it appeared as a headline in *Circus Magazine:* "Looney—Says Acme PR Man," Teddy was promptly given the sack and Tim Harrison, who thought the entire episode hilarious, got him the job doing tour p.r. for Jacar's artists.

Lindel and Jeff sat in Sommer's office, which was no more than a tiny cubicle with walls lined with posters advertising the performance of Bob Dylan at the Chicago Stadium, handbills of Alice

Cooper at the Agora; the usual stuff to prove that Teddy Sommer had been around. Lindel and Jeff sat in two black vinyl chairs facing Teddy, who sat behind the gray metal desk. His attitude was properly respectful, bordering on the worshipful one that she had grown accustomed to from record company people, but as Teddy ran down the itinerary, discussing the important journalists in each city, he began to get a bit more bold.

He put down the itinerary, looked at her, and said, "You know, I think you should re-mix your record."

Lindel just stared at him, and then at Jeff, who looked as if he was about to go for Sommer's throat.

"What did you say?" Jeff said.

"I think you should get the voice up front a bit more," he said stubbornly. "I know that I'm not supposed to say things like that, but I wouldn't feel right if I hadn't told you my true feelings . . . Even though it's probably too late . . ."

"*You're goddamned right you're not supposed to say a fucking thing!*" shouted Jeff, who stood up, grabbed his briefcase, put his arm around Lindel's shoulders and started to pull her out of the room. "And," he yelled, "even if it wasn't too late, what the fuck makes you think that we would even listen to what a putz like you has to say!"

Jeff and Lindel stood at the elevators. Jeff shaking, Lindel glaring.

"Okay, okay," he said. "Don't say it. He's a total shmuck. The asshole of the world. But the others aren't like that." He shook his head and pressed the elevator button again.

"Uh-uh, Jeff, that's it," she said. "No more. Unless you want me to start asking you if maybe he wasn't right, and maybe we should re-mix it. Do you understand me? No more meetings."

Marcia hung up the phone after confirming the plane tickets, hotel rooms and rent-a-cars with the travel agency. She still couldn't get over the name—Fly-By-Night. Where had Jeff found this one? She covered her typewriter, locked the desk drawer, and went to get her coat from behind the door. It was nearly seven o'clock and no one was left on the eleventh floor of the Jacar Building. She had no plans for the evening, except to look forward to a mindless night in front of the TV set.

Marcia had mixed feelings about Jeff accompanying Lindel on tour, and leaving her home to mind the store. Of course, there was no money for her to go along this time, and it would be somewhat of a relief to have him out of the office for a few weeks, not breathing down her neck every two seconds. Then again, she was still confused about him.

In the past three months she had thought that if she let herself, she could actually grow to like Lindel. There was a softness beneath the strong exterior, and it was apparent that Lindel, like Marcia, had no steady man in her life. Actually, Marcia thought with a smile, Lindel had been so obsessed with her album that she didn't seem to need any man in her life. Whereas she could not say the same for herself. *But I'm getting better,* Marcia thought. No longer was there an endless parade of one-night stands passing through on her sofa bed. She had far too much work to do these days. There were all the tour arrangements to make; rather than pay an agent's commission, Jeff insisted on booking it "himself." Which meant that Marcia ended up calling the club owners, the hotels, the concert hall promoters, the airlines, the car rental agencies—checking prices—then telling the travel agency what to book. She typed up the contracts and checked the riders that specified what expenses were to be covered by the clubs, and worked out a smooth schedule.

She had learned from Marty Paretta that there would be problems on the road; something always went wrong. But for the most part, Marcia had arranged a logistical triumph of a first tour.

When she discovered that Jeff hadn't even noticed that the contracts didn't state when Lindel would be paid, Marcia inserted a line in the contract that specified that Lindel would be paid on the night of the performance. Then, pretending to be filing something in the cabinet in his office, she made a point of watching Jeff when he went over the contracts. She had memorized every page, could read those contracts upside down, and from the corner of her eye she saw him get to the part where she had made the correction about payment. She saw him stop, quickly look up at her, and then continue reading without saying a word.

By now, Marcia had almost let go of those daydreams where she and Jeff, armed with contracts and file folders and demo tapes, would one day look at each other and realize that what was between them was movie magic. But she was still tied to him, felt a sense of loyalty, and worked hard for him. He was exciting to be around; he made things happen. Yet, at the end of a long day, when she often was too tired to go out, she resented what appeared to be Jeff's lively life. He had no romantic interest, of course, no woman, nor, for that matter—and she had considered the possibility—no man. He was too crazy about himself and his work. Still, he seemed to have a lot more fun than she did. And there was the matter of the lavish sums of money he always seemed to have at his disposal. He was generous with her salary, but she still had no expense account, and after that first mention about percentages of the acts, he had never referred to it again.

As she entered her apartment, turned on the lights and poured herself a large glass of vodka, Marcia wondered if she was still slightly jealous of Lindel. They'd only had one lunch together and Jeff's presence had prevented the immediate blossoming of any real friendship. They talked on the phone each day, but it was either Lindel's wakeup call or something to do with business. She had stayed away from Lindel's sessions because she had always believed that unless you were one of the musicians, there was no place on earth more boring than a recording studio. Marcia was cautious, she didn't want to get too close too soon. She wasn't crazy about Lucy, and then there was Jeff, who was still overly possessive of Lindel. She was better off keeping a certain distance. Now she resolved to spend the next few weeks enjoying the freedom. Without Jeff around, she could make lunch dates, stay out late at night, and not worry about what time she got to work. There were all kinds of new possibilities. It might turn out to be a plus, after all.

Lindel walked up the stairs to her apartment, with Lucy close behind. They both carried shopping bags and when they got to the door, Lindel fumbled around in her jeans pocket for her door key.

"Here, I've got mine," Lucy said, producing the key and opening the door.

They put the bags in the hallway. Lindel went straight for the new, dark green leather couch in the living room, took off her shoes and lay down.

"I'm exhausted," she said to Lucy, who stood in the doorway watching her. "I never realized shopping for clothes could be such hard work."

"We got some great stuff," Lucy said, starting to take clothes out of the bags and bring them into the bedroom to hang up.

"Don't do that now," Lindel said. "Forget it. I'll just take them folded right from the bags and put them in my suitcase tomorrow. Come and sit down. You must be wiped out. It was really sweet of you to come with me. And where did you find that fabulous designer? I could have bought ten more of those chiffon blouses if I'd had the money. They'll be perfect for the shows."

Lucy looked pleased, and came over to sit on the other end of the couch, facing Lindel.

"You could have bought more," she said. "I told you, she would have billed Jeff."

Lindel shook her head. "No . . . I'm scared about spending money so quickly. This couch . . . the new guitar . . . the clothes. It's enough."

Neither of them said anything for a few minutes. Lindel stretched her legs out in front of her. Wearing bleached, faded blue jeans and a tailored white silk shirt, her face seemed very pale, especially with the almost blue-black hair that surrounded it and fell down past her shoulders.

Lucy got up, went into the kitchen, and returned with a chilled bottle of white wine and two glasses. Lindel gave her a grateful look.

"I can't believe I'm actually leaving on this tour in two days," Lindel said.

Lucy went to the record player and put on a record. She turned the volume down low.

"After all this time waiting . . . and now it's here," Lindel continued. "I think I'm really nervous."

"That's understandable," Lucy said, and added, "but you've no reason to be nervous. You'll be fantastic."

Lindel thought Lucy's voice sounded strange. Actually, she

wished that Lucy hadn't come back to the apartment with her tonight. It was her next-to-last night before the tour and she would have preferred to be alone.

She looked at Lucy and immediately felt ungrateful. The girl had been such a help, figuring out what clothes she'd need for the tour, making lists of restaurants and checking the weather in each city. Lindel smiled at her. "It's seven o'clock. Are you hungry? We could go to dinner, or order something . . ."

"I'm not hungry," said Lucy, "but it's up to you. You might want to go someplace nice. After all, there really isn't a decent restaurant on your itinerary until you get to Boston."

She wasn't imagining it, Lucy did sound peculiar.

Lindel brought her legs up on the couch and curled one of them under her. Just then, in one split second, Lucy's hand accidentally brushed against Lindel's bare foot. Lucy made no move to take it away, and continued to drink her wine as if nothing unusual had happened.

Lindel was startled, and moved her leg ever so slightly toward the edge of the couch so it wouldn't be resting against Lucy's hand. She must have misinterpreted it, she thought, and dismissed the gesture from her mind.

"Well, I'm not really hungry," Lindel said. "I don't know, I thought I'd like an early night."

This time, there was no mistaking Lucy's intention as she casually put her hand back on Lindel's foot and started to rub it, ever so lightly. Lindel's mind raced, what was Lucy thinking? Maybe she was just being affectionate . . . Lindel's heart started to beat just a little bit faster. Neither of them said anything, but this time Lindel didn't move her foot. She was completely confused. She was only half conscious of some insinuating reggae music playing quietly on the stereo, and the feel of the silk blouse against her bare skin. Suddenly, she thought of Josie, her friend in junior high school. They had been inseparable. Josie, with her curly red hair and freckles. She had once slept over at Josie's house when she was thirteen, and in the middle of the night Josie had crawled into her bed and had kissed her, touched her in secret places, and Lindel had been frozen, stunned, but then, aroused, she had been unable to stop, and had submitted to the disturbing passion she shared with her friend. In the morning, neither of them had mentioned it; they had acted as if it had never happened. But when

Josie discovered boys a year later, discovered them with a vengeance, somehow Lindel felt betrayed. Josie had been her only really close friend, but as she became more and more involved with a teenage social life she drifted away from Lindel, who buried herself deeper into her music.

Now she didn't know what to do. Lucy, wearing her usual tight jeans and blouse unbuttoned almost to her waist, her face, at once familiar and yet strange. What would it be like to have Lucy kiss her, hold her . . .

She hadn't been with anyone since David. All those months, alone. She was used to being alone and she'd been so involved with the music, but all it took was this . . . gesture from Lucy to remind her that she was lonely. And even though there was something vaguely troublesome about Lucy, she was attractive. She was soft . . . sensual.

Lindel felt her face grow warm. She avoided Lucy's stare. She didn't know what to do, what to say. She didn't move her foot away from Lucy's touch. She longed to be held, to be touched, just for a little while . . .

Within seconds, thoughts flashed quickly through Lindel's mind. To feel Lucy's mouth on hers . . . to feel her skin . . . her warm arms, holding her. Then . . . her tour. She was going away in two days. Lucy was a friend. This was too complicated. It just didn't feel right.

She moved her foot away from Lucy's hand, and leaned down to pick up the bottle of wine. She poured another glass for herself and one for Lucy, who didn't say anything, whose hand didn't move from the couch—almost as a stark reminder of what had just happened.

"So," Lindel said, almost too loudly, "what should I wear in Buffalo? The new dress? Or jeans?"

Lucy looked at her and said quietly, "Lindel, why can't I come on the tour?"

Lindel was caught off guard. "I thought Jeff explained it to you. There isn't any money."

"I know, but I've figured it all out." Lucy's eyes began to sparkle. "I've got money, my parents send me money every month and I could pay my own way."

Lindel stared at her. "That's insane. Why on earth would you want to?"

"Oh," Lucy shrugged, "I think it would be fun. And frankly, I'd like to be part of it. Also," she gave a peculiar laugh, "I have nothing else to do."

"That's silly," Lindel said. "There's plenty of stuff you could do here. Not even necessarily for me, although I'm sure Marcia could use the help. And besides, this isn't exactly a glamorous tour. It's going to be half driving and nearly all Ramada Inns. It's *work*." She stopped, realizing that she was, perhaps, a little too adamant.

Lucy said, "But I thought you liked having me around."

"Well . . . of course, you've . . . you've been a . . . big help," Lindel stammered.

"And you're going to need me even more on the road," Lucy's words were coming faster now. "Believe me, I know, there are a million things that will have to be taken care of. Getting your clothes cleaned, packing, unpacking. Coordinating the interviews. And you'll need a friend along."

Lindel tuned her out. Was Lucy really a friend? She had done so many things these last few months that Lindel was beginning to forget what it was like to take care of herself. There was something about it that Lindel didn't feel comfortable with at all. No, she thought. I don't want her on my tour. I don't want her there with her drugs, creating possible problems with the band. I just want to go and make music and be with the band and be alone and not have any . . . complications.

She looked at Lucy and said gently, "Not this time, Lucy. It's really not a good idea."

Lucy's head was turned away from her and for a few seconds Lindel was afraid that Lucy might actually start to cry. Neither of them said anything, then Lucy turned and gave Lindel a blinding smile. "Oh well," she said, "maybe I can just come to Chicago, or L.A.—you know, the fun dates. Anyway, why don't we get started on the packing? You'll feel so much better tomorrow if it's all done."

Tim and Lucy sat at the usual corner table in the back room of the Grotto. It was two-thirty in the morning and the club was beginning to empty out. Tim handed the small glass vial to Lucy, who took two pinches of cocaine and smeared them on her eyelids.

"Don't waste it," Tim said.

"It makes them shine. It's pretty," she said.

"Did you ever think about how no one really spends much time in this place when they're happy?" said Tim.

Lucy didn't answer. She stared sullenly ahead, taking big gulps of what was clearly not her first drink of the evening.

"Why didn't Lindel come tonight?" Tim pressed. "I thought we were going to have a bon voyage."

"She said something about getting to bed early," Lucy mumbled. "They're leaving around noon, I think."

"You'd think she just couldn't wait to get to the Rochester Ramada Inn," said Tim.

"Buffalo," Lucy muttered."And it's not the Ramada Inn."

"Whatever, the first gig isn't until the next night. Why is Jeff spending money on an extra night in the hotel?"

"Not for the band, they're going Tuesday. But Lindel says she doesn't want to travel and sing on the same day if she can help it."

"Really? Good luck to her. She's going to have to do it about twenty-five times in the next six weeks. Anyway, I'm going to miss her, aren't you?"

Lucy said nothing.

"Of course, I'll probably go to Chicago, L.A., some of the better dates. Maybe New Orleans. Which ones are you going to?"

Lucy glared at him. "You know damn well I'm only going to L.A. If that."

"Oh?" Tim feigned surprise. "Tsk, tsk, what a mistake that is on Jeff's part. Leaving her at the mercy of what's out there on the road. He would be well advised to realize how lonely it gets . . ."

"She has the band, and Jeff."

"Well, it's hardly the same thing as having a . . . friend. My goodness, Lindel should have just told Jeff she couldn't do it without you."

"Oh, shut up," Lucy hissed. "First of all, you've never said 'my goodness' in your life. And you know that Lindel probably doesn't even want me on the damn tour. They're trying to keep expenses down . . ." Her voice faltered.

"Oh, surely you could have shared a room."

She ignored the innuendo, finished her drink, and wondered how the hell she was going to get out of here without him realizing that she was truly upset.

Well, maybe she wasn't wanted right now. Not yet. But wait until Lindel started going stark raving mad in the Midwest. Maybe she would just fly out there and surprise her. The prospect cheered her immensely.

"Why the Cheshire cat grin?" said Tim.

"Oh, nothing. Listen, it's dead in here. I know a great after hours place all the way downtown that's opening tonight. Want to go?"

"Don't you have to get up early to say your good-byes?"

"I did that already," Lucy murmured in what she hoped was a mysterious tone.

"No bags to pack?" Tim inquired.

Lucy laughed. "They're already packed."

"You don't miss a trick, do you?"

"I try not to," she said. "I try real hard not to."

9

At LaGuardia, Lindel and Jeff checked in, and then went to the bar near the gate to wait until the plane was ready to board. They both ordered bloody marys, and the waitress, who wore a black mini-skirt with a red halter top, brought them two glasses with large stalks of celery in each.

Lindel had checked her two large suitcases and carried only a small tote bag with some magazines, cosmetics, cigarettes, and a hair dryer. If anything should go wrong and her baggage was lost, she would at least be able to wash and dry her hair before the first show. Somehow, it was a comforting thought.

Jeff sat across from her at a small table in the airport bar. He was making notes in that book he carried everywhere. She now wished that the band, or Hank at least, had come with her instead of joining them the next day. She originally thought she wanted a day to settle in, to get used to the idea, to acclimate herself to the hotel. But faced with Jeff like this, just the two of them, now seemed ominous. It would have been more fun to start out with the band.

For the past four weeks they had rehearsed for eight hours a day, six days a week. They worked out a good thirty-five-minute set of eight songs from the album plus another one, in case there was a demand for an encore. Jeff wanted her to do some crowd pleaser like "Heat Wave," or another oldie from the 1960s for the encore, but she had just laughed at him, saying, "I'm not falling into that 'Johnny B. Goode' syndrome," and chose instead a Vipers song called "Not So Special" that she particularly liked. She knew she couldn't sing it the way Brian did, but she was proud of her version. She had rehearsed with the band over and over until she knew every single chord change, every drum beat, every song by heart. They were ready.

The flight to Buffalo was just long enough to drink another bloody mary and eat a minuscule packet of peanuts. After they landed, Jeff went to pick up the rent-a-car while Lindel waited for the bags. There wasn't a porter in sight, so she lugged her suitcases and Jeff's medium-sized one to the door to wait. Twenty minutes later, Jeff drove up in a brown station wagon. "I didn't realize that you'd be driving," Lindel smiled, as she got in the car.

"I figured we'd need an extra car. Johnny's driving up tonight with the equipment in the van, but we'll need to get you around the city tomorrow."

"It seems so official," she said, "having a road manager. Nice, actually. What's he like?"

"Johnny Paglioni? Exactly what his name sounds like. A hitter. But with a heart of gold. I remember him from the Grotto. He used to be a bouncer there a couple of years ago. You'll love him."

Neither of them said anything for the remainder of the dull gray ride from the airport to the hotel. They checked into adjoining rooms, and Jeff immediately went to the phone to call Marcia, in New York, to call the local promotion men at the Jacar branch office, the local radio stations and record stores (where he disguised his voice and asked if they had the new Lindel James album). Lindel, watching all this, said with amusement, "You don't have to change your voice. They don't know you. Yet."

She went into her own room, closed the door, and turned on the TV. Soap operas and game shows on all five channels. An orange shag carpet. So, it was all true. She felt like laughing; she felt giddy, free.

She lay down on the bed and picked up the room service menu. A cheese festival. Hand breaded shrimp. Tomato and egg wedges on a bed of lettuce. Kitchen fries. Nothing struck her as too appetizing, but she figured she should order something, just to have in the room. Room service closed at six o'clock and Lucy had warned her that the musicians she knew said you always got hungry in the middle of the night and there wasn't a thing you could do about it in a place like this.

Picking up the phone, she dialed room service, and seven minutes later someone answered.

"Can I get something sent to Room 703, please?" she said.

"It'll take an hour and a half," the woman answered. "We're very busy."

How could they be busy, Lindel wondered. They literally were in the middle of a highway. She considered going into the city and getting something from a supermarket and bringing it back to the room—surely that would take less than an hour and a half, but figured she ought to just get something . . . a piece of fruit.

"Do you have any oranges?" she said.

"No," the woman snapped. "Grapefruits."

"Okay, can I have a grapefruit and some coffee?"

"No grapefruit after ten A.M.," said the voice.

"What?"

"I said, no grapefruit after ten. It's a breakfast item."

"But you just said you had grapefruit."

"We *had* it, for breakfast, before ten o'clock. Now look, miss, we're very busy here. Why don't you decide what you want and call us back?"

"No, wait—don't hang up." Lindel looked frantically at the menu. "Do you have a sandwich that will keep a few hours? Something cold? A club sandwich maybe . . ."

"Miss, all of our food is wrapped in Saran wrap." The voice sounded annoyed. "It'll keep. One club. Anything to drink?"

"Do you have any wine?"

"Chablis. Seven ninety-eight the bottle."

"Uh . . . is it French?"

"This ain't Paris. It's American wine. From California. You want it or not?"

Lindel muttered yes, thinking that something awful would happen if she refused. They'd think her unpatriotic, word would get out, she'd get a terrible review . . .

She laughed to herself as she hung up the phone. She'd better calm down. Maybe she should unpack. She got up from the bed, and hauling her suitcases onto the two metal luggage racks, she opened them and began to unpack. She took the two black and white striped cotton toiletries bags into the bathroom and arranged her cosmetics. Shampoo, conditioner, razor and shaving cream on the edge of the corner of the tub. She took the tiny wrapped squares of hotel soap out of the soapdishes and substituted her own rose and glycerine brand. Her toothbrush and tube of Colgate toothpaste went into one of the plastic cups on the sink, and she neatly lined the bottles of moisturizer, aspirin, astringent, talcum powder, eyedrops and makeup on the shelves in the medicine cabinet. She looked at her diaphragm, in its turquoise plastic case and the accompanying tube of cream. No need to unpack that, she thought with a wry smile.

She walked back inside to the bedroom, and started hanging blouses, trousers, shawls, and dresses in the closet. There wouldn't be nearly enough hangers; after all, she had weeks' worth of clothes with her. Of course, she'd only be in Buffalo for two nights, no need to unpack everything, but she liked to have a choice. And it made her feel more settled, calmer, somehow, to have everything hanging neatly in place.

The door that separated her room from Jeff's opened and he walked in, full of enthusiasm.

"I'm ready to go to Jacar's local branch office to meet the guys. Want to come?"

She shook her head. "Definitely not," she said. "I'll see them tomorrow night at the club."

"No you won't," Jeff said, sitting down on her bed, leaning over to the television set and turning the dial. "You'll see them early tomorrow. There's two stops at radio stations and one in-store appearance before the sound check."

"So there's even less of a need to see them now," Lindel said, putting folded pairs of jeans into a dresser drawer.

Jeff stared at her. "You're going to be here less than forty-eight hours. For god's sake, why are you unpacking?"

"I like to," she said.

Jeff sighed. "Well, I'm off. We'll have dinner though, okay?"

She hesitated and he said quickly, "Just the two of us. And we could go to a drive-in movie, if you like." He seemed so eager to please.

"I'd love to," she said. "Really, I haven't been to one in ages."

She felt a sudden surge of affection for him, and leaned toward him and gave him a quick kiss. "Thanks, Jeff. Really. For everything."

After he left, she continued emptying out her suitcase. There wasn't enough space for everything so she left the sweaters and the shoes unpacked. She took out her robe to hang behind the bathroom door and she saw the box. Nestled in between her best white silk tunic blouse and a red cardigan sweater. Wrapped in bright pink foil paper with purple curled ribbon and a small white card. She tore off the paper; it was her favorite perfume. Joy. She looked at the card. Lucy, the card said, with love.

Lindel felt a pang of guilt. Lucy had seemed so hurt, being excluded from the tour. And now this expensive gesture. Maybe she should call her. No, she thought, remembering the other night. It wasn't a good idea.

She set up her travel clock next to the bed, and placed alongside it her new blank notebook and pen. Just in case she had any ideas for songs in the middle of the night. And then she knew what she wanted to do next.

She called to tell room service to leave the tray outside her door and went down to the lobby and out into the street. There were no cabs, so she went back in to the reception desk.

"Can I call a cab to take me downtown?" she asked the clerk.

He blinked at her. "Well, you could, but it would take about a half hour for one to get here. You'd be better off just walking."

"Walking? How far is it?"

"Oh, about four blocks to the center of town."

"It is?" You could have fooled me, she thought. It looks like the middle of a war zone. "Do you know a club called The Circle?" she said.

"Yes. It's about seven blocks from here. Just take a right when you go out of the hotel, and keep on walking. You can't miss it."

She saw the stage from the back of the club, and stopped for a moment, silent, considering what the place felt like. A large square room, with about twenty long tables crammed together down in front of the stage. One level up, there were more tables, with candles on them in red glass holders covered with plastic fishnet. A long bar to the left of the entrance, with the wall-length mirror reflecting the rows of liquor bottles.

She looked around, didn't see anyone, and walked onto the stage. Standing on this stage, she looked out front, then walked to the sides, to the back of the stage, wanting to feel it.

She took her shoes off and felt the hard wood against her bare feet. Putting the shoes back on, she walked to the front of the stage and looked out over the empty room. It smelled familiar and then she remembered. That bar, where David had worked. At four A.M. just before closing. An empty room that reeked of sour beer. She shuddered and closed her eyes for a few seconds. Opening them, she looked at the tables and tried to imagine them full of people. Would they be full of people? Who would come to see her? How would they react to her songs? What if she was so nervous that she dropped the microphone . . . or didn't start at the same time as the band? What on earth was she going to say between numbers—she hadn't really planned anything. Maybe she shouldn't say anything at all. She looked down at the edge of the apron of the stage. What if she fell? And what should she wear? Obviously, nothing too fancy. But people paid money to see a show, she should at least give them something more to look at than just jeans and a T-shirt . . .

She had never fully confided the depth of her fears to Jeff, to Hank, to anyone . . . Standing on the stage like this, with only the dim light from the club all around, it didn't seem like a stage at all. But the life of a stage, she knew, was the performance given on it.

She wondered where her dressing room was, and started to turn to go backstage when out of the darkness someone yelled, *"Who the hell are you and what are you doing on that stage?"*

"Oh . . . I'm sorry," she stammered. "I was just looking . . ." Should she say who she was? She was too embarrassed . . . she just wanted to slink out.

A tall black man came to the front of the stage. He looked at her. "You're not supposed to be here," he said. "The club doesn't open until nine o'clock tonight."

"Sorry," she mumbled, and turned to leave. Maybe he'd realize who she was. After all, her publicity photo was in one of the windows outside, listing her as a "coming attraction." But the man said nothing, just continued to stare at her accusingly until she was safely out the door. Show business, she thought with a little rueful grin. Who was it who said it was lonely at the top? It was pretty damn lonely down here at the bottom, too.

———————————

The next day she didn't feel worried and that worried her. After the radio and record store stops, she and Jeff went to the club to meet Hank, Tony and Eddie, who had already checked into the hotel and gone ahead for the sound check.

Hank was waiting for them outside the club. When he saw the car pull up, he walked over, and as Jeff rolled down the window, Hank said, "They're not letting us do a sound check."

"What?" said Jeff.

"The guy who runs this place says no sound check for opening acts."

Jeff turned off the ignition and practically flew out of the car.

"Wait here," he shouted to Lindel as he rushed into the club, with Hank following behind.

He found the club manager, a young man in his late twenties who still wore his hair shoulder length. He was smoking a joint. Jeff started to scream.

"What the fuck is this about no sound check?"

The man, who remained sitting on a chair, with his feet propped up on one of the long wooden tables, eyed Jeff lazily.

"Hey man, don't yell at me. I've got the headliners coming in here in about twenty minutes. You won't have enough time to set up."

"The headliners?" Jeff snorted. "You mean The Radios? That local band? You're putting me on."

Hank stood by, silently watching this exchange.

"Look," said the manager, dragging on the joint and offering it to Hank, who shook his head no. "I don't care if you never heard of them, The Radios draw big here. I assume you're Lindel James's manager, right? Well look, even if your record company did take a small ad in the local paper, these are the rules, so don't hit me with that next . . ."

"What the fuck is this?" Jeff broke in. "The Bottom Line? This is the goddamn *Circle* in *Buffalo,* for Christ's sake."

The club manager's expression didn't change. "We don't know what time those guys are getting here," he said patiently, "but whenever they do, they get to do their sound check immediately. And for as long as they want. If there's time when they're through, and it's okay with The Radios, then you can do one then. You can wait if you want to."

"We only need about twenty minutes," Hank said softly.

Jeff was seething. "We'll see about this," he snapped.

"Consider your first three songs tonight your sound check," laughed the manager as Jeff, with Hank behind him, stormed out of the club.

Eddie and Tony were standing by the car, talking to Lindel, who still sat inside.

"What happened?" Lindel said.

"Assholes," muttered Jeff, getting into the car. "Look, I'll take you back to the hotel. No need for you to hang around here. I'm going to make a few calls, see if I can exert some pressure. Where is the number for that local promo guy?" Jeff fished around in his pockets.

"We could do with ten minutes," Hank said. "We'll just wait here, and we can call you if the other band finishes in time. Then you can bring Lindel back. We should go over the set first with her."

"No," said Jeff. "I'll take her back and then come back here. Just wait for me here."

"Where would we go?" Eddie laughed. "There aren't many options in glamorous downtown Buffalo."

They all laughed except Jeff, who got into the car with a grim expression on his face, to drive Lindel back to the hotel.

At seven-thirty, Jeff called and said he'd pick her up in a half hour, but she should be ready to go right onstage, because the guy said he'd give them a short sound check before they opened the doors. She dressed, choosing the same tight black toreador pants, filmy black blouse and stiletto boots she had worn for her first gig at the Grotto, to give her luck. She looked at herself in the mirror. Maybe it's a bit much for Buffalo, she thought. *I look like a dominatrix.* Then she laughed. Might as well not start this tour on tiptoe.

She flipped her head down and brushed her hair from underneath, down toward the floor; the way she had done ever since she was a little girl and had read that Rita Hayworth brushed her hair that way to make it look fuller. It was amazing how she remembered all those movie magazine tips from her childhood. Vaseline on her lips to make them shiny. Kohl under her eyes so they'd look even bigger than they were. Shading on the cheekbones so they'd appear more prominent. She didn't fuss much, just used the little tricks that by now she took for granted, and went downstairs to meet Jeff in the lobby.

Jeff paced the floor at the back of the club for a few minutes, then finally sat down at the table that had been reserved for him and the promo man from Jacar. Of course, the promo guy hadn't shown up yet, so Jeff occupied the tiny black table alone. He hoped Lindel wouldn't be able to see him from the stage. He remembered that she'd once said if she ever saw anyone she knew in the audience it would make her nervous. He'd have to remember in cities like L.A. to have the press, and any friends, placed way in the back, and make sure that the lights were limited to the front tables only.

This was nerve wracking. It couldn't be any worse if he was onstage himself. He had already checked out the lights, the sound board, and he knew better than to hang out in the dressing room. Maybe later on, when they were all used to this, but not tonight. He'd better stay out of her way.

Two boys and a girl at the table next to his were arguing loudly about whether or not they should order a pizza. He turned to look at them. One of the boys was a large, red-faced blond kid, he looked to be about eighteen and was quite drunk. The other boy was older, he had a short haircut and a full beard. The girl was probably sixteen, maybe seventeen at most, and they continued to talk as a voice came over the P.A. to introduce Lindel.

Jeff leaned over the table and said, "Excuse me, do you think you could keep it down? The act is about to go on."

The three of them turned to look at Jeff.

"Who the fuck are you, man?" said the younger of the two boys.

"Listen," said Jeff, getting angry, "I want to hear this, okay? So keep it down."

"Hey man, we paid our five dollars. This ain't church, you know," said the one with the beard.

"I said," and he almost hissed the words, *"shut the fuck up or I'll have you thrown out of here, do you hear me?"*

They looked at him with incredulous stares.

"What's the matter with this guy?" said the beard to the blond. They all shook their heads and started to laugh, and at that moment, Lindel came onstage.

Jeff's heart was beating so loud he was sure it could be heard over the first few notes of the song she started to sing. He wasn't in Brandy's anymore, she was his, he'd made the commitment, his life was on the line as surely as if he was on that stage, under the spotlight, himself.

When Lindel stepped onstage, she was so thrown off by seeing faces in front of her that she missed her opening cue. The band picked it up again, but she had trouble hearing the small monitors at the front of the stage, and wasn't sure if she was in time. It was absurd; she had practiced "Roll On" hundreds of times, but now, on this stage, facing an audience, she was disoriented. By the time she got her bearings, they were into "White Bird," the second song, and she realized that the band was off. Eddie's drums were just a second behind Hank, and while she was sure it was nothing the audience would pick up on, it forced her to turn her attention to the overall sound of the band and lose her own concentration. Nothing clicked. They got the perfunctory applause after each song, but she saw one boy leave and it threw her into a panic. She wanted to get off the stage, instead of going through with her short set. She wanted to stop right in the middle and tell the audience, "Look, I know this is lousy. Honestly, we're better than this. I don't know if you've heard my record, but I can be good. Let me start the set again." But of course she couldn't do that. She saw Jeff standing in the back, applauding harder than anyone else when the set was over and it made her heart sink. Even with his applause attempting to spur the audience on, it was obvious that there was to be no encore, and Lindel left the stage feeling depressed.

"It sounded great out front," said Jeff jovially, when he came into the tiny dressing room. Lindel was sitting on a chair, staring into space. The band was lined up in the hallway, leaning against the wall, looking glum.

"I couldn't hear the goddamn monitors," Tony said, kicking his foot against the wall.

"This kid held up a napkin with 'you are boring' written on it," said Eddie, "and it threw me off from the minute I saw it."

"Come on," said Jeff, "it's the first fucking gig. That's why we're doing these dumps, to iron out all the kinks. Let's go get a drink."

The hotel bar didn't serve drinks after eleven, so they all went into Jeff's room and sprawled themselves over the green plaid-covered beds to rehash the show.

After a forty-five-minute discussion of everything each one of them thought had gone wrong, they all lapsed into silence. Lindel stared at the silent image of Johnny Carson on the TV screen. Hank sat next to her on the bed and studied the room service menu. Tony was slumped in his chair, smoking a joint, and Eddie was sprawled on the other bed, and appeared to be asleep. Only Jeff was in motion.

"Look," he said, pacing back and forth in front of the windows. "We can't tell anything yet. The record just shipped last week, and we can't be sure that people know who we are. It'll take time. These few dates—Buffalo, Syracuse, Rochester—they're just break-in dates. Glorified rehearsals. The real dates don't start until Boston and Philadelphia next week. Don't worry. Get some sleep. Trust me."

The next morning Jeff was at the biggest local record store by nine-thirty. Lindel's album wasn't in stock yet. They didn't think they'd get it for at least two weeks.

Back at the hotel, Jeff was on the phone, furious.

"We've blown Buffalo," he shouted to Larry Katz who was back in New York. "What the hell is the point of coming to play somewhere if they don't even have the fucking record in the stores yet?"

At Syracuse, the next stop on the tour, they also got no sound check. The set was slightly better than the night before, but not by much. The record wasn't in the stores there, either, and the local promotion man didn't even show up.

"This does not exactly fill me with confidence," Jeff complained long distance to Larry Katz the following day. "What's going to happen if it's the same story in Boston, or Philly?"

"Jeff," said Larry, "try and stay calm, will you? Guess what? This is what happens on tour. Things occasionally get screwed up. I don't know why the local guy didn't show . . . I forget his name . . . I think we just wooed him away from Acme . . ."

"Great. This you had to steal away from somewhere else?"

"Listen," said Larry, losing patience, "I'll check on it. But you'd better slow down."

"I will not slow down! Don't you fucking tell me to slow down. This frigging record is my life and my head is going to be up your asshole from now on!"

And with that, they both slammed down the phone.

In Rochester, Lindel was determined to do better than the two previous shows. Aside from the technical stuff that she couldn't control, she thought she knew what was wrong. So when she got on stage at The Haven, a club almost identical to the last two she had performed in, she shut her eyes. For just a few seconds she didn't want to look at the two hundred college kids who sat at the small wooden tables. She didn't want to see the waitresses wearing calico granny dresses carrying trays full of drinks, hamburgers, french fries. She didn't want to see the bar, or the men in the light booth opposite the stage. For just a few seconds, she wanted to pretend that she was completely alone with her music. It gave her less than a minute to enjoy a certain kind of privacy, but it made all the difference. It started the set on the exact right note, and when her eyes flew open and she confronted the audience with her stare, she saw the kind of stunned response on a few faces that she had seen at the Grotto. She felt the way she did when she used to sing alone, when she wasn't worried about the band.

The band, too, seemed aware of a subtle change in her attitude, and they picked up her confidence. It was a good set, and after the encore, the first she'd received since the Grotto, Lindel was elated.

Later on that night—after the band had gone with some girls to the local rock hangout—Lindel and Jeff sat alone in the bar of their hotel.

The red carpeting and red and black flocked wallpaper made the room look like every Holiday Inn bar or airport lounge Lindel had ever seen. Each small table and booth had its own brass-colored lamp with a triangular red shade. Hats, Lindel thought, those little red shades look like hats. People actually had designed them, made them, and bought them by the hundreds for rooms like these. There were only two other people sitting at a table off in a dimly lit corner, and Lindel and Jeff sat at the long black vinyl-covered bar. A cocktail pianist was finishing up for the night, singing "Feelings." Lindel turned to look at him for a minute, then turned back to Jeff.

"Sometimes I think that's how I'll end up," she said.

"Not with me around, you won't."

"Seriously, I really wonder about that sometimes. I mean, he's not bad. Don't you think he has dreams? Why has he settled for this?"

"Someone's got to do it," Jeff said.

"Sometimes I really wonder what the difference is."

"Oh, Lin," Jeff sounded impatient. "You're not even on the same planet. Your voice is a great gift—there's no comparison, and no matter what, I promise you, you are not going to ever consider singing 'Feelings' to an empty bar like this guy to whom, I assure you, it's just a job . . ."

"Sssh," she said. "Lower your voice."

"Anyway," said Jeff, "let's talk about you. The band's working out okay?" Jeff grabbed a fistful of the tiny, fish-shaped crackers from the plastic bowl in front of them on the bar.

"Mmm," Lindel said. "I mean, I've never worked with other musicians, so I have no basis for real comparison, but it feels right. I can't wait to hear us after three weeks. We'll be so tight." She finished her margarita, and lit a cigarette.

She had been pretty successful about cutting down on her smoking to less than half a pack a day. Her voice was strong, and she wasn't coughing in the morning the way she used to. Still, after the show, she needed to unwind.

"Hank is a dream," she continued. "He instinctively feels everything I'm doing onstage and his bass lines are so melodic, and his timing is perfect. It's a rare combination. Plus, he's such a calming force. Eddie is much more excitable, and I think he would rather play with a heavy rock band, but as long as he doesn't bash away too loud, it's okay. Tony is good except for one thing . . ." She hesitated.

"What?"

"Oh, he misses that girlfriend of his. I know he talks to her for hours every night on the phone. Hank said something about not being able to sleep or score last night with all the long-distance cooing going on in the room."

"He'd better not be putting those calls on his bills," muttered Jeff. "He certainly isn't making enough salary to pay for long-distance calls."

"I think he calls her collect, but I'm sure Hank is going to want to change rooms. Anyway, what's happening in New York? Lucy called me today and she said she saw the record in the window of the Eighth Street record store, but I haven't spoken to Tim in two days."

"Fine, fine, everything's fine."

Everything was not fine, but Jeff wasn't about to tell her that now. He was getting no satisfaction at all from Jacar. The records weren't in the stores, and after Buffalo he hadn't seen a promotion man. He called Marcia at least nine times a day to complain; she'd sigh, try to handle his requests as best she could, and then would call him back to report her lack of success. Everyone told him the same thing: calm down, don't worry. He worried. And he was beginning to wonder if it wouldn't be better for him to scream in person.

It was two in the afternoon on the day off in Boston, before the next night's show in Philadelphia. Lindel and Jeff were lying on two separate beds in her room at the Sheraton, watching some soap opera on TV, when she said, "Where are we staying in Philadelphia tomorrow night?"

"Don't you have the itinerary?" said Jeff, twirling one strand of hair around his forefinger in what, by now, was a familiar gesture.

"It's in one of the suitcases," she said. "I just don't remember which hotel . . ."

"I can call Johnny," said Jeff. "Although he may have left with the equipment already, in the van."

"Oh, never mind."

"Why?" he said.

"I just wondered." She didn't say anything for a few minutes. She leaned over to the TV set and turned the dial until she found the Red Sox–Yankees game. She turned up the sound and leaned back against the bed. "I should have gone to Fenway Park," she said. "Hank went with Eddie. It would have been a good way to spend the afternoon."

"Since when are you such a big baseball fan?" Jeff said. "This is the second game I've seen you watch on TV in two days."

"Oh . . . I haven't been for a long time," she said. "My father took me to see the Yankees when I was a little girl. It was so exciting. There's something about it I still like. It's so pretty."

"Too slow," said Jeff.

"No," Lindel said, "it's beautiful, really. It's like something out of the nineteen-forties, the way the players look on the field in blue and white uniforms on that bright green grass; those men in the red and blue uniforms who come out in the fifth inning to sweep up with those huge brooms. I even like watching it on TV. I remember all those years in school when the boys would get excited about the start of the season in the spring and they'd cut school, and then all summer long you'd hear the games on the radios at the beaches at the Shore. Then in the fall, there'd be a pennant race and everyone would run home from school to listen to the last innings of the game. It's like rock and roll. To me, even now, baseball sounds like school is out."

She stopped, realized that he was staring at her.

"Anyway," she was embarrassed, "we're staying at either a Holiday Inn or Ramada in Philadelphia, right?"

"I guess so," he said. "Why?"

"Do we have enough money for me to stay one night at the Barclay?"

"The Barclay? What's that?"

"Oh, it's a fancy hotel on Rittenhouse Square."

"Why?"

"I don't know. I just feel so . . . messy. I'd just like to pamper myself a little bit for one night. We have the whole Midwest coming up and that's all one big Holiday Inn until Los Angeles. Do we have the money? Please?"

"It's not a bad idea." Jeff looked thoughtful. "You do have a few interviews in Philly. Hopefully, with the *Inquirer* and one with the *Drummer*." He leaned over and reached into his briefcase and pulled out a copy of the *Drummer*. "Here, I got one at that out-of-town newsstand in Cambridge. It's like the *Village Voice* of Philly."

Then he said, "Why don't I see if I can get us a suite there, and then Jacar's publicity department can pay, and . . ."

"No," she broke in. "No suite. I just want a decent room. And I really feel like being by myself."

Jeff looked at her sharply, but said nothing. He had heard this tone of voice before. After a few seconds, he said, "Okay, I'll try and get it together."

After he left her room, Lindel lay on the bed for a long time. Then she got up, walked to the Formica dresser and opened the top drawer. She pulled out her copy of the *Drummer,* the one Marcia had sent, and turned to the page of ads for local clubs. It was such an astounding coincidence that the night before she was due to play in Philadelphia, The Vipers would be there. She hadn't even been sure that this short fall tour of theirs would bring them to the Northeast. Of course, she had no idea whether or not they'd stay the extra night, or where they were scheduled to go next. It was likely that she wouldn't connect with them at all.

She wasn't even sure of what she was thinking. Would she be able, upon first meeting Brian Davis, to take him back to her hotel room to spend the night?

Should she order a bottle of wine or champagne before she left the hotel for the gig, and leave it chilled in an ice bucket in her room? Leave just one light on, so the room would be properly dimmed? What would she say to him? It was silly, plotting it out like this. She learned a long time ago that life always happened to her when she was busy making other plans.

And yet she knew that if given the chance, she would have no defense against Brian Davis. Just from seeing him that one time onstage, and from listening to his records over and over, she knew that he touched something in her that had been dormant for a long time. It frightened her, yet she longed for it. There was no doubt that she wanted Brian Davis.

The next morning, Lindel was in the hotel lobby at nine, looking at postcards at the newsstand, waiting for the band to come downstairs for the drive to Philadelphia, when Jeff came up to her and said, "Listen, I spoke to Ian Bailey this morning. You know, that English lunatic who manages The Vipers?"

Lindel's heart froze.

"Did you know The Vipers were in Philly?" he said.

"No," she said, hoping desperately that he couldn't read her face. "How would I?"

"Well, I saw it in the *Drummer*. They did some club last night. A smaller one than you're doing." Jeff sounded pleased. He added, "I managed to track Ian down, and they're off tonight so I told him they should all come by."

Goddamn him. Always pushing. This was not the way she wanted to meet Brian Davis. To make it look like she was anxious to see him, to have her manager call and *ask*.

Then again, managers made such calls all the time. And in truth, she didn't know how else she would meet him. Someone had to make a move, and it might as well be Jeff. She tried to keep her tone noncommittal.

"I wish you hadn't done that," she said. "I don't need a bunch of English louts careening about during my show."

"What are you talking about?" he said, grabbing the two morning newspapers, a pack of Dentyne gum, and handing a dollar bill to the woman at the counter. "You flipped for them when you saw them at the Academy, remember? I was there. And I met Ian that night and we've been in touch." He picked up his change from the glass-topped counter.

"You have?" She was genuinely surprised.

"Yeah, you know. I told him to call me when they came back, stuff like that."

"Well, it seems a bit pushy, that's all."

"Don't be silly. It'll be great publicity for you. You're always kvetching that you don't want to be associated with folk rock. This will liven things up a bit."

"They probably won't even come."

"They'll come."

From the moment she stepped onstage at The Electric Factory, Lindel knew that this show would be different. Jeff hadn't mentioned it, and she didn't want to ask, but there was the chance that somewhere in that room was Brian Davis. Rather than unnerve her as she had feared, it pumped her up, made the adrenalin flow. For him, she would have to give a *performance*. She would show him . . . she wasn't sure exactly what, but it had something to do with all those moments she had thought about him since that one time she had seen him onstage at the Academy of Music.

The Electric Factory was Philadelphia's biggest club. It was smaller than the three-thousand-seat Tower Theater, but larger than the Grotto. Tim, who had taken the Metroliner down from New York to see the show, told her that the club *always* sold out on Friday nights. "Jeff and I could do a square dance on that stage," Tim said, "and if it was on a Friday night, there'd be a thousand people lined up to get in. It's a big pickup place." But Lindel wouldn't let that discourage her. She was too excited about the possibility of Brian Davis.

Before she was to go onstage, she stood in the wings backstage and looked out at the audience. They seemed older somehow, more sophisticated. Not quite so much of a college crowd as there had been in Boston. This was a city that was used to good music. Kenny Gamble and Leon Huff had been producing great R & B records here for years. The O'Jays recorded here, so did Teddy Pendergrass. There had even been a rumor printed in *Melody Maker* that The Vipers were considering recording here in the Gamble and Huff studios.

She wore the same outfit she'd worn at the Grotto, at the first show in Buffalo. She needed it to give her courage.

Usually she was just the slightest bit aloof onstage, holding back from the audience. But tonight, as soon as she faced the rows of people in that club, her eyes widened, she made instant connections with other eyes out there, she was full of flash and fire. Lindel's Philadelphia show was charged with magic. The audience response was overwhelming, and for just one minute she allowed herself the luxury of thinking that maybe, just maybe Jeff was right. Maybe she was a star. It felt so . . . *right* onstage; it was where she belonged. She couldn't get off the stage without doing three encores, and when she went back to her dressing room, she was dripping with sweat and flushed with excitement.

Jeff stood guard at the door until she had managed to dry off and change. Then he let people in, a few at a time. Lindel chatted with the local promotion man and a disc jockey, and then she saw him.

Dressed in faded blue jeans, a white T-shirt and an old black leather jacket, Brian Davis still made An Entrance. Lindel felt her heart lurch. She smiled at him and turned back to try to talk to someone whose name she no longer remembered. She was in a daze. She saw that he was with his manager, Ian Bailey, and what looked to be two other members of The Vipers. But for her, no one else was in that room except Brian Davis, who leaned against the wall, a bottle of beer in his hand, talking to Jeff.

From the minute Brian walked into the room Lindel felt a physical reaction so intense she was afraid that if he did come over to her she wouldn't be able to say a thing. Her knees felt weak, her heart was pounding and her face was flushed, hot. This is ridiculous, Lindel thought, I just did a fantastic show. He's here to see *me*. Besides, I don't even know him.

Her mind raced. Should she go over to him? No, it was her dressing room, he should come to her. But he didn't. She stood, surrounded by flattery, trying to decide what to do. She had thought about this man for months, fantasized about him, and now here he was, with no one to help her figure out how to act. Her instinct was to stay put.

After five interminable minutes, he ambled over to her and grinned.

"I'm impressed," he said.

She just stared at him. No introductions were necessary.

"Really," he said, looking into her eyes.

She held his stare, then reached over to her dressing table to get a cigarette. She looked around, and Ian was right there with a silver Dupont lighter. From the corner of her eye she saw both Tim and Jeff pretending not to watch her. Lindel leaned into the flame, relieved at having something to do for one second, just to have time to gather her confused thoughts.

Jeff rushed over to introduce Lindel to Ian, who was tall, very thin, and wore an unusual pair of purple leather cowboy boots. He had shoulder length curly hair and wore small, rounded granny glasses. The four of them—two musicians, two managers—stood there. There was silence for two seconds and then both Jeff and Ian started to talk at once.

"Sorry," laughed Ian. "You were saying?"

Jeff babbled on about something; Lindel wasn't listening. She tried not to stare at Brian, tried not to notice that he was staring at her. Jeff and Ian continued to talk to each other, and she turned her attention directly to Brian.

"How was your show last night?" she said. Jesus, she thought, is this the best I can do?

"It stunk," he said cheerfully.

"Oh, come on," she said, gathering strength, bantering now. "How is that possible?" Flattery. It's come to this.

"I don't know." He shrugged. "It doesn't matter. We're just doing a few of these gigs for American promoters to see us. We're trying to figure out what to do about America. Anyway, enough about us. You were really good, you know."

"Thanks." She started to feel better. Smiling. Waiting. What did he think about "Not So Special"? She *knew* she shouldn't have done his song. Not tonight.

"But you should sing more rock and roll," he said.

"Well, I suppose so," she said. "I seem to end up doing more ballads than I'd like . . . I don't know . . ." she drifted off.

Then she saw the girl.

Unnaturally blonde, poured into a tight red dress and platform heels and a high, squeaky giggle. All in one ridiculous package. She tottered over to Brian, put her arm around his shoulder and gave him a kiss, full on the mouth. Brian stood there and said nothing.

Lindel looked at Brian with a cold look of disbelief.

"Hi," squeaked the girl. "I'm Doe. Dee-oh-ee. But I pronounce it Do*ey*. Get it? You were terrific. Wasn't she terrific, honey?" She turned to Brian. Then back to Lindel. "He didn't take his eyes off you for the whole show," she breathed.

This isn't happening, thought Lindel. He can't really be with this person.

Brian smiled, a slow, lazy grin. "Yeah, I was just telling the lady how good she is."

Lindel smiled a tight smile and said, "Thank you. Really. Listen, I'm kind of tired. Where's Jeff?" And she looked around for assistance. Where the hell was Jeff? Even Tim had disappeared.

It was only a few seconds but it seemed like hours before Jeff appeared out of nowhere, and said, "Honey, we're all going to get a drink somewhere, okay?"

"No," she said, between clenched teeth. "I'm tired. You entertain everyone. But do me a favor, get me out of here. Now."

She turned and smiled at everyone in the room. The smile that didn't include her eyes. Jeff mumbled his apologies, and within seconds she was alone in a limousine, on her way back to the Barclay.

She walked into her room and didn't even pick up her messages under the door. The chilled wine in the silver bucket mocked her. At least she hadn't sprung for champagne. She turned the TV on, kept the sound off, and flopped down on the bed. Have some wine, she thought, quickly, before there was a chance to get truly depressed at what had just happened.

How dare he. Come to her dressing room with that . . . trash. Well, she thought, as she held up her glass and made a silent toast, here's to you, Brian Davis. You're no different from the rest, after all. Typical English rock star; be with someone who'll hang around until your head is on the bar at five in the morning, who will drag you home and say she scored, and you'll be too drunk to get it up. Lindel had seen similar stuff with her own band. It went with the territory, but it turned her stomach. She had been sure that Brian Davis was different.

Perhaps she was being unfair. After all, he might have already been with that girl, not knowing that he was going to see Lindel's show. Certainly he wouldn't have planned the meeting the way she had. What, after all, was he supposed to do?

Lindel lay on the bed, staring, but not focusing at the TV. She didn't like the way this episode with Brian had made her feel. Somehow she felt that there was a score to be settled. But she knew that if she were smart, she should never see Brian Davis again.

Lindel looked out over Sunset Strip from her tiny balcony at the Continental Hyatt House and saw Los Angeles twinkle back at her. It looked exactly like the still photo behind Rona Barrett on TV. Los Angeles smelled almost tropical. If she hadn't been so tired, she would have gone out with the band, but the plane ride from Dallas had been bumpy and long, and all she wanted to do was unpack, take a bath, turn the shower on and steam her clothes out in the bathroom, and then go to bed.

There was nothing planned for the next day until four o'clock, when Jeff got in from New York. He had left the tour two weeks ago, after Chicago, to go back to New York where, he claimed, he could better supervise the things that were going wrong. She hadn't been sorry to see him go at the time, but now she realized she had missed him just a little bit. It would be good to have him around again.

She had an interview to do, but that wasn't until five, so if she got up early enough she would have some time to wander around Hollywood as she pleased. Short of taking the bus trip to the stars' homes, she wanted to be a tourist, just for a few hours.

At twelve-thirty the next morning Lindel got into a cab in front of the hotel and told the driver to take her to Grauman's Chinese Theater. They drove by Hollywood High School and she remembered Hank and Tony joking about how they planned to cruise by the school at three o'clock. It was easier for the guys, on the road. Whenever she was asked in interviews, especially in those small Midwestern cities, "what it was like to be a girl on the road," she would inwardly groan, then answer that she'd never been a guy on the road, so how could she possibly compare? But what she could never say publicly was that it was easier for the guys in her band to dull the pain, to find companionship, to find someone to sleep with, than it ever could be for her.

The tour had its share of troubles and wonder, but most of it seemed to go by in a blur of similar days. She didn't get lonely until she thought about Brian. It was foolish, she knew; she had seen the man only twice. Once onstage, and once backstage when he had been with someone else. Still, she found herself thinking of him, far too often.

It was easy, on a tour like this, to need a fantasy escape. For several weeks they were in parts of the country that looked evacuated. Cities that came to life only at night when jubilant music fans filled the clubs, or the concert halls. Those moments onstage made up for the hours when the station wagon broke down or planes were late, for all the wrinkled clothes Lindel had to "press" in the steam of the shower, for the times the band got too drunk or too stoned, had too little sleep and bickered among themselves.

There were lonely times, when Hank, sensing her mood, would leave Eddie and Tony with the local groupies and stay with her, watching TV for hours, sometimes not even talking, until she had been able to fall asleep.

There had been the funny times, too—like the spontaneous food fight when they got pizza all over the inside of the car driving from Chicago to South Bend. Or the time when Eddie nailed a mattress against the door of Hank's room at Swingo's in Cleveland and Hank had to call the fire department to get out. When they put ice cubes in her bed. And eggs. Silly, giddy moments, but they relieved some of the tension. Those were the times it was good that Jeff hadn't been around. He wouldn't have understood at all.

Now she walked from Grauman's to Frederick's of Hollywood, and went in to look at the underwear. Red French lace crotchless bikinis, gold sequinned G-string panties, purple ribboned black lace garter belts, leopard print push-up bras, hot pink sheer nylon baby doll nightgowns with cutout nipples, fringed and sequin-trimmed black satin panties . . . The array was unbelievable. Who actually bought this stuff?

Would Brian think it sexy? She couldn't imagine ever really wearing any of it, but just for fun she bought a red and black lace garter belt and panties.

She walked into some of the movie memorabilia bookshops and looked through the bins of old black and white movie stills. There was a photo of Ava Gardner, with her ex-husband, musician Artie Shaw. Her hair was long and lustrous, and she wore a black suit with padded shoulders and metallic fabric leaves embroidered on the front. God, she had been gorgeous. Lindel stood there, staring at the photo. Something about it reminded her of the Rita Hayworth poster she had, rolled up at home. It was an ad for the movie *Gilda,* and Rita Hayworth wore a strapless shiny black gown and elbow-length black satin gloves. She was laughing, and her head was thrown back so her hair had swayed to one side. Lindel wondered if she'd ever be able to project that kind of confident sensuality onstage.

She was taking more care with her looks these days, experimenting with different makeups, aware when the cameras focused on her when she was onstage. But she had never thought all that much about *image.* Here, in Hollywood, it was inescapable.

On impulse, she took the photo of Ava Gardner to the cash register, paid the $2.95 for it, and went outside.

She watched the hookers, the junkies, the religious nuts, all walk by on Hollywood Boulevard in a sort of parade, and thought that, as rough as this scene was, it was still . . . California, after all. A living comic strip fantasy. She missed the streets of New York.

There were only four more days on the road; two shows at the Troubador tomorrow night, the Boarding House in San Francisco, and then home. There was so much pressure about this L.A. date. Jeff was acting as if this gig was the command performance. How big a deal could the Troubador be? She wouldn't think about it. It was just another show.

The phone was ringing as Lindel rushed into her room. It was Jeff. He was in the hotel.

"I've got great news for you," he said, not even asking how she was. "The album's finally starting to move. There are reorders all over the Northeast and the airplay in San Francisco is heavy. KSAN is really behind it. Where were you?"

"Welcome to L.A.," she said, really glad to hear from him. "I was in Hollywood, then I wandered around Rodeo Drive, North Camden, you know, Beverly Hills. I couldn't even afford to look in those stores."

"You will, you will . . . Anyway, the guy from the L.A. *Times* will be here any minute, and we should probably go downstairs to meet him."

"Come on, Jeff," she teased, "have you forgotten your road etiquette already? Let him call up when he gets here, then we'll go down."

"Right," Jeff laughed. "Sorry. But honey, it *is* Robert Hilburn. He's important. I've been looking forward to meeting him."

"Well, you can meet him, but no sitting in on the interview. I'll do it alone, then later we can go to dinner and talk."

"Oh, all right." He sounded disappointed. "By the way, I've arranged to have dinner with you and this guy from the distributors."

"Uh-oh. No more of those dinners, remember?"

"Lin, baby, this is no creep. This is the head of the distribution company. I've spent a lot of time cultivating him on the phone long distance. Now he wants to meet you."

"He can meet me in the dressing room. At the Troubador. After the show. Along with the rest of them."

"Lindel, he *distributes* your record."

"Look, I think we'd really better get this straight for the rest of our lives. Perhaps these really are decent people and they work hard for me and I should meet them. I'm sure it's good business. But if I let you, Jeff, and you know this is true, you'd have me doing this all the time. And I would be wiped out by the time I ever got on a stage. I have to keep something for myself."

"Lin, he's major. Just this once."

"You're here four minutes and already it starts. Please, stop. I'm used to being on my own, and it's important for the shows. I want to do the L.A. *Times* thing, have a quiet dinner, and get a lot of sleep before tomorrow. You can tell him that your artist needs rest. It's no lie." And she hung up the phone.

Jeff felt let down. He wanted L.A. to be special. So many people were here now. It had become more of a center for the music business than New York. And this was the first time Jeff was here with an artist, someone people were talking about. He wanted to make an impact.

He didn't know what to do. He figured he'd best leave Lindel alone. He'd even let her go and meet Hilburn without him. He left his room, walked to the elevator, and when it arrived, he pushed the button that would take him to the penthouse. He climbed a flight of stairs to the rooftop pool, where he saw Hank, Tony and Eddie and . . . that girlfriend of Tony's, Susie.

He walked over to them. Susie was all done up in a gold lamé bathing suit and backless fuck-me shoes. She was putting suntan oil on her fleshy thighs. Jeff tried to hide his displeasure.

"Hi guys. Susie, what a surprise."

"Hi, yes," she giggled. "I'm here. Tony just couldn't stand it another minute without me."

Tony avoided Jeff's eyes. Hank seemed to be asleep; Eddie was thumbing through a copy of *Rolling Stone*. Jeff pulled over a chair and listened to them talk about the last few weeks on the road, obviously leaving out a few details because of Susie's presence. Jeff looked at his watch. It really was hot up here. He never had the patience to lie in the sun. It seemed like such a waste of time. Maybe he should make a few phone calls, see if Tim's plane had gotten in yet.

"Hey man," said Tony as Jeff got up to leave, "stick around. You can pay for the drinks."

Everyone laughed.

"Put them on my bill," said Jeff, looking at his room key. "It's 2304. I have to see how she's doing."

"Who's she?" said Eddie and they all broke up laughing, started pushing each other into the pool and trying to get the attention of two stewardesses who had just settled into nearby lounge chairs.

Jeff's phone rang at ten o'clock the next morning. Jacar's West Coast publicity girl was on the line and she sounded frantic. "I can't believe what's going on," she said. "All of a sudden everyone's calling. Musicians, people in the business, Joni Mitchell, Lou Adler, Neil Bogart. They all called for tickets for tonight and I don't know where we're going to get them. Even," she paused, "*Jack Nicholson* called."

At the mention of Jack Nicholson, Jeff was instantly awake. "What are you talking about?"

"All hell broke loose because of the thing in the *Times* . . ."

"What thing in the *Times?*"

"The interview Lindel did with Hilburn yesterday."

"What? How did that get in? That was supposed to be a Calendar piece for next Sunday."

"Well, he must have really liked her because he rushed out a short interview and there's a record review, too."

"How is it?"

"Are you kidding? It's a *rave*. He doesn't waste that much space on someone he doesn't like. It says . . ."

"Never mind, I'll get it myself." Jeff hung up, jumped out of bed, pulled a T-shirt over his head and raced out the door, still zipping up his jeans. As he waited for the elevator, he realized he was barefoot.

He ran across the lobby to the newsstand, grabbed the L.A. *Times,* and turned to the "View" section. Barefoot, unshaven, with his hair sticking out in unruly curls, he read Hilburn's review. He smiled, then grinned, then laughed. Jeff threw a five-dollar bill on the counter, grabbed four more copies of the paper, and didn't wait for the change.

Back in his room, he sat on the bed and read the review, slowly. "Magnificent ... statuesque ... sincerity of the true artist ... thinks of her music first ... melancholy eyes ... haunting voice ... important new star."

This was it.

It couldn't have been better if Jeff had written the goddamn thing himself. Hilburn was heavy. The Troubador would be packed. Everyone would want to be in on The Beginning. This guaranteed airplay, ads ... he'd better call the local branch right away and make sure they had enough copies for the L.A. reorders that would inevitably follow this review. This also warranted an immediate call to Marc. It was one o'clock in New York, maybe he wouldn't be out to lunch yet. The New York *Times* would have to follow. John Rockwell wouldn't want to be outdone by his L.A. colleague. Certainly not on a New York act.

Jeff couldn't wait to tell Lindel. He picked up the phone to call her, then put it down. He couldn't wake her; she had two very important shows tonight.

First he would call Garnier.

Then he was going to get some Scotch tape and plaster this review all over Lindel's goddamn door.

10

AUTUMN 1975

Lindel opened the door to her apartment. The phone in the bedroom was ringing and she started to go to answer it, but changed her mind. There wasn't anyone she really wanted to talk to. Not yet.

She put the two suitcases in the hall, and turned on the light. Something didn't feel right. Then she laughed out loud. There was no orange shag rug on the floor or color TV on a Formica dresser. She stood, taking in the silence for a minute. The windows were closed and it was stifling. Her apartment was just as she'd left it.

She looked around, walked from the hallway to the living room, and into the bedroom. It felt too quiet. No clutter, no unmade bed, no red message light lit up on the phone, no scarves over the lamps to dim the light. There was no one down the hall in another room she could call to come and keep her company.

She instinctively turned on the TV but kept the sound off, and lay down on the bed. Maybe she should call someone, Tim, or Lucy, to tell them she was back. But she didn't have the strength to talk about what happened in the past two days. How immediately, suddenly, her whole life had changed.

It was mostly a blur. The Los Angeles *Times* review, the excitement at the Troubador, and the way she felt when she heard that kind of overwhelming applause for the first time. The dressing room afterward, filled with well-wishers, including her parents, who had flown from Phoenix to see her, and who were so proud. She had been propelled by some unknown force through that night, the next day, San Francisco, and then home. Jeff, leading her through it all; Jeff smiling, Jeff ecstatic. It had all been out of her hands.

Her apartment seemed surreal. Even the soft light in the bedroom was too bright. She reached into her handbag, took out a cigarette, and leaned back against the pillows.

She was home, but the tour was still on, they had a show tomorrow night at the Academy of Music. She wondered how it would feel to sing on a stage and go back to her own apartment, instead of a hotel. Actually, it was her apartment that was out of context now. Disorienting. And the Academy of Music was no ordinary stage. It was *New York*—and it was where she had seen Brian for the first time. She was nervous about the show. This one was special. She had to be great.

Even though Lindel was just the opening act at the Academy, she was treated as a star. Word had quickly reached New York about her Los Angeles reception, and there had already been advance pieces written about her in the New York *Times, Post, Daily News* and *Village Voice.* Cuts from her album were played several times a day on the city's top FM stations, and the concert was sold out. Her New York fans came to the show determined to create an event, and the concert was a triumph.

The next morning the New York *Times* review called Lindel an "extraordinary singer," a "promising artist," "musically striking," and referred to her songs as "passionate, stark, mystifying," and "sensitive and provocative."

Fifteen minutes after that review was on the stands, Jeff Stein rushed to his office to get ready to receive the phone calls. He sat back in the big new leather chair he had installed in his office, smiled, and even kept Marc Garnier on hold.

Twenty-five blocks uptown Alexis Garnier read the *Times* as the coffee got cold in the red and blue flowered china cup on her white breakfast tray. She put the paper down next to her on the bed, and pulled her pale gray silk robe tighter around her slim, elegant body. She reached over to the tray and absentmindedly picked at the flaky croissant and took a sip of the fresh orange juice.

Taking the hand mirror from the bedside table she looked closely at her eyes. Maybe that new Dior eye cream did help after all, the skin around her eyes looked taut, smoother than usual, even in this harsh morning daylight. Of course she was grateful for her good skin, and the almost perfect bone structure; so far she'd never had to have one of those terrifying face lifts that so many of her friends had with such alarming frequency. And her hair, shiny, blonde—the monthly touchups removed any noticeable gray. She put the mirror down and glanced again at the *Times.*

Marc would be so pleased, she thought. He had such plans for that girl. And she was a truly lovely girl. Not like the rest of the riffraff they usually had to associate with in that rock world. Of course her manager, Jeff Stein, was impossibly ill-mannered and vulgar; Alexis had met him only a few times—backstage at the Grotto, once coming out of Marc's office, and then of course last night—and every time he had been wearing sneakers. She never understood why so many of them had to wear sneakers all the time.

She pushed back the white silk sheets and got out of bed. Walking over to the small rosewood desk she opened the drawer and took out her calendar. She looked through it, and noted the nights this month that were free. She'd have to check with Marc, of course, but it really would be nice to do something special for that girl. Yes, she thought with a slow, easy smile, Lindel's success made it quite simple. This might prove to be an amusing diversion after all.

On Seventh Avenue and West Tenth Street Tim left his apartment, went to the corner newsstand and bought the *Times.* He folded it under his arm, and walked a block to the coffee shop at Sheridan Square. Jeff had called him an hour earlier, at ten o'clock, and read the review to him over the phone, but Tim had still been asleep and hadn't really been listening. He had heard just enough to know it was a rave and now he wanted to read it carefully, and alone.

He slid into a booth, took off his black leather jacket and sunglasses, ordered coffee, and turned to the entertainment page. Christ, there was a photo of Lindel. This was unusual for a debut, to say nothing of an opening act. Tim quickly scanned the review, and broke into a broad grin.

It was amazing that the *Times,* which still ran articles asking "Is Rock Dead?" had this power over the music business. Even though the show had been a smash, and the record was starting to sell, *this* would make Jacar take notice. It would influence airplay, get other magazines—ones read by kids who actually bought records—to do big stories on her. This was it. Lindel was in.

He drank his coffee in two big gulps. He'd better get to the office before those fools forgot who had discovered her. No doubt the old man was taking all the credit. Or that idiot Larry Katz. This was the first act that Tim had brought to Jacar that had the slightest chance of making money. Now he could keep his job. He just hoped it didn't ruin his reputation.

"Where *were* you after the show last night?" Tim's voice was unmistakable on the phone. "We all went to dinner at the Tea Room and *everyone* was wondering where you were. Have you seen the *Times?* Let me read you this *fabulous* review."

In her apartment on Ninth Street, between Fifth and Sixth Avenues, Lucy Walker was in a drugged stupor, but not so much so that she didn't hear what Tim was saying, or realize the impact of his words.

"I'm still asleep," she mumbled, "I'll call you later," and hung up.

She had been up all night, had taken two ten-milligram Valiums and finally, half a Quaalude at seven this morning when she was really desperate, but still, she couldn't sleep. She had seen Lindel's show from the audience—the *audience*—because Jeff had told Marcia to tell Lucy that Lindel didn't want anyone backstage until after the show. Lindel was nervous, he said. What a laugh. That girl wasn't nervous a day in her life.

Lindel barely had time to speak to Lucy after the show in the crowded dressing room. Later on, when she thought Lindel would be home, Lucy had tried to call, but there was no answer. She had thought at the time that Lindel might not be answering the phone, and had recklessly even considered surprising her, stopping by. After all, she still had the keys to Lindel's apartment. But she rejected the idea; she couldn't just show up at Lindel's apartment—what if someone was there with her?

Now Tim had confirmed her fears of last night. Lindel had been out, at a big celebration dinner. Probably with the Garniers. And Jeff . . . Certainly the band would have been there, and Marcia, too. A dinner to which she, Lucy, had not been invited.

Tim had said the *Times* review was fabulous. Lucy didn't even have to see it, or know what it said. She was only too aware of the power of such a review, and how it was going to change everything. Now there would be dozens of people who would crawl out of the woodwork, only too happy to perform a variety of services. It wouldn't matter that they hadn't been there at the beginning. Now Lindel was famous, and she, Lucy, wasn't needed anymore. Those little jaunts she had planned to take on Lindel's tour had never materialized. And even though she managed to get through to Lindel on the phone a few times a week on the tour, it was painfully apparent that they were drifting apart. Lucy had tried to keep busy, hang out with different people, get back in circulation, but Lindel had been a hard act to follow.

She had a sinking feeling in the pit of her stomach. What the hell was she going to do?

Ronnie Marren's two phone lines started to ring just after eleven o'clock. He rolled over in bed and bumped into the blonde who'd come home with him last night. He couldn't remember her name.

"Sweetheart," he mumbled to the girl who was wide awake and starting to cuddle up to him, "get me some coffee. Black." He patted her bare ass as she got out of bed. Nice ass, he thought, and then he reached over the side of his platform bed and answered the phone.

"Wait a minute," he said into the receiver, pressed the hold button and went to the other line. The first call was from Tim, the other from the lead singer of the Electric Toys. He told them both he'd call them back.

She returned with the coffee. Now he remembered. Donna.

That was her name. He hated when they were still here in the morning. He leaned back in bed and drank the coffee. Donna seemed annoyed and started to get dressed. Well, it was too bad. He was in no mood to talk, except maybe on the phone.

He heard the door slam. Donna was history. He finished the coffee and got up to get the paper. Donna had thoughtfully kicked the *Times* in the front door on her way out. He took it back to bed, and, turning to the "Food" section he passed the articles that would tell him where to get the best basil in New York and how to dry his homemade pasta, until he found the entertainment pages.

Jesus, look at that. All he needed to see was the photo, the headline—"A Fine Debut"—and the last line: *"the arrival of an extraordinary and remarkably fresh talent."* My god, he thought, I'd better send her some flowers.

He wondered if anyone would remember that Lindel James got her start in his club. She'd remember, but Jeff would be another story. Actually, he thought, it might be nice to do a special return engagement . . . Or have a party for her at the Grotto when the album hit the charts. He'd call Jeff about it. But first he had to call the florist.

"Hank, I'm scared," she had whispered into the phone.

"No you're not," he said, beaming, looking at the review, glad he had gotten to read it to her first. "This is it, Lindel, it's everything you've wanted, it's all going to happen now. Come on, aren't you happy? I know *I* am."

"I don't know what to do," she said. "I'm so tired, but I'll never sleep. Hank," she hesitated, then said, "could you come over?"

"Of course," he said. "Hang up. Take your phone off the hook."

"I just put it back on," she said. "Jeff called at about nine, screaming, but I was completely out of it, and after I hung up on him my parents called from Phoenix all excited. One of their friends from New Jersey called them and read the review to them over the phone. After I talked to them I took the phone off again. But it was no use, and I finally gave up on sleep."

"Take it off again," he instructed. "Or you won't get a minute's peace."

"Well, I better call Jeff first. He's probably been trying me for hours and if I don't talk to him soon he'll send the fire department here to break down the door. But come soon, okay?"

"You want any breakfast? Coffee?"

"No, I'm not hungry, thanks. Maybe just a pack of Merits. Oh, and there is one thing," she said.

"What?"

"Could you bring the paper?"

Hank had gotten only three hours of sleep, but he felt as though he could get on a stage right that minute and do a show. He was thrilled for Lindel, for the guys, for himself. Things would probably be easier now. Maybe he could get a new guitar for the next tour. And better amps. Maybe eventually even add a rhythm guitarist to help fill out the sound.

He took his money and his keys from the dresser and put them in his jeans pocket. He picked up the *Times* and read the review once again. His eyes searched quickly for the sentence about him: *"Mr. Cromwell's bass lines move fluidly from the solid, rhythm and blues feel of the best of the Memphis-Stax recordings to more contemporary experimentation."* That was it, but it was far more than he had expected. They usually didn't mention the band at all. He pulled the money out of his pocket to see if he had enough to buy something special for Lindel. Champagne, maybe, with orange juice. She'd probably like that. He only had eight dollars. Not enough for champagne. Well, he thought, walking out the door and down the stairs to the street, he could buy forty copies of the New York *Times*.

Marcia had to get out of the office. She couldn't stand to hear Jeff on that phone for another minute. Even with the door closed between them she could hear him, screaming, through the wall.

He'd be mad when he realized she had left, but she was, after all, entitled to a lunch hour. Even on the day that Lindel became a star. The offers would wait.

She walked out of the Jacar Building and turned up Sixth Avenue, walking to Fifty-seventh Street. To her, Fifty-seventh Street was a place of almost religious significance. It was like a shrine that she went to for relaxation; to think things out, to look in the store windows and fantasize. She liked to walk up to Park Avenue from Sixth Avenue and pass certain stores: James Robinson with the window full of cut glass, crystal and Georgian silver; Porthault, with the handmade sheets and pillowcases in beautiful dark colors and tiny floral prints; Dunhill tailors with their silk scarves and cashmere men's robes. Then she'd walk down past Tiffany's, and across Fifth Avenue to the best place of all, Henri Bendel.

Now she turned into Bendel's and walked to the back of the first floor, to her favorite part of the store, the shoe department. She couldn't afford these shoes, but she liked to come in here every few weeks to check out the new styles, just to stay in touch.

"No, I'm just looking," she murmured to the salesgirl who asked if she needed help. As she stood and looked at the rows of bright turquoise leather sandals, black suede pumps, red cowboy boots and purple lizard ballet shoes, she thought about Jeff. He was beside himself with ecstasy over this review. She was happy for him, and for Lindel too, of course, and for herself. So why did she feel so ... depressed? After all, it was Marcia's victory too. She had helped get that album out, booked the tour, and tried to smooth over the problems between Jeff and the Jacar staff. Working with the corporate mentality of the Jacar employees had been difficult, to say the least. She still couldn't get over the fact that the stationery provided by Jacar had a minuscule hole the size of a pinprick on the upper left hand corner, to indicate where to line up the margin. But she managed to represent Jeff, and Lindel, and people liked her and recognized that she worked hard.

If Lindel got onstage, or woke up at a certain hour in the morning, or did an interview on time, or had money regularly placed in her checking account, it was because of Marcia. Of course Lindel did the singing, but Marcia did most of the rest of the work. And here was Jeff, acting like he was about to burst with pride and self-importance.

Marcia really hadn't felt as though she'd been doing all this work for Lindel. She had thought she was doing it for Jeff. And for herself. But Lindel was the one who would get the glory, Jeff would do everything in his power to see that he shared it, and she, Marcia, felt let down. Nervous. Afraid of the next step.

It had never occurred to her that any of this might happen so soon.

Jeff wanted to savor every single precious minute of this glorious day. He had earned it, and lord knows, he had waited long enough for it. About twenty years, to be exact.

He didn't even mind that Marcia had left him in the office alone. This way, he'd have to answer both phones in a breathless voice, put people on hold and convey that he was rushed, that important things were happening.

He looked at the list of calls he still had to return. Marty Paretta. Jeff almost laughed out loud with glee. Paretta, who, if the word "toilet" wasn't in it, couldn't use it as a sentence. Who wouldn't even bother to come see Lindel that first time at the Grotto. Let him wait. And Larry Katz. Bet he'd be only too happy to agree to those fucking birds now. All these Jacar dummies would have no choice but to listen to him from now on. He remembered what Marcia had said when she went in his place to the Jacar singles meeting last week. She returned four hours later and he had stared at her in disbelief.

"What on earth do they do in those meetings for so long?" he had asked.

"Mostly," she said, "they try not to show fear."

Sometimes Marcia could get right to the heart of the matter. He made a mental note to give her a small raise. Also, he'd have to get at least another phone line in here. Despite the lunch hour, today the phones did not stop. And he was going to sit here and play Ping-Pong with those calls. He'd stay here until nine o'clock if necessary, to get the calls from California.

He stretched back in his new chair and put his arms behind his head. Tonight, he would take Lindel for dinner. Somewhere fancy, where he could order thick, juicy lamb chops with those little ruffled pink paper hats on them. The kind he'd never even known about when he was growing up. He'd never even seen a lamb chop until he was eighteen, waiting on tables in the Catskills.

Now he smiled and shook his head, and remembered . . .

It wasn't eight o'clock in the morning yet, but there they were, a crowd of them, eagerly pressing their noses to the glass doors of the dining room at Grossinger's.

"Are you open yet?" they would yell, a collective mass of ravenous, elderly Jewish vacationers.

"In a minute," Jeff, or one of the other waiters would grumble, placing on the tables huge trays of tiny danish pastries, slabs of cream cheese, platters of smoked whitefish and bright pink lox, and blue bottles of seltzer water. Then the door would open and in they'd rush, almost trampling over each other to get the choicest piece of fish, the first toasted bagel. Jeff felt a true kinship with these people. He understood that kind of hunger.

When Jeff was five his father had died of a heart attack, leaving Jeff's mother to raise him and his two older sisters on the small salary she made working in the lingerie department at Alexander's department store. There were nights when there was nothing more than a boiled potato and sour cream on the table for dinner, but as teenagers, Jeff's sisters had a plentiful supply of bras and girdles which his mother brought home from the store at a discount. Jeff didn't like his sisters much; they were always making fun of him and hanging their wet underwear in the bathroom. Those dripping wet, nylon and elastic girdles and brassieres were a constant reminder to him of his insignificance; so many women around all the time made Jeff feel small, uncomfortable.

But out on the street it was different. There was a whole world to conquer out there. It didn't matter that he was poor; so was everyone else in the South Bronx. The difference was that while others dreamed and then settled for less, Jeff *knew* he was going to be somebody, and never stopped plotting his way out.

"After my father died," Jeff had told Marcia when they first met in Max's three years ago, "I had to support the family."

She had looked properly sympathetic. "How old were you?"

"Fifteen."

"What did you do?"

"Anything I could. Grocery clerk. Ran errands. Waited on tables at Grossinger's. Put chairs by the pool. After all, I had two sisters, too, to take care of." By the time she finds out that they're older than I am, she'll forget this version, he thought.

"Are you still close with your family?"

"Extremely," he had lied, thinking that he hadn't called his mother in nearly a month. His sisters, of course, he didn't care if he never saw again.

He had elaborated. He took the basic structure of his Bronx boyhood and added details as his imagination saw fit. Jeff never told the same story of his life twice. With Marcia, he emphasized the loneliness, the hard knocks, the determination. Was she impressed? He couldn't immediately tell. But when she offered to help him get the job in the ACS mailroom, he knew he was on his way.

Sometimes he knew he was too impatient, that he almost went too far. Like the time he returned to New York during Lindel's tour and confronted Marc Garnier with the problems of the road.

"You've never been on the road, have you?" Jeff accused him, sitting on one of Marc's leather chairs, staring at him from across his desk. "I mean other than just flying in on the company jet to see some big gig at the L.A. Forum?"

Marc had bristled. "Don't tell me how to do my job. Being on the road hasn't got a damn thing to do with the running of this company. I've got six thousand employees to worry about in addition to my personal relationships with artists and their managers. I've got the pressing plants threatening to go on strike, the corporate people upstairs . . . please. Don't waste my time."

Jeff ignored Marc's anger and continued to talk. "Listen to me, Marc. When you're out there, I'm telling you, it's like war. Some of the places she's playing are real hellholes. We're talking no dressing room, sometimes there's not even a fucking *bathroom* backstage . . ."

Marc interrupted, "Jeff, we didn't book the tour."

Jeff waved his hands. "That's not the point. I'm saying the conditions stink, okay? That's a given. In some of those cities there's not a damn thing to do after eleven o'clock at night except sit in a motel and drink water out of a paper cup. So, when you see the simple business things that haven't been done—like *not getting the record in the fucking stores*—it is a real crime. Hardly any of the promo guys show up, where the hell are they? Ads not placed. No posters outside the gigs. Maybe one album cover, tacked up somewhere near the box office, and that's *it*. I'm sparing you the usual road horrors like no sound checks, truck breakdown, electricity fuckups—those things don't concern you. But the hardcore business shit that Jacar is supposed to do, the assurance we were given, what about that?"

That meeting with Garnier had not gone well. But at least he was back in New York where he could keep an eye on things. He told Marcia to arrange with a florist to send Lindel flowers in every city with a card from "Your Friends at Jacar," and to send Garnier the bills. He got a list of promotion men from Larry Katz and started to personally make individual phone calls to them. As someone had once told him, it was hard to make permanent deals with temporary help, but it was a start.

In order for it to be done right, he had to do everything himself.

Lindel's album was selling as fast as Jacar could get it into the stores. Magazines and TV talk shows called for interviews. *Vogue* wanted Richard Avedon to take her picture. Charities asked Jeff if she would consider doing benefit concerts—Jeff said no—and advertising agencies wanted her to endorse their products—this, he considered. Other musicians wanted to record her songs. Marty Paretta wanted to be her agent. Her phone rang so much she had to get an unlisted number, with a cutoff bell and an answering service. Musicians she barely knew from the Village from two years ago asked to borrow money. She hadn't seen a dime of any of her money yet, but no one believed her. Strangers sent her flowers, presents, and tapes of songs they wanted her to record. Jeff had to hire another girl just to answer the phone and to handle the mail.

Lindel was invited to Andy Warhol's parties. Columnists wrote that she was at parties whether she was or not. A movie company wanted her to sing the title song about the rock deaths of the 1960s. Whenever she went to concerts people took her picture and constantly offered her drugs. Jane Fonda wanted to meet her. So did Warren Beatty. She was not at all sure of how she was supposed to act. She felt giddy, overexcited, confused.

She wished she could talk to someone else to whom this had happened. But all the musicians she knew were still struggling in the Village and they resented her sudden success. The more established rock stars all wanted to meet her, but such introductions took place backstage in someone's dressing room, or in front of a camera. She couldn't very well go up to some stranger and ask, point blank, "How did you handle this when it happened to you?"

When she started to get recognized on the street, she thought it was just people looking at her the way they always had, construction workers whistling, that sort of thing. But then she noticed the pointing, people stopping and whispering to their companions when she passed. People came up to her to tell her they liked her record, or they had seen her concert. She was asked for autographs. Sometimes she liked it, other times it felt just too peculiar. She learned quickly that if she walked down the street one way, she was sure to get recognized, but that there was another, totally different way of walking that would ensure anonymity. She never got mobbed, but talking to strangers on the street became a part of her everyday life.

Most of all, she realized that she didn't have one special person to share any of this with. No one really close enough to let go and rejoice with, or to confide in late at night when she felt lonely. It seemed an isolating thing, this sudden fame, not unlike all of those years she had spent alone in her room daydreaming and making up songs.

It was four o'clock and Lindel had an hour and a half before that kid was coming from the Long Island paper to do an interview. Normally she did them in Jeff's office. She didn't like reporters coming to her apartment, but lately there had been so many that she decided to have them come to her, rather than having to go to midtown.

She cleaned up the newspapers that were scattered on the floor. She went into the kitchen and leaned down to open the door to the cabinet where she had lined up the liquor bottles. She had always wanted to be able to buy all those exotic liquors: tequila, anisette, Pernod . . . It was silly—they'd probably stay on the shelf and get dusty for years, as would the case of champagne Marc Garnier had sent when her album had gone top fifty. Everyone she knew drank beer or white wine, but it gave her pleasure to have a good bottle of brandy, those champagne bottles . . . black, almost religious-looking champagne bottles, all lined up, ready for someone to share with her.

The doorbell rang. Damn, it wasn't four-thirty yet; the reporter was early. She hoped this wouldn't be too long.

The kid was nervous, fumbling with his tape recorder. He was definitely younger than she was, had long, greasy hair, wore very thick glasses, a plaid shirt and jeans. He worked for a big Long Island paper and was considered a serious rock critic. Not her favorite type.

"How has the success of your album changed your life and your perspective on your art?"

Oh, Jesus. "Well, I started smoking more."

Not a smile from this kid.

"Oh, look," she said, "it's like anything. I got a chance to do what I always wanted to do. You just do what you can and hope people will like it."

She trotted out all the familiar answers and he droned on with his humorless questions. Why did she always get these intellectual types who wanted to discuss the poetry of her lyrics? They were writing, after all, about music that was supposed to be fun, and they all used ten-dollar words to describe two-dollar actions. She'd really rather gossip with someone who had a decent sense of humor, and there were only one or two journalists who were capable of that. The rest of them . . . She hadn't even wanted to do any more interviews; she had told Jeff that she felt her record said it all.

Two days earlier when Jeff had handed her the schedule for the week, she said, "I'm so tired of explaining, of defining everything."

"Lindel, it comes with the territory. It helps you sell the record."

"How many more can we sell, for god's sake? It's already sold—how many hundreds of thousands?"

"It'll go platinum," he predicted with confidence, "but it can always sell more. Oh, I forgot to tell you. *Newsweek* called. They're doing a story on us."

"I know. They called me, too."

"Well, I told them you were the voice of this generation. I said that you were calm, unassuming, mature."

"I didn't tell them what you were really like either," she laughed.

They were in his office and he was going through the mail. Most of it he threw into the garbage, but some he handed to her to acknowledge.

"You know I don't want to go to this," she said, looking at the invitation. "I feel trapped when I'm sitting in a theater. You really are turning into Mr. Two-on-the-Aisle."

"I like opening nights," he said. "Why not?"

"I don't want to go to this party, either," she tossed another invitation back to him.

"Well, that's important. Alexis Garnier doesn't invite just anybody. We have to go."

"I don't see your name on the invitation," she said.

"You don't?" he asked. "Right there, where I'm writing in 'and guest.' That's me."

"No, Jeff," she said. "I mean it. I don't want to go. I wouldn't feel right. I really don't want to turn overnight into one of those professional celebrities who—what is it Marcia says—goes to the opening of an envelope. Make some excuse. Tell Alexis Garnier that I'm in rehearsals."

Jeff seemed disappointed and slightly annoyed, but he said nothing, and Lindel watched him as he continued to make notes in his ever-present little looseleaf book.

Jeff was looking different these days. He had cut his hair in what seemed to be a more fashionable style. He wore a better version of his old fake Cartier watch. His shirts were unbuttoned lower. At least, Lindel thought, he doesn't have a coke spoon or razor blade on a gold chain around his neck yet. All of her success had seemed to go straight to his head. He was considering signing two new bands—the Electric Toys and the Marquis de Sade—to

Valhalla. He solicited film scripts for Lindel. When she had told him that she wanted to do a surprise set at the Grotto, as a way of saying "thank you" to Ronnie Marren, Jeff talked her out of it. "You're too big now," he had said. "It would be a mob scene. We've got to be careful." He planned her time. She had one more week of this promotional activity and a week of rehearsals before the quickie European tour. One more week of interviews with European press flown in to talk to her in advance of her shows in London, Paris, Amsterdam and Brussels; one more week of radio stations and in-store record signings, where she had to stand in the middle of a record store during business hours, meet the public and autograph copies of her album.

"When I went to Sam Goody's they had this *throne* for me to sit on," she complained to Jeff. "I think it was left over from Santa Claus. I don't mind seeing kids waiting by a backstage door after a show. That seems natural, wonderful. But these things . . . I hate feeling like I'm a box of detergent."

After the European tour she would write songs for the next album. She'd have two months to get the record done, followed by another tour to sell the rush-released album. Then the whole thing would start all over again. Lindel wasn't at all sure that she liked knowing exactly what she was going to be doing for the next year of her life. And, in the back of her mind, with all of this whirling around her, she couldn't help but wonder if Brian Davis had heard about her success.

11

On December 9 Lindel and Jeff boarded Pan Am's morning flight to London. Jeff had surprised her with two first-class tickets.

"First class?" she said.

"From Jacar International," he said, smiling. "We're not paying for it."

She leaned back in the roomy, cushioned seat. "That's why you wanted the boys to go alone tonight."

"Well, yes. Also, if they fly at night we save on one day's hotel. Don't be mad, but you're staying in a different hotel than they are."

"Jeff," she warned, "I told you, I hate all that prima donna stuff."

"Look, this is Europe. The hotels stink unless they're really good. And you're going to have to do some interviews, so we're in the Ritz. The boys will be perfectly happy at Blake's. They wouldn't know the difference anyway."

Lindel didn't say anything. She took a glass of champagne from the stewardess. Jeff pulled out some papers from his attache case and put them in the pocket of the seat in front of him.

"Don't you think this is all happening too fast?" she said.

"Here we go again," he sighed. "No one said you had to get tuberculosis doing this. Where is it written that it has to be a long, lonely climb to the top? This is why you have me. I told you I could pull it off. Will you just relax and enjoy it?"

"I don't know . . . It all seems like bad karma. Like one day it's going to come back and haunt me in one horrible swoop."

"You've seen too many movies. Come on, dammit. I'm not spending the next six hours on this plane listening to you moan." He laughed. "You're only a star once. Then you start having comebacks."

Even Jeff was surprised at the grandeur that was the lobby of the Ritz. Just past the wood-paneled reception area was the large Edwardian Palm Court, with fifty small white wooden tables surrounded by chairs covered in pink velvet. In the corners, waiters hovered around the dusty rose velvet couches and tapestry damask armchairs where tea was served. Thick rose-colored carpets and gilt crystal chandeliers were reminiscent of another era. At the front reception desk, porters wore black cutaways.

A tiny elevator took guests up to their rooms. The hotel was old, fading, and elegant, and Lindel and Jeff were entranced.

The rooms were not as splendid as the lobby, but Lindel loved the salmon-colored satin bedspreads, the high, marble fireplace, the ornate moldings. Best of all was the bathroom. It had beautiful tile, old fixtures and a huge marble tub.

Lindel ran across the hall to Jeff's room and knocked on his door. "Does your bathroom have that incredible tub?" she said.

"Yes, and two sinks," he said, dragging her inside.

"I can't, I left my door open."

"It's London, it's safe here."

"No, I want to go back and unpack. There's a magnum of champagne, if you want to come have some with me, it's from Jacar. And there are some flowers. There's no card with the flowers, though."

"I have them too," he said. "They're from Harvey Goldsmith, he's the promoter."

"Oh," she said. She sounded disappointed.

"Look, it's eleven-thirty," he said. "I don't know if anything's open, but maybe we could run around to the Speakeasy, and . . ."

"No. I hear it's full of roadies throwing food. I'm in no mood for that. I want to unpack and get a good night's sleep."

"I can't believe you. Always this routine when you arrive at a hotel. What is it?"

"I don't know, it helps me get my bearings. I hate flying, I'm nervous about the show . . ."

"All right. I guess I'll go check it out alone. You do have a lot of stuff to do tomorrow. Tim and the Garniers are coming, there are those interviews, and then you'll have to go over to Manchester Square and meet the people at International. There's probably some kind of dinner, and if you want, we can go see The Vipers."

She avoided looking directly into his eyes.

"Oh," she said, "where are they?"

"The Rainbow. I thought I mentioned it to you. It's an old, art deco movie theater way out in Finsbury Park. Supposed to be beautiful."

"Mmmm, I don't know. I'm not in the mood to go see another show when I've got to perform the next night."

"We can go to the party if you like. Think about it."

"Okay. I'll leave a wakeup call for noon."

The dark blue Daimler limousine pulled up to the front door of The Generation. A few people ran over and looked into the car's blacked-out windows, some recognized Lindel from the photo of her on the cover of that week's *Melody Maker,* and called out her name. Jeff and Tim quickly moved her through the crush, past the security at the door, and into the club.

Lindel was high from a champagne supper with six people who worked for Jacar International, her face was flushed, her hair was wavy and soft around her face. She wore a long, shiny black dress, and she knew she looked good.

She was glad that Tim had come; he'd flown over with Marc and Alexis Garnier on Jacar's private jet and although the Garniers had jet lag and sent their regrets, Tim was always up for a party. She was happy he was there; she needed all the moral support she could get.

This was London, Brian's turf; here, he was the star. But she had come in triumph, too, with that big cover story in *Melody Maker,* and there was no way he could not notice.

Inside the dark, crowded club, Lindel immediately spotted The Vipers at a large corner table, surrounded by beefy security guards. As soon as her eyes got accustomed to the dim light, she saw Brian, with a girl on each arm. The usual: blondes, with the flowers in the hair and the frilly chiffon dresses. Rock star ornaments. Everyone kept looking over at Brian. He was like a powerful magnet. All eyes in the room were on him. Lindel recognized the girl next to Brian from the copy of British *Vogue* she had read on the plane. She was Lady Sarah Ashley, this year's society groupie; pretty in a pale, fragile sort of way.

Ian Bailey, The Vipers' manager, came over to Lindel, Jeff and Tim and steered them over to The Vipers' table, pulling out a chair for Lindel.

"Bri," he said, "you remember Lindel James from America?"

Brian looked up. He, too, was dressed all in black. Lindel was aware of her heart beating, fast. She sat down opposite him, a cool smile on her face.

"It's you," he smiled. He seemed glad to see her. "Why didn't you come backstage?"

"I didn't see the show," she said.

"Good reason." He laughed.

They just sat there, staring at each other. He looked slightly drunk. Despite the fact that there was something about this man that made her feel like she was about to go to pieces the minute she saw him, this time she felt brazen. She didn't take her eyes off his face.

Jeff broke in. "Brian," he stuck out his hand. "Good to see you. Sorry we missed the show. We had to go to dinner with the people from International."

Tim wandered off. Ian poured Lindel a glass of champagne. Jeff stood there, looking around for a chair.

"Don't you have a concert tomorrow night?" Brian asked Lindel.

"Yes . . ." she said. "At the Hammersmith Odeon."

"I'd love for you guys to come," Jeff broke in, pulling over an empty chair he took from an adjacent table. "Why don't I send some tickets around in the morning?"

Lindel shot Jeff a furious look.

"I'd like that," Brian said. "You know, we're even," he said to Lindel. "I still haven't heard your record."

"I'll send that over too," Jeff practically bellowed. Why doesn't Jeff just go away, Lindel thought.

Still staring straight at her, Brian said, "I hear you're a big star in America now."

"Oh," she shrugged, "I've been pretty lucky."

"Are you kidding?" Jeff was really shouting now. "She's *huge*. Lucky, my ass. She's probably going to be *Billboard's* Top New Artist of the year, I'll lay anything that she'll get the Grammy for Best New Artist. The album's already sold five hundred thousand copies . . ."

"Jeff," she hissed, "stop it."

This was not at all the way she had planned it. Jeff was impossible. But Brian seemed amused. And he continued to stare at her.

Lady Sarah leaned across the table, put a cigarette in a long ivory holder, and said to Jeff, "You must be from New York. I keep telling Bri he should go back there. There's so much energy. I can't believe he was only there for a day and a half on that last silly tour. Don't you agree?"

She and Jeff discussed the merits of New York versus London while Lindel and Brian sat in silence. Lindel was thankful for the long-stemmed tulip-shaped glass of champagne to hold, to play with, to keep her busy. She watched more girls come over and talk to Brian.

Ian sat down next to Lindel. Looking at Brian he said, "Tracy just tried to get in. Big row at the door. We got rid of her, though." Brian nodded, and looked up at a girl who couldn't be more than sixteen who was leaning over and whispering something in his ear.

Lindel turned to Ian and said, "All these women here, Ian. All you need is a few children and it would look like the Grateful Dead entourage . . ."

Ian laughed. "Well, that's Brian for you. Of course, the women around Brian are much more glamorous than the ones around the Grateful Dead."

She wondered if she should leave.

Then she felt Brian's knee press against hers under the table.

It must be a mistake, she thought, and moved her leg away slightly. His knee followed hers, and continued its gentle pressure. There was no mistake. Brian leaned over to light her cigarette, and she saw the smile. She suddenly felt giddy. Lindel's heart began to race. She felt like laughing. Maybe not tonight, not with that fancy groupie ensconced, but Lindel was certain that they would be together. She felt a wave of elation.

Jeff was taking down the address of Ian's office so he could send over the record and tickets in the morning and Lindel was relieved that he wasn't inviting them all over on the spot to have a listen. Jeff mumbled something about Lindel needing her sleep, and they got up to leave. For once, Jeff had made a clever first move. Brian was one of those stars who kept a room filled merely by his presence. When he left, so would all the energy. On her own, it would have been impossible to leave the room while he was still there, and Lindel had been afraid that she would sit there, rooted to her chair, and Brian would be the one to leave first.

On the way back to the hotel, Lindel stared straight ahead, as if to warn Jeff that conversation was totally out of the question. The car slowly made its way through the wet streets, around Berkeley Square, into Mayfair.

"He's *sooo* cute," said Tim, from the front seat.

"Who?" said Jeff.

"Brian Davis, of course," said Tim.

Lindel hoped she looked indifferent.

"He's violently sexy," said Tim. "Think he's straight? I guess so, that girl with him is really beautiful. Don't you think?"

He really is getting to be a pain in the ass, thought Lindel.

"Lady Sarah?" said Jeff. "She's okay, but she talks too much. I hear that she's a total speed freak. Of course, Brian's no day at the beach either . . . the stories about him . . ." He shook his head.

Lindel looked at him sharply. "You phony. You'd sign him in a minute if he was available."

"Signing him is one thing," said Jeff, looking directly at her. "Getting involved is something altogether different."

She had no privacy whatsoever. Everyone knew everything on her mind, it seemed, even before it happened. She wished that they'd get back to the Ritz and she could just go and hide in her room. And wait for Brian's call.

At three A.M. Lindel checked with the hotel operator to see if any calls for her had, by mistake, been put through to the wrong room. By the fifth time she checked, the cold, English operator's voice said, "Madam, there have been no calls for you, at all," and Lindel was mortified. She finally fell asleep at six in the morning, only to have her eyes fly open at ten-thirty. She was exhausted, and needed more sleep, but couldn't take a pill; she'd be too groggy for the show. She had to perform in ten hours, and do a sound check at four o'clock—damn Brian Davis. What was all that knee pressing about, anyway?

She could have sworn that he was attracted to her. Maybe he had just been drunk. She tried to go back to sleep, but gave up at noon and ordered breakfast. She phoned Jeff, who was out, but had left a number.

A woman's voice answered the phone.

"Is Jeff Stein there?" Lindel said.

"Lindel," said the voice, "it's me, Alexis Garnier. I'm so glad that we'll have a chance to spend some time together at last."

"Oh, that's right, you arrived with Tim last night," said Lindel. Then, confused, "Where is this I'm calling?"

Alexis' laugh was low. "It's our apartment. We keep one, out here in Belgravia, because Marc has occasion to be here so much. Wait, I'll get your manager for you. But don't go away, darling. I want to make some plans to see you. Tea, perhaps? Today? At the Ritz?"

"I think I've got a sound check later on, and then the show, but . . ."

"No matter," Alexis interrupted smoothly. "We'll see you tonight, Marc and I are giving you a little party after the show at Mr. Chow's."

"Alexis, thank you, I didn't know . . ." But Alexis Garnier had already pressed the hold button.

"Hello?" It was Jeff.

"What's going on?"

"You should see this apartment," Jeff was talking low. "They've got a sauna bath in here the size of a small ballroom."

"Jeff, what are you doing there?"

"What am I doing here?" He sounded offended. "I have business with the man, remember? We have your album to talk about, plans, the party tonight . . ."

"I don't want a party."

"Don't be ridiculous." He laughed.

"I don't," she insisted. "I have the show to do and in two days

I have to go and do the same thing all over again in Paris. I didn't sleep much, I'm wiped out."

"So, I'll get you something to help you stay awake."

She was annoyed. "I don't want anything. Anyway, whose idea was this party? The Garniers? Or yours?"

"Absolutely not. Alexis suggested it herself, and you wouldn't believe the trouble she's gone to. She's ordered flowers especially from some fancy place on Berkeley Square, and told Chow's to be sure that they have ten cases of Cristal champagne."

"What does all of this have to do with rock and roll?"

Jeff's voice changed. "Yes, I know, it's fabulous, isn't it? I told Alexis you'd be thrilled. Well, okay, I'll be back at the hotel in about an hour . . ."

"Cut it out," she said. "I don't care if she is in the room. Call me as soon as you get back. I want to talk to you. Who's invited to this thing?"

"Yes," said Jeff. "Alexis took care of all that. See you soon." And they both hung up.

Lindel lay on the bed for a long time, staring at the phone. A party. Brian. No doubt Jeff had made sure that The Vipers had been invited. He'd think it was good publicity. Dammit, it wasn't the way she wanted to see Brian again. She wondered if he would even show up, if he would come to her concert. She had eight hours before she would find out.

At precisely eight o'clock that night Lindel stood in front of the mirror in her dressing room at the Hammersmith Odeon. She was pleased at the way she looked, and was ready to go onstage. But at the back of her mind she couldn't stop wondering if Brian was there. Jeff and Tim had cleared everyone out of her dressing room—all the press, people from Jacar, all those who wanted to be able to say they saw her before the show—and now she was alone. The band had their own dressing room, but they were probably already in the wings, and now Jeff waited outside her door to take Lindel downstairs to the stage. In the distance she heard the sounds of the audience: taped music that sounded like The Eagles, the crowd was clapping, yelling in anticipation. There was no opening act; Jeff had insisted that this show was to be treated as a special event, and it surprised Lindel when he got his way.

She was actually going to be singing—headlining—in London, where so many American musicians she admired had come before and had done so well. Otis Redding. Jimi Hendrix. Lou Reed. Bruce Springsteen. A city that for the past ten years had exported some of the most exciting, the very best music: The Rolling Stones, The Kinks, The Who, The Yardbirds, Roxy Music. She had to be great tonight. Not only because a success in London was important for building her reputation in Europe, or that it added prestige at home. She wanted this audience to like her, she wanted their respect.

She wished Hank hadn't gone downstairs with the rest of the band. Just having him here, with her, in the dressing room for a few minutes would have given her a bit more courage.

All around the room there were baskets of flowers, arrangements that went from the seriously funereal to those big sprays that the English did so well. The Garniers sent one, so had Jacar International. One was from Marcia, another still from Harvey Goldsmith, the promoter. Some publishing company that Jeff said administered her songs in Europe sent a hideous bunch of gladiolas. She hadn't even known she was signed to a publishing company in Europe. But it was the odd combination of lilacs and birds of paradise that troubled her. The card read, simply: "Ian Bailey." No mention of Brian. Was he here? It wasn't possible that he would sit in that sold-out audience; he was far too famous. But Jeff had insisted that no one stand in the wings during the show, and this time she was grateful for his arrogance. She hated the kinds of shows where forty or fifty hangers-on spilled forth from the wings, practically onto the stage where they could be seen by the audience. "Liggers," they called them here in London. Well, there wouldn't be any liggers at her show.

She wouldn't have been able to sing one note if she saw Brian in the wings. But knowing that there was a possibility that he was there ... somewhere ... well, she was up for the challenge. "Ready?" Jeff yelled through the door. "Yes," she said softly, almost whispering to herself. Ready for the best part of the day.

The audience greeted her finale with silence, and for five seconds Lindel was frightened. Then it began, the applause that was, at first, enthusiastic, then overwhelming, and then turned into a roar. Lindel had heard that London audiences were worse than New York's; that they were jaded, concerned with fashion, unwilling to lavish approval right away. But now, three thousand people were standing and cheering what even Lindel had to agree was a great show. She was soaked through to the skin. She rushed off-stage into Jeff's arms, grabbed a towel from Tim and wiped her face, her hair, took off her purple satin blouse and quickly changed into a black T-shirt. She was ready for her encore, she could go all night. She felt as if this show should begin *now*. The blood pumped through her veins, she was exhilarated. She wished she could do another show. As good as that one had been, she just knew that another one—right now—would be better. She wondered if Brian had seen it.

Tim sat on one side of Lindel, Jeff on the other, as the big black car made its way to Mr. Chow's restaurant. Lindel leaned her head against the tan leather seat, her eyes closed, pretending she was dozing off to sleep so she wouldn't have to talk.

"Wake up, baby." Jeff prodded her arm. "You're the guest of honor, remember?"

"Mmm," she said, turning her head away from him, eyes still closed.

The car drove through the park on its way to Knightsbridge. It was just starting to rain, and the reflection of the car lights against the wet street pavement made everything look shiny. It was beautiful, toylike, and glistening.

Alexis and Marc Garnier stood at the front entrance of Mr. Chow's, right by the small spiral staircase that led upstairs. The restaurant was all chrome and mirrored glass with bright-colored Warhol and Hockney prints lining the walls. The main, downstairs dining room had two sections of white linen-covered tables. On each table there was an exquisite floral arrangement in a Lalique bud vase, and a bottle of Cristal champagne stuck in a gleaming silver ice bucket. Platters of spring rolls and a dark green seaweed dish called *gambei* were brought to each guest by waiters dressed in tuxedos who talked softly to each other in Italian. In the middle of the room a man wearing a white chef's hat was applauded as he made long, white, Chinese noodles. The conversation was lively and the lights were low. Lindel's record was piped in over the sound system.

Jeff looked around with a gleam in his eye. Turning to the Garniers he said, "Marc, Alexis, this is gorgeous. It was really incredible of you to do this."

Alexis leaned over and gave Lindel two kisses in the air, took her hands, and looked at her.

"My dear," said Alexis, "you were just splendid. I can't remember when I've seen such . . . energy."

Alexis wore a heavily brocaded red Chinese jacket over black satin trousers and very high heels. Her blonde hair was pulled back behind her ears into a tight chignon and she wore huge ruby earrings. Lindel, wearing black leather jeans and a black silk blouse, looked spectacular, but felt underdressed next to Alexis, who looked elegant, imposing.

"Come," said Alexis, taking Lindel by the hand and leading her up the winding metal stairs. "There are loads of our friends here who want to meet you."

Lindel cast a frantic look behind her at Jeff and Tim, but they were both engrossed in conversation with Marc. *Where was Brian?* she wondered, as Alexis took her around the upstairs tables, introducing her to people whose names she vaguely recognized from fashion magazines. She posed for photos, sipped from a glass of champagne, and accepted compliments—all in a daze.

Then she saw him. He was alone. Alexis was on one side of her, talking about plans for lunch the following day, Hank was on her other side, talking with an anorexic teenage blonde model. Brian was halfway across the room, leaning against the bar that had been placed at the front of the room for this party. He was wearing black denim jeans and a black jacket, with a white silk shirt and a few black and white silk scarves around his neck. He looked right at Lindel, smiled, and then walked over to her.

They just stood there, staring at each other. Lindel didn't know what she would do if he didn't say something soon. All she could think of was that she wanted to feel him next to her, to have him hold her in his arms. How could it be possible for her to feel this way unless he felt it too?

Then he said, softly, "Do you have to stay long?" He sounded strangely urgent.

Her heart was pounding.

"Well," she heard herself say, "I guess for a little while. I just got here . . ."

They just looked at each other. Right at that moment, she wanted to touch his face, be in his arms, have him kiss her.

He took her arm and walked with her to the bar. They leaned against it, both of them drinking champagne. Out of the corner of her eye, she saw Alexis look after her. It was probably rude to just walk away like that with Brian. She didn't care. She knew that she had no choice.

"You're good," he said. "Better than when I saw you in Philadelphia. You have much more presence."

"You know it's strange," she said, not feeling at all self-conscious. "You sort of become what they think you are. First, you present yourself a certain way, and maybe they believe it. Then, without knowing exactly when, you actually become it."

"Well, you'll find, too, that if you try to take it back, they just expect it more."

She smiled.

"Where are you staying?" he asked.

"The Ritz," she said.

His eyebrows went up. "Mmm, posh. What are the rooms like there?"

"Why don't you come with me and see?" She couldn't believe that she had actually said it.

"Let's go," he said, finishing his champagne.

And, ignoring Jeff, Ian, Tim, the Garniers and the photographers who tried to get a shot of them together, they ran down the stairs, hand in hand, laughing, into the waiting Rolls Royce limousine.

Lindel woke up the next morning in a room full of pink roses. Brian was asleep next to her. The heavy satin draperies were closed tight and she had no idea what time it was. She focused quickly, trying to remember the details of the night before. They had stopped at Covent Garden and Brian had rushed out and bought four bouquets of pink roses. When they knocked on the door of the hotel, Brian's arms filled with flowers, Lindel holding her high-heeled sandals in her hands, the elderly hall porter didn't even blink an eye. Up in her room, when they couldn't find enough vases, Brian tossed the roses along the fireplace mantel, on a chair, across the bed. Then he turned off the light and lay down on the bed. She went over and sat next to him in the dark.

"Are you passing out on me?" she whispered.

"No," he mumbled. "I'm just lying down."

She leaned over to touch him; his arm went around her. They lay there for a few minutes, just holding each other.

"Your heart's beating much too fast," he whispered. "Tell it to slow down."

She started to kiss him; his neck, his face, his eyes, his hair. He wouldn't turn his face to her, and they just lay there, his arms locking her in; touching, reaching, all over. Slowly, up and down, touching her face, touching his face, her eyes. She biting his head, digging her fingers into his scalp, him groaning. Reaching for her more, enveloping her in his arms, long arms, wrapped around her. She reached under his thin silk shirt. His skin was velvet smooth, reaching up to his head, pulling his hair tight, making him groan again.

Trying to reach his mouth with her mouth, he resisting. He, kissing her cheeks, her neck, her eyes, keeping his lips away from hers, as if kissing her on the mouth meant he would be giving in to something . . . something he wasn't ready to admit, she thought, until finally he looked at her, pulled her head back, pulled on her hair and whispered, "Okay."

"What?" she asked puzzled.

"Okay," he said looking at her. She could barely see his face in the dark. *"Okay,"* he said, more urgently now, and he put his lips over her mouth, wet, engulfing, and drew her in. He moved on top of her, and within seconds he took off his clothes, then hers; he touched her, and was inside her.

They moved slowly at first, their bodies fit so perfectly. Then he moved more insistently, faster, then stopped. He rolled over to his side, holding her, taking her with him, still inside her. He held her tightly in his arms, and for a few seconds they were very quiet, very still. Kissing, holding each other, and then he started the rhythm faster. Soon, she thought, soon, and then he put his hand there, making love to her, all the while still hard inside her until with him, she came so completely—as if she had let out everything that had been kept in for so long, just let go, all over him.

In a near daze, Lindel realized that this was Brian in bed with her. Brian, the fantasy, no longer a fantasy; he was there, he had made love to her. *Oh god,* she thought, *I'm sunk.* And then they had drifted off into a deep sleep.

Now, and whether it was morning or afternoon she didn't know, she just wanted to lie there in silence, to savor the memory. He woke up, smiled, and reached out for her. They were ready for each other, and came together hungrily as if they had been waiting for this, for each other, and they couldn't waste any precious time. He could not know how special this was for her, or how long she had waited. She felt alive in a way that she hadn't, ever, and she was aggressive, demonstrative in her lovemaking in a way that surprised her. He looked so beautiful; he was so long and thin, he seemed to just curl around her. He started to touch her, very slowly, with light fingers, all along her body, accompanied by little tender kisses. On her forehead, her eyes, her neck, down along her arms, on the insides of her arms, her legs, her feet. She lay perfectly still for a minute and let him make love to her in this tantalizing way. He was so sensual; she had never known anything like it. He makes love the way he performs on stage, she thought, he completely gives himself to it.

They stayed in bed all day, alternately falling asleep and making love, and when Jeff knocked on her door, calling out, "Lindel?" they huddled under the blankets, giggling, hiding, as if afraid to be caught. When at last Lindel called the hotel operator, she was astonished to find out that it was seven in the evening.

Brian got up, turned on the light next to the bed and reached for his clothes.

"Where are you going?" she asked.

"To the studio. We're in the middle of doing the next record."

Careful, she thought, and said, "Oh, what time do you finish?"

"Oh, six, seven in the morning. You know, whenever we finish."

The words came out before she could stop them.

"But I'm going to Paris in the morning."

He just looked at her.

"I mean . . . Well, I guess I won't see you," she faltered.

"Yeah. Well, you know, that's rock and roll." He grinned and pulled his wrinkled silk shirt over his head.

She just lay there. She was instantly depressed. Let him go, she thought, say nothing.

She got out of bed and put on her apricot silk robe. He was looking around for his scarves, but found only one. She started to help him look.

"Forget it," he said. He seemed in a rush to leave. "If you find it, hold on to it until I see you again."

When will that be? she wanted to cry out. Say nothing, the voice inside her said.

He picked up the rumpled pack of cigarettes, put them in his jacket pocket, and looked around for some matches. He picked up one of the small blue boxes of matches that had the Ritz insignia on it. He looked at her for a minute, leaned over to where she was sitting on the bed, and kissed her.

"Bye," he whispered.

And then he was gone.

After he left, she lay on the bed for a long time. She smoked cigarettes. The room seemed so quiet, so empty.

She knew he had to leave. And there were some people who just weren't good at good-byes. But this had been so special for her. It must have been for him, too. Maybe he was scared. That must be it. He had studio time booked and he was scared of his feelings . . .

He was gone, and she had no idea when she would see him again. If she would see him again. She looked at the ashtrays on each side of the bed. Hers, filled with Marlboro stubs, his with the butts of strong French cigarettes. She looked at the flowers; their petals in sad little designs on the floor. She remembered how excited she had been when they came in, just seventeen hours ago. Now those dead flowers looked so lonely, lying around the room like so many tears. She buried her head in the pillow, she still smelled him, them—the combination of sweat and sex and her perfume and his cigarettes. She hugged the pillow to her, wishing he was still there, wanting him to come back. She lay very still for a few minutes, listening for a sound in the hall, thinking that maybe he would rush back, come to tell her he didn't want to leave, couldn't leave.

After a long time, she got up, turned on the overhead light and the television. A show called "Inside Business" was on BBC 1; BBC 2 had a panel discussion on the war—what war, she wondered—and on the commercial station a woman was demonstrating how to decorate a plate. Lindel opted for the plate decoration and started, slowly and deliberately, to pick up the flowers and throw them into the wastebasket.

It was nine o'clock and even though Jeff thought he heard Lindel's door close a little while ago, he almost gave up on hearing from her that night.

"Coming up for air?" he said when he picked up his ringing phone and heard her voice.

"Don't be bitchy. Were there any reviews of last night?"

"Of the show?"

"Jeff," she warned.

"You were a smash," he said dully. "Of course those were just the dailies. The music papers won't be out until later in the week. I tried to call you, but you had that 'Do Not Disturb' . . ."

"Listen," she interrupted, "I'm going to take a nice long, hot bath. Then, if you like, you can take me somewhere fabulous for dinner."

"What, you, me, and the living god?"

"He's gone. I meant the two of us. Unless Tim's still around."

Jeff perked up. "Well, okay. I told a few people I might join them but it's nothing heavy. Tim's gone. So are the Garniers. They left this afternoon. You know, you were really rude to Alexis. She called two times today. Something about a lunch at San Lorenzo . . ."

"Look, I'll see you in an hour. Let's go somewhere really nice." And she hung up.

Lindel turned on the water in the tub, running it full blast and very hot. She dialed the housekeeper and asked the night maid to please come in and make up the bed. She wasn't going to think about Brian now. She had work to do.

12

Back in New York, Jeff kept Lindel so busy she shouldn't have had time to think about Brian. It had been two weeks since she had spent the night with Brian in London, and she could not get him out of her mind. Nothing helped. The ten-day European tour after London didn't help either; even with triumphant concerts in Paris, Brussels, Amsterdam and Frankfurt. Except when she was onstage, Lindel had gone through those cities in a trance; unfamiliar surroundings, the babble of foreign languages and old, magnificent hotels all added to her feelings of isolation and increased her thoughts of Brian.

Nor was she distracted from thinking about him during band rehearsals when she returned to New York, or while she auditioned rhythm guitarists.

It was strange; for almost a year she had existed in this music world being only vaguely aware of Brian Davis. Now, whenever she opened a rock magazine it seemed as though his face jumped out at her, looking at her in that taunting way. Wherever she went, Lindel heard Brian's newest single: blasting from the jukebox at the Grotto, or from the open window of a car passing in the street. "In Ruins" was far too threatening to be a mainstream hit, but the more adventurous stations played it, and it seemed as though everyone Lindel knew loved the record.

When she got back from Europe she had half expected to find a letter, or a postcard from Brian in her mailbox. When there wasn't one, she felt let down. Of course, he probably wasn't a letter writer. When Marcia gave her the neatly typed list of phone calls she'd received while she was away, Lindel quickly scanned it, looking for Brian's name. He hadn't called, and then she felt foolish; there was no way he would have known her address, or her phone number.

Still, each day she woke up with the thought that maybe he'd call. If she was thinking about him so much, didn't he have to be thinking about her just a little bit too?

She allowed Jeff to plan most of her days and some of her nights. Jeff insisted that she do another photo session; the publicity shots she had taken five months ago had been used too often and she looked much more beautiful these days. Jeff was positive he could get Annie Leibovitz to take the photographs, and they might be able to get the next album cover out of it as well.

He set up meetings for her with video directors to discuss a concept for a promotional videotape that could be used on rock TV shows to publicize the next album. She did more interviews, even though she warned Jeff that she was starting to get tired of talking about herself. Each day she talked on the phone to Marcia, who made her appointments, gave her a wakeup call, told her that day's schedule, and relayed phone messages. People she didn't know called all the time.

"How can he call to invite me to dinner?" she asked Marcia. about one well-known movie star whose stud reputation was legendary. "I don't even know him."

"You're famous," Marcia said. "It's like a club. Famous people just assume they can meet any other famous people they want. Anyway, you're crazy not to want to meet him. He's gorgeous."

"Marcia, he comes on to everyone. It's hardly a compliment."

"He can insult *me* anytime he likes," Marcia had said.

And still, there was no word from Brian.

Lindel wondered if she should go out with someone, try to meet new men, get her mind off Brian. But no one else interested her; next to Brian, all other men paled by comparison.

Jeff didn't understand her attitude at all. Had it been totally up to him, they would have accepted every invitation. He constantly bemoaned the fact that Lindel was ruining what could have been his new, glamorous social life. New York was hustle and glitter; it was the media power gathered for lunch at the Russian Tea Room, the table hopping and dinner gossip at Elaine's, it was the green room at the Academy of Music, Ronnie Marren's office at the Grotto, backstage at the Garden. He thought that Lindel just didn't *get* it. What he didn't understand was that she was truly not interested.

She did like to go with Tim to hear the new bands that played in the tiny clubs downtown; bands like The Ramones, Talking Heads, Television, Blondie. She was inspired by their energy, and often would get home at four in the morning and start to write songs and not stop until way after dawn, when, exhausted, she would turn off her phone and fall asleep.

A few nights a week she would go with Tim to the Grotto, sometimes Hank would come too. Ronnie would join them and Lucy would sit with them, and everyone said it was like old times. Except that so much had changed. Tim encouraged Lucy as always, and Hank seemed to enjoy having her around, but Lindel had mixed feelings. She needed to keep her distance, even though she wasn't exactly sure why she felt that way. It would have been so easy to let Lucy back in her life; after all, she was jammed with work, and lonely, and Lucy was as attentive and persevering as ever. But it was as if a red flag was up somewhere in the back of Lindel's mind, and she heeded the warning.

Four weeks passed since she'd returned from Europe, and Jeff was pressing her to choose a rhythm guitarist from the three she liked best of fifty who had tried out. He wanted her to make a decision about a producer for the next album, and a commitment for a short winter tour. She and Hank thought it might be a good idea to work out the new material live, on the road, before going into the studio.

Then, in a flash, the idea came to her. And she knew exactly what she was going to do.

The engineers had all gone home and Lindel and Jeff were alone in Studio A of the Sound Factory. They sat next to each other behind the console, passing a joint back and forth.

Finally Lindel said, "I'm not trying to be difficult."

"I know," said Jeff, "but I really think the second one was better."

"Oh, I don't mean about the edit. The second one is better for the new single. I mean about what to do next."

"Honey, you said you wanted to hold off on the new album until the spring, that you wanted to work on the songs more. I agreed. Now what?"

"I mean about the tour."

Jeff widened his eyes. "You agreed to do this tour, you said you wanted to get out in front of audiences again . . ."

"No," she interrupted. "You said you want me out in front of audiences again. God forbid I shouldn't be working."

Jeff looked hurt. "Lin, what do you want to do? You can't put out one album, have it be such a phenomenal hit, then sit around."

"I'm not suggesting that I sit around." She reached for the glass of orange juice on the console, and picked at a piece of stale coffee cake.

"So, what's the problem?" said Jeff. "All the three-thousand seaters are dying for you. I've already put holds on dates with Bill Graham in San Francisco, Larry Magid in Philly, Barry Fey in Denver, Don Law in Boston, Ronnie Delsener in New York—all the bigs. All you have to do is give me the go-ahead to okay the deals. L.A. is the only hassle. I'd rather you do five nights at the Roxy, because it would be such an event, but if you can't stomach five days at the Beverly Hills Hotel . . ."

"It's not that." She reached across the console for her cigarettes. "It's the concept of showing up in the same place every night for a week. It seems too much like a job. I like it to be fast, to move." She lit a cigarette, coughed, ignored Jeff's raised eyebrows and said, "Anyway, I want this tour to be different, to be fun. I don't know if you can completely understand, but after awhile the tour got so . . . strange. It's like the only people who exist are the ones on the tour; everyone else looks like they're wearing Halloween masks."

He waited.

"I've been thinking about it," she said, "and I don't want to go out and just do the predictable tour with one of those 'let's boogie' opening acts."

He still said nothing.

"You know," she went on, talking faster now, "one of those bands that Tim says always sing songs called 'Carolina' or 'West Virginia'."

She got up, and walked around the console to the window that looked into the studio. She stared into the empty studio for a few seconds and then turned to face Jeff.

"Wouldn't it be a gas," she said, her eyes sparkling, "to have The Vipers as an opening act?"

"You're not serious." He stared at her.

"Oh, but I am."

"That is just about the *worst* idea I've ever heard," Jeff said, rolling back his chair, almost toppling it over.

"Why?" She sat down on the couch.

"Don't give me that innocent look," said Jeff, getting up and starting to pace back and forth in the small control room. "Okay, forget the obvious personal problem. The fact that you just want to get laid."

"Jeff . . ."

"Professionally," he continued, "it's a disaster. No one knows who they are yet. Not really, especially your audience. The combination is totally fucked."

"I don't think so," she shot back. "I want a different audience. I'm tired of this folk rock princess. It's bullshit, and you know it. It's only because the press was so bored with glitter rock that they latched onto me this way and put me in this ridiculous category. I never wanted to do palatable, grown-up rock and roll, and I think this would be a great move. A great career move, as you would put it."

Jeff stopped still, and looked at her. Almost pleading, he said, "Lindel, it's insane, it's trouble."

"Why? Give me one good reason."

"The last thing in the world we want to worry about is carting around a bunch of English rock and roll musicians, with their girls, their drugs, all that looning about. Come on, cut it out, you know what I'm talking about."

"Look Jeff," she said, putting out one cigarette and lighting another. "I want the road to be fun this time. What's the point if it's not? Why should it be drudgery? I like Brian. I'm not saying I don't. I'd like some company . . ."

"We'll send Marcia, Tim, anybody. But not him."

"Tim?" Lindel laughed. "That's great. A gay guide to America. That would help me out a lot during all those lonely nights. And, by the way, what is this Tim mentioned to me last night about my low royalty rate? I forgot to ask you."

"What about royalties?" Jeff looked at her sharply and sat down.

"He said I have a low royalty rate. What's that supposed to mean?"

Jeff frowned. "It's nothing. I worked it out that way in the production deal so you'd have less taxable income. It saves you money in the end. We make it up on your expenses. What's the matter? You need more bread?"

"No, I was just wondering . . ."

"Tim should mind his own business," Jeff muttered. Then he smiled quickly and said, "All right, about the tour. I'll go with you."

She looked at him and burst out laughing. "I think you're missing the point," she said. "You coming on the tour has nothing to do with it. First of all, I don't want you on the tour. We fight too much on the road. No, I've thought about this a lot."

"I'll bet you have."

"So, I want you to check it out, okay? Who's the agent for The Vipers? Marty Paretta? Call him." Her voice was like a command.

"Lindel," he pleaded, "it's suicide."

She got up from the couch, put her cigarettes in the pocket of her black linen jacket, and turned to face him.

"I really don't want to discuss it, but I know what's best for me and my music, no matter what you think. I want a band with us this time that's going to shake us up a little bit, give us a challenge every night. I don't want it to be easy just because we could get away with it."

She stopped, and then added, quietly, "I love this music. I don't think about it the way you do. And," she lowered her voice to almost a whisper, "I didn't get into this so I could get a good table in a fancy restaurant."

And then she was gone.

Jeff sat there, alone. Jesus, what was that restaurant crack about? He didn't like this at all. Here she was, a recognized new superstar. In *Billboard*'s Top Ten for eight weeks. He barely had time to really enjoy all this before she was starting up. He knew that since London she had been thinking about Brian Davis. She seemed distant, distracted; she didn't finish sentences, she was off in some private little world. He heard all about the problems other managers had when their female artists started thinking with their cunts. Even with guys—wives and girlfriends always broke up bands. He had just never thought about this happening with Lindel.

She was too smart for this. How would it look, shlepping some two-bit cult band with them across the country? Marty Paretta had been shmoozing him for weeks; it was obvious he wanted to be Lindel's agent. How the hell could he, Jeff, call Marty to ask for The Vipers? Marty surely would make it seem like a favor. Goddamn her. Why couldn't she just fuck her lead guitarist like every other girl singer did on the road? Her rap about the music; what a crock of shit. Here he had a chance on this tour to do himself some good. A few favors for promoters in different cities who had local bands of their own they wanted to stick on the shows. Maybe use the Electric Toys or the Marquis de Sade, bands he would soon sign to Valhalla, as opening acts in some of the Northeastern cities. Help his own cause with other record companies by booking some new bands they wanted to break to open the shows. All his plans down the drain.

Maybe, he thought with a faint glimmer of hope, maybe The Vipers will be busy. Perhaps he could even lie to Lindel and say they were unavailable. But he knew that was impossible; Lindel was determined and she'd just find out. Christ, for all he knew, she might have already discussed it, planned it with Brian.

With reluctance, he went into his office the next morning and dialed Marty Paretta's number. Marty came on the line right away.

"Jeff, how are you? I hear Lindel's going to go out on tour. *Bubi,* you really should let me book it for you. Save you all that grief . . ."

"Well, maybe. But I want to ask you something. For some reason, god knows why, Lindel has this bug up her ass to shlep those Vipers on tour with her. They busy for the next few months?" He hoped, please, let them be busy.

"What? She's crazy. Why them? She doesn't need them."

"We know that Marty, we know that. But we've been thinking," *my nose shouldn't grow from this lie,* he thought, "we've been thinking, Marty. She wants to do something that will give this tour a certain . . . ah . . . edge. You know, give it some balls. And it would be a helluva publicity gimmick."

"What, she wants to shack up with Brian?"

"Marty, *please.*"

"Listen, he's not *my* type, but you should see the broads that guy gets. Of all the artists I've got—Jesus, can you believe they're called artists?—half of them don't even flush the toilet. Anyway . . ."

"Look," said Jeff, cutting Marty off, "I just think she's had it with this rock princess bit. Her music is getting funkier, and she's got this thing about them opening for her. And," he nearly choked on the words, "I think it would be an interesting career move."

Marty groaned. Jeff heard him rustle some papers.

"Well, I'll look into it. But I'll be honest with you, Jeff. I book them, yes, but that Davis kid has to approve everything. I never saw anything like it. I'm used to dealing with agents, lawyers, managers, whatever. And now, every decision with this cockama-mie band has to go through this kid, and you can't imagine how it slows things up. It takes days to get an answer out of him."

"So?"

"Well, I'd have to 'present' Lindel to him."

"What?!" Jeff exploded. "Well, *fuck that.* We don't need him that bad. We can get some other asshole limey band."

"Wait, wait. Don't get your balls in an uproar. Let me see what I can do."

Here it comes, thought Jeff.

"I mean," said Marty, his tone soothing now, "how much does she want them?"

"Not enough to beg," said Jeff, ready to hang up the phone.

"Of course not, of course not. I know that. But like, for instance, what else is going on?"

"You know, Marty, wouldn't it be nice if this whole business wasn't done on favors? If everyone could be above board with everyone else, and things were just judged on merit . . ."

"Oh, give me a break," said Marty. "We'd all be bored in two minutes and you know it."

Jeff sighed. "Well, it just so happens that I am sending the Electric Toys into the studio next week and they haven't made an agency deal yet. Neither have the Marquis . . ."

"You can take those junkies and shove 'em," said Marty. "But the Toys, well, I'd be interested. Of course Lindel is the one who should be signing with us. But you know, Jeff, we really don't like to take an artist this way. It's not the way we do business."

"Sure, Marty, sure," Jeff said, laughing, and they hung up after making a lunch date for the following week that they both knew they would break.

When the tour had finally been arranged, Lindel was nervous. Six weeks on the road with Brian. His first real American tour. She would have someone with her at night. She wouldn't be alone.

But what if he resented it, what if he didn't want to be with her? After all, he hadn't called her after that night in London. She wouldn't think about that now. He had agreed to the tour, and he must know, as she did, that there was a reason why they came together at this time in their lives.

She was sure that everyone—Jeff, Marcia, Tim—thought they knew what she was up to. But they didn't know all of it. They didn't know how much she wanted, needed, to see him onstage. This tour was going to be for her music. And for her heart.

The next three weeks were taken up with rehearsals with the band, breaking in Rob Gilbert—the new rhythm guitarist—and going over hotel and transportation arrangements with Marcia. This time, Lindel wanted nothing left to chance. She kept a careful eye on the concert dates, making sure that there were at least two days off each week, that there weren't many early morning flights and that there were as few Ramada Inns as possible. She insisted that money be allotted for The Vipers to stay in the same hotel that she and her band stayed in, and when Jeff had a fit, screaming that at this rate she was going to lose money, she simply told him that if they weren't all in the same hotels, she wasn't going.

She took money from her checking account and bought new clothes for the tour. With every new dress, blouse or jacket she bought, she wondered if Brian would approve. She paid one hundred and fifty dollars for a pale gray silk nightgown, then felt ridiculous about it, and packed and unpacked it in her suitcase ten times. Each day that passed without a call from Brian added to her nagging fears. What if this whole thing had been a mistake?

Around four in the afternoon on the day before the tour began, she figured she should pack. She had no plans for the evening, but maybe she'd do something with Tim. The phone rang, and she debated whether to answer it or not. It was probably just Marcia or Jeff with another detail. She reached for it, and picked it up on the fourth ring.

"Hi," said the unmistakable English accent.

She grabbed the receiver tighter in her fist, lit a cigarette with her free hand, and tried to keep her voice steady.

"Brian?"

"Very good," he said. "I just got in."

"Where—where are you?" she stammered.

"At the airport. Waiting for my bags."

"I thought you were all going straight to New Orleans."

"I had to stop here and have my visa fixed first."

Brian. Here. And they were babbling about visas and luggage.

"Welcome," she managed to say. "Where are you staying?"

"Well," he sounded as if he was smiling, "I was going to ask you a favor. Do you think I could sleep on your floor?"

Her heart was going crazy. Surely he could hear it over the phone wire.

She laughed, a low, sexy laugh. "You don't have to sleep on my floor, Brian." And then she gave him her address.

She hung up the phone and hugged herself. Brian was here. Typical of him to call like this: unannounced, at the last minute. Or was it?

He was here. He wanted to see her. He'd be in her apartment in an hour or so, and her tour—their tour—started tomorrow. She'd better get ready. She got into the shower, washed her hair, and as it dried she ran around the apartment, frantically trying to pack for six weeks in forty minutes. She checked the refrigerator, there was some wine and a few bottles of beer. If he was hungry, they'd have to go out. Maybe she should call Marcia and have a limousine on hand.

She looked at the fireplace; she had run out of firewood, but at least she could turn the lights down low. She emptied the waste-baskets and ashtrays, and left the flowers she had bought a few days ago in the vase on the mantel. She wondered if he would think someone else had bought them for her. She debated whether or not to put a record on the stereo, she wasn't sure what he would like to hear. She would have plenty of time in the next few weeks to find out.

At five-thirty he was at her door, with two large suitcases in his hands and a sloppy grin on his face. They stood there, smiling foolishly at each other, and then she leaned over to hug him. He kissed her lightly on the mouth and still, they stood there.

"How's London?" She didn't know what else to say.

"The usual bright gray."

"I guess you should come inside."

He put down his suitcase and looked around the living room. "What a great apartment," he said.

"There's not much furniture."

"I like that," he said. "Most people clutter up their lives far too much."

"Do you want something to drink?"

"Yes, please. What do you have?"

"Some wine, beer, whiskey . . . whatever you want."

"Do you have any brandy?"

"Well, yes, actually, I do." She was thrilled to have a reason to open the bottle of Remy.

He walked over to her record player and thumbed through the stack of records as she went to get the drinks. She was glad to have something to do, even if it just was to pour the brandy. She, who had performed to thousands of strangers, still felt like Jell-O alone in a room with this man.

She handed him his glass, and sat in the chair across from him. He was quiet, just sat there on the couch sipping the brandy, and looked at her. He had such an unsettling stare, and she fought the impulse to chatter. This is silly, she thought, and went to sit next to him on the couch. With one motion, he put his arm around her, drew her into his embrace, and kissed her, long and hard. Not yet, she thought, *not yet,* and pulled away.

"How do you feel?" she said. "Tired? Want to unpack or anything? Have a bath? Go out?"

"Whatever you like. I'm a guest in your country. You be social director. I'm not at all tired. I took a pill on the plane and slept the whole way. I'm not in the mood to go hear any music though, if that's what you mean."

She thought for a minute, then blurted out, "Have you ever been to Coney Island?"

"No. It's an amusement park, isn't it? Like Disneyland?"

She laughed. "It's not quite as clean as Disneyland. It's kind of sleazy, but it's fun. They have the best hot dogs and a huge ferris wheel and bumper cars. It's right on the beach in Brooklyn, although it's a hideous beach . . . with a boardwalk . . ." Now why did I bring this up, she thought, wildly.

"Like Brighton?"

"Brighton Beach?" She was surprised he had heard of it.

"Brighton. In England."

"Oh," she said. "I've never been there. No, what I meant is right near Coney Island there's a section called Brighton Beach, where old people live . . ."

"Brighton in England is a lovely old seaside resort. I went there once for a vacation when I was a kid. It's also the place where all the Mods and Rockers fights were. Anyway, sure, let's go. I've never seen Brooklyn."

"There are actually some pretty places in Brooklyn. My father's from there and he used to take me there when I was a little girl. You can't really see much at night. Coney is fun, even though most of the rides are closed in the winter."

She stopped, realizing that she had been talking too fast. Why was it that Brian caused her to feel like she could either say nothing at all, or want to tell him the story of her life? She went to the phone in the bedroom and called Dav-El Livery herself to ask them to send a car. Marcia didn't need to know about this just yet. Lindel was glad they were going out. She wanted tonight to be special, to take him somewhere that he would find exotic. It was a laugh to think that anyone would find Coney Island exotic but one never knew with the British. The next six weeks would put her in very close proximity with this man. She had no intention of falling into bed with him the minute he walked in the door. After all this time, she could wait three more hours.

The car sped down Broadway, past Seventh Avenue in the Village, to lower Manhattan. City Hall and the federal courthouse were lit up and reflected against the sky. There was a large, full moon overlooking the city. It looked like a big white balloon; eerie, yet quiet beautiful. Brian and Lindel sat close together in the back seat, with a black radio station on full blast. Brian had eagerly turned on the radio the minute they got into the car, saying, "This is really the best thing about America. Your radio. You don't know how lucky you are."

An old Ike and Tina Turner song came on the radio and Brian turned it up louder.

"I love this song," said Lindel. "It was on an early live album they did."

Brian turned to her. "You had that album too? I wore mine out eight years ago."

"Me, too . . ."

"It was my favorite album . . ."

"I know, I couldn't believe when Tina Turner did that 'battle' on it with Vanetta Fields. It took my breath away."

They were both talking now, fast, talking over each other in their enthusiasm. Lindel felt excited, giddy.

They drove over the Brooklyn Bridge and rode through the quiet, residential streets of Brooklyn in silence. Brian's arm was around her, and Lindel felt the same way she had on the other occasion when she'd been with him: that there was nowhere else she wanted to be. The car stopped in front of Nathan's at Surf and Stillwell, and Lindel pressed the button that lowered the partition and told the driver to wait as they got out of the car.

"We can go around the back and sit down to eat if we want to," she said to Brian, "but it's faster, really, and more fun, I think, to eat out here."

Brian looked around. She couldn't read his face, but she felt that this had been the right choice. If he thought that she was some sort of prima donna, one look at Nathan's would put that idea right out of his mind.

The large room was brightly lit and even though it was the off season, a few people stood around eating hot dogs, bright yellow ears of corn, greasy french fries in paper cups, and fish sticks dipped into a sticky red sauce.

"This is great," Brian mumbled.

"I thought you'd like it," she said. "The best way to do this is for one of us to get the hot dogs, the other one can get the french fries, and drinks, or whatever you want, and then meet back here with everything."

He looked at her. "Are you always so organized?"

"Well," she stammered, "it's faster that way."

"What's the rush?"

"Sorry . . ."

"You just wait here, and I'll go and get everything."

She smiled. "I forgot about you British male chauvinists."

"I hate that bloody expression . . ."

"Me, too," she said quickly. "It was a joke."

"Anyway," he said, smiling, "I just remembered I have no money. Didn't have time to change it at the airport. I barely had enough to pay the taxi in. So you'll have to do it after all."

"Aha!" she said, smiling. "Some male chauvinist. Okay, we'll go together. I'll pay. But dinner in New Orleans is on you."

He just looked at her. Had she imagined it, or did he look annoyed? Damn. There she went, making a few plans. She had to control her eagerness.

They ate hot dogs, drank beer, walked hand in hand to the boardwalk. The large gray ferris wheel was silent and still and outlined against the full moon sky. The booths all along the board-walk were closed with wooden shutters, but they found one bumper car concession open and they bought tickets and Brian purposely crashed into her every time they passed each other's car. They went into a game arcade and Brian aimed a water pistol at a doll's mouth until a balloon broke and he won a stuffed dog. A man incorrectly guessed their ages and Brian picked out two plaid barrettes for her prize. They won the bowling game, and with their tickets got two whistles: a blue one for him, red for her. They walked by the seedy, rundown Surf Hotel and Lindel said, "I always thought it would be really sexy to get a room there."

"Sexy?" Brian looked at her. "Nothing sexy about rats, dear. Believe me, I know." She realized once again how little she did know about him.

Around ten o'clock he started to yawn.

"Jet lag?" she said, worried that he might be bored.

"I guess so. I think I'm going to have to crash."

"Let's go."

In the car on the way back to Manhattan he leaned his head against her shoulder. She was wondering whether she should get the gray nightgown out of her suitcase and wear it tonight. It was only ten o'clock—although it was four in the morning his time— maybe there'd be a good movie on the late show. It would be so wonderful to have Brian with her, in her bed, where she'd been alone, thinking of him for all these weeks. Suddenly, she realized he was fast asleep. When the car pulled up to her building, she had to prod him awake and he practically stumbled up the stairs and inside the apartment. She led him toward the bed, and he collapsed, fully dressed, on top of the covers.

Lindel looked at him. There was no waking him, no getting him undressed. She would just have to slip into her side of the bed. She'd deal with everything else in the morning. Brian was here. It was a strange beginning.

The Royal Orleans was a large, expensive hotel in the heart of the French Quarter. Horse-drawn carriages were lined up on the street in front of the main entrance and the doormen wore red waistcoats and white cotton gloves. A spacious lobby had Oriental rugs on the blond wooden floor, and large twinkling glass chandeliers hung from the ceiling.

From the minute she landed at the airport, Lindel felt a strong physical reaction to New Orleans. It was one of those romantic Southern full moon nights and Lindel felt as if she'd been embraced with a whispered, sensual welcome.

Her large room had two double beds and a small balcony that looked out onto Royal Street. She stood on the balcony for a few minutes, feeling the air, and looking at all the other wrought-iron balconies that were like bracelets on the buildings that lined the streets.

She wanted Brian here, next to her, right now. They could sit on this balcony and look at the moon and drink one of those sweet, tropical drinks. It was only eight o'clock, and they had nothing to do until the sound check the next day for the first show that night. She wanted to get all dressed up and go with him to the wood-paneled Antoine's restaurant, where she had heard that big old-fashioned fans cooled the air and the waiters spoke patois and the French food was out of this world. Then afterward, they would walk down Bourbon Street, and stop in the topless bars and drink Hurricanes and go hear some music. She had already looked in the paper to see who was playing: Professor Longhair, Clarence "Frogman" Henry, The Meters, Frankie Ford. She knew what those names would mean to an English musician.

Then, when it was very, very late, they would take one of those carriages to the all-night Cafe du Monde, and drink coffee and eat freshly baked hot doughnuts and get the powdered sugar all over their faces.

Lindel changed from her jeans into white linen trousers and a black shirt. She sat down on the bed and picked up the phone to dial his room. Tomorrow morning, or whatever time they woke up, they could go to breakfast at Brennan's, and sit in the lush, enclosed garden and eat blueberry pancakes.

There was no answer in Brian's room.

She didn't understand. They had just checked in. She looked at the room list for the two bands. Maybe she had tried the wrong room. She dialed it again; still no answer. She tried Bernie, The Vipers' road manager. No answer. She methodically went down the rooms of everyone in his band. No answer in any of their rooms.

She lit a cigarette. They were probably in the bar. She dialed the extension for the bar, and asked the maître d' if there were some English musicians there. There weren't.

She waited ten minutes, and then tried his room again. Still, no answer. She dialed again, and when she got a busy signal she was relieved, until she realized that she had tried her own room. This was ridiculous. She tried her own road manager.

"Johnny, did The Vipers ask for a car?"

"Yeah. The road manager, Bernie, called me about half an hour ago."

"Where did they go?"

"I think he said down to the hall."

"The hall? That's in Baton Rouge. Isn't it about an hour away? What on earth did they go down there for?"

"I think he said something about a rehearsal."

Lindel was stunned. A rehearsal? Now? They'd get a sound check the next afternoon. She never even considered rehearsing on the road. But then, she had just spent three weeks rehearsing with her band in New York. Maybe he hadn't spent three weeks in rehearsals. Or maybe he just liked to play.

She had so looked forward to this night. Last night he had just passed out, and today they had spent the whole day arranging his visa, and getting plane tickets and hotel vouchers from Jeff. There hadn't been any time for them to be alone.

Now, she didn't know what to do. She had purposely avoided making plans with the guys in her band because she was sure she would be alone with Brian. He hadn't said anything; she had just taken it for granted.

She could watch TV, or read a book. Surely she had some inner resources. It was just so . . . empty in this room, and her expectations had been so high. She'd go out. No reason why she should sit here waiting for him.

It would take about an hour for The Vipers to get to the University of Louisiana at Baton Rouge, maybe they'd rehearse two hours, and then it would take another hour to get back. He should be back at midnight. No, she would not wait here for him.

At nine she met Johnny and Hank in the Touche Lounge in the lobby. They sat and listened to the cocktail pianist for an hour and a half. Lindel drank four margaritas, and she was quite drunk when around eleven o'clock she saw some of The Vipers straggling into the hotel. She didn't see Brian. *Where was he?* She saw Bernie go over to use the house phone. He hung it up, came into the lounge, and walked over to her.

"Bri's lookin' for you," he said.

"Oh?" she tried to sound casual. "Where is he?"

"He went with the guys to the place where Frankie Ford's playing. He said if you wanted to, you should join up with him there."

She hesitated. "Are you going?" she asked Bernie.

"Yeah. I love that geezer. I wore out my copy of *Sea Cruise* when I was fifteen."

For one second she thought that maybe she shouldn't go. Maybe she should just disappear for the rest of the night, let him miss her. But as soon as she thought it, she knew it wasn't even an option. She wanted to be with Brian and she wanted to be with him right now. She never had been very good at playing games.

It was four-thirty in the morning and Lindel and Brian walked slowly up Bourbon Street, their arms wrapped around each other. Lindel had taken off her shoes—high-heeled, strappy sandals—and carried them in her hand just as she had that night with Brian in London.

A girl on a swing rocked back and forth in a second-story window, advertising the sex show inside. From the street, Lindel could see inside the Baby Doll Bar where men stuffed dollar bills into sequinned G-strings worn by two overweight strippers. A loud Dixieland trumpet played in the Sho-Lounge, while next door the Stones' "Brown Sugar" was the musicial accompaniment for a transvestite revue. Down the street, an elderly group of black men played ragtime in the dimly lit Crazy Shirley's. It was sleazy, it was honky-tonk, and Lindel thought she had never been anywhere quite so beautiful in her life.

Back at the hotel, her room was stuffy and Lindel went to turn on the air conditioner.

"No," said Brian, "don't. Bad for the voice." And he pulled her toward him and turned out the light. The curtains were opened, and the light of the moon filled the room.

Standing there, leaning against the wall, he started to kiss her. He stopped, and stared at her. She tried to kiss him, but he turned his head away. He teased her, he took her head and turned it to face him. Her knees felt weak, she wanted to lie down. They were standing inches away from the bed, but he wouldn't let her move.

His grip on her was firm. He took his finger, put it in his mouth, wet it, then put it against her lips to make them wet. It was unbelievable the way he touched her, the way he made her feel.

She tried to pull him onto the bed. He shook his head, still staring at her, took her hand and put it against his chest. She started to move her hand . . . down . . . he didn't close his eyes, just continued to stare at her.

"Please," she whispered, "couldn't we lie down?"

He shook his head no, and covered her mouth with his hand. She started to kiss his hand, lick it with her tongue, and he laughed, a low laugh, and then at last he pulled her down onto the bed.

He kissed her, hungrily, hard, and she responded: grabbing his head, kissing his mouth, his hair, his eyes. He undressed them both, and with his mouth on her mouth, not giving her a chance to breathe, he took his hands and moved them slowly down her body. She was ready for him; had been ready for weeks, months. How many times, alone in her bed, had she gone over in her mind that night in London when they had first been together. And now here he was, inside of her, their bodies hot and sweaty as they reached for each other, into each other, more. She couldn't get enough of him, she wanted it never to stop.

Afterward, in the dark, the glow from their cigarettes silhouetted their naked bodies against the white sheets. He was so beautiful. He had that amazing velvet skin—how did he get such skin, she wondered—and his legs were so long, they seemed to curl around her entire body and still kept going. The curve of his back down to his legs was magnificent; surely there had never been such a gorgeous body on a man. She didn't want him to see how much she was looking at him, drinking him in. Even though she had seen his face in countless photographs, she wanted now to memorize each feature, to remember him lying here next to her in a way she would never see from just watching him onstage, or in a bar, in real life. It wasn't fair for a man to have such long eyelashes, such great cheekbones . . . He had an elusive quality. Even lying next to her, naked in bed, there was something about his presence that was not quite real.

His arms were so long, tapering down to those graceful fingers. Just thinking of those fingers on her skin again made her breath quicken . . . she wanted him so much. He turned to her with a smile, put his cigarette out in the ashtray, and pulled her toward him again. She was sure that he knew she had been staring. And this night, he did not fall asleep before she did. He made love to her once more, and then again, until the sun came up over the sleepy French Quarter and, as she heard the early morning sounds of window shutters open and people talking in the street, she fell asleep, safe, in Brian's arms.

13

Marcia walked into her darkened apartment and put her brief-case on the table. She went to the refrigerator and took out a can of Tab, then went to turn on the answering machine for her messages.

"It's Jeff. I'm in a phone booth and I don't have the itinerary with me. What time does Lindel's plane get into Detroit? Call me immediately. Leave a message with my service." . . . *"Marcia, it's Dad. I missed you at the office, but I have that information you wanted. If you need me tonight, I'll be home."* . . . *"Hi, it's Tim. Are you going to The Studs concert tonight? Call me if you want to share a cab."* . . . *"Marcia, it's Greg. Call me if you're free tonight. Maybe we could see a movie."* . . . *"It's me again. I've got to find Lindel before eight. Call me as soon as you hear this."*

She turned the machine off and sat down on the couch. She kicked off her shoes and put her feet up. She didn't need to look at the itinerary; she knew Lindel's schedule by heart. The plane got into Detroit at nine, she'd be at the Pontchartrain by ten. It was seven forty-five now—there was nothing Jeff could do about finding Lindel for two hours, and Marcia was in no rush to call him. He'd call back.

She was exhausted. No way could she go to the Academy with Tim. She probably should see The Studs, especially since Jeff had been mumbling about signing them. But not tonight.

Greg. He was sweet. Too sweet, actually. Why was it that the men who seemed to really like her were the ones she didn't care about at all? She probably should see Greg tonight, but it had just been too long a day.

She picked up the phone to call her father. His number was busy, and the instant she replaced the receiver, the phone started to ring.

It was Jeff. "Where've you been?" he demanded. "I have to get in touch with her."

"What's the problem?"

"No problem," Jeff snapped. "I just want to talk to her about the TV show."

"Now? She won't be in L.A. for another three weeks. Why ask her about it now?"

"I know what I'm doing." Jeff sounded annoyed. "They have to book these things in advance. What time does she get in? What hotel? What name is she registered under?"

"She's using her own name. She'll be at the hotel by ten. The Pontchartrain."

Jeff sighed. "Shit. I'll miss her. Unless I can call from a pay phone."

"Are you going to see The Studs?"

"Probably," he said. "I've got those Japs from International in tonight."

"I hope you're not calling them that to their faces."

"It doesn't matter what I call them. They don't speak a word of English. It'll be an evening of sight gags. Want to come?"

"No, thanks. In the words of the immortal Sam Goldwyn, include me out."

"Oh, come on. I want you to see The Studs anyway, and you'd really be a help with these Japs."

"Jeff, I've been at the office since eight-thirty this morning trying to call London to find Ian Bailey to work out those problems with The Vipers' visas if we do more shows in New York at the end of the tour. Then there were those meetings with Larry Katz about the budget for the live album . . ."

"Oh, listen," Jeff interrupted. "You didn't mention that to Lindel, did you?"

"What?"

"The live album."

"She doesn't know?"

"Well . . . not exactly."

"Then how are you going to tape the shows? I've arranged for a mobile recording unit to be with them in L.A. Richie is going. I just assumed you had discussed this all with her."

"I want to give her another week or so to settle into the tour. I know what I'm doing. Trust me on this one. Don't mention anything about it just yet."

"Well, anyway, I'm not going out tonight. As a matter of fact, I'm passing up a date with a lovely, respectable man who's not in this business, because I'm wiped out. I'm not about to spend my night watching you work." Helping you work, she wanted to add.

"I'll call you later," he said, and hung up.

Marcia walked over to her briefcase and took out the copy of the new *Vogue*. Taking it back with her to the couch, she picked up the phone and dialed Szechuan East. She'd have a spring roll, some sesame noodles, and beef with broccoli. And some ice cream. She'd start the new diet tomorrow. She went to the closet and, hanging up her purple T-shirt and salmon pink overalls, she changed into a long white cotton flannel nightgown covered with a tiny red apple print.

It was only eight o'clock, but she was going to get into bed and pretend she was sick. Just indulge herself with the new *Vogue* and some TV and the Chinese food. Maybe she'd call Greg and make a date with him for next week. He was nice enough, just kind of dull. The sort of man her mother would love for her to marry. Nothing at all like Jeff.

Jeff. What was he up to now? How could he commit Lindel to a live album without her approval? And there was that little thing that she had accidentally stumbled upon yesterday while organizing the files. It was probably nothing, but she was curious why Jeff would have put such a clause in Lindel's management contract. She looked at the clock. It was early, her father would still be awake. She couldn't discuss this with any of the lawyers she knew in the business. But her father was different; she trusted him. Maybe he'd be able to explain it to her.

The next morning, Jeff was already at his desk when Marcia got to the office at ten-thirty.

She looked in at him. He was dressed up more than usual, wearing a blue plaid collarless shirt and a darker blue velvet jacket with jeans. His hair looked like it had been cut in a new style.

"Coffee?" she asked.

He shook his head. "No, I've had some. I put the receipts on your desk, plus the bills that go to Jacar. I'm going to be tied up on conference calls for about an hour. Hold my calls."

She shut the door behind her and went to her desk. Pulling the expense forms from the left hand drawer, she took the pocket calculator out of her handbag and started to check the bills. She looked at Jeff's restaurant receipts. The Russian Tea Room, fifty-seven dollars. Patsy's, sixty-three dollars. The Ginger Man, forty-four dollars. Elaine's, one hundred and sixteen dollars. La Scala, fifty dollars. He certainly was eating well. She looked at the backs of the credit card slips. They were all blank. None of the phone lines were lit up, so Marcia buzzed the intercom.

"You didn't put any names on these restaurant charges," she said to Jeff. "What do you want me to do, round up the usual suspects?"

"Yeah, whatever. Put down some disc jockeys, writers. Make sure they're not the same ones we used last week."

She hesitated, then said, "Jeff, I want to ask you something."

"Yes?" He was impatient.

"Who pays the phone bill?"

"Jacar, of course. What do you mean?"

She stopped for a second, then continued. "Well, I know our two regular lines go through the switchboard and Jacar pays for that, and for the Wats line, too, and that you bill them for your private line, but . . . you know this statement they send us each month?"

"Marcia, I'm in a hurry. What are you getting at?"

"Well, they apply that monthly phone bill—as well as your travel and entertainment expenses, recording costs, rehearsal time, my salary—toward the annual Valhalla budget, right?"

"Yes. So?"

"So I don't know if you've noticed, Jeff, but you've been spending money like you're Jackie Kennedy with Ari Onassis. It's eight months into the fiscal year and taking Lindel's recording costs into account, along with the rest of the bills, I think you're almost over budget."

"Is that all?" Jeff gave a little laugh. "Of course we're over budget. They expect that. They wouldn't have any respect for us if we weren't."

"But," she went on, "doesn't that mean that the money is then taken out of Lindel's royalties?"

The phone clicked in her ear and, within three seconds, he was in her office.

"What's all this about?" He smiled at her. "Why are you so worried all of a sudden about the bills?"

"It's not the bills," she insisted. "I'm just trying to figure out how this all works."

"Marcia, you've been around the music business for years." He walked back and forth in front of her desk. "You know that these sort of things are always charged to the act. We're doing her business, after all. But don't forget," he added, "I have my own production deal with Jacar. They take it out of my royalties."

She didn't say anything for a minute; she just watched him flip through the copy of Kal Rudman's tip sheet that lay on her desk. He had never told her how much of a royalty he got from Jacar and also, how much of that amount he then gave to Lindel. Marcia knew that those contracts—the ones dealing directly with the record company—were locked in the safe in his office, but he had never told her the combination to that safe.

"Marsh, what's the problem?" He stared at her.

"Oh . . . nothing, I guess," she mumbled. "I just get worried when I think you're . . . we're spending too much. Last month's phone bill was twelve hundred dollars."

Jeff grinned. "Sweetheart, twelve hundred bucks is paper clip money to Jacar. Lindel's had a monster hit. We don't have to hassle this shit. Now I've got to go and run up some more phone bills. And don't forget—confirm my twelve-thirty at the Tea Room."

It was high noon at the Russian Tea Room. A line of people waiting to be seated extended from the end of the bar to the front door. The small bar booths had "Reserved" signs on the tables as did the larger, more prestigious front four booths in the main room. Miss Rosa and Mr. Camillucci escorted the regulars to their usual booths, while lesser knowns and tourists waited impatiently on line.

The room was like a brightly lit Christmas tree, with dark green painted walls and red vinyl chairs and banquettes, pink linen tablecloths and brass lighting fixtures. The actual Christmas decorations on the chandeliers were a year-round feature of the room; no one was sure how that tradition began, but it never would have occurred to anyone to take them down. Waiters wearing red, gold and black Cossack uniforms rushed by carrying trays loaded with plates of blini, small bowls of Beluga caviar on crushed ice, bright pink borscht with globs of sour cream, rich creamy beef Stroganoff, and plump, breaded chicken Kiev, oozing butter.

The Tea Room at lunch was all about power: media power, movie power, and music business power, and Jeff was thrilled to be able to have had the chance to overtip and be seen with Lindel enough in the last six months to rate a "regular," perfectly respectable—in fact, desirable—bar booth.

The real stars—Woody Allen, Liza Minnelli, Robert Redford, Dustin Hoffman, Bette Midler—wouldn't come in until one o'clock, and Nureyev usually waited until two to make his Grand Entrance. But all around him were faces Jeff recognized, and people he had come to know through his success with Lindel. He belonged here. It was a good feeling. And, it was a long way from 161st Street off the Grand Concourse.

"What a gratifying success this must be for you," said Carl Willis, the president of Acme Records, as he sat across from Jeff.

"Well, I needn't tell you how thrilled we all are," said Jeff, taking a sip from his glass of ginger ale.

"Lindel is a very special artist," said Carl. "Very special. Lovely girl. Truly unique voice. You know, we've never really been properly introduced. I'm going to try to get to one of the shows on the tour, maybe L.A. After all," he said, smiling, "I do have one of my bands on her tour."

Jeff smiled back at him. "They're going over really well," he said, making a mental note to call Lindel that afternoon. He hadn't been able to reach her for three days.

"I suppose we should thank you," said Carl. "After all, we've rush released the new Vipers album to coincide with this tour, and I don't have to tell you how much being on this kind of a prestigious tour will mean for their album sales."

"A three percent royalty will be fine," said Jeff with a straight face.

Carl laughed. "Not so loud, Jeff, not so loud. Someone might hear you and take that seriously. But, really, I want you to know that we appreciate it over at Acme. After all, I understand that you're thinking of signing some new bands yourself. It would have been much easier for you to put one of those bands on this tour, give them exposure."

Damn right, thought Jeff.

"Or," Carl continued smoothly, "you could have used one of Jacar's acts, one of the new bands that they can't seem to break. Surely then they would have helped you with extra tour support."

My sentiments exactly, thought Jeff. He looked closely at Carl Willis. The man was in his mid-forties, and almost completely bald. He was tanned and in fairly good shape, but his designer clothes—Armani or Cardin, Jeff wasn't sure—looked as if they didn't really fit. Of course Carl Willis was no Marc Garnier. Willis was still, after three years of success at Acme, considered "up and coming." The really important record company presidents like Ahmet Ertegun, Marc Garnier and Walter Yetnikoff ate lunch in their private dining rooms and would never consider going out to the Russian Tea Room. What Willis was, was a Brooklyn born and raised music business lawyer who worked his way up through Acme's legal department until he was the president of the company, and, in the process, tried to develop a rarefied manner that was never totally convincing.

Jeff wondered how much Carl knew about the Valhalla deal with Jacar. Did he know that Jacar only had the right of first refusal on the new bands Jeff wanted to sign, or that Jacar wasn't obligated to sign just any act with whom he waltzed in the door. After Lindel's success, it was unlikely that they would turn him down. But he wanted to be safe. It wouldn't hurt to just talk to other companies. Jeff knew that, within hours, it would be all over the Jacar Building that he had met the president of a rival record company for lunch. Just to be sure, he had mentioned it to Tim, whose reaction had been merely to raise an eyebrow and say,

"That pompous ass?" But he was positive that seconds after he left Tim's office, Tim was on the phone about it to Marc Garnier. Yes, this lunch, and this restaurant, had definitely been the right idea.

Marcia was on the telephone when Jeff returned from lunch. "I'm sending the refreshment rider over," she was saying, "but it's only one page, and I don't want to pay to Federal Express it, so I'll just mail it. Call me when you get it." She hung up, smiled at Jeff, and said, "How was Carl Willis?"

Jeff shrugged. "Okay. He seems like a nice enough guy. He wanted to talk to me about The Vipers. To see if we needed any help with them on the tour."

Marcia seemed surprised. "That was nice of him," she said.

The phone rang and she picked it up. She listened for a minute, then said, "Send the check and we'll keep it in escrow. There can't be any percentages until there's billing. Well, Jeff doesn't want to announce it until a week from now, then we'll put the first night tickets on sale." She listened for a few seconds, then said, "No, not until the first night sells out. Well, then you can add three more shows by popular demand. It's the way Jeff wants it."

She hung up. Jeff looked at her questioningly.

"L.A.?" he asked.

She nodded.

"Problems?"

"No. Although the guy's a creep. He wants to make a big personal splash by taking a full-page ad out in the L.A. *Times* announcing the four nights . . ."

"I told him no," said Jeff.

"I know, I know," said Marcia. "By special popular demand extra shows added. It's all been worked out. It's just that he's—" She shuddered.

"What?"

"Have you ever met him?"

Jeff shook his head no.

"Well," she said, "he used to be a promo guy at CBS before he moved out there and opened that club. He's the kind with the yech physique who wears his shirt unbuttoned to the waist with the black, hairy chest and a *chai* the size of a golf ball . . . not only the *chai,* but more stuff hanging around his neck, all gold."

Jeff nodded, turned and started to walk into his office. He stopped and turned back to face Marcia.

"By the way, have you spoken to Lindel recently?"

"Yesterday. Why?"

Jeff frowned. "I haven't been able to get her on the phone for a few days. Every time I've called there's a 'Do Not Disturb' on her line."

"I've been speaking to her every other day, each time for only about ten minutes."

"What does she say?" he said.

"Oh, nothing much. She sounds good, the shows have been great. Mainly she's needed a few little things done—she wanted some money, she forgot a pair of shoes she needed, things like that."

Jeff looked at her curiously. "How are you getting along with her?" he asked.

"Fine," said Marcia. "You know, I think she really likes me."

He looked at her for a minute, and then he said, "Well, she may like you. But don't forget, Marcia, she *loves* me." And he turned around and walked into his office and closed the door.

Jeff and Tim sat at a small table in the Blue Grotto. They had left the Academy after the performance by the Electric Toys, and now were having a drink before deciding where to go next. It was only eleven o'clock, and the club was empty. Even Ronnie Marren was nowhere in sight.

"I don't get it," said Tim, his arms folded, his dark glasses on, and a frown on his face.

"What?" said Jeff.

"I saw four unknown bands at a Polish dance hall last week that were better than this band."

"You're wrong. They're going to be very big."

"You liked the midget rhythm guitarist who kept racing across the stage with the no shirt and the rolls of fat hanging over his pants?"

"He'll go on a diet," said Jeff.

"You should tell him also not to jump from the drum riser to the stage. For him it's too big a leap. And what about the singer, with all that 'Come on, New York, you can do better than this' bit to the audience?"

"They were an opening act." Jeff was defensive. "It's the first time they've played a big hall. I'm not saying they don't need work. But they write catchy, melodic, pop songs and they're cute."

Tim rolled his eyes.

"Girls will think they're cute," Jeff insisted. "Especially the singer. And that's all that matters. You'll see. I'm going to make them as big as The Beatles."

Tim feigned a yawn and said, "What does Lindel think of all this?"

"Of what?"

"Of you signing them."

"She knows I'm planning to sign other bands."

"They hardly seem like her type of band."

"So what?" said Jeff. "I couldn't care less if she likes them or not. She doesn't own the company."

The waitress came over and Tim ordered wine; Jeff asked for a hamburger and french fries. He thought about the way he was playing it with the Toys. He wouldn't chase them the way some managers were doing; he didn't have to. The band was grateful for his interest and the longer he held out, the better percentage he could get. He mentally calculated: twenty, no, maybe twenty-five percent of their gross income for management, which, with their advance from Jacar, could mean twenty thousand for him alone. Of course, Jacar would advance Valhalla the eighty thousand, Jeff would take his commission on that, but he'd only give the band forty thousand. The other twenty thousand would have to go toward his expenses in running their business. Their first tour would net him the ten percent agent's commission as well as the management percentage of their concert fees, and maybe he'd start to think about getting into merchandising. He had been thinking about that for Lindel, too. After all, why should he just license the rights for someone else to make and sell the T-shirts and the posters at the concerts when he could do it himself and make all the profit . . . Then there would be the record royalties, the foreign distribution deals, and the song publishing, which he'd own, of course. Yes, he stood to make a lot of money with the Electric Toys.

" . . . have you decided?" asked Tim.

"What? Sorry, I wasn't listening."

"When you're joining the tour?" Tim was leaning back in his chair.

"Oh, probably L.A."

Tim looked surprised and said slowly, "That's three weeks away. Not until then?"

"I just have too much to do here."

The waitress brought the carafe of white wine and Jeff's food. The room was starting to fill up. Jeff poured ketchup on the hamburger and started to eat.

Tim waved to someone and Jeff turned around to see who it was. He didn't recognize anyone he knew, and said to Tim, "Who are you waving at?"

"Lucy," said Tim.

"Where?" asked Jeff.

"Right over there, at the big round table."

"That's Lucy? My god, I wouldn't have recognized her. Jesus," Jeff muttered, "she looks like hell."

Tim didn't say anything; he just squinted in the direction of Lucy's table. She was sitting with a group of actors from the Theater of the Ridiculous and London's newest androgynous rock singer. Lucy had lost about ten pounds since Jeff had seen her last, and there were deep circles under her eyes. She wore a man's leather motorcycle jacket, blue jeans and a blue silk blouse unbuttoned nearly to her waist.

"I'd invite her to come over here," said Tim, "but I think she's very much with that kid. He's got a really hot new band. Trust Lucy to get to him first."

Jeff looked over at the table, then said to Tim, "I seem to remember that you were the one who thought she should work for Lindel. I thought you two were friends."

"We're the best of friends," said Tim. "Who said not?"

"So why does she look so strung out?"

"Oh, I don't know . . . I think she looks kind of fabulous. Gaunt . . . and mysterious."

"She looks sick," said Jeff. "What is it, downs?"

Tim shrugged. "I guess so. I was at Ronnie's house the other night and she was there and she just sat there for hours, staring into space with headphones on, listening to Pink Floyd, or something, not saying a word. And then she just picked up the first boy she saw on her way out the door, and took him home. She told me the next day that she didn't remember any of it. She also told me that she couldn't stand to sleep alone. She said she didn't care if whoever she brought home just turned full ashtrays upside down on the floor and she had to clean them up—she couldn't bear to be alone in her apartment at night."

Jeff looked over at the table again. "I hope she doesn't come over here."

"She won't," said Tim. "She doesn't really like you."

Jeff's eyebrows shot up. "Me? Why? I've always been perfectly nice to her."

"I think she thinks you didn't want her on Lindel's first tour."

"That's ridiculous," Jeff broke in. "It never even came up."

"But I think it bothered her a lot. She's not used to not winning."

"Winning?" asked Jeff, staring at him. "Winning what?"

"Oh, you know." Tim signaled the waitress to bring some more wine. "Lucy's used to getting what she wants. Anyway, the other night she was so loaded on downs she could barely speak. Then there are periods when she's so coked up and fragmented that if she misplaces a barrette it's as important to her as if her mother had jumped out of a window."

Jeff shook his head in disgust. "That's so dumb. I mean, I myself like a little coke now and then, but these extremes . . . And I'll never understand downs. Why anyone would want to make life slower is beyond me."

"Oh, it can be kind of fabulous," Tim argued. "You feel like you just don't have a care in the world, nothing matters, nothing can get to you."

"Such a waste. Anyway, as I was telling you before, I can't join Lindel for a while—I have to go to London next week to see the Marquis de Sade."

"Did I *tell* you about Steve?" Tim asked, instantly alert.

"Steve?" asked Jeff, picking up french fries with his fingers, dipping them in a pool of ketchup on his plate and then putting them in his mouth.

"Yes, Steve." Tim was impatient. "The junkie lead singer of the Marquis."

"He's not a junkie," said Jeff. "So he did a little too much tootski. Who doesn't?"

"Darling, I'm not talking about what he put up his nose. I'm talking mainlining two, three times a day. But no more."

"I heard he was clean," Jeff said, looking up from his food. "That's why I want to go there and check them out. I still have that option on their first album."

"Well, you'll find he's clean," Tim said, similing. "Lucy told me *all* about it."

"About what? Tim, get to the point."

"He's found God."

"What?" Jeff put down the half-eaten hamburger and stared at Tim.

"Yes," Tim said, "isn't it *fabulous?* He's with some guru called Sri Rama, whose name I'm sure used to be Isadore Epstein, and this ... holy man," Tim rolled his eyes, "tells him when he can record, or perform, or when he should eat, or go to the bathroom."

"I can't take that seriously," said Jeff, picking up the hamburger. "It's like astrology."

"No, it's much more serious. Lucy says not only has he stopped all drugs, he doesn't drink or smoke anymore. And ..." Tim's eyes widened in disbelief, "he's not even *fucking.*"

Jeff finished his hamburger, picked at the remaining french fries, and said nothing. He had a feeling that his own lack of a sex life was a subject of some speculation and gossip. As far as he was concerned, it was simple: his obligatory teenage advances to girls had not been born out of any real desire and, although he had gone to bed with several women when he was a waiter in the mountains, the experience had left him feeling almost disgusted. He felt unprotected; he didn't want anyone to get too close. The whole thing of grappling around undressed in the dark seemed so silly, when there were much more gratifying ways he could spend his time.

"How does Lucy know all of this?" he asked Tim.

"Oh, she keeps in touch with her old friends. Anyway, I think this swami or whatever is one of those who has a racket that can't be believed. He's a real ten percenter. All you have to do is cut him in—it's like the Mafia. You cut the guru in for a piece of the action and he says that god says it's okay to sing."

Jeff shook his head. "Are you sure we're talking about Steve Elliot? Who up until ... when did I see him ... three months ago

. . . was living with that Chinese stripper and talking about using whips onstage? The one who wears black leather all the time?"

Tim smiled. "The very one. Although I assure you, he's not wearing black leather these days. You'll probably find him with his head shaved, wearing a long white dress. Maybe we'll even see him in front of Bonwit's with the peach-colored *shmatahs* and the bells on his feet . . ."

"Stop it," Jeff said.

"You *know* how *extreme* some of these musicians are," Tim added.

Already the problems were starting. No sooner had he made Lindel a success than she had insisted on dragging that Brian with her across the country. The rhythm guitarist for the Electric Toys had to lose at least fifteen pounds. He couldn't give Chuckie Fisher an answer about Lindel taping *Rock Show* because he couldn't get Lindel on the phone. And in order to get the Toys, or the Marquis on *Rock Show,* he knew he had to deliver Lindel. He wanted to get the Toys in the studio next month to do a demo and would have to find the money for it somewhere. Jacar still hadn't paid him the royalties on Lindel's record because they hadn't been paid by their distributors. Jeff was practically living on credit. There was increased talk in the industry of massive returns on hit albums because of piracy; records that looked and sounded exactly like the originals but were bootlegged and sold at half price to stores for which neither the artist nor the record company received a dime. And now the lead singer of what was a promising new band had discovered God.

But Jeff knew he'd work all of it out. He thrived on the action and, yes, even the problems. No matter how much money he got from the artists, it wasn't enough. How could it possibly be enough when his mind was always clicking, working, thinking? He wasn't like the artists who could crash after a show or sleep all day. He never really could stop, not for a minute.

Marcia turned the key in the front door lock and walked into her apartment, Arnie Kaplan following close behind. He looked around and said, "Nice place. You don't have any cats, do you? Can't stand cats."

"No cats," Marcia said, going to the refrigerator to open a bottle of wine.

"Got any Stoli?" Arnie said.

Marcia turned to look at him. He had great eyes, she thought. The kind they used to call bedroom eyes. They were his best feature. Otherwise he was slightly chunky.

"Stoli?" she said.

"Yeah, you know. Stolichnaya vodka."

"Oh," she said. "No, I'm ... um ... out of vodka. I have wine ..."

"Beer? Got any beer?"

"Yes," she said, grateful for the two bottles of Heineken stuck in the back of the refrigerator. She couldn't even remember when she had bought them.

As she poured drinks, Marcia watched Arnie Kaplan out of the corner of her eye as he walked to the stereo and turned on the radio. He switched the dial from one FM rock station to another. Typical promotion man, she thought, always checking out what was being played whenever he was near a radio.

She walked over to him and handed him the beer. She smiled, and then realized that there was no need to try to seduce this man; it was obvious what he was here for. All of that had been taken care of at the beginning of the evening when he had said to her, "You know, when I first saw you in Jeff's office last month I thought you were pretty cute. I was going to hit on you."

And Marcia, feeling high, brazen, had smiled flirtatiously and said, "But?"

"Well," Arnie Kaplan had paused, "I'm married."

"So?" Marcia had retorted. "Does that stop you?"

"No," Arnie had smiled with a glint in those eyes, "but it slowed me down a little."

"I'll say," Marcia had murmured, and knew right then that she and Arnie Kaplan would end up in bed. Even so, there was still something exciting about the sexual tension. Something about that intricate dance they did around each other all night that caused Marcia's heart to beat just a tiny bit faster, that made her flesh feel as if it was a little bit on fire when he touched her arm, or her knee, or leaned over so that his lips accidentally brushed against her hair.

Marcia sat down next to Arnie on the couch.

"Where do you sleep?" Arnie said.

"On this," Marcia pointed down to the couch. "It opens up."

Arnie looked directly into her eyes. "Well, then, why don't we open it?"

Marcia felt that burning sensation beginning, down below her belly and into her legs. She felt weak as she stood up and proceeded to open the couch into the instant double bed.

Arnie leaned over and turned off the lamp. Only the light from the hallway remained on, illuminating their faces as they quickly got undressed.

In bed, Arnie reached for Marcia and pulled her into his arms. She was surprised at how strong he was. She felt enveloped by his muscular arms, his chest covered with soft hair. There was something warm, comforting, almost furry about the way his body felt. His legs were smooth, solid and Marcia just wanted to be wrapped inside, wanted him to hold her tight, hard; she wanted him to crush her, she wanted to feel small.

Arnie was kissing her breasts, then licking, moving his head down, resting between her legs, sucking, kissing, devouring her as he held on to her, stopping and smiling with obvious pleasure at her moans, then turning her over and entering her before she could stop him.

"No," she whispered. "No. Please stop. Not that way . . . you're hurting me . . ."

Arnie laughed. "Sssh," he said, grabbing her roughly. "You'll love it. You want it. I know you do. You want me to hurt you just a little bit, don't you? Relax. Come on, baby, give in to me."

Despite herself, the more she heard his voice murmuring, low, sexy, the more Marcia felt herself submit. Yes, she thought, talk to me. Don't stop. Keep talking . . . And she realized that she was saying these things out loud. Arnie kept up the smooth, steady rhythm while he took her hand and moved it so that she was touching herself.

"Go ahead," he whispered. "You know how you like it. Do it for me. Come on, baby, make yourself feel good. Make yourself all nice and wet. Make yourself come. Be a good girl."

Marcia felt wild, out of control. She did as she was told, feeling an almost unbearable pain as he tore through her, and continued to whisper softly, moving his hand on top of hers, around, more, refusing to stop until she felt she was about to break and he grabbed the pillow and covered her face with it as she cried out with release.

Afterward, she watched him smoke a cigarette in the dark. She felt warm, soft . . . She ran her fingers along his arm, realizing that it was probably too soon but wanting, needing him again. Differently this time. So that she could kiss him while they made love.

Suddenly, Arnie jumped up out of the bed and started to put on his jeans and his shirt; to look around for his socks. He turned on the lamp and Marcia quickly covered her face. She pulled the sheet up around her and reached over for her glass of wine.

Fully dressed, Arnie Kaplan stood up, walked over to the mirror that hung above the sink, and ran a comb through his hair. He walked back to the bed, leaned down and kissed Marcia on the top of her head.

"Hey," he said, sounding altogether too smug, "I feel like a million bucks."

And the next thing she knew, the door closed and Arnie Kaplan walked out of her apartment and, more than likely, out of her life. Marcia sat up in bed and pulled the blankets off the floor and covered herself. She felt cold. She took another sip of white wine. It tasted sour and warm.

It was just as well, she thought, that Arnie Kaplan had to go home to his wife. It wasn't as if she was in love with him. So why did she feel so unsettled, as if he had trespassed?

The phone rang. It was two o'clock, and could be anyone. Marcia debated whether or not to answer it and then picked it up.

It was Lindel. "I didn't wake you, did I?" she asked.

"No, not at all," Marcia said, glad to have someone to talk to. "The man who just walked out the door wasn't Mr. Right."

"Oh," Lindel hesitated. "Are you okay?"

"Yeah, I'm all right. I'm glad you called. Where are you, Milwaukee? Where's Brian?"

"He's asleep. I got a small suite in this hotel, I think by mistake. Anyway, I'm in the other room."

"You all right?" asked Marcia.

"I'm terrific. But tell me about this guy. What happened?"

"There's nothing to tell." Marcia fluffed the pillows behind her and leaned back in the bed. "I went to the screening of the new Scorcese movie with some people from Jacar, and this guy was along. He's one of Jacar's promo men. Good-looking, dark hair, tan, could be thinner, but very smooth. Also married."

"What's his name?" asked Lindel.

"Arnie Kaplan."

"Arnie Kaplan . . . Do I know him?"

"Probably not," said Marcia. "Jeff does. Jeff thinks he's smart. I think he wants to get him to work for Valhalla one day. Anyway, we all went to this big party afterward and there was a lot of coke, and . . ."

"Marcia," Lindel sounded surprised, "since when do you do that?"

"Oh, you know, once in a while. It's no big deal. Anyway, he had been checking me out all night, and I was feeling high, and I figured what the hell. So I took him home."

"And?"

"And nothing. He made it very clear that he couldn't stay over. The wife and new infant son and all that. Not that I was already brewing the breakfast coffee. But he's one of these honest types. You know, the kind who tells you that he probably won't call you again."

"Did you like him?"

"He was good in bed. But otherwise—it's like a time warp. He asked me why I wasn't married. I should introduce him to my mother, they'd have a lot to discuss. And he literally told me that he didn't really like rock music, that his taste leaned more toward Sammy Davis, Jr."

Lindel laughed.

"Can you imagine?" Marcia said. "The two things I hate most in this world are the Long Island Rail Road and Sammy Davis, Jr."

"So you're not upset that he left?" asked Lindel gently.

"No," Marcia said. "But I do feel kind of funny . . . I don't know. It just all seems like something I've done before, and too many times. Anyway, what's with you?"

"Oh, too much to go into now. I have a lot to tell you though. I just got your message and wanted to call you back. Anything important?"

"No, just some business details. They can wait until tomorrow. You sound great."

"Marcia, I'm afraid to say it, but I've never been happier in my life."

After they hung up, Marcia lay in bed and stared at the blank TV screen. She didn't even have the energy to pick up the remote control and turn it on.

Lindel was in love, and Marcia was genuinely happy for her. Funny, how she used to think of Lindel as a threat. Of course that had a lot to do with Jeff, and Marcia's feelings about Jeff were mixed these days.

She didn't feel romantic about him; she no longer had those kinds of expectations. Still, despite her occasional suspicions, or distaste for the way he did business, there was still no one like him. She had yet to meet a man with his energy.

Maybe she should stay away from men for a while. They were either too nice and boring, like Greg, whom she really didn't want to see, or sexy, sleazy bastards, like Arnie Kaplan. Tonight had been a mistake. It made her feel a way she hadn't felt in a long time. Used. Anxious. Trying to please. Insecure. Wondering if he liked her. Whereas all day long she felt important in that office. Jeff needed her, Lindel needed her, she was appreciated. What was the point of taking a man home and making love if afterward you felt more alone, emptier than before? It was as if she had taken two giant steps backward into her old life, and didn't like what she saw there at all.

14

For Lindel this was the tour she had hoped for, dreamed about. From that first night in New Orleans, she and Brian were insep-arable. After the shows they usually went back to the hotel and stayed together in her room. Sometimes they went out, exploring whatever city they happened to be in, finding little jazz clubs or all-night diners. If it wasn't a travel day, they slept until the after-noon, watched daytime TV, ordered room service, and made love.

Lindel began to see a side of Brian that up until then she had only suspected—like the times he surprised her with flowers, always delivered in an offhand way, propped up against the door to the room, hidden in the bathtub, or stuck inside her guitar case. Whenever Brian brought her flowers, she was careful to quietly remove the bouquet already in her room sent by the hotel manager or the concert promoter. She wanted to be sure that there was nothing else around to compete with his tangible displays of affection.

They found delicious spareribs at four A.M. in Milwaukee, and a great old record store in St. Paul. In Cleveland they took the limo without the driver, did Kid Leo's radio show on WMMS, and then went to a sexy drive-in movie. In Buffalo they went to Niag-ara and looked at the falls, got soaked in the spray and they hugged and kissed like newlyweds.

In Philadelphia they sat in the bar of the Barclay drinking brandy and Brian talked about Italy. He told her how he once took the overnight train from France to Italy and stayed up looking at the Swiss mountains and drinking wine. He didn't say, but she was sure that he hadn't been alone. She knew not to ask. She wondered why he even told her about it. Maybe he wanted to take that trip with her. If he asked, she would go anywhere with him. Then he surprised her with his next words.

"I feel good when I'm with you," he said.

"Why?"

"You're so damned cheerful all the time. Some of it is bound to rub off."

"Well, things are good, sometimes."

"No," he said. "Usually they're not."

"Why are you so negative? Whatever happened to you to make you think that the bad stuff is the norm?"

"I can reverse that, you know. What makes you think otherwise?"

She didn't answer right away. She toyed with the red plaid barrette in her hair, the one he had picked out in Coney Island. Then she said, "I don't know. Maybe I've just had some good luck. But it's just that somehow, living seems so amazing."

Brian gave her a cynical grin, and leaned over to rumple her hair. She wanted to say more. To tell him how, for her, rock and roll was such a joyous reaffirmation of life. To Brian, it was a sneer, a slap in the face. Yet she was sure that they both felt the same things. He wouldn't dampen her spirit; she refused to let him take her hope away.

They were getting ready to leave the hotel for Philadelphia's Tower Theater, and Lindel was sitting on the bed, strumming the guitar chords to "White Bird." Brian was in the shower. She started to sing softly, and was only vaguely aware that Brian had turned the water off and was standing in the doorway, a towel wrapped around his waist, watching her.

She stopped, embarrassed. "I'm so tired of that damn song," she said. "But there's no way they'll let me off the stage alive without my doing it."

He walked over to her and sat down next to her. Lindel still felt a tight choking in her chest whenever he was near.

"Play it again," he said.

"Why?"

"Just do it. I want to see something."

"Brian, this is silly. What's the matter, you haven't heard me do it enough—every night for almost three weeks?"

"C'mon," he said, pushing her hair out of her face, giving her a kiss. "I want to hear it."

She started to strum the all too familiar chords and to sing the words she had written over two years ago. Brian began to sing with her, and she looked at him, amazed. He shook his head, "Keep going," he commanded, and she realized that he was encouraging her to sing it faster. He had changed keys, so she had to switch to major chords, and his voice, blending in harmony with hers, was stretching out certain words, evoking a sense of anger that subtly, but totally, changed the meaning of the song. It was stronger now, and faster, and she was excited.

"Brian . . ."

"Sssh. Don't stop."

They continued to sing; he with a harsh, uncompromising sound, forcing her to sing louder, faster, to keep up with him. It was joyous, yet angry, it was her song, but he had put himself all over it, making it better, bigger, louder, sexier.

When it was over, she was stunned, and he looked at her and said, "There. Now it's a rock and roll song."

"Brian, what did we just do? My god, it sounds completely different . . ."

"We just changed to major chords, sang it faster, gave it some more strength. It was there all along. If you de-emphasize the plaintive sound, it has more rage, that's all. Simple."

"Easy for you to say," she muttered. "I never thought of it. Damn, I wish we had taped that. Could we try it again?"

He smiled at her.

"No, I mean it," she said. "Please?"

"Why don't I do it with you onstage tonight?"

"What?"

"Unless you mind."

"Mind? Are you mad? I'd love it. Oh, Brian." She leaned over to grab him, and fell on top of him with her guitar between them.

She sat up quickly, and looked into his eyes. "Are you sure? What a fantastic idea . . . You know, you changed it in such a subtle way. It sounds so ambiguous, like you could interpret the words any way you like."

"Well, yes. That's the point. People want real life, in terms they almost can't understand. Works all the time."

She just stared at him.

"C'mon." He smiled. "Time to punch the clock."

In San Antonio, Brian woke up at nine-thirty in the morning, took Lindel in his arms and said, "Let's go for a walk along the river and stop in one of those terrible taco places."

"Let's put on silly sunglasses and hats and no one will recognize us and we can drink tequila sunrises," she said.

"I want four tequila sunrises," he said, burying his face in her neck.

"Don't forget we have a sound check at three."

"But then after the show we can come back here and order two bottles of champagne and we'll get in bed and hope for a good late movie and then, when we're good and drunk, I'll slowly take all of your clothes off and make love to you all night long."

"Mmmmm," she said. "You're not getting out of here so fast," and she rolled over and lunged at him, kicking and tickling, biting, teasing and hugging and kissing, until she thought she couldn't stand it, not one more second, if he didn't make love to her right that minute. How did she exist before him, and what on earth would she do if he were gone?

In Boston she bought him a tie, and even though he made a face, he gave in and borrowed a jacket from Tony to go with her for drinks at the Ritz Carlton. They sat at a small white table in the lounge on the hotel's second floor and listened to the pianist play Cole Porter songs. They ate salted nuts and drank gin and tonics. Whenever Lindel was with Brian in this kind of setting, so out of context, she felt as though she was drifting through a movie she'd written for herself to star in. With Brian as her leading man.

The past year, the success, and now, this love affair had turned Lindel into an even more magnificent looking woman. Her eyes flashed, her body—always voluptuous—now moved with a new and sensual grace.

That afternoon, sitting in the quiet elegance of the Ritz Carlton, Brian said softly, "You look beautiful."

She smiled at him. Her heart was full of love.

He added, "You have a much softer look these days. A lot of your previous . . . harder edge is gone."

"Well," she joked, "sex will do that every time."

"I hope it's more than that," he said, and she was surprised. In the three weeks they'd been together, he'd rarely expressed any such emotion. If she stopped to seriously think about things, she was scared to death. The tour would be over and Brian would probably go back to London. It was, after all, only rock and roll. But still she had to follow her heart.

Her life revolved around Brian. She never woke up until he did, and she couldn't make a plan until she knew what he wanted to do. She thought about him always; when she was alone, when they were together. She wanted to take care of him, to make sure his stage clothes got to the hotel valet on time, to see that his bags were packed. And so their days, and nights, fell into a comfortable pattern. Except that there was nothing comfortable about the way she felt about Brian Davis.

The Lindel James–Vipers tour made music history. The critics applauded Lindel's daring in appearing with one of the world's most brilliant rock bands, and never before could anyone recall such chemistry as when Brian joined Lindel onstage nightly for their duet of "White Bird." Lindel was praised for taking a chance, for refusing to do a predictable, easy tour. Each night she would watch Brian's set from the wings, and realize that she thought of him—up there—as a person other than the one to whom she had made love the night before. As she watched him perform, and saw thousands of fans scream, demand his return to the stage, she realized more than ever that his music had to be the most important thing in his life. It was unsettling, for she was afraid that the most important thing in her life was Brian.

In Chicago, at the end of the fourth week of the tour, Lindel and Brian were in Buster's Bar on the South Side, watching Buddy Guy play guitar with a tiny amp perched on top of a pinball machine.

Lindel's hair was tied back with a plaid satin ribbon, and she wore a red dress and red leather boots. She was aware that people were staring at her, but she was never truly cognizant of how beautiful she was. She thought that because Brian was so special, and Brian looked so handsome he made her look better, and together, she was convinced, they gave off a special glow.

Not taking his eyes off Buddy Guy, Brian turned to Lindel and mumbled, "Jesus, I can't believe I'm seeing that man. I used to listen to his records when I was a kid, and now we're seeing him in this dump while we play to three thousand kids across town." He stopped talking.

He seemed depressed. Lindel was becoming used to his occasional moods; he'd often be excited one minute and sulking the next. He usually snapped out of it, but now he didn't say one word to her all the way back to the hotel, and when they were back in her room, he flopped on the bed, turned on the television, and stared straight ahead.

"Brian, what is it?"

"Nothing."

"Look," she said, "it's not our fault if the music we do is more . . . accessible, or if we have a bigger audience. That doesn't mean that what we do isn't valid."

Brian said nothing, but he gave her a peculiar little smile, and she felt ashamed. Then she was angry, angry at them both; at him for being so righteous, and herself for feeling guilty.

"Dammit," she raised her voice, "talk to me! You just sit there, looking so goddamn smug. What is it?"

He looked at her. "I think I still have my room key," he said quietly. "See you later."

And before she could even think about trying to stop him, he was out the door.

She debated whether or not to follow him. He'd call her, she figured, he wouldn't stay away. After all, he had practically all of his things in her room.

One hour later, at four A.M., she tried his room. No answer. *Where was he?* Why had she let him leave like that? She knew she would not sleep this night. At least this was Chicago—civilization—where there would be something she could watch on TV.

There was nothing on TV except test patterns. She turned down the sound and left the most colorful test pattern on, it made her feel less alone. She tried his room again at five, and then again at five-thirty. She smoked cigarettes, tried to read but couldn't concentrate, took half a Valium and still, sleep did not come.

He'd come back. They had three more weeks on tour together. She'd probably be laughing with him about this later tonight.

At six o'clock in the morning she felt as though she was going to jump out of her skin. She decided to take a walk, and put on a coat and took the elevator down to the lobby. Once outside, she looked up and down the street. To the left was the lake, to her right, a row of quiet townhouses. The sun was just starting to come up and the view of the lake, with the Marina Twin Towers and the Chicago skyline, would be beautiful. But what good was it if she couldn't share it with Brian? And what if he were trying to call her right now, or even knocking on the door?

She raced back to her room and, breathless, she opened the door and looked at the hotel phone. The red message light wasn't on. She picked up the receiver and called the front desk.

"This is Miss James, in Room 1616. I think I just heard my phone ring as I was opening the door and I wondered if you had a message for me . . . Are you sure? . . . All right, thank you."

Unable to stop herself, she tried his room again. No answer. *Where could he have gone?* She had too much pride to call Bernie, his road manager. Nor would she call anyone else in his band. It was far too early to call Marcia and wake her up; she didn't know what to do.

She tried watching TV, at least the early morning shows were on. She ordered a huge room service breakfast, and when it was delivered, surprisingly quickly, she couldn't eat a thing. She looked at his clothes, hanging in her closet. Reaching into his jacket pockets, looking into his flight bag. Bits of paper, napkins, matchbook covers with scribbled lyrics, notes for possible future songs. She studied them closely, searching for clues—something that would tell her more about him than she already knew.

At twelve noon she finally fell asleep, and at two-thirty Bernie called to wake her for the sound check.

"Johnny's gone ahead," he said, "so I said I'd call. Tell Bri to bring an extra set of strings. Dave's guitar is badly in need of some tuning."

"He's not here," she said. "I . . . um, don't know where he is."

"Oh well, then," Bernie said easily. "Never mind. I'll get it myself. Ta." He hung up.

Her head was throbbing. How was she going to do a show tonight? Goddamn him. Where the hell was he?

He didn't show up for the sound check, but none of The Vipers seemed concerned. "He'll show," said Bernie. "He's done this before."

Lindel wanted to scream, *not with me he hasn't*. She hoped she projected an air of detached unconcern. Inside, she was furious. But most of all she missed him.

That night, when she was filled with a mixture of anxiety and rage, it happened for the first time. Lindel was onstage at The Auditorium and, bathed in a blue spotlight, one leg up on the monitors, she leaned into the audience. The kids were jammed right up to the stage, and they reached out for her, arms waving wildly. Somewhere in the back of her mind, she thought that the scene resembled the movie *Suddenly Last Summer*. There was something different about this performance. She felt wired, burning with a crazy kind of energy. She punched the air with her arms, her hands balled into tight fists. She was almost lost, perilously close to stepping over that invisible line: the one that if she went over, she might go so far she'd never come back. The audience wanted to get to her, and she was ready to submit. High on nothing but the power of her own voice, she felt that she could do anything.

She sang her songs in the usual order, but in a new way. She stopped several times to talk to the audience. Later, she would not be able to remember a thing she had said. She waved to the band to lower the volume, she chanted, shouted, she whispered words she had never sung in these songs before. It all came from somewhere else and she went with it, let it take over. She was unafraid. She wanted to dance, to spin around, to go out over the heads of the crowd, and gave in to it all. No longer did she want to be in control on that stage, she wanted to fly.

Lindel realized that this was the effect that Brian had. Almost by osmosis, he had dared her to take the chance. He gave her the courage to be out of control.

After the show she sat soaked with sweat in the dressing room she shared with the band. The band knew instinctively to stay away from her as they changed, made their arrangements for the night, packed their guitars. She looked around for Brian. She had seen him for two seconds when he had raced in late to do his set, and then later when he joined her onstage to do their number together. She needed to talk to him to know what he thought of her set, to feel that everything between them was still all right.

After what seemed like forever, but was probably only ten minutes, Brian came into her dressing room, walked over, and sat down next to her on the couch. He leaned across to the table in front of them and grabbed a handful of potato chips and a piece of salami from the tray of soggy cold cuts. "Amazing," he said softly.

"It was good, wasn't it?" she said. "Brian, where have you been?"

"Yeah," he said slowly, "it was good." Then he looked at her, and said, "But you have a responsibility as a performer."

"What do you mean?"

He went on, speaking so softly that she had to lean her head close to him to hear. "You're at the ultimate point of a certain hierarchy, and you have to hold something back for yourself. If you give everything to that audience, and especially if you're filled with any negative or paranoid feelings, it can get out of hand, and you won't know when to stop."

Then he stopped. He seemed embarrassed, as if he'd said too much.

She leaned over and took his hand. "Can't we go back to the hotel and talk?" she asked. "I really need to talk to you. About last night . . ."

He smiled and looked around the dressing room. Tony sat on a couch in the corner talking to a plump Oriental girl who couldn't have been more than fifteen. Hank was packing up his guitars, Eddie was blow drying his hair. Rob was talking to two disc jockeys. Bernie came to the door and looked at Brian questioningly. Brian shook his head.

"Right then," Bernie said. "We're off. See you tomorrow. Remember, in the lobby at eleven for the drive to South Bend."

"You didn't answer me," Lindel said to Brian. "And what does all of that mean—what you just said?"

He looked at her and smiled. He seemed tired. "It's after midnight," he said. "No serious discussions after midnight. Let's go and get some sleep. We'll talk tomorrow."

They were in Kansas City and Brian had been with Lindel again for five days and nights. They had made love, made music, and acted as if nothing had happened in Chicago. But ever since that night when he left her room, and still had not made any explanation, Lindel felt a nagging anxiety. It reminded her of David. There was always the chance that Brian would do it again. She knew better than to press, but she tried to draw him out, to have a real talk with him.

"What do you want out of all of this?" she asked him when they were getting ready to leave for the hall.

Brian was putting a hairbrush, some small bottles of pills, tinted sunglasses, and a few possible shirt changes into his dark green flight bag. He tossed it on the bed, sat down in a chair, and turned on the television. Lindel leaned against the back of the bed, smoked a cigarette and thought to herself, he's so beautiful; *why can't I just leave it alone?* Why were explanations necessary? And she thought about how the TV set was always on.

"Seriously, what do you want out of this?"

"Out of what?" he said, changing the channel.

"You know . . . rock and roll."

He continued to stare at the soundless television screen, with its flickering image of an old Bette Davis movie.

He took another drag on the joint he was smoking and said, "Well, I don't think about anything permanent, if that's what you mean."

"Personally or professionally?"

He shot her a smile, and said, "Look, I like this life. No responsibilities. No wife, no kids, no mortgage on a house. If I'd done what my old man wanted me to do, I'd have been a chartered accountant. This music was the only way out."

"Sometimes I think I could so easily tire of this life," said Lindel, leaning forward. "The planes. The no sleep. Worrying about the band down the hall, making sure that they have something to do. Knowing that they're always thinking about me, worrying that I'm all right. It's just a different kind of responsibility. It's not summer camp and braces, but don't kid yourself, you're not totally free."

"Oh, but I am, darlin'," he said. "It doesn't feel like work to me; it never did. I like being in a different city every day, even if sometimes I have no idea where I am. I like that. So far, it's never let me down. But I hate talking about it. You know why we do it. We don't have a choice."

In Denver, Brian disappeared after the show at the Regis. They hadn't even had a quarrel—he just took off, and Lindel, determined not to go through another one of those long, sleepless nights, called Hank.

She was about to hang up when he answered the phone on the sixth ring.

"Hello." He sounded sleepy.

"Hank, I'm sorry. Go back to sleep."

"No, no, it's okay. What time is it?"

"It's around one-thirty. I'm sorry, I never thought you'd be asleep yet."

"It's okay, I guess I just crashed."

"Go back to sleep, I'm sorry . . ."

"Stop it. What's up?"

"Well . . ." She hesitated. "Are you alone?"

"Wait a minute, let me look." He laughed. "No, but it doesn't matter."

"Oh, look, I didn't want to bother you."

"What's wrong?"

She realized how discreet he was; he didn't even mention her name.

"Well, it's Brian," she said. "He's just gone off somewhere, and I'm trying not to get freaked about it."

"I'll be right there," he said, and hung up.

Within five minutes, Hank was at her door. Barefoot, wearing jeans, a black T-shirt, and a sleepy expression.

"Hank, I'm really sorry . . ."

"Don't be ridiculous. What are friends for?"

He came inside and lay down on the king-size bed.

"Want anything?"

"Beer, if you have it."

She took a bottle of Heineken out of the small refrigerator, opened it, and handed it to him. She sat down in the easy chair facing the bed. Before she said anything, the phone rang. Hank raised an eyebrow, and Lindel grabbed the receiver.

"Oh. Hi Jeff." She made a face at Hank, who walked over to the tape recorder on the dresser and started looking through the stack of cassettes.

"Look," she said, "I'm tired; we have another show tomorrow night. I'll talk to you about this when I see you in L.A." She gave Hank an exasperated look.

"I've told you, bring any papers that need my signature to L.A.," she continued. "This pouch business is a pain in the ass. The last time you rushed some contract for me to sign, Federal Express arrived at my door at ten in the morning, and they insisted on waiting for my signature. God knows what I signed, I had just fallen asleep."

Hank put a Wailers tape on the machine, and turned the volume up high.

Lindel laughed. "No, that's just Hank putting a tape on. Yeah, he says hi to you, too. No, of course I don't mean that I don't trust you, it's just that I think you forget what it's like out here. I know you've offered to come. I'm not saying you should be here— Christ—" She rolled her eyes at Hank, who pulled a joint from his pocket and handed it to her.

"Look," she went on, "I'm wiped out. I said I'd do all the interviews in L.A. except that one with Brian." She paused. "Yes, I know it's a great idea, gimmick, as you so delicately put it, but no, I haven't asked him about it and I won't. You don't know Brian. He wouldn't do an interview with me as if we're some kind of vaudeville team." She held the phone away from her ear. Hank could hear Jeff shouting. "The song is different, and so was Kid Leo's Show. We played records on that," Lindel said. "Anyway, we can talk about the next album and all of the rest of it when I see you in L.A. I have to go now, we're in the middle of a band meeting. Bye-bye." And she hung up.

She turned back to Hank and sat down next to him on the bed.

"The man makes me so mad sometimes," she said. "Can you

imagine, first he couldn't stand the thought of The Vipers being on tour with me, and now he wants to see how much mileage he can get out of it. Plus, he's asking me about a TV special. And a film. Now. He says it's the only time he can get me on the phone. He's mad as a hatter. I call that office twice a day and he's either at lunch or out of the office. Last week he was in London, doing god knows what."

"I think he went to see the Marquis de Sade. I heard they're living there now, and he wants to sign them. Lucy told me."

"Lucy told you?" Lindel looked startled. "When?"

"Oh, didn't I tell you? She called me last week. She said she had been trying to reach you, and couldn't so she thought she'd just say hello. I just assumed she would have left you a message."

"No ..." Lindel said thoughtfully. "No, she didn't. What else did she say?"

"To tell the truth, I couldn't make much out of anything she said. She sounded really wrecked. But I do remember her babbling about the Marquis, something about Steve Elliot and some guru. And she said Tim told her Jeff wanted to sign them, that's all."

"Well, anyway, whatever. I've told him to handle all the business stuff himself, and stop bothering me in the middle of the night. There's nothing that can't wait. He was talking about a private plane that he wants to lease for the next tour. Let me get through this tour first, I told him. I think he's on speed."

They both lay on the bed listening to the music. The smoke from Hank's cigarette curled slowly above their heads. Lindel got up and poured herself a glass of wine.

"Where'd you get this tape?" asked Hank.

"It's great, isn't it?" said Lindel. "It's a live tape of the Lyceum concert. Marley really is incredible. It's one of Brian's, the sound man there gave it to him."

"What's happening with you two?"

"I don't know. I'm so hung up on him, and every so often he just ... disappears." Lindel sat down on the edge of the bed. "Even when he doesn't physically disappear, it's like he has this way of retreating into himself. I never know what he's thinking."

"He seems to be pretty heavily involved with you."

"But I have no idea what will happen when the tour's over. We've never discussed it."

"You know, your hair looks great with those little braids in the front."

"Really?" She turned and looked in the mirror, shrugged, and turned back to Hank.

"Look," he said, "why don't you just take it as it comes? He's a vague kind of guy. He obviously has a different sense of time than you do . . ."

"Tell me something," she broke in. "What do you think he does when he splits?"

"I have no idea. It could be anything. But it doesn't matter. Obviously, you mean a lot to him, and the rest of that stuff doesn't really count. Let me ask you, what do *you* do when he splits?"

"Well, it only happened once before at night. I don't know. Go crazy, watch TV."

Neither of them said anything for a minute. Then she added, "You know, I purposely kept myself apart from his band. I didn't get at all buddy-buddy. I thought it was better that way, but I wonder if it was a mistake. Maybe they think I'm a snob."

"I don't know them very well, either. They've hung out a few times with Tony and Eddie, but they're a bit rough for me."

"What do you mean?" she asked.

"Oh, you know. They have a lot of scenes." He took a swallow of the beer. "Parties every night. Some really sleazy drug people around them. That bass player, Brad, drags that groupie Dr. Bob around with him, at his own expense. Supposedly, he's there to give everyone vitamin shots, but I think there's more than that in his little black bag."

"This is just a side of Brian that I haven't seen at all," she said, shaking her head.

"Well, he's not involved with it that much. But there have been some moments. They wheeled Brad, naked, into one of the rooms on a room service table one night, covered him with whipped cream, and these two girls had a go at licking it all off. And in Kansas City, I think, the promoter sent the band a package, all wrapped up with a bow, and when they opened it, these two girls jumped out, all dressed in Nazi leather outfits. And then Bernie rode the motorcycle into the lobby . . ."

"What?"

"Didn't you hear about it?" he asked.

"No." She was agitated now, walking to the window. Turning to face him, she said, "See, this is what I mean. Even though I see everyone on the plane, and backstage, I've been pretty much in my own little world with Brian. And I guess Johnny makes sure that I'm shielded from things."

"Johnny is rather protective of you. He's the perfect road manager and bodyguard rolled into one."

"Except," she said, "sometimes he's so damn solicitous of me that I feel like the Queen Mother. What happened with Bernie?"

"I can't believe you didn't hear about it," he said, smiling. "It was really dumb; it happened yesterday morning, and they threatened to kick us all out of the hotel. Johnny gave some money to the manager and smoothed it all over. Oh, and also, they had these two girls tie up the writer from *Melody Maker* and lock him in his room. Listen, even their roadies get blow jobs from the groupies who want to get backstage. But, Lindel, Brian's not really a part of all of that."

"I can't believe no one told me. Jeff didn't even say anything to me about this . . ."

"Well, I don't think Jeff knows. Johnny takes care of these things as quietly as he can. But frankly, when would someone have told you? You're in your room most of the day with the phone off the hook, or the two of you go out somewhere. After the gig, we're all off on our own."

"Are you angry at me?"

"Of course not." Hank regarded her with affection. "Your singing's never been better, the shows have really hit some amazing high peaks, and you look incredible. Obviously, he's had a good effect on you."

"But do you . . . do the boys feel that I've let them down? Have I been just with him too much? It is true that none of us hang out anymore the way we used to on the first tour. I kind of miss it."

"Things have changed," said Hank, starting to roll another joint. "You're famous now. It wouldn't really be cool for you to come with us to some of the dumps we check out in each city. You'd be surprised at the stir even we cause in these places."

"You know," she said softly, "I feel sad. I don't like change. I'm not even sure when all of this happened. Or what to do about any of it."

"Ssssh," said Hank, leaning over and putting his arm around

her. "Don't get all depressed. Nothing has happened. We're all making dynamite, incredible music, and the Lindel James Band gives all of us more money, and more of a chance to play, than we've ever had in our lives. You've met the love of your life, and everything's going to be all right. I don't think we should worry tonight. Why not take advantage of the 'night off' and let me take you to the local rock dive where everyone will make a big fuss over you and we'll get all the free drinks we want."

"I don't think so, but thanks."

"Come on, put some boots on with that fabulous dress or whatever it is . . ."

"It's a nightgown," Lindel said, laughing.

"Well, whatever. I think you need a reminder that you're a star."

"I'd be nervous that Brian would come back, that I wouldn't be here."

Hank just looked at her.

"I know what you're thinking," she said. "But I just can't play those games. I wouldn't have a good time. I'd just be a drag. No, I think I'll stay here. Go back to whoever you were with, I'm sorry."

"I kicked her out as soon as I hung up the phone. I'm sure she's found one of The Vipers by now. Uh, sorry." He grimaced. "But I'm sure Brian wouldn't look at her twice. You know me and my peculiar taste for seventeen-year-olds."

"Still?" Lindel shook her head. "I hope at least that you're careful."

"I try."

"It seems like such a serious flaw in your otherwise perfect personality," she said.

"I know." He smiled. "I'm just not ready for a really serious, deep, grown-up relationship with an intelligent, mature woman . . ."

"All right, all right, enough. Do you think we could con room service into sending something up? Anything?"

"Are you kidding? It's two in the morning. This is *Denver*. Room service closes in the entire state of Colorado at six-thirty. As a matter of fact, room service west of Chicago closes at six-thirty."

She didn't say anything for a minute.

Then, "I'm really starved," she said. "There must be a diner, or something . . ."

He didn't answer. Finally she said, "Okay, let's go out. I'll call Johnny for the car, fix my makeup, you go put your shoes on. And Hank?" she called to him as he was halfway out the door.

"What?"

"Thanks."

15

Jeff looked at his brand-new tank watch and saw that he had one hour to get to the airport, check in, and make that flight. Usually, it would be no problem; Dav-El's limo could get him from the office to JFK in thirty-five minutes, but it was Friday, and rush hour.

He grabbed his leather jacket, briefcase and overnight bag and, as he raced past Marcia, he shouted, "I'll call from the airport if there's time, otherwise from the hotel."

"Which hotel?" Marcia asked.

He stopped. "Aren't I in the Hills?"

"You are," she said, "but you also said to get you a room at the Sunset Chateau so you could pretend to be staying with the band."

"I did?" Then he laughed. "Marsh, it must have been a little joke."

"Very little," she muttered.

"Well, fuck all that. I'll be at the Hills. Christ, I run a successful record company. I can't stay in that hellhole."

"Well, I apparently will be in that hellhole when I come out on Monday."

"Marcia, we've been through all that. You said you wanted to stay in the same hotel as Lindel . . ."

"I know, forget it. You'd better go, you'll miss your flight."

After he left, Marcia got up from behind her desk and walked inside to Jeff's office. His desk was piled high with papers—contracts, computer printouts of record sales, a stack of demo tapes, copies of the trades, radio airplay tip sheets. She considered cleaning it up, then decided against it. In his own way, he knew where everything was, and would go nuts if she moved things back to their proper places.

She walked to the window and looked out at the row of glass skyscrapers that lined Sixth Avenue. To her right she could see the limousines parked in front of the glamorous "21" Club. This view—the one that had so pleased Jeff when they moved up to these bigger offices in the Jacar Building—was a constant reminder of the size and power of this city. It could easily intimidate, but today Marcia felt up to the challenge.

After a few minutes, she went back to her desk, and stared at herself in the round silver paperweight she had bought at Tiffany's. In the year since she'd been working with Jeff at Valhalla, she had made a real change in her looks. She lost weight, cut her hair short and dyed it a bright, sort of aubergine color. She knew that she projected an aura of confidence. Jeff liked to say that Lindel's success had touched them all; they had more money, more power, more prestige, he said. Marcia just laughed at him, saying that they all just had better clothes. But it was true that she now had a certain position in the industry. She was assistant to the president of a successful independent label. She was friendly with that label's most important artist. She was politically adept at her job, and she knew every clause in every contract that dealt with Jeff's business. That knowledge had become a cause of some concern. It was for that reason that she chose to stay in New York and not accompany Jeff to Los Angeles this weekend.

She needed some time alone. She needed to do some quiet, calm thinking before she saw Lindel. She wanted to go over the books again, to try and figure out what was going on. And to decide what to do.

Jeff still felt a slight thrill each time he checked into the Beverly Hills Hotel. Every time he had been there in the last year he had overtipped the staff; so by now most of them jumped to attention when they saw him come their way.

The assistant reservations manager, Edmond Zoghaib, greeted him at the reception desk with a stack of phone messages. "Good evening, Mr. Stein," he said. "So good to see you again. I have the usual suite reserved for you. But, if I may suggest, there's a lovely small bungalow available in case you think you're going to want to entertain?"

Jeff hesitated. It was tempting. But he really couldn't afford to. Plus, then he'd have to have all those musicians over. "No, thanks, Edmond," he said. "The suite's okay."

As he accompanied the bellman to his ground floor suite, he was already making plans. Tonight he could see Clive Davis and Bob Feiden at the cocktail party for Paul Drew, at RKO Radio. He'd have to look at his book and see what else he could squeeze into the evening. He tipped the bellman ten dollars and closed the door behind him. He loved this suite, with its large living room furnished in red and green. Of course, he never understood why they had these cabinets filled with fancy china dishes, but he supposed it added a note of elegance.

The stereo and tape deck were already in the room. Good, he'd be able to play the Eyeteeth tape for people, but he'd have to keep the volume down. Last time there had been several complaints.

He walked to the sliding glass doors, opened them, and stepped out onto the patio. There was a smell about Beverly Hills; a combination of soft warm air, flowers and money. The thick, rubbery plants on the patio, the green and white lounge furniture, the pink stucco walls—everything about the place felt familiar and special. The basket of fresh fruit and the vase of carnations left in his suite by the management acknowledged that he was a favored guest. Even the pink note pad next to the telephone gave him a feeling of reassurance; he liked to collect those pads to use for phone messages, notes to himself, lists, and he made no secret of the fact that he pocketed as many of them as possible when he passed the laundry carts in the hallway.

His phone was ringing and he went back inside to take the call.

"Carl, I just got in. I was going to call you." He fished around in his briefcase for the small bottle of cocaine. "Well, I couldn't agree more. Right. The album is done, and it's fantastic. I can't wait to play it for you."

He listened to the other end of the conversation as he laid out three fine lines on a small square piece of metal.

"Of course I realize how valuable your inputs would be. Well, I think there are at least two singles, maybe three, but ultimately, that would be your decision."

He pressed the phone to his ear with his shoulder, covered the mouthpiece with one hand and, while listening, leaned down to snort the drug. "Look, if you come up with the dollars, then we have a deal. My lawyer told me to be more diplomatic, more of a statesman, but I said don't give me that statesman bit. I'm a Jew from the Bronx. So, I'll be honest with you. I'm free to take the Marquis de Sade anywhere I want. My deal with Jacar, aside from Lindel, of course, is to give them first refusal on two other albums a year. They've already picked up the Electric Toys but they passed on Eyeteeth and they're stalling on the Marquis."

He listened, then said, "Well, of course Steve Elliot is healthy. You have my personal guarantee. I wouldn't get involved if he wasn't. I just think for the time being it wouldn't be wise to announce that he's into this religious thing. Who knows how long it will last? Let's just keep that quiet, hmmm? Also, that we're talking. I haven't mentioned it to anyone, and . . . wait, can you hang on a sec? My other phone is ringing."

Jeff ran into the bedroom to answer the phone next to the bed.

"Tim. Hang on a minute, I'm on the other phone."

He raced back into the living room. "Hi. Listen, why don't we talk later? I can see you at this RKO thing, or you can come here for a drink if you like. Great. See you then."

He went back into the bedroom, lay back on the king-size bed, noticed with annoyance that it really was two mattresses pushed together, and picked up the phone.

"Hi, I just got in. What's up?" As he listened to Tim, he opened the drawer of the night table next to the bed, took out the Bible, and shoved it under the bed. He reached around behind him, and took one of the pillows out from under the bedspread and put it behind his back. He took the pink pad from the night table and scribbled a few notes to himself.

"Well, I've got to go to the Roxy tonight and see how many tickets they've held out. I know it's sold out, but you don't mean to tell me that if Barbra Streisand or Diana Ross wants to come at the last minute they're not going to have seats for them. Right . . . Well, we can check out the Record Plant tomorrow. The mobile is all set for Monday night. What? Oh, don't worry about it, that's my problem. It'll all work out. How was San Francisco? Did you see Bill Graham?"

Only half listening to Tim, he looked at his watch. He'd better unpack and get moving. Carl was coming in a half hour, then there was the Paul Drew thing, and the Roxy . . .

"She is?" He frowned, not liking at all what he'd just heard. "Well, when the prick stands up, the brains go right in the ground. Right, that *is* why I'm all business. Look, you can tell me all about it later, or tomorrow. Now I've got to do something about Eye-teeth. I can't even start to think of where to bring them because the goddamn lead singer's wife wanted all the birthdays of the record company presidents so she could write them on pieces of paper and throw them into their baby's crib and the paper the kid picked would be the winner. No, I wish I *was* making it up."

He began to twist a strand of hair around his finger and continued talking. "Carl Willis says his tape recorder is broken and he can't listen to the tape for a few days, the guy at Epic who's in charge of A & R has a *hearing* problem and he can't listen to anything, can you believe this? I'm seeing Clive later. The whole thing has turned into a . . . *mishagothic*, as Marcia would say. Anyway, come with me to the Valley, after I go to the Roxy. Joni Mitchell's musicians have formed their own band, and they're looking for a manager. I told her I'd see them as a favor to her. Okay, see you later."

There was so much to do. This time he had to leave L.A. with something sewn up for the Marquis and Eyeteeth. The Electric Toys were due to go into the studio and he had already spent the advance he got for them from Jacar. Even though Lindel's concerts were sold out in every city, her tour expenses were so high that he wasn't making any money from her at the moment either. On paper, Jacar still owed them record royalties but he wouldn't see a dime of it until the end of the fiscal year. He made a note to change the payment schedule when he renegotiated Lindel's contract. Meanwhile, his overhead was so high that he was quickly running out of a ready cash flow. If Carl Willis didn't want these acts, he'd try one of the L.A. companies like A & M, Casablanca, or Warners. He wasn't going home empty-handed.

Jeff pressed down the button on the phone, then picked it up again. "Room service, please," he said.

After far too long a wait, room service answered.

"This is Jeff Stein in Suite 183. I need a bowl of guacamole, some chips, you know, whatever also comes with it when you serve it in the Polo Lounge. And a few bowls of nuts, a bottle of white wine . . . Oh, I don't care, any good, dry French white. And send some Perriers, and ice, and a bottle of Chivas, Stolichnaya, and some mixers. Oh, that's a good idea. Yes, let them arrange a small bar, I didn't have time to take care of it before I left New York." He hung up. He thought, this was something Marcia could have taken care of.

He picked up the phone and asked for the housekeeper.

"It's Jeff Stein in Suite 183. I *specifically* asked for a king-size bed when I made the reservation, and *not* one with two mattresses pushed together. I don't know . . . wait." He pulled the dark blue bedspread away from the pillows. "Yes, it has been made up with the sheet covering the two mattresses, but that isn't what I want. No. I'd rather not wait until the morning. Well, do what you can. And I need some more hangers, another pillow, and some bath towels. Oh—and also send someone to clean the patio, it's filthy." He paused. "I have to call maintenance? Jesus," he muttered, and hung up.

He called maintenance, then the valet, who would agree to take only the clothes for pressing because it was after five o'clock, then he called the hotel drugstore.

"This is Suite 183. I want the New York and L.A. *Times, Daily Variety* and *Hollywood Reporter* sent to me every day. I'll be here about a week, I'll let you know. Bill it to the room."

He looked at his watch. It had taken him over a year to get this watch, and now the damn Rolex was the one to have. Well, it would be a legitimate business expense. After all, how could he do business unless he knew the time? And image. People had no idea how the right clothes immediately escalated the level of negotiation. To say nothing of a car. Especially out here. People would drive their houses around if they could. He picked up the phone and asked for Edmond.

"It's Jeff Stein. Edmond, I'm going to need a limousine on call for my stay. And could you call Svend in the morning and get me a cabana? I'd better take one of the upper ones so I can be on the phone and still try and get some sun. And I don't want any cabana after Number Five; there's no sun in those after one in the afternoon."

That done, he leaned back against the headboard and thought about Lindel. Tim had just told him that she'd been sequestered with Brian the whole two days they were in San Francisco. He'd have to find out more about this. He'd have plenty of time with her during the next few days. And maybe he'd be able to get to know Brian a little bit, too. Perhaps he should take the band to dinner after the shows. They would expect it. What the hell, he thought, as he went to answer the door for room service, she was paying for it.

In upper cabana Number Five Jeff slammed down the phone and turned to Tim with an exasperated look.

"She checked in ten minutes ago and already there's a 'Do Not Disturb' on her line."

Tim adjusted his sunglasses, lay back against the yellow terry-covered chaise lounge, and began to apply cocoa butter to his body. He wore a brief, black bathing suit and sipped a piña colada.

"What do you think she's doing?" demanded Jeff.

"What do I think she's doing?"

"Don't answer a question with a question," snapped Jeff.

"I think she's probably sleeping," said Tim. "It's only twelve-thirty, and they got up early to leave San Francisco. Why did she have to leave so early, anyway?"

"She's taping the *Rock Show* TV show at four-thirty."

Tim widened his eyes. "She agreed to do that?"

"Why wouldn't she? It's on in one hundred markets, for Christ's sake."

"I just thought you turned down all that TV stuff."

"When the album was hot we turned a few things down. This won't air until November. Who knows if the new album will be ready. If it is, this'll help sales. If not, it keeps her in the public eye. Besides, the producer is a good friend."

"Mmmm," said Tim, reaching for the sun reflector. "Are the Toys or the Marquis doing the show, too?"

"I suppose they will when their records are out. Anyway," he reached for the phone, "if she's asleep, I'd better tell Johnny to get her up by three."

"Maybe she's fucking," offered Tim.

"Not on my time, she'd better not be." Jeff waited for the operator. "Yeah, give me the Sunset Chateau, I need Johnny Paglioni there." He hung up. "She had all the time in the world to fuck in Cleveland and San Diego, Kansas City and Buffalo. I purposely stayed away from this tour so she and the living god could get it on, as per her request practically. But this . . ." he paused significantly, "is *Los Angeles*. Business time."

He stood up and looked around. In the cabana next to him was Barry Manilow, eating lunch with three men Jeff recognized as music publishers. To his right, the pool attendant was adjusting the yellow awning and curtain, taking down the white vinyl partition to make two cabanas into one large one.

Jeff pushed his mirrored sunglasses against the bridge of his nose, leaned over the railing to look down at the pool. Ahmet Ertegun, dressed in tennis clothes, stopped to talk to Irving Mansfield in lower cabana Number Eight. In lower cabana Number One, Donald Brooks talked on the phone. John Denver and his wife, Annie, sunbathed outside of lower cabana Number Two. All around were the bright, hot colors of a tropical resort: the pink hotel with its green shuttered windows, and green and white striped awnings; the turquoise pool, trimmed by neat rows of yellow chairs; tanned bodies glistening in the sun, and waiters carrying trays laden with Perrier and bloody marys, setting up luncheon tables with shrimp salads and French rolls. It all looked like a big holiday, yet it was deceptive. Business was done here.

Jeff removed the plaid, collarless Sea Island cotton shirt he had purchased that morning at Maxfield Bleu, and lay down on the chaise lounge next to Tim's. God, how he loved this place.

"I guess we have a few hours before we get to see Her Highness," said Jeff. "Want lunch?"

"Let me finish this drink first. I never like to eat on an empty stomach."

After a few moments of silence, broken only by the consistent telephone paging, Tim said, "So, how's everything in New York? I've been gone a week, it feels like a month. I can't believe people can last on tour for so long. Just one week on the West Coast, and I really miss the Grotto. Have you been there?"

"I was there two nights ago," said Jeff. "Oh, you'll be interested in this, Carl Willis was in there again. He was with that singer, Sandra Lewis."

Tim smiled.

"What's so amusing?" asked Jeff.

"Oh . . . nothing. I just know Sandra Lewis from the old days. Did he sign her to Acme?"

"I think he's about to. I guess he's hoping she'll be another Lindel. What's she like?"

"It's too long a story."

"Well, then tell me about Lindel. What else happened? So far, you've told me that she's lost weight, smoking too much, drinking more than she ever has, that her eyes follow Brian wherever he is in a room, and that the shows are unbelievable, but that she seems fucked up."

"Right. That about covers it."

"In what way is she fucked up? If the shows are good . . ."

"The shows are inspired. That's just it. I think she's in some kind of obsessive trance. You know how Lindel and I used to dish, pal around, hang out. Now she's holding something back . . . she's off somewhere else. Like this whole number with Brian and the music is all interwoven—I think she thinks she needs him in order to sing well."

Jeff noticed Svend arranging the chaise lounges in lower cabana Number Six for Michael York. The hotel operator's voice called out over the loudspeaker: "Paging Mark Goodson, telephone puh-leeze. Mark Goodson, telephone puh-leeze." He couldn't remember a time when he had been in this hotel when they had not been paging Mark Goodson at the pool. He was convinced some people even left provisions in their wills to be paged at the Beverly Hills Hotel pool after their deaths.

Jeff turned to Tim. "What are you talking about? She always sang well. Well? She's fucking dynamite."

"You don't get what I mean. It's something else."

The phone in the cabana rang and Jeff reached up over his head to pick it up.

"Johnny, hi, it sure took long enough for me to get through to you. Yeah, I tried her. I know. Well, she has to be there, with the guys, on stage, for a sound check at four-thirty. You'd better tell her four." He paused. "Really? It's that bad? Well, okay, do your best. Wake her at two, tell her you've got to leave at exactly three to be there at three-thirty. I'll be there with the limo at three. You can send the band earlier, I need some time with her alone . . . Why does Hank have to go with her?" He was silent. "I see. I'll see you at three."

He hung up the phone, lay back down, and turned to Tim.

"She has to have Hank in the car with her if she's not with Brian?"

"I'm trying to tell you. It's some weird trip. She was always close to Hank, but now I think it's that he and Marcia are the only ones she trusts to talk about the Big Love."

"I know she's been talking to Marcia," said Jeff, sounding slightly peeved. "I just figured it was girl talk."

"She's got this thing in her head," Tim continued. "Like she's involved in some kind of mystical . . . religious . . . project that no one else can understand. You've got to see them together. It's like no one else is in the room. Then when he splits . . ."

"Splits?"

"Apparently he's been known to take off some nights . . ."

"And?"

"She goes nuts. Can't sleep. The whole number. Always takes him back, no questions asked. But you can tell she's not smiling."

"Who told you all this?"

"Eddie. Tony. Johnny. Please, the whole tour knows about it."

"Shit. This is exactly what I was afraid of. With L.A. and New York left to do."

"Well, she usually doesn't show it onstage. Sometimes, on the days after he's gone she gives even a better show that night. Almost as if she's proving something to him. Then, I've been told that there were one or two that were slightly dodgy, that seemed fucked up."

"Dammit, and then what? This was exactly what I did not want. What are her expectations?"

"You got me. I haven't talked to her about any of this. I told you, I barely saw her. I just get the feeling that she's all caught up with him, and it's all tied to the music. She also seems to depend a lot on Hank. They have this weird kind of silent communication. Of course, Brian is the main thing. But I don't trust any of it. What's she going to do when he goes back to London?"

"Well, at least if the shows are good this week, we'll get a hell of a live album."

"You didn't tell me that she didn't know about that," said Tim. "You *didn't* tell her."

"Well," Tim tried to look sheepish, "not exactly. I managed to stop myself in time, when I realized that she didn't know. But you should have told me. You should have told *her*. Why didn't you?"

"I know her, that's all. If she thought there was a big recording number going on out here she'd panic. And she doesn't like live albums. I was just going to casually mention it, tie it in somehow with that concert show that DIR Broadcasting does on the radio. Let her think it's for that, later on. Meanwhile, we'll have it on tape. It's a great idea." Jeff was warming to the subject, hyping himself as much as he was Tim. "I'm going to hire Paul Wasserman to do the p.r. He does Dylan, Ronstadt, the Stones, Paul Simon . . ."

"I know Wasso. I'm still telling you, she won't be amused."

"She'll love it when she hears it." Jeff gave Tim an accusing look. "Are you sure you didn't tell her? I'll kill you if this thing is fucked."

"I didn't tell her. I still don't think she's going to like it."

"She'll do as she's told," muttered Jeff. "Look, I'm starving. Want food?"

"Okay. A Monte Cristo sandwich."

Jeff ordered from room service and hung up the phone.

Tim sat up and looked out over the pool. "This place is great. Much nicer than the pool at my hotel. Jacar is really being a pain in the ass about expenses."

"I keep telling you to come and work for me," said Jeff.

Tim ignored Jeff's suggestion and said, "I just thought after Lindel that it would be different. I thought they'd jump if I so much as mentioned a new band. But it's the same old bullshit."

"Why don't you tell me about these bands? I could sign them to Valhalla, or do a co-management with you and get them a deal elsewhere . . ."

"I thought Jacar has all your bands," said Tim.

"Not if they turn them down. Then I'm free to go to another company."

"Is that what you're doing with the Marquis?"

"Jacar hasn't turned them down yet," said Jeff. "Unless you know something I don't."

"Me? They don't tell me anything," said Tim, reaching into his leather case and pulling out the small vial. "Anyway," he said, after he had snorted a small pinch of cocaine, and handed the vial to Jeff, "how could I work for you? We have different tastes, and I'd never be able to convince you that the bands I like are on the right track. But you'll see, in three years it'll be like a new . . . wave of groups. It always happens in rock and roll. Just as it gets mellow, someone comes along and says 'fuck you' all over again. That spirit just won't go away. Unless, of course, video completely wipes out records. Or the economy does."

"That's nonsense. The industry's never been in better shape."

"Wait. You'll see. I told Garnier three years ago to start video-taping the bands. He looked at me like I was crazy. He said . . ."

"No one wants to look at those groups playing live," argued Jeff.

Tim laughed. "That's exactly what he said to me. Jesus."

"Kids want records," said Jeff. "They want to be able to hold the album in their hands, read the liner notes, look at the photo on the cover."

Tim looked disgusted. "I swear, you're all the same. When I talked to Marc about this, it was as if it was nineteen-sixty-five and I walked in with an electric guitar and he was telling me that acoustic was still good enough. *Now* maybe kids want records. But wait until the equipment to show videotapes is as cheap as a stereo. They'll want to *see* David Bowie or The Rolling Stones as well as hear them. From a business standpoint, wouldn't it make sense for you to tape Lindel and use that tape for six different TV shows rather than dragging her around the country—with the band— for tapings? I'm telling you, in ten years, maybe less, records will be like sheet music."

They heard the room service waiter wheeling a table outside the cabana.

Jeff walked to the door and stuck his head outside. "That ours?" he said, sounding surprised. "So soon?"

"Are you Garnier?" the waiter asked, looking at the bill.

"Garnier?" Jeff looked at Tim. "Isn't Marc in London?"

"Maybe it's her," said Tim.

"What number cabana do you want?"

The waiter looked at the check. "Three and four," he said. "They've been joined together. There's lunch for three here."

"No, that's not us," said Jeff, as he stood by the doorway of cabana four, watching the waiter move the lounge chairs and set up the round table. A bottle of Pouilly-Fuissé was stuck in a silver bucket full of ice. There were two avocado pears on lettuce leaves, with an accompanying small silver pitcher of vinaigrette. Two chicken salad platters with fruit and cottage cheese and a Neil McCarthy salad were placed next to a wicker basket of a few crisp rolls and a lot of dry melba toast. There were four bottles of Perrier water. Women, thought Jeff. It looked like a ladies' lunch. Then again, you couldn't tell, what with everyone on diets these days.

Just then, Alexis Garnier came through the swinging door that led to the upper row of cabanas. She wore white linen trousers, a bright turquoise silk overblouse, and she had on huge dark sunglasses and a white, floppy straw hat.

"Jeff Stein," she said in her full, throaty voice. "Why, how nice. I had no idea you were here. Marc never said a word."

She leaned toward him to accept his kiss.

"Lindel's at the Roxy for five nights," said Jeff, beaming. "She'll be so glad you're here. Tim's here, too." He pointed inside to his cabana. Tim got up to say hello.

"Well, what a fortunate coincidence. I'm just on my way back from Japan and stopped here for a day's breather between flights. Does she have a show tonight?"

"No, not until Monday," said Jeff. "Can you stay?"

Alexis looked over the arrangements in her cabana, instructed the waiter to open the wine, put down her pocketbook and tossed her hat on a chair. "Thank you," she said to the waiter, and signed the bill. Turning to Jeff, she smiled. "No, I'm afraid I can't stay for her show, although it would be marvelous, wouldn't it? But is she here? In the hotel, I mean."

"No, she's staying with her band over at the Sunset Chateau."

Alexis poured a glass of wine. "Will you have one?" she said to Jeff and Tim, who stood in the doorway of the cabana.

Tim shook his head, holding up his half-empty glass of piña colada, and Jeff said, "No, thanks. We've just ordered."

Alexis sat down and motioned for them to sit down, too. The three of them faced the pool, and for a moment no one said anything.

"You know," Alexis said, taking a sip of the wine, "some very interesting people are meeting me for lunch. You might like to meet them. I'm sure you've heard of Dick Marsden? From Gemco Management?"

Jeff was impressed. And surprised, too, that Tim seemed to have no reaction to Dick Marsden's name. Dick Marsden was very big time. A former corporate lawyer, he had gone into artist management a few years ago and had put together the most prestigious stable of stars in show business. Dick Marsden not only represented major superstars, he represented legends. As far as Jeff knew, he managed no musicians, unless it was a singer of the caliber of a Sinatra. But Oscar-winning actors and actresses, pillars of the theatrical world, and major television personalities were the norm at Gemco.

Alexis went on. "Dick is a very old, dear friend of ours. And his wife, Sue, is an utter delight."

"Well, I've heard of him, of course," said Jeff. "Obviously, he's an inspiration to a novice like myself."

Alexis laughed. "Now don't be modest, Jeff. You've helped create one of the major success stories of the past few years."

"Jeff? Modest?" said Tim, his face deadpan.

Jeff shot him a dark look and said, "Well, obviously I'm pleased about Lindel's success. But don't underestimate Marc's role in all of it." God help me, he thought. She's a success despite Jacar's bungling.

At that moment Dick and Susan Marsden appeared at the door of the cabana. Alexis stood up to kiss them both, and introduced the couple to Tim and Jeff. Sue Marsden was a short, bubbly-looking brunette who wore tennis clothes and was deeply tanned. Her husband towered over her and looked starched and flawless in a dove gray summer suit. It was unusual to see anyone dressed in a suit and tie in the middle of a sunny afternoon in Los Angeles, Jeff thought, but then, Dick Marsden was an unusual man.

His handshake was firm, polite, and Alexis said, "Jeff is in your line of work, Dick. He manages that wonderful new singer Marc signed. I'm sure you've heard of her. Lindel James?"

Dick Marsden looked intently at Jeff. "Ah . . . yes," he said, "I've heard of her. *Walk on Glass,* wasn't it?"

"It still is," said Jeff. "It's double platinum and we're releasing the third single from the album next week."

"Congratulations." Dick Marsden had a bemused smile on his face and Jeff wondered if he'd sounded too braggy.

"I'm starved," said Sue in a high, nasal voice, walking to the table. "Alexis, darling, have you ordered us bird food again?"

Tim gave a slight nod of his head to indicate to Jeff that they should leave but Jeff was unsure. He really would like to talk to this man . . . Then he had an idea.

"I've got to go," said Jeff. "I have to wake up my artist, get her ready for TV. I'm sure you know what that's like," he said to Dick, regretting it in the next instant. Surely this man never did anything so menial as having to awaken one of his stars.

"Anyway," Jeff went on, as Alexis and Sue sat down at the table and Dick continued to stare at him, "I'm having a party in my suite tonight. After Lindel's TV taping. Just a few friends, and Lindel, of course. I'd love for you to meet her."

"How nice," said Alexis, smiling. "I'd love to. Do you think you two could make it?" She turned to the Marsdens.

Sue looked at Dick and an imperceptible glance passed between them.

"Well, we'll certainly try," said Dick smoothly. "What time?"

"Oh . . . how about seven-thirty? For cocktails. We should be through with the taping by then," said Jeff.

"Then I'll take you all to dinner afterward," said Alexis. "I'm just dying to see Lindel again."

"We can't make dinner," Sue said quickly, as she picked up a white linen napkin and started to pour vinaigrette dressing over the avocado. "We have a nine o'clock at Chasen's with the world's leading Shakesperean actor."

Dick laughed. "She's right; we do. But I'm sure we can fit in a drink first. I'm looking forward to it, Jeff. Thanks."

Jeff and Tim walked back into Jeff's cabana and sat down.

"I didn't know she'd be here," he said in a low voice.

"Lindel will be happy that you've signed away the evening," said Tim.

"If she dares to give me trouble," he whispered. "Jesus, it's

Alexis Garnier, for god's sake. How many musicians get a chance to socialize with the wife of the recording company president?" To say nothing of Dick Marsden, he thought.

"Mmmm," said Tim, rolling over on his stomach. "Is Brian invited, too?"

"Fuck him. This is business."

"I warn you. If she can, she goes nowhere without him."

"You mean to tell me that she'd throw away all that we've worked for for the last year because of a fuck?"

Tim smiled.

"Get that dumb grin off your face," said Jeff, annoyed. "So, she thinks she's in love. I don't care what she calls it. See, this is why I have no involvement at all."

"Don't you ever get horny?"

"Only for more money," he retorted. "And I'm better for it. Nothing stands in the way of my plans. She already stood Alexis up in London; she's going to make up for it this time."

"I don't think we ought to talk about it here," said Tim, indicating the thin vinyl partition that separated their cabanas.

Jeff picked up the phone. "Room service," he said. He waited. "Yeah, room service. Listen this is Jeff Stein; I'm in upper cabana Number Five. I ordered some food over a half hour ago. Has it left yet? Well, send it to my suite, instead. I'm on my way there now. Right. 183."

He stood up and put on his shirt. "Come on," he said to Tim. "You can get sun on my patio until three o'clock."

"But it's so much cuter here," Tim complained.

"Come on. I want to hear more about Lindel. I might as well be prepared for the worst."

16

"I'm not going." Lindel stared defiantly at Jeff.

He sat on the edge of the large double bed in her suite at the Sunset Chateau. He thought about how, on Lindel's last tour, he would have been thrilled to stay in the three-room setup that they gave you here, instead of the Hyatt. But now, particularly compared to the Hills, this place looked shabby.

Lindel sat in a chair next to the window. She was barefoot and wore a black silk robe and her hair fell way down past her shoulders in soft curls. She was thin, and looked exhausted, but she was breathtaking. There was something in her eyes—she looked haunted, possessed.

"You know," he said, "it's only been five weeks since I've seen you, but you look unbelievable."

"Don't change the subject," she warned. "We might as well get this all straight right now."

Lindel got up and walked to the sliding doors that led to the small terrace that overlooked the pool. She opened the doors and a blast of music drifted up from a tape recorder, the sound of someone being tossed into the pool, English accents, laughter.

She turned to face Jeff and said, very quietly, "I've changed, Jeff. I think you'll find that the music is going in a slightly different direction. Wait until you see the show." Her eyes sparkled.

Jeff chose his next words carefully. "Well, that's great, Lin. I'm really excited. But what exactly is it that you're telling me? After all, who could be happier than I if it's going well? That's good for all of us, right? I want you to be happy."

She sat down in a chair, and lit a cigarette.

"I don't know if I can explain it," she said. "Something has happened to me on this tour."

"You fell in love," Jeff said.

"I suppose I did," she said.

"How could you fall in love with someone who lives in a foreign country?" he asked.

"Don't joke about it. You can't imagine how much this has helped me, how much I've needed this. I feel charged with energy, I have so many ideas for new songs. I can't wait for the shows each night, and when they're over, I want to do them again."

"Well, that's wonderful," said Jeff. "What's that on your wrist?"

"Oh, it's a piece of string. I wear it all the time. It's just a superstition . . ."

"What's the matter? Afraid you're going to forget something?"

"Don't be silly," she snapped. "It's just a private thing between Brian and me."

"Listen, don't you think you should get dressed? It's after three. We could talk in the car."

"I want to settle this now. I know you have my best interests at heart . . ."

Did he imagine it, or was that sarcasm he heard in her voice?

" . . . but I am not going to dinner with Alexis Garnier. It's not fair of you, Jeff. It's not as if I'm canceling her, I never made the date in the first place. You should have at least told her that you had to ask me. It is possible that I have other plans."

"Do you?" he countered.

"As a matter of fact, yes. I do."

"Lin, this is Alexis Garnier. You already were rude to her once in London because of Brian, you just can't do it again. This is important." His voice was pleading. "There used to be a time when I could make a plan for you if it was good for business, if it was part of what we were working for."

"Things have changed." Her voice was cold.

"Well, I don't know what to say. Look, why don't you ask Brian? Maybe he would like to come."

"Brian," she laughed. "And Alexis? In some fancy restaurant? You don't know him."

"Well, she suggested we go to a 'fun' place. Maybe it doesn't have to be so fancy."

"Brian's idea of a fun place is to go get hamburgers, and preferably hamburgers that aren't too thick. Or watch TV. Or go to a blues bar. Think Alexis would like that?"

Jeff groaned inwardly. So this was what he was up against. Her pride in his . . . funkiness.

"Listen, I'm the one who's going to have to deal with Alexis. What should I do? She really was looking forward to seeing you."

"Tell her the taping isn't going well," she said. "Tell her we have to do it a few more times and we'll be there until midnight. Tell her you'll try to get away and meet her yourself. I don't care what you tell her. I'm not going. I'll call her if you like."

She got up and walked to the closet and started pulling clothes off hangers. Dammit, he thought, how was he going to deal with this? It wasn't only Alexis, it was Dick Marsden, too.

"Tell me the rest of the stuff you said you had to talk to me about," Lindel said.

Jeff sighed. "You definitely won't come?"

"Nope," she said cheerfully, still pulling clothes out of the closet and flinging them onto the bed.

"Well, everything's set for the taping," he said. "The lights are set up for 'Roll On' and 'White Bird.' If you want to do different songs, let me know now."

"No," she said, holding a black satin blouse up against a pair of red leather pants. "Are these okay for TV?"

"Fine, great. What about the songs?"

"Those two are okay."

"And Chuckie wants to introduce you onstage, to make it special, like a bigger deal."

"Why does everyone call the producer Chuckie? He's a grown man."

"Lindel," Jeff warned, "he's the sweetest guy in the world."

"I didn't say he wasn't. I just asked why a grown man is called Chuckie . . ." Her voice trailed off, and she started to throw things into a small carrying case. Makeup, a hairbursh, some T-shirts; she hung a plastic cover over the black blouse, and turned to Jeff.

"Now, what's this about recording the Roxy shows?" she said.

"What?"

"You can't call Hank and Johnny and ask all those questions about EQ's and equipment and levels and have my producer show up and expect that I'm not going to catch on."

"You always tape your shows," he began.

"For the *band,*" she emphasized, pulling off the robe and getting into blue jeans. Christ, he thought, she was thin. "So they can listen to the set after the shows," she continued, "and see what went wrong. Not for an *album.* We never talked about this. You know I don't like live albums."

"Look," he said, "I never said this has to be an album. Maybe one day you'll want DIR Broadcasting to run it as a radio special. But think of this," he said, faster now, gathering momentum, "this tour with The Vipers has generated a lot of excitement. There's a real buzz about it, the New York shows have been sold out for weeks, and the Roxy is an event. Your finale with him is, from what I've heard, a magic moment. I just thought, why not get it down on tape, now, while it's happening? We can stick the tapes in the vault for all I care. We can listen to them again in a year, whatever. It's just dumb not to take advantage of it now, while you're already into it. I'm sorry you didn't do it on the first tour."

"Well, I'm not sorry we didn't," she said, as she snapped the carrying case shut. "That was amateur time compared to this tour."

"Great, great. That just makes it even better."

She didn't say anything, just stood there and looked at him for a minute.

"So, it's okay then?" he said. "I can go ahead with the plans for the mobile?"

"If you promise that it's not already in the catalogue," she said. "Just to tape it, okay? There is no way I want it released as an album."

"Of course, baby, absolutely."

"I mean it," she warned.

"Hey, I said okay. But remember, if we ever wanted to release it . . ." He noticed her face. "I said *if* we ever wanted to, it should be in a couple of years."

"All right. What else?"

"Lin, we have all weekend to talk. Why the rush act?"

"Hank will be in the car with us, and then we'll be with a TV crew, and right after the show Brian and I are driving to the beach."

"You're not coming to my party?"

"What party?"

"I *told* you," his voice was, by now, a wail. "I definitely told you about this. I'm having some people over to the suite for cocktails after the taping. Originally I wanted to have a late afternoon thing, with champagne and strawberries and chocolate soufflés, but when the taping got moved up we had to make it cocktails. It's for you. Hilburn's going to be there, and lord knows you owe him a thank you, and some radio people . . ."

"Champagne, and strawberries and chocolate soufflés?" She looked amused. "Who on earth came up with that idea?"

"Tim. Look, you can't let me down. They're all expecting to see you. And I did tell you about it. Jesus, Lindel, how the hell do you expect me to act as your manager if every time I want to take a shit I have to get your okay. I have to be free to move without asking you."

"I thought our arrangement was that we decided together," she said softly.

"Read your contract," he snapped. "Technically, I don't need your approval for a goddamn thing. But," he added quickly, "of course this is all based on mutual trust and mutual goals. And love. We both want the same thing here. And honey, it hasn't been exactly easy on this tour to get answers from you."

The phone rang, and Lindel practically ran across the room to pick it up.

"Hello. Oh, hi." Instantly, her voice changed. "Hold on a second, can you?" she said softly, in a tone Jeff had not heard before.

She covered the mouthpiece with her hand, and looked at Jeff. "It's Brian," she whispered.

"So?" Jeff said.

She frantically pointed in the direction of the other room.

"I don't believe this," Jeff muttered, staring at her. As he turned to walk out of the room, he heard her say, again in that strange, almost strangled voice, "Close the door, will you?"

When Marcia knocked on Lindel's door at the Sunset Chateau on Monday afternoon, it was with a combined feeling of anticipation and dread. She had not slept at all the night before, and even the wine she sipped for five hours on the flight from New York didn't help. What was she going to say to Lindel? Where, in fact, did her loyalty really lie? With Jeff—who had pulled her out of the ACS secretarial pool and had given her a new career, a future, in the music business? Or with Lindel, who had become her friend? And what if Lindel knew everything? Marcia could seem foolish, overprotective, meddling.

Lindel opened the door wearing a black silk bathrobe tied at the waist, and gave Marcia a hug.

"I'm so glad you're here," she said.

Marcia walked into the large living room, and looked around. The curtains were pulled tight, but with the tiny crack of light that shone through, she saw a familiar tableau: empty bottles of beer were on every table top, ashtrays overflowing with cigarette butts, magazines and newspapers were scattered on the floor. Lamps covered with scarves. A Fender guitar was plugged into a tiny Pignose amp and there were stacks of cassettes next to a large, portable Sony tape machine.

"At least you don't have room service tables full of last night's french fries," Marcia smiled. "Lindel, you used to be so neat."

Lindel looked around. "I guess I forgot what this must look like to a normal person. Anyway, it's mostly Brian's. And there's no room service here."

"So I've found out," Marcia said dryly.

"Do you want something? I've got a huge basket of fruit, and I think there's some cheese, too. Some Perrier? Wine?"

"I could do with some cheese," Marcia said. "I drank all the way out here, and my blood sugar has probably sunk so low that I'll be a real bitch by tonight."

The two of them walked into the small kitchen. Marcia's boots clicked against the linoleum floor. Lindel looked at her appreciatively. "You certainly look festive," she said.

Marcia laughed, looking at her orange cashmere turtleneck sweater, the green and purple tweed knickers and the high-heeled purple boots. She wore a chunky art deco necklace of green and turquoise Bakelite and had three matching bracelets on her arm.

"I know," she said. "Tim says I dress like a carnival in Costa Rica."

"I think you look great."

"And you look spectacular, as always."

Lindel made a face. "I've lost too much weight."

"There is no such thing."

"And I haven't seen the sun in three weeks."

"Well, you can lie at the pool with me while I'm here. I fully intend to be tan and gorgeous by the end of the week." She took the Perrier Lindel handed her. "God, I still feel shaky."

"Still afraid of planes?" said Lindel, as she put some cheese on a plate.

"Aren't you?"

"Not so much anymore. After so many flights, it's almost like just another ride. Brian keeps telling me that my destiny doesn't include dying in a plane crash. There was one flight he didn't make, though. It was from Washington to Memphis, and we got caught in a storm . . ."

"Where was he?"

"He overslept. On one of those nights when he disappeared. Anyway, I was convinced that he did it purposely. That he knew something I didn't. It was the worse flight I've ever been on."

Lindel took the two glasses of Perrier and, handing the plate of cheese and fruit to Marcia, said, "Let's go inside. I'm never comfortable anymore unless I'm lying down."

"Isn't that a problem onstage?" Marcia said, laughing.

"Oh, stage. Stage is something else."

They walked into the bedroom, and Lindel turned on the lamp next to the bed. She sat down amidst the rumpled sheets, and Marcia took the easy chair across from the bed.

"Where's Brian?" Marcia asked.

"I don't know."

Marcia raised an eyebrow.

Lindel sighed. "I know. The thing is, he's pulled this about six times on the tour . . ."

" . . . about?"

Lindel tried to smile. "No, exactly six times. He split after the show in Phoenix. I'm sure it was because he couldn't handle meeting my parents. I had to act like nothing was wrong . . ."

"Do they know about him?"

"No. I've never been much for confiding in them. Actually, you're the only one I've really talked to about it. And Hank, of course. Anyway, he's pulled this enough times that by now you would think I'd be used to it. Then it happens again, and it just drives me crazy. Here we are, I'm opening tonight at the Roxy, and I'm a wreck."

Lindel took a cigarette from the pack next to the bed. "Want one?" she said to Marcia.

Marcia was surprised. "You know I don't smoke."

"Oh, right. Sorry. Anyway, I don't care what I look like. Although Jeff did say I looked gaunt. And he actually had the nerve," Lindel gave a short laugh, "to tell me after the taping that my tits looked terrible. But about Brian . . ."

"Well, what does he say about his disappearing act? Haven't you confronted him yet?"

"You don't know what he's like. There's a part of him that's so unbelievably soft, and sweet, and . . . loving. Then, it's as if he shuts everything out and has a sign on his forehead saying, 'Don't trespass.' When he's in that mood, which is often these days, there's absolutely no use trying to talk to him. He just wouldn't answer."

"Is he doing a lot of drugs?"

"I don't know. I don't see him do it, if he does. As the tour went on, The Vipers started carrying on. Different girls in every city, of course, but sometimes really wild scenes, with lots of girls at one time, things hushed up. I don't think some of those girls were more than fourteen years old. I've heard rumors about Brad and junk, but no one tells me, really. I don't know . . ." She picked at her thumb with her fingernail. It made a strange, clicking sound.

"What if you just went off with someone else?" Marcia said, leaning over and taking a piece of cheddar cheese from the plate on the bed.

Lindel's voice lowered. "I can't. You know I can't. It's the last thing I'm interested in. He's the only one I care about. Even before Brian, I wasn't much for one-night stands."

[248]

"Me neither," said Marcia. "I need a minimum of two, maybe three years of heartache."

Lindel laughed out loud. "Listen, here I've been going on and on about myself. I haven't even asked how you are. What's going on back in New York?"

"Nothing," Marcia said. "Everything's the same. No new men in my life. Lots of work. You've seen Jeff . . ."

Lindel rolled her eyes. "He's a pain in the ass," she said. "He thinks of me as something to constantly sell, sell, sell. It's always Alexis Garnier or some rack jobber or journalist. If I let him, I'd have no free time, ever. I have to fight for whatever privacy I can get. And, he's going to be in for a big surprise when he wants me to go into the studio next month and there are no songs written."

"Still?"

"Marsh, how can I write songs in the middle of this?" Lindel spread her hands out. "Some people can, Brian's written eight songs on this tour and they're all incredible, but I really need to be alone, to be quiet."

Marcia looked at Lindel's hands. The cuticles on both hands had obviously been picked at relentlessly; there were red, raw spots where the skin had been torn away. Lindel noticed Marcia looking at them, and folded her hands across her chest. "I've lost ten pounds on this tour. I'm smoking two packs a day which, along with the air conditioning in the halls and the planes and some of the hotels where you can't turn it off, is hell for my voice. And I don't want to go back to New York, because then it'll be over."

"What's he going to do?"

"I have no idea. I haven't had the guts to ask him."

"You've got more self-control than I do, I'll tell you that. I would have asked him the second day of the tour."

"Well, it wouldn't matter when I asked if he didn't want to say. He might not even know. They have an album to do, and I heard Bernie say something about booking time in London. So, I guess they'll go back soon."

"Why couldn't you go too?" said Marcia. "There are great studios in London, maybe you could do your next record there." .

"I thought of that, and if he'd asked, or seemed the slightest bit concerned about what I was going to do after the tour, I would consider it. But he's so vague. Sometimes, there's a real barrier between us. He seems so . . . detached."

"Maybe it's the cocaine."

"Maybe."

"You don't have any idea how much he takes?"

"Well, I don't think he buys. Although he might, he's always broke. You know how it is, people are just around . . . they give it to him. Brian calls it the 'can't say no drug.' "

Marcia didn't know what to say. She had listened to Lindel talk about Brian for hours on the phone a few of those nights when he disappeared. Other than seeing him onstage once at the Academy, Marcia had only met Brian once, on that day the tour was to begin, when Lindel—all flushed and hopeful—brought him into the office. Marcia thought then that he was one of the sexiest men she had ever seen. And that he was going to be Big Trouble.

Now she offered, "Maybe he's scared of his feelings for you. Maybe he needs that distance every so often."

"Maybe." Lindel didn't sound convinced.

"Why don't you get dressed," Marcia suggested, "and we'll call for a car and we'll go over to Jeff's suite and order champagne and lie in the sun until it's time for the sound check?"

"Can you believe, he's my manager and we have to go to his room to order champagne? There's something screwy about that." Lindel sounded annoyed.

"You could have stayed there if you wanted to. You wanted to be with Brian, and the band. You know Jeff, he's there because he thinks it's . . ."

" . . . good for business," Lindel finished the sentence. "Well, that's ridiculous. Anyone with real style or power could stay anywhere, and people would want to come to them. Anyway, thanks, Marsh, but I think I'd rather stay here. Brian might come back and I wouldn't want to miss him. Besides, I have to talk to him. I haven't had a chance to tell him yet that we're recording these shows."

Marcia's eyes widened. "Don't you know?" she blurted out.

"Know what?"

Marcia hesitated.

"Know *what?*" Lindel's tone was impatient.

"Brian knows about it. Ian and Jeff talked about it ages ago."

"What?"

"Oh, honey, he had to approve it before they could tape him singing the finale with you. Also, you do 'In Ruins' and if it ever comes to putting out a record, some kind of publishing arrangement had to be made."

"What?" Lindel was in a rage. "How come Brian knew about it and I didn't? Why did he have to approve and I didn't?"

"First of all, I don't know why no one told you until this weekend. I just assumed you knew. I can't imagine Jeff being so dumb, but maybe he had his reasons. Maybe Brian just assumed you knew too. It's not such a big deal, is it?"

Marcia felt sick. She was tired of constantly being in the middle of Lindel and Jeff, soothing sore egos, covering for Jeff. Lindel was her friend. She deserved better than this.

"Marsh, it's my music." Lindel stared straight ahead. Her eyes looked tired. "Jeff can't make all these decisions without consulting me, can he?"

Marcia didn't know what to say. If she started now, it would take hours to explain, and everything would be in shambles. Lindel was too upset about Brian, and she had a big show tonight. Besides, maybe it was premature; maybe it would all work out.

"Lin, you've been so preoccupied on this tour, Jeff probably figured it was better this way. I wouldn't make a big deal of it with Brian, either. What I think is that you should get out of this room for awhile, get some fresh air—what there is of it in this town. We could go have a big lunch at Musso and Frank's."

"No, I don't think so."

"But you told me that you love Musso and Frank's."

"I think maybe I'm not such good company right now." Lindel looked at the travel clock next to her bed. "I'll be okay. Maybe I just need to be alone for awhile."

Marcia looked at her.

"Please?" Lindel said. "I'm just going to wait for Brian. Maybe take a nap. I'll be fine . . . really."

Only one more week, Lindel thought. Seven days. Two more shows at the Roxy, two in New York at the Academy of Music, and then he'll be gone. He still hadn't said anything about what would follow, about whether they'd be together or not. The whole week in L.A. had been so crazed, with Jeff and Ian around, Tim,

Marcia, both bands, Carl Willis from Acme, all the press; they hadn't had much of a chance to be alone. There were the usual drunken rock and roll banquets after the shows each night, and it was five o'clock in the morning before they got back to the hotel and staggered into bed.

They had not made love all week. Brian passed out the instant his head touched the pillow, and it was a struggle to rouse him up in time to get ready for the shows.

In two days they'd be on their way to New York. She tried to hide her anxiety from Jeff, from the band, but she couldn't fool Marcia. Marcia knew how upset she really was.

"Why don't you just kick him out?" Marcia had asked her. "Let him stay in his own room. You don't need this. I think he's incredibly selfish."

"He's not always this way," Lindel argued. "He's probably nervous about the Roxy, about New York . . . He just needs to retreat sometimes. He's just naturally mysterious."

"You know," said Marcia, "sometimes people who create mystery around them have nothing to hide."

Lindel couldn't explain. She felt tied to Brian, bound by an almost spiritual commitment. This was just a stage he was going through. It would change. It would get better. It would, once again, be the way it was.

Hours later, she sat in her dressing room after the show, eyes darting nervously toward the door. Brian always came to her dressing room after the show, but she'd waited a half hour and there was no sign of him. Reluctantly, she went to look for him, and found him downstairs, at the bar, talking to a pretty blonde girl.

"Brian," Lindel said softly, "I want to leave."

He just looked at her. Lindel looked closely at the girl sitting next to him. She had, Lindel recalled, been with various members of Lindel's band on previous evenings.

"Brian," Lindel started again.

"I don't want to go just yet," he said, slurring his words. The girl next to him looked smug.

"Fine," Lindel said, coldly. "See you later," and she turned around to leave.

"No wait," he said, getting off the barstool and following her outside into the hallway. "Look," he said, grabbing her arm, "I just felt like staying here for awhile. I like to unwind after a show."

"And just what am I supposed to do while you . . . unwind?" she said between clenched teeth. She started to walk out again, and he grabbed her by the arm.

"Please," he said, "I don't want you to get angry."

"I should wait for you, is that it? Until you're drunk enough so that your head is on the bar and then I scoop you up and take you home? That's what . . . *they* do," she nodded her head in the direction of the bar. "Well, I'm sure that they provide a necessary service for the lonely rock star, but I don't know who you think I am." She turned around again to leave, but his hold on her arm was firm.

He leaned back against the wall, and still holding her hand, he locked his fingers into hers. "It's nothing, you know it's just harmless flirtation. It helps me relax. But I need an emotional base," he said softly. "Why can't you be my emotional base?"

"Because you haven't earned it," she hissed, and ran out of the club and into the empty black limousine that waited at the curb.

Back at the hotel, she regretted what she had said. She hadn't been fair. He had been—most of the time—loving toward her. He had changed her way of thinking about herself onstage, had encouraged her to take chances, to dare. He *had* earned it. She wanted to get back into the car and go get him, to tell him she was sorry. To tell him . . . what? That she'd wait?

She looked around the bedroom for his flight bag. She searched through it, for what, she didn't know. There was just the usual: an assortment of sunglasses, hairbrush, combs, vitamins, Valium, a few books, a toothbrush. Bits of paper with words scribbled on them. His address book. She'd seen it all before. No new clues. But looking at the flight bag made her feel secure. It meant that he had to come back.

Several hours later, she heard him turn the key in the lock. He came in and sat down on the bed in the darkened room. She could tell he was very drunk.

"Are you angry with me?" he said.

She didn't answer.

"Are you going to give me a lecture?" he said.

"No, Brian," she whispered. "I don't want that role."

And they went to sleep.

Lindel's final L.A. show was a screaming, stomping affair. The audience refused to let her off the stage until she did six encores. Afterward, the celebrity crowd had overflowed to On The Rox, the private club upstairs from the Roxy where Jeff hosted a party.

The lights were dim, the room was hot, the music was loud. Jeff had allowed the photographers to take pictures for fifteen minutes, then had them all cleared out. Diana Ross danced with movie producer Howard Rosenman on the tiny dance floor. Peter Boyle and Robert DeNiro sat in the corner on an art deco couch. Joni Mitchell and Hiram Keller whispered to each other at a table near the bar. Lindel sat with her band, Marcia, and Jeff on a large bank of couches in a corner, roped off by two security guards. Lindel felt the beginnings of a headache.

Tim came over, looked at her questioningly, and pointed to the dance floor. She shook her head no, but patted the space next to her on the couch. He came and sat down, and said, "Where's Brian?"

"In the men's room."

"Oh, that euphemism."

She shot him a look. "Don't start. I'm in no mood."

"But darling, this is your big night. You were wonderful. Nothing should spoil this for you."

To her left, Jeff was busy talking to Ian. Their heads were close together, and Jeff's hands were waving wildly. Marcia sat on the couch next to Ian; she wore a gold lamé jumpsuit and a fixed smile. Her face was flushed from the sun, or the champagne, or both, and she listened as Hank and Eddie talked across her about that night's set.

Lindel looked at Marcia with affection. She was really her friend, in a way that Tim, or Jeff, could never be. But what did Marcia want from this life, Lindel wondered. Could she be content just working for Jeff, having no real boyfriends, devoting herself to Lindel's career? Lindel had been so preoccupied with Brian all week that she hadn't really spent much time with Marcia. Well, she'd make it up to her in New York. She'd have plenty of time, then.

She looked around again for Brian. Where was he? Maybe she should get out of here. She wasn't enjoying the party at all.

She tapped Jeff's shoulder. "I'm wiped out. I'm going to take the car, and . . ."

" . . . I'll go with you," he said quickly.

"No," she was firm. "You're having fun, you stay. I just want to go to sleep." And, she thought, be out of here when Brian decides to return. Force him to come and find me. Maybe even to talk to me about what we're going to do after next week.

She blew a good-bye kiss to Marcia, and with Jeff by her side and a professional smile on her face, walked past the people who reached out for her, to congratulate her. Downstairs, into the waiting car, alone. She leaned back against the soft, gray-cushioned seat and closed her eyes. She felt a tremendous letdown. She knew what Jeff would say: If you had to be miserable, you might as well be miserable in the back of a limousine. Better still, she smiled sadly—be miserable in the back of a limousine with a top twenty single.

It was a lively, noisy group that boarded the Starship for the afternoon flight back to New York. Jeff thought it would be fun to rent the private plane for the return flight; and he arranged full press coverage for their arrival at LaGuardia's Butler Aviation.

Lindel thought it a tacky plane, but The Vipers couldn't get over the plush velour maroon couches that lined the main cabin, the gold piano bar, and the two bedrooms in back.

It took only a few minutes for the twenty people on board to settle down. Lindel and Brian sat together in the front two seats. Lindel looked through an old issue of *Newsweek,* as Brian stared out the window. The plane was readying for takeoff, when he turned to her and said, "I'm probably going to stay at the hotel with the guys in New York, okay?"

An alarm went off in her body.

"Why?" she said, hoping that the panic she felt was not in her voice.

"I just feel I should spend some more time with them, that's all," he said.

She couldn't stop herself. "Brian, what am I to you? Where do I fit in your life?"

"Well," he countered, "what am I to you?"

"Not fair," she tried to smile, looking at him. Wearing dark glasses, with his hair all mussed up, right now he looked all of fourteen years old. She just wanted to touch his face. "I asked you first," she said.

He didn't answer right away. Then he said, "Well, I have a good time with you. I care about you, and I think we have a very loving feeling about each other. And I can talk to you more than I can to most people." He stopped.

She waited.

"Oh, I'm not very good at this. You know that. I don't know, what do you want me to say?"

I want you to say that you love me, Lindel's voice shouted inside her head, but she said nothing. *I want you to tell me either to come with you to London or that you'll stay in New York. At least for awhile. I want it to have meant something to you. I don't want us to be over.*

But she said, simply, "Well, what are your plans?" And then, before she could stop herself, she blurted out, "What about us?"

"You know," he said suddenly, "I really like to gamble, don't you?"

"Yes," said Lindel, wondering about the change of subject. "I wish we had had time to sneak in a night in Las Vegas."

"It's just as well that we didn't," he said, looking out the window. "I only like to gamble when I have a lot of money. When you don't care about losing, that's how you always win."

17

Lucy sat up in the bed and stared into space. She held a half-empty bottle of warm beer in one hand and a slow-burning joint in the other. The sheets on the bed were all rumpled, and the room was stuffy and close. Her hair was damp, stuck to her forehead, and she knew that her makeup must be smeared across her face.

Next to her Hank lay asleep. She couldn't remember how they had gotten back to her apartment. The last thing she did remember was being at the Grotto, at a large table with a few of The Vipers and Hank, Eddie and Tony. Everyone was expecting Lindel to come in with Brian, it was all they talked about. Lindel and Brian on the tour; how their song together was magic, how they'd been inseparable, what would happen now that the tour was almost over. Hank thought that Brian might stay in New York for awhile, Eddie said Lindel would record in London. Lucy tried not to listen to any of it, she just wanted to drink enough to blot it all out. She remembered thinking how it would serve Lindel right if she, Lucy, started something with Lindel's precious bass guitarist. Hank seemed pretty drunk, and although Lucy couldn't remember how they actually ended up together, here they were.

She looked at Hank. He was totally out. Her pill case was open, next to the bed, and she remembered the sleeping pills. Hank had said something about needing a lot of sleep this week. He was wiped out from the tour, he said, and the New York dates were important. Lucy couldn't remember how many pills they had taken. She was used to them, she could even sleep behind them, but Hank looked zonked.

She stumbled out of bed and went into the bathroom. Turning on the light, she shielded her eyes from the glare. She looked in the mirror and quickly turned away. She couldn't bear to look at herself. In the past few months her skin had become slack, and blotchy. Her eyes were lackluster. She just felt so . . . awful all the time. Some days the pills got her through, but on others, everything seemed to be just too much to deal with.

She walked back into the bedroom and bumped into the television set. The screen flickered, the sound was down, and she stared at Hank. Maybe she should try to wake him. On the other hand, she almost giggled, what would Lindel say if he just slept for—oh, a few days. Nothing really serious of course. Just long enough to miss the first sound check at the Academy. Lucy had often slept for a day or two after being up for nearly a week, but Hank didn't seem the type. Still, he was here, and he'd passed out. It would be easy enough to just take a few of those Seconal capsules apart and pour the powder into a drink when he woke up.

Lucy took a sip of the beer, made a face, and walked into the kitchen. She opened the refrigerator and took out an opened bottle of ice-cold white wine. Clutching the bottle in her hand, she went into the living room and sat down next to the small cabinet near the window. There it was, right on the bottom shelf, in a big box, behind some record albums, hidden from view. She took the large cardboard box off the shelf and put it next to her on the floor. The wood floor was cold next to her naked skin, but she didn't move. Taking the top off the box, she slowly picked through the contents.

Polaroid pictures of Lindel; dozens of them, at the recording studio, in her apartment, at the Grotto. Lindel smiling, with a guitar, with Jeff, with Tim, with Lucy. The two of them last summer, before Lindel's first tour, at the zoo in Central Park. Lindel on the merry-go-round. And the clippings: the signing photo in *Billboard,* the itinerary from the first tour—the one Lucy had been so sure she would be a part of—the New York *Times* review. The charts, ripped out of *Billboard,* tracing the rise of Lindel's album. Lucy remembered that she had once planned to laminate those chart listings for Lindel and have them framed.

She knew she should have thrown this stuff out ages ago. But somehow, she never did. She needed it; it was proof that she had once been a part of Lindel's life. It had been an exciting time and dammit, she had helped. It wasn't fair that she hadn't been allowed to stick around long enough to get some of the reflected glory.

Tears of frustration welled up in Lucy's eyes. Don't get mad, she told herself over and over; get even. She covered the box and put it back on the shelf. She went into the bathroom and opened the medicine cabinet. She took two blue ten-milligram Valiums out of the large orange bottle and swallowed them down with wine. She stood in the bathroom, staring down at the sink for a long time. She wondered what Lindel was doing now. Probably she was with Brian, laughing, or making love. Or maybe they were out at a party, or a club, with the Garniers, or some of those celebrities Lindel had always sworn didn't interest her. Lucy was sure that things were different now, with Brian in the picture. The perfect rock couple.

Lucy stumbled back into the bedroom. She needed to lie down. She was too numb to think, but maybe if she could sleep just for a little while, she would figure out what to do. Perhaps Hank would help without his even realizing it. After all, he was so naive, and he had no regular girlfriend. Maybe there was room for her in his life. Lucy was sure she could still be quite persuasive if she wanted to.

At two-thirty in the morning Lindel and Brian sat with Tim at a corner table in CBGB's, watching The Studs. Despite a wooden barricade that separated them from the main part of the room, people kept coming over to ask for autographs and take Instamatic photos. Brian seemed uncomfortable; Lindel knew he would have preferred to anonymously watch the band.

Brian drank a bottle of Heineken, Lindel sipped from a glass of white wine, and Tim fussed over them both. He knew just how much publicity value their presence would have for The Studs— a band he had decided to manage.

After The Studs had finished their earshattering set, Tim ushered Lindel and Brian into the tiny backstage dressing room so that photographer Bob Gruen could take a picture of them with the band. Then they left the club by the back door, through a dark alley littered with broken bottles and into their waiting black limousine.

"Where now?" said Tim.

"Oh, anywhere," said Lindel, thinking that she would in fact go anywhere, do anything not to stop the night. Otherwise she was afraid that Brian would go back to the hotel, alone. Tomorrow night was the first of the two Academy shows, and then . . . she didn't want to think about it now; she'd deal with it when it happened.

Tim was listing places where they could go. " . . . and then there's Le Jardin, it's a disco. It's not that fashionable anymore, but most of the good gay clubs are only on weekends. And it's the only place that's probably still open at this hour."

"I don't care," said Lindel. "Brian, what do you want to do?"

"Whatever you like. I'm just a guest in your country."

Lindel felt a pang of sadness. He had said that to her the night he had come to New York for the tour. When they went to Coney Island. She'd been so excited then, so full of plans and hope. And now she just felt as if she'd been put on hold, awaiting some kind of decision.

There was silence as the car drove uptown to West Forty-fourth Street and the fading Diplomat Hotel. The three of them walked into the lobby and down two flights of stairs to the basement, and Le Jardin.

The disco was decorated all in white. Huge potted palm trees painted white sunk in Astroturf dominated the room. Large clusters of white balloons hung from the ceiling. Strobe lights flashed on and off making the dancers look like they were in an old, silent movie. "Rock Your Baby" blasted out from the massive sound system. The crowd was glamorous; thin young boys danced with each other, tall, gorgeous models in jeans and sneakers danced as though they were in a gym, taking exercise. Brian looked around and smiled. Lindel felt relieved.

But she also felt compelled to say, "I thought you hated disco."

"I like a good sound system," he said.

With a sinking feeling, she watched him look at the girls. Tim went to the bar and returned with a round of drinks. They sat down on a banquette along the back wall of the dance floor, and watched the dancers for awhile. This was a more sophisticated crowd than in the rock and roll hangouts. If anyone recognized Lindel and Brian, they didn't let on. After awhile Brian said, "Come on, let's dance."

Dancing with him was like being onstage: it felt as if they were all alone out there—even on that crowded floor—no photographers, no roadies, no musicians, just the two of them. And she threw herself completely into the dance.

Watching him dance, his ass outlined tightly in faded blue jeans, she thought of him onstage. Onstage Brian seduced the audience, his performance was conquest on a massive scale. Here, on this dance floor, he directed his energy to her. The music didn't stop; hot, sexy, pulsating sound and then Brian, eyes gleaming, grabbed her arm and pulled her off the dance floor toward the stairwell.

Lindel's heart began to race. "Brian," she murmured. "What are you doing?"

"Ssh," he said, "just come with me." And he took her into the small, dark stairwell.

"You're mad," she whispered. "What if someone comes in here . . ."

"Sssh," he whispered, kissing her hair, her forehead, her lips, her eyes. "Ssh, don't say a word. I'm going to touch you here . . . and here . . . "

He took her hand and held it next to his lips. Then, very slowly, he took one finger after another and kissed them, and licked them, and one at a time, put them in his mouth while he took his hand and lifted her dress.

Lindel was floating, she was wet and hot and all she could think of was how she wanted him . . . the feeling just got bigger until she felt that surely she could not contain all this feeling anymore. He took his hand and put it to her mouth and she tasted herself, and he made his hand wetter and then put it back on her again. Moving it, slowly, increasing her desire. Continuing to kiss her, long, hungry kisses.

With one quick motion, he moved her around so that she was sitting on top of him, and he could enter her.

Oh my god, Lindel thought. I'm drowning. I can't keep my

hands off this man and I don't want this to ever stop and what am I going to do?

"Kiss me," Brian whispered. "Don't stop kissing me."

And Lindel, shaking now, unable to control the passion that consumed her body, kissed him, again and again, trying to memorize with her lips every inch of his face until she could no longer hold back and she gave in to him completely with a deep, shuddering sigh.

And then, without saying a word, he fixed her clothes and took her arm and led her back to the dance floor before she had a chance to catch her breath.

Later that night, she wanted to ask him about it, but changed her mind. Brian never talked about their lovemaking. It was enough that he came back with her to her apartment instead of going to his room at the hotel.

He was asleep, and she stared at him for at least an hour before she, too, finally fell asleep cradled against his smooth, naked back.

———

At seven in the morning on the day of Lindel's first Academy show, Jeff called Marcia at home.

"Marcia, wake up. I need you to help me with my tickets."

"What? Jeff, it's seven in the morning, can't it wait until we get in the office? What tickets?"

"My fifty for tomorrow night. You know, I told you."

"Fifty?" Marcia sounded alarmed. "What fifty?"

"I told you I needed fifty. Didn't you put them aside?"

"Jeff, you don't really need fifty, do you? I don't think I have more than sixty altogether and the band wants tickets, and The Vipers . . . "

"Fuck The Vipers. Acme bought some. Let them take from their supply. These are for me, personally."

"But why do you need fifty? Who are they for?"

"Relatives," Jeff mumbled.

"Who?" Marcia said. "I don't think I heard you."

"I said relatives," Jeff said, louder now.

"All of a sudden you have relatives? Where did they come from?"

"Well, it's my mother . . . and her sister, and my sisters and their kids. Look, I can't help it. I guess my mother wants to . . ."

" . . . show off," Marcia suggested.

"Look, I can give her some pleasure." Jeff was annoyed.

"I thought you told me that you weren't that close to them. Didn't you say you hated your sisters?"

"I never said that. Anyway, what difference does it make, I have to get these tickets."

"I don't think we have them."

"Well," said Jeff, "find them. Get them from Jacar."

Marcia laughed. "Jeff, you're kidding. You know that these shows are sold out. Jacar doesn't have any tickets, either. No one has tickets. I've been answering the phone for days saying, 'The answer is no' before anyone even says hello. It's been a nightmare. I never want to hear the word 'ticket' again. Anyway, we need Jacar for more ads, a bigger recording budget for the next album. And you want me to *hondle* them for tickets? You're nuts."

"I don't care how you get them," Jeff said. "Get them from scalpers if you have to. But get them."

And he hung up.

That afternoon, Jeff came into the office and stopped in front of Marcia's desk.

"You know those fifty tickets I need?" he said.

He'd just assumed she'd gotten them.

"What?" She eyed him suspiciously.

"Take them and come into my office with the seating plan of the Academy."

"Why?"

Jeff sighed. "Apparently some of my relatives don't talk to others," he said, "and I have to make sure that my Aunt Ruth isn't anywhere near my Aunt Jessie . . ."

"I'm not hearing this," she said.

Jeff's voice rose. "Look, do you think I need to worry about this now? I've got enough on my mind. But my mother is making the big deal about it, and even though she said if it was too much trouble I should forget it, I know she doesn't mean that for a minute. I'll never hear the end of it if I don't do this. We can get it done in five minutes," he said, walking past her desk and into his office.

It took three and a half hours to decide who sat where because the fifty tickets Marcia had managed to obtain were scattered all over the hall.

"I don't know who should get the better tickets," Jeff said.

"Just put the shorter ones up front," Marcia suggested, "and the taller ones in the back."

"Don't be stupid. I'm not about to call my mother for measurements."

"I'm sure she could get them."

"Don't be catty. What should we do?"

"Put the women in the better seats."

"You know these people. These women sit with their husbands."

The two of them stared at the brightly colored tickets.

"Look," Marcia said, "it seems to me that the only real problem is Ruth and Jessie, right?"

"No. Harold lent Arthur money once and never got it back . . . "

"Please," she broke in. "Spare me any more of the family history than I need to know. I give up. Someone in your family is just going to have to be insulted. Let's just throw the tickets up in the air, and pick them up as we scream out a different name."

Jeff shot her a furious look. "You're not being helpful," he said. "This is serious."

"Oh come on," she said. "Serious, it isn't. Besides, where have you been?" Marcia seemed amused. "For months now I've had to get tickets, and albums, and autographed pictures, and T-shirts, for the children of people who work in this business. You'd be surprised at the people who get offended when I can't get their hairdressers backstage passes to Lindel's concerts."

He just stared at her.

"Jeff," Marcia said, the smile no longer on her face, "when you had nothing, you couldn't give it away. You wanted the big time. This is it."

At the back of the Academy of Music Jeff looked at Tim with alarm. "What the fuck is going on?" Jeff hissed.

Onstage Hank was looking at Lindel with concern in his eyes. Something was wrong. She wasn't making the connection with the band, or even with her own voice. The concentration wasn't there.

Midway through the second number Lindel appeared to completely forget the words and just stood there. Jeff raced backstage, into the wings, not knowing what to do, but he knew he'd better be near her if things got much worse.

Hank broke into the chords for the next tune and Lindel just stared at him as if she wasn't sure of where she was. *What the hell was she on,* Jeff wondered, in a panic. This was *New York,* for Christ's sake. He turned around and raced up the narrow backstage stairs until he got to The Vipers' dressing room. He'd find that fucking limey bastard and get him on the goddamn stage with her. No doubt this had something to do with him. She had never pulled anything like this before.

The Vipers' dressing room was crowded with girls. Jeff grabbed Bernie by the arm and screamed, "Where the fuck is he?"

"Who?" Bernie said.

"Brian."

"Man, I dunno. He split awhile back. Right after his set. Don't fucking ask *me* where he goes."

Jeff raced back down the stairs. Split. Was he planning to come back and do the encore? Goddamn him. Goddamn her. She's supposed to be a professional. With all these radio people here tonight. And his family. And, Jeff's heart sank as he realized Alexis had brought Dick Marsden. And Lindel had to go and have a fucking nervous breakdown. She was making a fool out of him.

On the stage, Lindel was confused. She couldn't remember the order of the set. She kept forgetting the words. She felt like she just couldn't go on anymore, she was so tired, she just wanted to sit down. Maybe if she sat down on the edge of the stage and explained things to the audience, she was sure they'd understand. Sometimes it just got to be too much for her . . .

Where was Brian? Why wasn't he in the wings? She needed him there . . .

Standing in the wings, Jeff was in a rage. He signaled to Hank to speed things up. If they played faster, louder, maybe they could get through the set without any major catastrophe. He'd pull her off the stage without a fucking encore. Fuck Brian and their song together. He wasn't letting Dick Marsden see any more of this.

After the set Jeff told Johnny to stand guard at the door, and not let anyone inside Lindel's dressing room. She sat on a chair, and Hank stood quietly in a corner, leaning against the wall, while Jeff paced back and forth.

"Maybe you'd like to explain what the fuck that was about," he said, his teeth clenched.

"Jeff," said Hank, "Lindel's exhausted, maybe this can wait until tomorrow."

Jeff whirled around to face Hank, his eyes blazing. "Who asked you? And by the way, where the fuck were you during the sound check today?"

Hank looked at Lindel and said, softly, "I'm sorry. It's a long story. I . . . overslept. It won't happen again."

"It's all right," Lindel said, almost in a whisper, her eyes wide. "Jeff, I can't argue with you. I don't know what happened up there tonight. Something snapped. I have a lot on my mind."

"So who doesn't?" Jeff raised his voice. "You *owed* something to those kids who paid eight bucks apiece to see you. To say nothing of all the radio people I invited, and . . . "

"Stop it," she said. "I can't listen to it. Not tonight." She thought, I don't want to hear about how I'm supposed to be a professional. This isn't a job to me. Sometimes I get scared, or have too much to drink, or I need Brian there to give me moral support and when he's not I'm afraid I can't do it all. She couldn't explain to Jeff that Brian had left her apartment that morning without a word and she hadn't seen him at all the whole day. Jeff wouldn't understand why that would make a difference. So she just sat there, saying nothing, in a daze, as Jeff stormed out of the room and slammed the door.

It was well after one-thirty in the morning when Lindel and Brian managed to get away from all of the people gathered in her dressing room at the Academy. Lindel had been determined to make up for the night before and the second and final show had gone off without a hitch. Her finale with Brian was the best they had ever done—maybe because she was uncertain if they would ever do it again, and she wanted it to be right. As she sang she shut her eyes tight and remembered the joy she'd felt—always—singing with him; how their eyes met and there was instant, silent communication with not even a second's delay before that understanding was translated into song.

The audience had gone wild; they stomped and hollered and shouted her name until she was forced back for encore after encore, and the line of people waiting to greet her backstage was all the way down the stairs. When she and Brian finally slipped out with Johnny Paglioni to the Thirteenth Street stage door where a few hundred fans waited, they had to sign dozens of autographs before they could get into their limousine.

Her apartment seemed especially silent after this final show. Lindel automatically handed Brian the ice-cold bottle of champagne, and he opened it. She poured two glasses full as he sat down on her bed and leaned across to turn on the TV set. She stood there, then walked over to the bed and lay down. She knew the minute he turned on that damn TV, there was to be no talk.

Brian looked tired. He wore a white collarless shirt and tight black corduroy jeans. Lindel had changed into the gray silk nightgown she had never worn on the tour. She still had her stage makeup on, and her eyes were dark, and wide, and questioning. But, even though she couldn't stand not knowing, she would not ask him about his plans. She was too afraid of what she might hear. And so, on this, the final night of the tour, the two of them lay on her bed, sipping champagne, saying little and watching television until many hours later, they fell asleep.

The next morning Brian jumped out of bed. He started to put on his clothes and Lindel felt a stab of fear.

"What are your plans?" she said, sitting up and pulling the sheet around her.

"I'm taking a one o'clock flight."

"What?"

He turned to her, and with a small smile on his face he said, "I've got to get back, love. I've got an album to do."

Her heart turned into an ice ball. She didn't know what to do, what to say. Could he just walk out of here? She didn't believe it. Then she knew that faced with disaster, she had to remain in control. She couldn't say anything. She'd make him say it.

When he was dressed, he came over to her and sat down on the edge of the bed. He looked at her for a long minute.

"Bye," he whispered, leaning toward her to give her a kiss. "It's been lovely."

She smiled, her heart pounding so loud she was sure she was going to faint. In that instant, she thought, *he'll stay, he isn't going anywhere.*

He smiled. He kissed her again, and then he was gone.

Just like that. Like the first time in London. After six weeks, he just walked out. No word about when he would call, when they would see each other again.

Lindel lay in bed for a very long time. She wanted to cry, but no tears came. It hadn't sunk in yet. He was still in the city, his plane wouldn't leave for another few hours. Surely he would call her from his hotel, or the airport.

After twenty minutes, she called Marcia.

"He's gone," Lindel said.

"What happened?" Marcia said.

"Nothing. He just left. Said nothing about seeing me again. I don't know what to do. I think I'm in a state of shock."

"Don't worry. He's probably not very good at saying good-bye. Didn't you tell me that the exact same thing happened in London?"

"But that was after one night. We've been practically inseparable for the past six weeks. I can't believe he thinks he can just drift in and out of my life like this."

"Well," said Marcia, gently, "he probably didn't know how else to leave you. He knows you have work to do, too. Think about it. It was probably as hard for him as it was for you. I'm sure this isn't the end of it."

"I don't know. I can't believe it. Maybe you're right. Maybe he'll call. But it seems so quiet without him. The tour over, Brian not here, it's like the curtain fell."

"Why don't you meet me for lunch? Don't lie around in bed all day, gloomy. Let's go somewhere fabulous."

"You always think lunch is a remedy."

"Sorry, I was just trying to help . . ."

"I know, I'm sorry, Marcia. I didn't mean to snap at you. I'm tired. Maybe I'll try to go back to sleep."

"Call me later."

"Okay, thanks."

Lindel hung up the phone and lit a cigarette. She leaned back against the pillows, and realized that they hadn't even made love before he left. She put the cigarette out, and turned over to try to go back to sleep. After a few minutes, she knew it was useless, and got up out of bed. She saw the remains of the night all around her. Dead flowers rotting in a vase. The empty champagne bottle. Moldy cherries in a bowl next to the bed. An empty pack of those French cigarettes he smoked. In the bathroom, two toothbrushes in a glass on the sink. Hers, and the one she'd bought for him. The one that wouldn't be needed tonight.

He would be leaving the hotel now. Bernie would be rounding up the band, and they'd be on their way to JFK. In a few more minutes, she wouldn't be able to call him.

She walked into the living room, and almost unconsciously went over to the record player. She flipped through a few albums until she found the one she was looking for. A few seconds later, Brian's voice, Brian's presence, filled the room. She sat on the couch and closed her eyes, listening to him sing, imagining him onstage.

She got up and turned the record off. It was too soon, he was still too close. She wouldn't sit here like some groupie and listen to his album. Slowly, she took the record off the turntable, put it back in its jacket, and put it away, in the back of the bookcase.

18

The next day, Lindel refused to leave her apartment, certain that if she did, she would miss Brian's phone call. She couldn't believe that he hadn't called before he left New York, or from the airport, or when he arrived in London. She even phoned BOAC to make sure that his plane had landed safely.

"Honey," Marcia told her, "if it hadn't landed, believe me, you would have heard."

She looked at the clock all the time; her mind always six hours ahead, on London time, trying to imagine what Brian might be doing. She was tempted to just get on a plane and follow him there.

Lindel thought about Brian constantly. Brian coming out of the shower, dripping in a puddle of water on the bathroom mat. Combing his hair, absentmindedly drying himself with a large white towel. Brian, waking in the morning; yawning, stretching, rolling over on top of her. Brian, eating pizza, putting grapes in her mouth. Grinning when she sat on his lap. Watching television. Looking at himself in the mirror. But most of all, she still thought about Brian onstage.

With Brian, she had felt that she was part of a team, that she didn't have to bear the burdens of touring, and travel, and stage fright; and insomnia—alone. With Brian she slept peacefully. With Brian she felt that she could do anything. And now, all of that was gone.

As the days went on, she felt listless, depressed, empty. When she went out, and saw couples laughing together on the street or in restaurants, she felt as though she was the only person in the world who was alone. So she started to stay inside her apartment, and smoked cigarettes, talked to Marcia and Hank on the phone, and listened to Brian's first album. She had vowed not to play it, then couldn't help it, and then would feel worse after she heard his voice. She didn't even try to write a song, she was far too numb. All she wanted to do was relive and rethink every moment of the tour. To remember what they had done together, what it had felt like, and try to figure out where she had gone wrong.

Several weeks later, Marcia phoned Jeff in L.A. and told him he'd better get back and do something about Lindel. He had been out there finalizing a deal, he said, for Eyeteeth, and he hated to leave to come back to New York. There was so much happening in L.A. now—he was seriously considering moving his office there—and he just couldn't believe that things were as bad with Lindel as Marcia said. But he figured he ought to check it out for himself.

Jeff went directly from the airport to Lindel's apartment, and, as he got to her front door, he was not pleased to hear Brian's album blasting over the stereo. Christ, he thought, no wonder her neighbors had complained. He rang the bell a dozen times, and, after she had turned off the record, a few minutes later, Lindel opened the door.

Jeff was shocked by her appearance. Her hair looked as if it had not been washed in days, and her face was pale and drawn. She wore a baggy pair of faded blue jeans and an old gray sweatshirt and looked ten pounds thinner than the last time he had seen her.

She just stared at him.

"I want to talk to you," he said, brushing by her into the apartment. Opened containers of Chinese food were on the floor, ashtrays overflowed with cigarette butts, newspapers and magazines were strewn about—and it looked like this had been going on for weeks. Lindel seemed oblivious to the fact that she was living in utter chaos.

He looked at her and said, "What the fuck is happening here?"

She lit a cigarette and averted her eyes. "What are you talking about?"

"You know damn well what I'm talking about. You haven't been out of this apartment in weeks. Your band is waiting around, they have no idea when you're going back into the studio. You miss photo sessions, you cancel interviews, you don't return my calls, are you out of your mind?"

"I'm *exhausted*," she said, and went to sit down on the couch. She curled her legs under her. "I did six weeks of gigs and I need a rest."

"Fine. You've had it. Now what?"

"I probably just should have gone somewhere . . ."

"Oh? Where? London?"

She looked at him with narrowed eyes. "And what was that supposed to mean?"

"Oh, come on, this is Jeff. I know this is all about Brian."

"It is not." She raised her voice. "I'm tired. Don't you get it? You didn't have to get onstage every night, fly somewhere every day. Christ, I can't believe I have to justify a few weeks off to you. I am *not* a machine."

She started to cry. She looked beaten, defeated. The color was drained out of her face.

Jeff sat down next to her, and put his arms around her. She moved away. "Lin, I'm sorry, honey. I guess I shot my mouth off too much. But baby, I'm worried about you."

She just sat there, her head leaning back against the corner of the couch, saying nothing, tears rolling down her face.

She reached for a tissue from the box on the floor and wiped her eyes. She put out her cigarette, lit another, and almost immediately she started to cough, violently, and Jeff tried to grab the cigarette out of her hand. She jerked her hand away, and Jeff said, "You're supposed to be a *singer,* remember? That hacking sounds awful."

She didn't say anything, but continued to smoke.

"Lin," Jeff said quietly now, "you do this to yourself. You've created the whole problem yourself. You just get too involved."

"What do you know about it?" she whispered. "I haven't been

'involved' since you've known me except for this one time. And this was different."

"It's always different," Jeff sighed. "Why do you think I don't even consider these kinds of . . . relationships. It just screws up your life."

"Well, I'm sorry, Jeff, I'm not like you."

"Fine. So you're different. Where does it get you now, this big love, this big romance?"

"It was special," she insisted.

"It was six weeks on a rock and roll tour. Didn't you ever go to camp? What is it Linda Ronstadt calls it? Roadmance, that's it."

"It wasn't like that," she said. "We shared something. And it was more than just us. It was all tied up with the music, the shows . . . I can't help it, I just can't turn off and forget about my real life."

His eyes widened. "Your music, the shows, that's not your real life?"

"Come on, Jeff, for most people their love life is their real life. Just let something go wrong with it and it's all they think about."

Jeff stood up and started to pace in front of the couch. "Look, he's a musician. And I don't care what anyone says, it's different for a guy. You knew what you signed up for with him. I tried to warn you. You were drawn to him because he was wild, or elusive, or whatever, and then you tried to tame him. It just doesn't work. He had to go back to London to do what he's supposed to do. I only wish you felt the same about your work."

She glared at him. "I don't think you get it. You seem to act as though this was a long, sleazy one-night stand. We really cared for each other. It was the only . . . private thing I had. I need someone to share my life. And he may not admit it, but I think he needs me too."

"Fine. If he does, then he'll let you know. But until he realizes it, you should not spend your time moping around. I can assure you, he isn't moping around in London."

He looked at her. "And when the hell are you going to take that goddamned piece of string off your wrist?"

She didn't say anything.

He tried to change the subject. "Look, whatever. Let's not talk about it anymore today. What about you, have you written any songs at all? Anything you think you'd like to try and record?"

"No."

"Well," he tried to sound cheerful, "take some more time if you need it. But be ready to go in next month. It was a bitch getting the Record Plant to postpone the time, and we can't juggle it around much longer."

Lindel turned on the light next to her bed and looked at the clock. Five-thirty in the morning. Ten-thirty in London. It was useless, she just couldn't sleep. Brian would probably still be sleeping. She opened the drawer of the night table and pulled out the piece of paper with his unlisted London phone number on it. Lindel didn't want anyone to know she didn't have his number, so it had taken Marcia over a week to wrangle it out of Marty Paretta's secretary. Marcia invented some excuse about tax forms and money owed to The Vipers from the tour, and managed to get a copy of Brian's work permit with his phone number and address.

"Why don't you just go there and ring his bell?" Marcia had suggested.

"Don't be crazy," Lindel said. "I couldn't do that."

"Didn't he practically do that when he came over here for the tour?" Marcia said.

"That was different."

"I don't see how," Marcia said. "Anyway, now you have his number, why don't you call him?"

Lindel hadn't been able to explain. Something just . . . stopped her. She felt that if she had to call him, to ask him if there was anything between them anymore, then she already had his answer. She was once again reminded of David, and how it never was any good when you had to chase after someone. And she remembered something Brian had once said: " . . . *when you don't care about losing, that's how you always win.*" She couldn't bring herself to call him, to look like she was afraid she'd lost him.

On the other hand, surely after four weeks apart she had the right to call and just tell him she missed him. She'd be glad to hear from him; why wouldn't he be glad to hear from her?

Lindel picked up the phone and dialed the operator. She lit a cigarette and started to place the transatlantic call. What if his voice was cold? What if a girl answered his phone? Before she finished giving the London number to the operator, Lindel hung up. It was too early to call Brian. She didn't want to wake him up. She'd try him later. Maybe.

Lindel walked back upstairs to her apartment, holding the morning's mail in her hand. Again, nothing from Brian. Actually, it had been two months since he'd gone; she would have been surprised if there had been a letter from him. All there was was the usual junk mail, and a thick, cream-colored envelope with no return address that looked like an invitation. Even the fan mail had radically tapered off to almost nothing these days.

She walked into the bedroom and sat down on the bed. The cream-colored envelope was a mystery. She ran her finger under the sealed flap, and took out a piece of paper with a rubber band around it. Inside the paper were three Polaroid photos. Of Brian. Naked in bed, laughing, with a girl on either side of him. There was nothing written on the piece of paper.

Lindel threw the photos on the floor, then immediately leaned over and picked them up. For once, the tears wouldn't come; she just felt sick.

It was no surprise that he slept with other girls, but when were these taken? On tour? On one of those nights when he had disappeared? She couldn't recognize the hotel room—after awhile they all looked the same. And who had sent these to her; who wanted to hurt her that much?

That week she saw a photo of Brian in *Melody Maker* with the model Nina Hawthorne, at some party in London. Two days later, Tim called to tell her that Brian and Nina were in Liz Smith's column. They were, he couldn't wait to tell her, on some island. Mustique, he thought it was. Vacationing. Tim said that Liz had referred to him as the "former close friend of superstar Lindel James."

"Get angry," Marcia had said to her when Lindel phoned in tears. "First of all, notice that she refers to you as the superstar, and to him as 'your former close friend.' You made him famous in this country, you should be furious. Don't sit around and sulk, you know what they say: get even. Go and make the best possible record you can make."

"Oh, Marsh," Lindel wailed, "I don't even care about making a record. I just don't have the strength . . ."

"I'd also like to say," Marcia continued, "that I don't think you should even talk to Tim when you're in this mood. He's probably sleeping peacefully now, while you're all upset, which is exactly what he wanted. And, what is Brian doing in Mustique, of all places? Since when did he get so fancy? I thought all he cared about was rock and roll . . . Anyway, have you tried to call him yet?"

"No," Lindel mumbled.

"After all I went through to get the number?" Marcia joked. "Well, why not?"

"I don't know. Every time I think of it, it's either too early in the morning or the middle of the night."

"That's not the reason."

"I know . . . I don't know, Hank said I should send him something."

"Like what?"

"Oh . . . a letter, or a card, or something personal."

"How about that piece of string around your wrist? Sorry, I guess that wasn't so funny."

"Marsh, I don't know what to do, I don't know what to think anymore. Hank was here last night and we were going to go to see a movie and we just ended up talking about this until four in the morning. I feel like such a drain on him, on you."

"Stop it," Marcia said. "We love you, we're your friends. And besides, I'm sure you'll have to go through something like this with me one day. But I wish you'd call him, or something."

"What do you think he's thinking about me?"

Marcia sighed. They had been through this many times. "I think the same thing I've always thought. That he wasn't ready for you. He was afraid of his feelings for you. And, to tell you the truth, I think he just couldn't be with someone who was more famous than he was. I think his ego couldn't take being with a woman who had her own identity . . ."

"I can't really believe that," said Lindel. "But now, it's just gone too far . . . we've really drifted."

"You have to wait for him to make a move. He will. I promise you."

"When?"

"I don't know. Probably when you least expect it. Or maybe when you don't care anymore. That's usually the way it happens."

It was twelve-thirty at night when Lindel and Tim arrived at the Electric Toys party in the Belvedere Suite on top of Rockefeller Center. The room was crowded, hot and smoky. She saw Jeff right away, posing for pictures with the band. As she looked around for a table, there was an explosion of flashbulbs in her face. She smiled automatically, then, temporarily blinded by the light, she turned to Tim for help.

"Get us a table, will you?" she said softly. "And then get me a drink."

Lindel wore a clingy black jersey minidress and thigh-high black suede boots. Her hair was fluffed out around her face in dozens of long, curly ringlets, and her eyes were lined with kohl. She knew she was thin, but she knew too, that she would look good in the photos. And maybe Brian would see one of them.

Tim grabbed a waiter and ordered drinks, then led Lindel over to a roped-off table in the corner. The Belvedere Suite offered a spectacular view of the city: the Empire State Building all lit up in red, white and blue; the shiny, silver Chrysler Building, and the big red RCA sign that flashed out in the midst of thousands of twinkling lights.

She wondered how much longer she could do nothing and still get this kind of star treatment. It had been three months since the end of the tour and she still hadn't gone back into a studio. She hadn't wanted to come to this party and answer all the inevitable questions about what she was doing, but Jeff had made it seem like a dare. He had sent a limousine and had called every half hour all night long pleading with her to make an appearance. Almost in spite of herself, she began to relax just a little bit, to enjoy the stares, the attention.

She looked around. Jeff was everywhere: at the buffet table, loading up on plates of food, scurrying back to the bar, stopping to greet people, posing for photos. All with the same frightening energy.

He came over, carrying two plates of food, and sat down with her and Tim.

"I brought you some food," he said, pushing over a plate filled with cold roast beef, cheese and salad.

"I'm not hungry," she said. "But thanks."

"Well, thanks for coming." He turned and looked at her closely. "You look great," he said.

"You sound surprised," she said, with a faint smile.

"Not at all," he said, picking up a fork, and attacking the food on his own plate. "I'm starved."

She watched him with distaste. "Why do you always eat as if you're on your way to the electric chair?"

He smiled, didn't miss a beat, and continued putting food in his mouth.

"Who's here?" said Tim.

"Everybody," said Jeff, taking a gulp of Perrier water. "Garnier's not, but all the vice-presidents are. And Kal Rudman. Steve Paul. Ron Delsener. Nat Weiss. Carly Simon. Jagger's supposed to come later."

Lindel groaned. "Oh, Jeff, that old line. You don't have to impress us."

"No, really," Jeff insisted. "He is. He was backstage at the concert. He likes the band. Maybe I can get him to produce." His eyes gleamed at the thought.

Lindel said nothing, and sipped the white wine.

"Hmmmm." Jeff was pointing to the far end of the room. "There's Peter Frampton." And he jumped up, saying, "Be right back," as he raced away.

Lindel looked after him. "I can't believe how he still loves all of this. Maybe this was a mistake, my coming here."

"You can't leave yet. He'll be so upset."

"He's off ass-kissing everyone in the place. He won't even notice I'm gone."

"Lindel, look," said Tim, sounding pleased, "it's Lucy."

Lindel looked up to see Lucy stagger toward their table.

"My god," Lindel muttered. "I never would have recognized her."

Lucy looked like she weighed ninety pounds, maybe less; it was hard to tell because she wore a baggy hip-length navy blue sweater over loose, harem-style white pants. Her clothes looked like they were about to fall off her pitifully thin frame, and there were huge circles under her eyes. Her hair was cut very short, almost to her skull, and her eyes looked twice as large as usual and totally crazed.

"Lindel, it's so good to see you," Lucy said, slurring her words, and sitting down in the chair vacated by Jeff.

"Lucy, you look adorable," said Tim.

Lindel shot him a look, then turned to Lucy. "How are you?"

"I'm great, great," said Lucy, her eyes vacant.

"I'll get you a drink," said Tim, standing up and ignoring Lindel's warning look. "I know you two gals must have *so* much to talk about."

He left the table, and Lindel looked at Lucy with concern.

"What have you been up to?" Lindel said.

"Oh . . . you know. I've been getting it together. I saw this incredible movie the other day, *The Man Who Fell to Earth*. With Bowie. It was really amazing. Did you see it? No? Oh, you've got to see it, he was unbelievable. It was so . . . real. I sat through it three times. You know, the summers are kind of a real drag. Not that much going on. I've been getting into some interesting stuff, you know, just doing my thing. Oh, there's Jeff. Talking to Peter. Isn't Peter cute? . . ." Lucy's voice trailed off as she stared at Lindel.

Lucy continued. "Man, I saw you at the Academy and wow, you were so happy . . . you know . . . I just couldn't believe it. You made me cry . . . you know?"

"Thanks," Lindel made a face. "I just wish I could write some new songs. I've been kind of . . . ah . . . blocked lately."

"Oh, you'll get it together. You know, I really wanted to tell you, 'cause I haven't seen you in such a long time. I mean we haven't really talked in such a long time, but I thought the stuff you did at the Academy with Brian was really super . . . Tim said it might be on a live album?"

"No," said Lindel, "we taped it, but just to have."

Where was Tim? He must be purposely staying away. And where was Jeff? Lucy was still talking, not making much sense, and Lindel didn't know what to say, what to do.

" . . . and I thought Hank was going to come tonight," Lucy continued, "but when I called him he said he wasn't up to it. Hank's so beautiful, you know, he's got such a fantastic . . . thing about him." Lucy lapsed into silence for a few seconds and stared into space.

"Oh, have you seen him lately?" Lindel said.

"What?" Lucy just stared.

"Hank," Lindel said. "You were talking about Hank. Do you see him?"

"Oh . . . no. You know, I think of you often, Lindel, I really do." Lucy leaned across the table and put her hand on Lindel's arm.

Lindel was immediately uncomfortable, and tried to gently move her arm away. Lucy grabbed it tighter.

"I miss you," Lucy whispered, tears welling up in her eyes.

Lindel didn't know what to say. This whole encounter with Lucy had made her even more depressed. Fortunately, Tim came back to the table, carrying drinks, a broad smile on his face.

"You two look cozy," he said, sitting down. "Lindel, this is just like old times, isn't it?"

Lindel didn't respond, and Lucy started to get up. She bumped into Lindel's chair, and holding on to the back of it, she straightened up.

"I've . . . got to go to the bathroom," she said. "Anyone want to join me?"

Lindel shook her head no and Tim said, "No, thanks. But don't leave, darling. Come back and chat with us. It's *so* good to see you."

When she was gone, Tim muttered, "I'll bet she's got to go to the bathroom. She'd better fix her nose quick or she'll be on the floor."

"She seems really out of control," Lindel said.

"Too many downs," Tim agreed. "Quaaludes mostly. They're so addictive. Then when she's too high, and starts to nod, she takes a lot of coke to wake up."

Lindel felt awful. Seeing Lucy like this was like some kind of twisted acknowledgment of what had become of her own early hopes. Again, she thought of leaving.

Tim nudged her.

"Your guitar player is on his way over to say hello."

"Tony? What's he doing here?"

Tony came to the table and leaned over to kiss Lindel. She felt a quick stab of guilt; she hadn't even called anyone in the band except Hank in weeks. He pulled a chair over and sat down next to her.

"How are you?" he said.

"Oh, you know . . . I'm sorry I haven't called, but I've really been wiped out. What about you? Tim told me you jammed with Eyeteeth at the Grotto a few weeks ago?"

Tony looked uncomfortable. "Ah . . . yeah. I wanted to talk to you about that, but maybe this isn't the right time."

"No, go on," said Lindel. "What's the matter?"

Tim got up and motioned that he was going to the bar. A photographer ran over and snapped a picture of Lindel. She turned back to Tony.

"Jeff says we're not going into the studio," said Tony.

"Well, not yet. I'm having trouble with the songs. I thought about asking you or Hank to write with me, but I've always done them alone before, and I thought . . ." she trailed off.

"So, when do you think we're going to go in?"

"Why? What's the matter? I thought you all were on a salary during this time off."

"We are," Tony said, his voice getting louder. "But Lindel, you know I like to play."

She didn't answer.

"And . . . well, Eyeteeth were thinking of adding another guitarist just for this tour, and I thought . . ."

She waited.

He wouldn't look her in the eye. "Well . . . Jeff thought . . ."

"Jeff thought? Since when did Jeff have a thought about your career?" The instant she said it, she regretted it. She wasn't herself these days.

"Look, Lindel, I'm sorry," Tony was talking faster now, reaching for her hand. "I love you, you know that. There's nobody else I would rather play with. But I can't sit around for two months waiting while you get the songs together. Why should you care if I go out and join them for a few dates? I just want a gig, that's all."

It hadn't occurred to her that this might happen. Was she going to lose the rest of her band, too? She wondered how much of this had to do with Jeff.

"Tony, I don't know what to say, I'm sorry. I've been in a weird mood. I didn't mean to take it out on you."

"You're tired," said Tony. "You just went through a grueling tour. You're more sensitive . . ."

"Did Jeff tell you to say that?"

Tony looked hurt. "No, he didn't. I care about you, Lindel. We all do. But I'll go stir crazy if I don't play soon. The others are different, they all have various little projects that keep them busy, but this gig is the only chance I have to stay active."

"It's okay, Tony, of course I understand. And good luck, I'll look forward to seeing you play soon. But remember, I'm going to need you in a . . . few months."

"Of course." He leaned over and kissed her. "I wouldn't let you go into the studio with another lead guitarist."

Jeff came over to the table, a big smile on his face.

"Hi, kids," he said. "What's happening?"

Tony looked relieved to have an excuse to get up and give Jeff his seat. Lindel stared at him as he walked away, then turned to Jeff, a small, tight smile on her face.

"You bastard," she whispered to Jeff.

"That's a nice thing to say to the man who just arranged to have Peter Frampton record two of your songs."

"Don't con me," she hissed. "I don't want Peter Frampton to do my songs. I did want to hold on to my lead guitarist."

"So?"

"So, I know that you arranged to have him play with your new band."

"I did nothing of the sort," said Jeff. "As a matter of fact, Tony came to me and said that he ran into them in Max's and they asked him to sit in on one number. They made him the offer. I tried to stop it, as a matter of fact."

"Mmmmm," said Lindel, "and there is a Shubert Theater in San Francisco."

"What?"

"Oh, something Tim says. *All About Eve.* Forget it. I don't even care anymore," she said, dully. "He'll get what he's always wanted. Satin pants and lots of groupies. Listen," she said, reaching for her bag, and her cigarettes, "I hope you don't mind, but I'm going."

"Lindel, I'm not letting you go home."

"Not letting me?" She got up.

His hand stopped her. "Listen to me," his voice was urgent. "How the hell do you think it looks when everyone is always asking me what you're doing, why they never see you, what's wrong. It is not good business. Why, the offers I've had to turn down for you

... Lindel, there's a real buzz around, that you're fucked up, washed up ..."

"Is that what you think?" she whispered.

"*Me*? Of course not, baby. I know how great you are, and how you've been having a ... reaction to all of this. It'll pass. But someone's got to have a clear head, and think about the product. If you want to go ahead and make me the bad guy, go ahead. I guess it comes with the territory."

"The product," she said, shaking her head slowly. "You know, I've always heard these kinds of stories, but I never really believed that it happened that way. Let me tell you something, my friend. I am a singer. And a songwriter. And I have thoughts and demons whirling around in my head driving me nearly half crazy all the time and you couldn't begin to understand."

"Lindel, ssssh, please," Jeff tried to calm her down. "Let's not have a scene here, okay? Honey, you're an artist, I know that. I'm just the shleppadick manager, trying to keep it all together. But you have to admit that you have been indulging yourself ...."

"I didn't come here for a lecture," she broke in. "Goodnight." She turned and quickly left the room.

Tim raced over to the table. "What happened?" he said. "I was watching at the bar, but I couldn't bear to interrupt ... Shall I go after her?"

"I suppose so." Jeff sat there looking as if the air had been let out of him.

He watched Tim rush out of the room in search of Lindel. He didn't know what to do about her anymore, but he knew he desperately needed her to get back to work. Without that advance toward the recording budget, he was in real trouble. He had to hustle every minute for money: to get Eyeteeth into the studio and out on the road, for new equipment for the Electric Toys, to get the Marquis back from London and set up in L. A. But the bottom line was Lindel. Without her working, there wasn't enough money to operate Valhalla in the style to which he'd become accustomed. Her record had net him nearly three quarters of a million dollars but his operating costs were nearly that much. Her tour had practically lost money, and he wouldn't see dollar one of her foreign sales or publishing for at least six months. And the style to which he'd been accustomed was the only way in this business where what you acted like was even more important than what you were.

He got up from the table. He'd better work the room. If she wanted to wreck her career that was one thing, but she wasn't going to stop him. Not now, not after he was almost where he wanted to be.

Lindel walked in the door to her apartment and went directly to the bedroom. She turned on the air conditioner, lay down on the bed and lit a cigarette. It had been a mistake to let Jeff talk her into going to that party. Seeing Tony . . . Lucy . . . it had all just made her more depressed. There really was no one she wanted to be with except Brian.

On impulse, she picked up the phone. She didn't need the piece of paper, she knew his phone number by heart. It was around five in the morning in London but she didn't care. She missed him and needed to talk to him. This silence had gone on too long.

The operator made the connection, Lindel heard the double ring, and she felt her heart start to pound. *Your heart's beating much too fast,* Brian had told her that first night they were together. *Tell it to slow down,* he had said.

She let the phone ring a long time. Marcia had once told her that the British took forever to answer their phones. Just as she was about to hang up, she heard the click that meant someone had picked up the phone.

"Hello?" It was Brian.

Lindel grabbed the receiver tight, she didn't say anything for a few seconds. She felt paralyzed.

"Hello?" He sounded annoyed.

"Brian, it's me," she practically whispered. "Lindel."

"Oh . . . hi." His voice softened. She couldn't really tell, but he sounded pleased to hear from her.

"I . . . just wanted to see how you were," she stammered. "I mean, it's been awhile . . ." Dammit, that wasn't what she had wanted to say.

There was silence on the other end of the line.

"Hello?" she said. "Are you still there?"

"Yes," he said. "But there's a terrible echo on the line. Listen, love, do you think I could . . . uh, call you back in a bit?"

"Did I wake you? I'm sorry . . ."

"No, no, it's not that. It's just that I really should call you back. Give me your number."

You used to have my number, she wanted to scream, but instead just said, "I see," in a cold voice, gave him the number, and hung up.

She felt like a fool. Obviously someone had been there with him. But the worst thing was that he sounded like such a stranger.

She picked up the phone to call Marcia and then changed her mind. She didn't want to talk about this to anyone. She wished she had never called him, never left herself open to wait for his next move. To wait for a phone call that she was almost certain was not going to come.

The next morning, Tim called. "I didn't wake you, did I?"

From his eager tone, Lindel just knew he had some bad news.

"Darling," he went on, "I hope you're not upset."

"Why should I be?"

"Didn't you see that bitchy item Bob Weiner had about you in his column in the *Soho*?"

"Tim, please. Who reads that?"

"What? Why, everyone, of course. It says . . ."

"I have to get the door . . ."

"Who's at the door at eleven-thirty in the morning?"

"Look, I've got to go."

"I'll hold on," he said. "I have some other stuff to tell you."

"I'll call you back," she said, and hung up.

A few hours later, he called back.

"Whatever happened to you?" he said. "I thought you were going to call me back."

"Persistent, aren't you?" she mumbled.

"What?"

"Nothing."

"Well," he said. "I thought that you would want to know that there's another big picture of Brian with Nina Hawthorne in the new *Rolling Stone*. It isn't out yet, they sent me an advance copy."

"How fortunate," said Lindel, reaching for a cigarette.

"At some party for David Bowie at Mr. Chow's in London. She's wearing one of those 'I mustn't be late for the duchess's party' hats. Want me to read the caption?"

"No . . ."

"Brian Davis and model Nina Hawthorne at Bowie's bash at Mr. Chow's," he read. *"The lovely Nina said she was thinking of accompanying Brian when The Vipers tour, following the release of their new album."*

She hung up the phone. That was it. No more. From now on, she'd call Marcia to check in, then keep her phone off the hook. If Brian hadn't called her by now, and was involved with someone else, he wasn't going to call at all. She didn't need her friends calling her with bad news.

Brian. With someone else. And, of all places, at Mr. Chow's. Where she had been with him that first night they had spent together.

Lindel felt a kind of helpless rage. Didn't he think of *her* when he was in Mr. Chow's? What did he think? It was almost as if Lindel had ceased to exist for him. The whole affair wiped out, negated. Declared null and void.

What if he did come back here on tour and brought that . . . model with him? Would he take her to Coney Island? To the Ritz Carlton?

She looked at the piece of string on the wrist of her right hand. Brian had put it there one night, when they were in the dimly lit bar of the Stamford Court hotel in San Francisco. "Jewelry," he had mumbled, smiling, and she hadn't removed it since. Now she didn't want to look at it anymore, and slowly, she took it off her wrist and dropped it into the wastebasket next to her bed.

How could she have so misjudged him? It seemed as though he just needed someone—anyone—propped up by his side so he didn't have to be alone. Now he was stepping on, no, *stealing* her memories. She couldn't stand thinking about it anymore. She just wanted to sleep, not talk to anyone, watch daytime television. Get completely immersed in her own silence. Maybe a drink would help. No one understood. She just had to be alone with this pain.

19

SUMMER, 1976

Alexis Garnier pulled the gray satin blindfold off her eyes and looked at the clock. She'd better get out of bed, it was ten-thirty, and she had a lot to do today. She absolutely had to talk to Marc about Lindel.

She looked over at the phone on her white lacquered night table. One of the four lines was lit; that meant Marc was already up.

The cool sea air drifted in through the slightly open window, and Alexis got out of bed and walked over to the sliding doors that opened onto the deck. It was cool for August, usually her least favorite month, and she reached into the closet for a light wool navy blue robe and put it on over her white silk pajamas. She stepped outside onto the deck and stared straight ahead to the ocean. Everything was so calm, so peaceful, here. All grays and slate blue and sandy beige colors. Her house in East Hampton was pleasing to her, especially her bedroom: white lace curtains, linen sheets on the four-poster bed, and a blue and white Oriental rug on the pale gray wooden floor. White lacquered night tables, a dressing table and puffy white chair, and the walls, stark and white. Color was provided by the sand and the sea outside, by the lavender freesia in a Lalique crystal vase, and, of course, by Alexis herself. Alexis designed the rooms in which she lived as colorless props for her striking presence.

She decided not to get dressed, nor ring for breakfast. First she wanted to speak to Marc. She wasn't really concerned; she just wanted his approval that she was doing the right thing. She was certain that Marc would be pleased, they usually agreed about everything.

She looked into Marc's bedroom next door. The bed was made, and the room was empty. She walked down the long hallway to the living room. A large wine and blue Chinese rug took up the middle of an impressive room that contained only a massive white sofa and one glass table. Huge bouquets of fresh summer flowers were placed in vases on opposite sides of an imposing fireplace.

She found Marc in his office. Unlike his offices at Jacar, which resembled a men's club library, this room was streamlined: with white Formica cabinets enclosing stereo and video equipment. On one wall there were three television screens in a panel, and in the center of the room was a large white Formica desk with two soft gray leather chairs facing Marc's beige leather recliner. Alexis had designed the office as a surprise for his birthday three years ago, and she liked to say that from behind his desk Marc could press a few buttons and control all the technology in the room.

Marc was on the phone, and motioned for her to come inside and sit down. She blew him a kiss, and sat across from him in one of the two gray leather chairs.

He put down the phone and regarded her with pleasure. "I don't know how you do it," he said, smiling. "You must be the only woman in the world who can look so radiant in the morning."

Marc wore a pale pink Lacoste shirt and a pair of khaki trousers. He was tan, and the sun shining in through the window made highlights on his silver-gray hair. Looking at him, so trim and fit at sixty years old, Alexis thought that she had made the right choice when she married him eighteen years ago. *We make a good team.*

"I wanted to talk to you about Jeff Stein," Alexis began.

"Ah, yes," he said, rustling some papers until he found the one he was looking for. "Well, I have all the information."

"How bad is it?" she said.

"It's quite grim." Marc smiled.

"Oh good," she said. "Tell me."

"Well, first of all Lindel is in far worse shape than Jeff is willing to admit. She's nowhere near ready to record her second album, she's not even writing songs. Apparently, she's in a very deep depression. Tim says it all has to do with that singer she was with on the tour. Brian Davis."

Alexis nodded. She had quietly followed their affair from that night in London at Mr. Chow's through to the final shows at the Academy. It had been a very different Lindel who had run out of Mr. Chow's hand in hand with Brian last winter and the nervous anxious woman Alexis saw backstage in the dressing room on the last night of the tour five months ago. Alexis understood such things, and it was clear to her that Lindel was in pain.

"What else?" she said to Marc.

"Jeff is planning to release a live album of the L.A. shows. Brian's on it. Lindel doesn't know about it, hasn't approved."

Alexis raised an eyebrow. "How could he make a live album without her knowledge?"

"Oh, she knew he recorded it, but he probably just said he was doing it so they'd have it, maybe use it in the future for a radio show, that sort of thing."

"Can he release it if she doesn't want him to?"

"It happens all the time," he said. "And with the contract he has with her, he can damn well do anything he likes, it seems."

"Have you seen the management contracts?"

"No. But I've a pretty good idea of what's in it from the way he's been talking his fool head off for the past year and a half."

Alexis didn't say anything for a minute. She leaned over to the desk and took a cigarette out of a silver box. Lighting it, she leaned back in her chair and looked directly into Marc's bright blue eyes.

"You like her, don't you?" he said suddenly.

Her heart skipped a tiny fraction of a beat, and she didn't answer. Marc knew her so well, he understood her so completely. And there was such trust and honesty between them. Honor among thieves, she thought, wildly.

"Yes," she said softly, "I do." She didn't need to go into it any more than that. It wasn't necessary for him to know the extent of her interest. And, she rationalized, it was understandable that she'd want to set right the embarrassing snubs she had received from Lindel. Although Alexis was sure that it was probably Jeff's fault that she and Lindel had never gotten together; he wouldn't know how to correctly handle such things.

Marc smiled. "Well then, what do you have in mind?"

"First, tell me more."

Marc looked at the sheet of paper in front of him on his desk. "I don't know much more about her. Tim says she looks awful . . ."

"I can't imagine that darling girl looking awful," Alexis muttered.

"Tell me something," Marc said. "As a woman, do you understand the fatal attraction of Brian Davis?"

Alexis paused. "Would you sign him to your label?"

"Of course. He's a great rock singer. One day he'll even be a really great blues singer. And he does have charisma. But I'm talking about as a lover." Marc shook his head. "Someone would have to be insane to get . . . hung up over a musician like that."

Alexis was thoughtful. "Well," she said, softly, "very often the object of an obsession is not nearly as compelling as the obsession itself."

"Perhaps," said Marc. Then, his eyes returning to the paper, he continued, "Jeff's problems, of course, are not unique. Everyone got greedy. So far, Jacar is still doing well, but how could we have known four years ago that the industry would now be in trouble."

"Trouble?"

Marc laughed. "Don't sound so alarmed, my dear. It doesn't affect *us*. But the signs are everywhere. Cutbacks on advances to new groups, smaller promotional and advertising budgets, eliminating lavish press parties and junkets. I've even heard that Acme Records has stopped making promotional T-shirts."

He chuckled. "When they stop making the promotional T-shirts, you know that there's trouble."

"What is Jeff's situation?"

Marc ran his fingers through his hair. He got up and walked to the window, then turned to face Alexis and leaned against the windowsill.

"Well, as I've told you," he said, "the entire industry has become—out of necessity—much more corporate. The companies don't want to take so many chances anymore. People don't have the kind of money to buy records that they did even two years ago. These days if someone has an extra five dollars they'll put gas in their car and go to the beach. Or, they're starting to buy blank cassettes and taping off the radio. I predict that in five—well, maybe eight, years there'll only be four major record companies.

The independent labels will be forced out, it's too difficult for them to financially survive."

"But Valhalla isn't really independent," Alexis argued. "Jacar distributes the records. It's a subsidiary label, really."

"True. So, he needs us for his budget, for his expenses. And," Marc walked behind the desk and sat down, "he's in way over his head. Spends money like a madman. He has practically no capital left and he's made commitments to bands all over the place. As well as being in debt to us."

"But he had a big hit. Surely he made money from her album?"

"When you consider his advances, and his overhead, and tour support, and all the rest of the expenses that ultimately get charged back to her, he's not left with much. He's quite seriously mismanaged it all."

Alexis looked at him. "So what do you have in mind?"

"Well, I have several options. One, I want the girl well, and working again. I believe she has a splendid future. She just needs to get through this bad time. And I have a feeling that you can be a tremendous help with this."

"How?"

"Well, she's going to need some comfort . . ."

"A trip?" Alexis suggested.

"Exactly," said Marc.

"Europe," said Alexis. "Paris . . . Italy . . . the collections. She could come with me to the collections."

Marc smiled. "First let's get Jeff out of the picture, darling."

"Why do you dislike him so much? He doesn't seem so different from a lot of the others."

Marc was silent for a minute. He picked up the phone and pressed the intercom. "Yes, we're in my office. Can we have two coffees? Wait, I'll see." He looked at Alexis. "I already had breakfast, but are you hungry?"

She shook her head no.

"No thanks, just coffee," he said into the phone. Then, hanging up and looking at her again, he said, "I'm not sure what it is about Jeff Stein that bothers me the most. But I get so . . . annoyed at these kids coming in and thinking they can outsmart me. Oh, I know what they say behind my back. They call me the old man, they think I never listen to music anymore. But I was out on the streets along with Jerry Wexler and Ahmet Ertegun discovering some of the greatest singers that ever stood in front of a microphone before the Jeff Steins of the world were even born. You're right, I don't like him, but it's more than his greed, or his attitude, or his . . . almost singular lack of grace. I do not like the way he handles what potentially is one of the really special talents of this time. Lindel should be with us, on Jacar, and I'm determined to move him out of the way."

"Well," smiled Alexis, "I might have a little surprise for you. Remember I told you how I introduced Jeff to Dick in L.A.?"

"Marsden?"

"Yes. I found out that Jeff was in the hotel and I set up a lunch with Dick and Sue. Coincidentally, we just happened to be in the cabana next to Jeff."

Marc smiled. "Go on," he said.

"Well, you should have seen Jeff. He could barely contain his excitement at meeting the great Dick Marsden. It was as if a little kid who just picked up an electric guitar for the first time met . . ." She stopped.

"Eric Clapton," offered Marc.

"Yes. Anyway, Jeff was drooling at the mouth. Dick was perfect. Later, in Jeff's suite, we had cocktails and Dick asked just enough questions about Lindel to get Jeff wondering about his interest. Then Jeff invited Dick to come see her shows, but he was busy and couldn't get to the Roxy. I told Jeff I'd bring him to the Academy, but Dick couldn't make that either. It was just as well. Lindel was so . . . strange that night."

"I remember," said Marc. "Well, well, you are a sly one. So, have they talked since?"

"No, but Dick is waiting for the word from us. If you think it's a good idea, he'll make Jeff an offer."

"I'm pretty sure there's an assignment clause in the management contract," Marc said. "But it would have to be a big offer; it would have to really tempt Jeff, really cover his losses in order for him to consider selling his interest in her. And we wouldn't want Lindel to know right away. Jeff would still have to act as her manager."

"Well, I'm sure that's what Jeff would want, too," said Alexis, excited now. "And Dick understands."

"Of course, I could offer to buy Valhalla from Jeff," Marc said slowly. "There are several options . . ." His voice trailed off. He looked out the window. Alexis lit another cigarette.

Marc turned to Alexis and said, "Tell me, what do you want from all of this?"

"Why . . ." she seemed surprised, "to help you, of course. To do whatever you want to do. And of course," her eyes sparkled, "to have some fun."

Marc laughed. "I do adore you," he said, and just then a maid knocked on the door and came into the room with two coffee cups on a tray.

"I love you too, darling." And Alexis smiled as she accepted the cup of coffee, and began to make plans.

Jeff tossed his brown leather overnight bag into the back seat of his rented chocolate-brown Mercedes. The Garniers had not invited him for the weekend, but he was prepared, just in case. As he drove through the Midtown Tunnel to the Long Island Expressway he planned in his mind just how he would handle this meeting.

It was not unusual for Marc Garnier to hold meetings at his home in East Hampton. During the summers, everyone took long weekends and more business got done in the Hamptons than anywhere else.

So many of the important record people were there; it was much more than a summer vacation and it had nothing to do with rest. It was a place to be seen, a place to wheel and deal, and as such, a house there was a business necessity. Next summer, he vowed, he was going to rent a house there.

Two and a half hours after leaving the city, Jeff pulled up to the large, modern house on the beach. He walked up the steps to the patio that overlooked the ocean. No one was around, and Jeff looked at his watch. He wasn't early; Marc had said to come for lunch at one, and it was exactly one o'clock. He didn't know whether to go into the house or not. He peered through the sliding glass doors but didn't see anyone inside.

He sat down on one of the soft white-cushioned lounge chairs, and looked out at the ocean. A white phone was on a glass table next to him and he resisted the urge to pick it up and call his answering service. The large, round table shaded by a pink umbrella had been set with five places for lunch. Alexis hadn't mentioned who else was coming. He got up and walked to the edge of the patio. There was a pool on the level below, surrounded by bright blue and white striped tentlike cabanas and white terry-covered chaise lounges. No one was there, either.

He looked at the glass doors again, but there was no sign of a doorbell. Maybe this was the back entrance; perhaps he should have come to the front of the house, wherever it was.

This was silly, after all, he had been invited. He went to the door and started to pull it open when a loud alarm suddenly went off. A maid rushed into the living room, Jeff tried to close the door—anything to make that hideous ringing stop—and there was Alexis, cool and poised in a pair of white linen trousers and a long, black, man-tailored silk shirt. She held a drink of something red in her hand—blood, Jeff thought wildly—and she was laughing.

"Jeff, how silly of me. I must have forgotten to turn the blasted thing off. I'm sorry." She walked to the door, turned off a switch, and the alarm stopped.

"I'm mortified," he said. "I didn't see another entrance, and I didn't know what to do . . ."

"Sssh." Alexis came over to him and gave him two kisses in the air. "Let me get you a drink, darling."

A waiter, or houseman, Jeff didn't know which, appeared, and looked inquiringly at Jeff.

"Oh, ummmm, a bloody mary, please."

Alexis nodded her approval, and sat down on one of the lounges. Her hair was pulled off her face into a tight knot, and large, dark sunglasses shielded her eyes. "This is a very mysterious house," she said. "It really changes with the seasons in extremely peculiar ways. In the summer, you absolutely don't see any other entrance except to this patio . . . And there are two entrances. I'll show you later. It's as if the house is so proud of the view back here that it almost commands you to come and look at it at once."

Jeff accepted the drink from the silent houseman and thought to himself how really different rich people were. Alexis probably believed all that stuff about the house, whereas to Jeff a house was either small or large, depending on how much money you had. He remembered with a tight, nostalgic feeling across his chest of how, as a boy, he had gone to visit his grandparents in that little bungalow at Brighton Beach. It had been no more than a tiny, run-down shack, and he had stayed with them for only one week each year. But to him, coming from the Bronx, far away from the ocean, it had seemed as though this was the most glamorous, exciting vacation there could possibly be on earth. Thinking of his grandmother now, living in that old-age home in New Jersey, while he sat here surrounded by pink linen and bloody marys, filled him with a rare sadness. He remembered when he went to visit her in the home and told her that he was president of his own record company. The shrunken, tanned old woman had looked at him with sharp suspicion. Clearly, this was not to be considered a legitimate job. For the rest of that afternoon she had introduced him to her friends: "This is my grandson. He's the president of a major concern." Even now, thinking about it, he had to suppress a smile.

Alexis was still talking about the house and the trouble with the damp and the art. All that was required from him, it seemed, was to nod, look alert, and make a perfunctory noise. His mother . . . why should his mother come to mind? He had bought her the condo in Miami this year and the car and driver on call to take her shopping or to visit her friends. He knew how she bragged about him: "My son, he bought me an apartment. The apartment has a doorman. Then he buys me a car. The car has a driver. So where do I go? From the apartment to the car back to the apartment. My son, he's fixed it so I never have to open a door for myself again."

It was all a far cry from where he sat now. He wondered if he'd ever feel really at home with any of this. He wished he could excuse himself and go into the bathroom for a minute. He needed a bit of cocaine, after that long drive, just to be sure that he'd be sharp for this lunch. Or meeting, whatever it was. On the phone, Alexis had made it sound social, but she did say that Marc had some business thing he wanted to discuss. He hoped it wasn't about Lindel. He was beginning to run out of lies.

Jeff felt his armpits start to get damp. He was nervous, but his mind kept saying that it had to be all right. The old man couldn't have dragged him all the way out here for something unpleasant. After all, his artist was still one of Jacar's top five sellers this last year, and the buzz on his newly signed Electric Toys was good. No, Marc Garnier was no fool. Surely he realized how valuable

Jeff was to the company. Especially in these shaky times, they need all the new, young executive talent they could get. Maybe he could even convince Marc to sign the Marquis. Maybe here, with Marc and Alexis, as a guest in their home, he could turn on the charm and walk away with more than he'd bargained for. If he could just have one little bit of the white powder in the vial in his jeans pocket, he'd feel so much better . . .

Alexis' voice interrupted his thoughts.

" . . . and Marc was telling me you have a wonderful live album of her L.A. shows?"

"It's fantastic," Jeff said, hoping he sounded confident. He couldn't let on that Lindel didn't want it released. "It'll be a smash."

"When do you think you'll release it?" Alexis regarded him closely.

"Well, I'd like to get it out in time for Christmas of course. If we just rush release it we could probably have it in the stores by next month."

"How is Lindel?"

Alexis' penetrating look made him uncomfortable. He wished he could just get away from her for one minute, or that Marc would join them.

"Lindel's great," he said, a bit too loudly. He wondered how much Alexis knew. "She's had kind of a rough time getting used to being back home, and all, and writing new songs was always difficult. It's even harder now that the pressure is on her to top the first album."

Jeff stopped, thinking that perhaps he had talked too much. But Alexis turned her face to the sun, and seemed satisfied with his answer.

Jeff sat for a minute in silence, wondering again where Marc was, and why he had been invited here. Just then, a car pulled into the driveway. Alexis got up and walked to the side of the deck. She waved, and turned to face Jeff.

"You remember Dick and Sue Marsden, don't you?" she said. "They're joining us for lunch."

"Yes," Jeff said, "of course I remember. That's fantastic. It'll be great to talk to him . . . to them, again."

Jeff couldn't believe his good luck. Then he wondered, perhaps it wasn't luck at all. Maybe Dick Marsden had arranged this in order to see *him* again.

As Jeff got up from his chair to greet the Marsdens, he calculated in his head: a half hour for more drinks and casual conversation, then, lunch, maybe another hour. He looked at his watch. By two-thirty he should know exactly what this was all about.

20

"Well, where the hell is he?" Lindel shouted into the phone.

"Don't yell at me," Marcia said calmly. "I just work for the man."

"Oh, I'm sorry, Marsh. I really am. I don't mean to take it out on you. It's just that I'm so nervous, so upset, and I want to find out what's going on."

Marcia transferred the call to the speaker phone on her desk, telling Lindel, "You're on the machine now, so we can talk while I go across the room. But don't worry, no one else is here. Wait, let me close the door."

She got up from behind her desk and closed the door that separated her office from the hallway.

"Okay, let me look through the files again while we talk," Marcia said.

"I cannot believe he thinks he can put that album out. I don't want that album out. He told me he wasn't going to . . ."

"Okay, okay. Now listen, I'm reading the contract."

"What does it say about this?"

Marcia felt sick. She didn't know how to answer Lindel's question without opening up that huge can of worms. Maybe she should just tell her to go to an impartial lawyer.

"Well," Lindel's voice was impatient. "Are you there?"

"I'm looking at it. Lindel, have you read your contract recently?"

"No. You know I hate all that paper. Why?"

"I just can't believe you signed this," she muttered.

"What? I can't hear you. You sound like you're under water."

"I said," Marcia's voice was clearer, stronger now, "I can't believe you signed this."

Lindel sighed. "I was just so anxious to have someone come and take care of all of it, I wanted to make a record so badly. I would have signed a hamburger."

Marcia didn't laugh. She flipped pages. "Well, it doesn't say anything at all in your management contract about whether or not you have to approve of what he does. And in the recording contract, wait ... hold on ... no. He can put out what he likes, according to the way I understand it. Of course, as you've always said, these things aren't written in English, they're just meant to confuse."

"What should I do?"

"Honey, I'm not a lawyer, I can't tell you what to do. Wait a minute." Marcia closed the filing cabinet, went back to the phone, and picked up the receiver. "Okay, I'm back on the phone again."

"Good, I hate that machine. Marcia, I don't know what to do ..."

"Look," said Marcia, "this is the way I see it. You don't want the live album out, right?"

"Right."

"Why not?" Marcia said.

"You know why not. I hate live albums. It's always the obvious move the record company makes when they can't get ... product. They put out live albums when the band is breaking up or when someone's too fucked up to go into the studio ..." She stopped. Neither of them said anything for a few seconds.

Then Lindel continued, "Or they put it out when they've exhausted all the possible singles on the studio album. Too bad I've only got three, because I'll bet if he could, Jeff would have loved to get out a "Greatest Hits" album. Live albums are just a way of milking more money out of the fans. It's obscene to put it out now. It's not as if I've had a five-year career and this represents the best of many tours and it made some sense. This was only my second tour. And, we recorded just the L.A. shows. It represents nothing but one week, and those concerts were meant to be enjoyed and just sort of go out . . . in the air. I never intended for those to be put down as something permanent. A record is . . . *forever,* you know. And Jeff lied to me."

Marcia didn't say anything. She hadn't heard Lindel this impassioned about her music, her work, in a long time.

Then Lindel added, "And honestly Marcia, it's just too painful for me. I don't want to have to hear it. It's a part of my life I want to forget."

"Have you heard the album?"

"I don't have to. I lived it."

"It's not the same. I know how you feel, but maybe you should hear it. It's pretty amazing, really it is. Lindel, a lot of us really miss your voice."

"That's not the point. Jeff misled me. He recorded it under the assumption that it would stay in the vault for years. That's what he said. Not release it now, six months after the tour, just in time for Christmas. If that's not the cheesiest . . ."

"All right, look, calm down. You're going to have to talk to him about it. He's probably on the plane now, in between L.A. and Chicago."

"Why Chicago?"

"He's going to some video convention. He was in L.A. all week with Eyeteeth."

"What were they doing there?"

"Recording. With Robert Diamond."

Lindel gave a short, unpleasant laugh. "Perfect. Jeff's been dying to get a star producer to do something . . . anything. How's Tony?"

"Oh, I guess he's all right," Marcia said. "I don't have that much to do with the band. The girl in Jacar's L.A. office handles Jeff's 'L.A. acts.' You know, though," Marcia felt compelled to say, "Jeff did try to call you several times, he said, last week. He said your line was always busy."

"That's ridiculous. You know I don't take the phone off the hook anymore, I let the service pick up. And I didn't get any messages."

Marcia sighed. She ran her fingers through her short, newly permed auburn hair. "Lin, I don't know what to tell you. He'll call me when he lands in Chicago. Or when he checks into the hotel."

"Which one?"

"Ritz Carlton. So, I'll tell him to call you. But if you don't answer the phone . . ."

"Oh, what difference is it going to make?" Lindel sounded resigned. "I don't know if I even have the strength to fight with him about this right now. I haven't even seen him in nearly a month. Some manager."

Marcia tried to change the subject. "What have you been doing? I miss you. Want me to come over with some dinner and we'll just eat in front of the TV and gossip?"

"No, thanks anyway. I'm really not up for much social conversation. The place is a mess."

"Want me to arrange for a maid?"

"No. I don't want anyone in here."

"I don't like the way you sound."

"Yes, well, I know. I'm just in a funk. Every day I wake up thinking I can make the day be different. I think to myself, this is the day I'm going to just wash my hair, put on some makeup, make a good meal for myself, try to write a song. And then, before I know it, it's eight o'clock at night and I'm still in bed. I've smoked three packs of cigarettes and had nothing to eat and I've done nothing and there's nothing to look forward to except have some wine and passing out in front of the television. And still, Brian won't have called. I remember being with him at night, in different hotel rooms, watching him write songs, listening to him, helping him, encouraging him. And then I think about why isn't he here now, helping me, listening to me? Day after day I think I'll snap out of it. But I'm beginning to think that maybe I won't." She tried to laugh, but her voice cracked. "You know, maybe there really is a thin line between depression and running through the streets naked, screaming . . . putting mashed potatoes in your hair." She stopped, and then said, softly, "Marcia, he just broke my heart."

"I'm coming down there," Marcia said. "I'm really worried, I mean it. I think you need some help. Why should you have to go through this alone?"

"No, I don't want you to come here." Lindel was firm. "Anyway, I wasn't serious. I just need to be alone for a little while longer . . . Promise me you're not coming. Look, I've got to get off. I'll call you later."

The phone clicked in Marcia's ear, and slowly, she replaced the receiver. She sat for a very long time, staring at her desk; at the new carriage clock Marc Garnier had given her for her birthday, at her maroon leather appointment book. Lindel sounded worse than ever. Even though Lindel seemed genuinely upset about the live record, Marcia wondered if her concern about it was real, or just a momentary distraction until her mind switched back to Brian. Something absolutely had to be done.

The next morning Marcia called Jeff and, after he kept her on hold for a full three minutes, he got on the wire and said, "Can we release another single from her record this month?"

"No, I've looked into it," said Marcia. "The pressing plant is way behind because of some fuel problem, and they're not pressing anything other than what they've got on schedule for at least another month."

"Shit," he muttered. "Even with the live album, that's at least another month without any news or product out on her. People are really starting to wonder, there are rumors already in the press. If she keeps this up much longer, her whole career is going to be Pasadena . . ."

Marcia waited.

"What if we put out a story that she's missing?" Jeff said.

"Another one of your great promotional gimmicks," said Marcia. "Like hanging the lead singer."

"Well, goddammit, then think of something. Each day she sits on her ass having a nervous breakdown we're losing money."

"I hate to be the one to mention this," Marcia said, "but could you stop thinking of money for one minute and think about her state of mind? She's really fucked up. You used to care about Lindel, Jeff. What happened to you?"

"Don't give me that human shit," he snapped. "I'm concerned with her state of mind as much as you are, but someone has to think of the practical here. We didn't put two years into this to have it all fall apart now for no good reason. I don't assume that that's what you were working for, either."

"No, but I care about Lindel . . ."

". . . and you think I don't? Jesus, Marcia, you are getting awfully smug. I don't need my secretary to be the best friend of the artist . . ."

"... *what* did you call me?"

"Oh, fuck. You know what I mean. Dammit Marcia, I'm upset. You know I don't think of you as a secretary."

Marcia's voice was cold. "Jeff, I think you'd better come to New York. Lindel needs you." She hung up the phone.

Two weeks later, Jeff stood at Lindel's front door. If it was possible, he thought, Lindel looked even worse than the last time he had seen her.

She just stared at him.

"Aren't you going to ask me in?" he said.

"What happened?" she said. "The phone lines go dead in L.A. and you got restless?"

He walked past her into the apartment. "What the hell has been going on here?" he demanded.

"Not much," she mumbled.

"Lin, baby, what is this? You're falling apart, there's no need for this . . ."

"I'm in no mood for a discussion."

"You're never in the mood for a discussion. What are we going to do?"

"We?" she said.

"Yes, dammit, we. We were supposed to be a team, remember?"

He looked around for a place to sit. The pillows on the couch were dusty, there were clothes thrown all over the room, there wasn't an inch of clean space anywhere. She noticed him looking around.

"Come into the bedroom," she said. "I have to lie down."

The bedroom was worse. The sheets looked as if they hadn't been changed in weeks. Jeff nearly gagged at the sight of the half-eaten hamburger still in its Styrofoam container on the bed, moved it aside, and sat down. He had gotten used to the mess in which musicians lived, but Lindel had been different, and this was worse than anything he'd ever seen.

Lindel lay on the bed, her head against the headboard, lit a cigarette, and stared at him.

"I guess this is the inevitable nervous breakdown," she attempted to joke.

"It's not funny. Maybe you really need some help."

"Oh, please." She made a face. "Don't worry, Jeff, I'll eventually make the next record. You'll get your percentage."

Jeff looked as if she'd struck him. "Lindel," he said, "when did all this happen? I thought we used to be friends. What went wrong?"

She didn't answer.

"I know I've been spending a lot of time in California lately," he said, "with the Toys and Eyeteeth, but a lot of it has to do with you, too. There's so much of the business there now. And besides, I didn't think you wanted me around that much. You didn't want me on the tour . . ."

She put out one cigarette, and almost immediately lit another.

"I shouldn't have let you go off on that tour with Brian," he said. "I knew it. I should have gone with you."

"Oh, stop it." She nearly spat out the words. "I wanted that tour, and I still don't regret it. You never saw me sing better than I did on that tour. Lord knows, you've got the album to prove it."

She stopped, and he didn't say anything. He wouldn't get into a discussion about that album now.

"I don't think there is any way I can possibly explain it to you, Jeff, but I'll try. I've spent weeks, months, trying to sort this thing out. And I think it was just that I wanted something for myself, something that had nothing to do with the business aspect of this music . . . and I got in way over my head. See, I told you it wouldn't make sense."

"Lindel," he said, patiently, "you had a love affair. It's over. It's not so goddamn epic. It happens all the time. You have now spent more time agonizing over it than the amount of time you were with him."

"Talking to you about this," she said, "is like talking to someone on Mars. You've never been involved with anyone, not in this way, you don't feel like this, you're not me."

He tried a different tactic. "I know I'm not you. But this doesn't have to do with love. You know what I think? I'm no shrink, but I think that you're punishing yourself for your success. You don't think you deserve it, so you had to destroy it. Did you ever think about that?"

"Why would I do that?" she said, her eyes wide. "I love to sing. I wanted people to like my music. Stop playing lay analyst."

"Well, did you ever think that he's jealous of you? He sabotaged you, and it worked."

"Brian? Jealous of me? You're crazy."

But he knew he had her interest. She had the kind of attention span so indigenous to one who was obsessively in love. Stay on The Subject—and if possible introduce A New Theory, and you had her completely for as long as you were willing to talk about it.

"I don't think it's so crazy," Jeff said, talking faster now. "He's jealous of you. I saw him in Los Angeles, watching you at the Roxy. He had this look on his face . . ."

"He was probably drunk . . ."

"Honey, I've been around musicians long enough to know drunk when I see it. No, this was something else. It was proud, resentful . . . You do something he can't do. You've got a special kind of sexuality and no matter how great he is onstage, he can't get the same thing across. He's determined to be the best, and nothing, but *nothing* will stand in his way. It doesn't matter if you two had some great . . . common bond, shared, inspired whatever. The minute he feels that you might stand in his way, or take something away from him . . . he had to leave. He's selfish. That's what I think. Notice, you're lying here in this bed, and *he's* in the studio in London."

"I thought he had some feeling for me . . ." Her voice trailed off.

Jeff got up from the bed and started pacing back and forth across the room. "He had as much feeling for you as he can have for anyone other than himself. I'm sure he tried, but believe me, you don't grow up on the streets of London and work your way through that sleazy English music business without learning something about survival. In some instinctive way, hell, it's no secret— he knew that his career would benefit from your relationship."

"So," she looked at him, "you're saying he used me?"

"Partly. I'm sure he did have feelings for you. But I don't think he was ready to settle down and get married just because you two had some great moments together."

"Don't be stupid," she snapped. "Who said anything about settling down? I just didn't want it to end . . . so abruptly . . . like this."

He went over to open the window.

"No, don't," she said.

"It's so stuffy in here," he complained. "Just a crack, it's nice outside. You need some air in here."

He sat down on the bed, facing her. Neither of them said anything for a minute. Then she said, "Look, I'm as smart as you are . . ."

"Oh?" he broke in. "Then why are you lying here, helpless, in this bed?"

"Well, these are my feelings. I can't just turn them off."

"Well then," he put his hands out in an imploring gesture, "take those goddamn feelings and make them work for you. Use them for something positive. Stop seeing your happiness as something he holds in his hands. No one can be that important."

"You're wrong. One person can be that important. People do have great loves."

"But you act as if . . . what? One night he's going to come charging in here, and save you in some spiritual, mystical way? Realize that he can't live without you? Lin, it isn't going to happen. He can live without you very well."

She started to cry. He leaned over to try and comfort her, to take her hand, but she brushed it away.

"Baby, please stop, listen, I'm sorry. Let's not talk about this anymore. I really am just trying to help. Why don't you change your clothes and tie your hair back and we'll go for a walk. You look like you could use some fresh air."

"No," she muttered, as large tears rolled slowly down her cheeks.

"Baby, we've got to pull you out of this. I'm surprised at you."

"Just go away, Jeff. Go away and leave me alone."

Jeff canceled all his appointments in L.A. for the following week, planning instead to stay in New York to see what he could do about Lindel. He tried to get her to go to lunch at the Tea Room, dinner at Elaine's, to the Led Zeppelin concert at the Garden, to Bette Midler's opening on Broadway. She refused to leave her apartment. Even Hank said he couldn't get her to go out.

He went shopping with Marcia to buy Lindel some new clothes; they sent her cartons of groceries, and arranged for a maid to clean up her apartment. None of it seemed to make a difference; she was in a daze, and the pushier Jeff got, the more distant Lindel was.

When she wouldn't pin herself down to a recording schedule, Jeff sent an announcement to the trades that the next studio album had been postponed. She told him that she didn't want the live album out but Jeff went ahead anyway with the plans for its release. He was frustrated, irritated at being in New York with a sick, helpless singer on his hands when he had two working bands who needed him desperately back in L.A. He tried to cheer her up, to get her to react. He suggested going to the Bahamas to record the next album, he mentioned that Madison Square Garden was a very real possibility for the next tour. She seemed completely uninterested.

He left her alone for three days; didn't call or stop by her apartment. He stayed in the office and even worked through lunch nearly every day. Two more days, he decided. I don't hear from her in two days, I go back to the coast.

He wanted to see Lindel one more time before he left. So, after he had packed his suitcase, and made arrangements for a car to pick him up, Jeff figured that he had an hour to go to her apartment, talk to her for a little while, and still make the nine o'clock to L.A.

He could hear The Vipers' record on full blast through the door. This was not a good sign. He rang the bell. No answer. He started banging on the door. Finally, she opened the door. She looked funny; drunk, maybe, and angry.

"Why the hell are you barging in here every two minutes?" she shouted.

"I haven't been here in over a week," he said, pushing past her into the living room, over to the stereo, to turn off the record.

"I call and call and you never answer," he said.

"You know," she said, arms folded, glaring at him, "I really have no privacy at all when you're around."

"What the fuck am I supposed to do?" he yelled. "We were supposed to be a team! We were out to conquer the goddamn *world*. Then we do it, and now what? Is *this* what it's come to? You have really let yourself, and me, down."

They stood there, looking at each other.

"Don't you see what you've done?" he continued. "You've let your emotional problems take over your whole life, and you act as if this just happened to you. You have turned yourself into some pathetic . . . *victim,* like the tragic, rejected lover, and it didn't have to be that way at all."

She didn't say anything, she just stared at him.

"He could have been someone who could have just come in and out of your life," Jeff continued. "It could have been a nice thing when you were together, you didn't have to turn into . . . *Camille* over it."

"Are you through attacking me?" she said, very quietly.

"I am not attacking you," he said, trying to calm down. He went and sat on the couch, and turned around to face her. "I care about you; why do you think I've put so much emotional time and energy into you?"

She laughed, a short, bitter laugh. "I suppose the twenty-five percent had nothing to do with it."

"I'll walk right out of here if you insult me again." He was clearly upset. "I can get twenty-five percent, and more, from any of the fifty bands who have been begging me to manage them for the past year. Anyway, I don't fucking need to be here. Technically I'm not even your manager anymore . . ."

"What?" She stared at him.

His mind was racing. He hadn't meant to say that.

"What did you say?"

He fumbled with the thin gold chain around his neck and desperately wondered how he was going to be able to explain. Finally, he said, "Oh, fuck it, you might as well know the truth. We needed money, so I sold my interest in you to Dick Marsden. He's got a big management company in L.A. But it doesn't really affect you, it's just a technicality."

"What do you mean, you sold your interest in me? What do you mean, *we* needed money? What are you talking about?" Her eyes were blazing.

He paced back and forth, avoiding her eyes, talking quickly. "Lin, baby, it's just business. Details. It doesn't really change anything. There were over a hundred thousand dollars in recording costs before we recouped a dime, and who the hell do you think paid for you and The Vipers to fly around the country and stay in all those fancy hotels . . ."

"How much did you get for me, Jeff? How much was I worth?"

"Lin, baby, cut it out." He reached for her hand, but she shoved it away. She jumped up from the couch, walked to the fireplace, and gave him an accusing stare.

"I'm still acting as your manager," he said quickly. "You don't even have to know about it. It doesn't make a difference."

"I asked you," she hissed, *"how much did I go for?"*

He tried a different tone. "I am not going to fight about this. I did what I had to do for business. It was as much for you as it was for me. When you're calmer, and feeling better, we can sit down and I'll explain the whole thing to you. But now . . ."

"Get out!"

"What?"

"I said," she shrieked, *"get out of here! Now. I don't care if I ever see you again!"*

Something exploded in his brain. Artists. They were all alike. So ungrateful. If she had any idea of what he had gone through for her . . .

"I said get out!" She was screaming now, her face red and twisted.

He grabbed his suitcase, and, shaking with rage, he looked at her.

"Go to hell, Lindel," he said, between clenched teeth, and walked past her, and slammed the door.

She immediately went to the bedroom, picked up the phone and dialed Marcia's number.

"Why didn't you tell me?" Lindel cried into the phone.

"What are you talking about?" Marcia sounded sleepy.

"Are you asleep?"

"No . . . I guess I dozed off. What time is it? What happened?"

"Jeff . . . He said that he sold his twenty-five percent of me. What does that mean? How could he do that? And why?"

Marcia was silent.

"Hello?" Lindel said.

"I'm still here. Oh, god, this is such a mess . . ."

"Marcia, what is going on?"

"All right, I'll probably be fired, maybe even sued, but you're my friend and I love you and I better give it to you straight."

Lindel waited.

"He is acting as your manager, for a rather large fee, I might add, but he sold his interest in you to Dick Marsden."

Lindel turned on the small lamp next to her bed, put out her cigarette, and immediately lit another one.

"That's what he told me," Lindel said, "but I don't understand any of this."

"Marsden Management. Apparently they handle all these movie stars, actors, I think politicians too. And they have some video interests, something to do with cable television. And Jeff is interested in cable, all of a sudden. Between you and me, I think he eventually wants to phase out of the record business. Although, who knows anymore with him, he probably thinks he can do both . . ."

"Go on." Lindel's voice was impatient.

"And so," Marcia continued, "when it became painfully apparent that he was broke . . ."

"Broke?"

"Broke. He needed money. Fast. He had no money to pay for the Toys' recording sessions, and he needed money for operating expenses—his operating expenses are very high—and so, well, he sold his interest in you to them. Just the management part, though, not the records, or the publishing . . ."

"How much was I worth?"

"Lindel, please, I know you're upset . . ."

"I'm curious, really. How much was I worth?"

"Lindel, I don't even know. I only found out two weeks ago. He doesn't even know that I know. I mean I've been suspecting for some time that things weren't right, but . . ."

"Why didn't you tell me?"

"Oh, god," Marcia's voice cracked. "Don't you think I wanted to? At first, I thought he told you. Then, when I realized that he hadn't, I didn't know what to do. You were so upset about Brian and I just didn't think I'd be a good friend by dumping all of this on you now."

"How could he just 'sell' me like that?"

"Well, I did try to tell you about your contract. He can, because there's an assignment clause in there that gives him the right. But it's worse. You've got to see a lawyer. I think he's really mismanaged you."

"I can't believe this . . . I'm not hearing this . . ."

"Listen to me." Marcia's voice was firm. "I'm not sure of all the details, but I've been quietly keeping my eye on things for some time, and I talked to a lawyer. Honey, Jeff's been ripping you off. He charges things to your account that have nothing to do with you. Unbelievable long-distance phone bills. Travel. For other bands. His car. His apartment. Things related to the Toys . . . to Eyeteeth . . . He misled you, he takes percentages from your records as your manager, but there's a specific clause in your contract that says he doesn't have to act on your behalf as manager when dealing with his own record company. He's been talking about leasing a private plane for your next tour from a company he owns part of. I'm sure he gets kickbacks from that Fly-By-Night travel agency he uses which his *cousin* owns. Your insurance hasn't been taken care of . . ." Marcia sighed.

Then she said, "Lindel, you told me you'd sign anything back in those days, and I hate to say it honey, but you did. But there really is a helluva case against him, and . . ."

"Stop it," Lindel said. "Don't go on, I can't bear to listen. I know you're trying to help, but . . . not now. I'll call you in the morning." She hung up.

Lindel couldn't believe it. He did this. To her. Sold her. Betrayed her.

First Brian, now Jeff. She fought with him, sometimes she hated his guts, but he had been her manager for almost two years. She had trusted him.

What on earth was she going to do?

21

Marc Garnier didn't seem at all surprised when Lindel telephoned. He suggested that she see him in his office as soon as possible. "Don't worry," he said, sounding his paternal best, "I'll take care of this. Come for lunch."

The morning of the lunch with Marc, Lindel took special pains with her makeup, and wore what Tim had once laughingly referred to as her best rock star outfit: tight black leather jeans, a sheer red chiffon blouse, black silk jacket, and thigh-high black leather boots. Marc Garnier would see her looking good.

She was on time, and was ushered into the executive dining room where Marc was waiting. He greeted her with a hug, looked at her and said, "Lindel, you look fabulous."

She smiled. "Thanks, but I have seen better days."

The last time she'd been in here was with Jeff, when she had posed for photos with the platinum album. Things were so different now; there was no celebratory spirit, it was just the two of them, fussed over by a waiter wearing a tuxedo. Lindel felt sad.

Lunch was shrimp cocktail, steak au poivre, watercress salad, and red wine. Lindel barely touched her food, and Marc made no reference to the fact that she smoked through the entire meal.

"How can he do this?" Lindel came straight to the point.

Marc sighed. "Lindel, I saw this coming. But I can't get in the middle of our artists and their managers. He has gotten completely out of hand. Do you know at the convention, right next to the cardboard cutouts of you, the Electric Toys, all the bands, he had one of himself? He absolutely thinks he's as important as the artists."

"What am I going to do?"

"First of all, you are not to worry about it. I promise you, we'll take care of it. There are things you don't know about that he did involving your publishing, your foreign rights . . ."

"Like what?"

"Oh," Marc waved his hands, "it's not necessary for us to go into that now."

"No, please. I want to know."

"Well, for a start, he sold your publishing, which was always in his name, completely, to Royal Records, in return for a deal for Eyeteeth. That's just one thing."

"And selling my management like that," Lindel shook her head. "How did that happen? I can't even remember if he ever mentioned Dick Marsden to me. I have no idea how he met him, how it happened. . ."

"Lindel, don't worry about any of these details," Marc said smoothly. "This isn't your job."

"But there was that assignment clause in the contract," Lindel said. "I was dumb enough to sign it . . ."

"It doesn't matter," said Marc, drinking the wine. "There is something called a breach of trust . . . fiduciary duty . . . fraud, undue influence, the lawyers can explain it to you. He may have had the right under that contract to do what he did, but that contract is, from what I've been able to figure out, worthless. It was misleading. You didn't have a lawyer at the time, he misrepresented himself to you, he didn't give you accurate accountings of album or publishing royalties, of expenses. Believe me, he did not look out for your best interests. Obviously, he looked out for *his* best interests. It's an old story, Lindel, and I'm sorry you got caught up in it, but I must say I have never seen quite so many indignities brought to bear on one artist."

"Why did he do it? How could he have been so . . . stupid?"

"He didn't think he was being stupid. I'm sure he can justify it. You have to understand one thing about this business. Just as there is the old cliché about the artists getting ripped off, there have been those artists who have had one hit, and then decide to drop their managers, thinking they don't need them anymore. I'm sure he was just trying to protect himself."

"Marcia said it was like divorce. Two people who start out loving and trusting each other . . . and then . . ."

"I know, it is most unpleasant. Most unpleasant. But I assure you, he doesn't have a leg to stand on. Particularly with the battery of lawyers we have here." Marc chuckled. "There's no way he'll be able to hold on to you."

"What can I do?" Lindel looked at him. She was upset.

"Well, what do you want to do?"

She didn't answer right away. She looked down at her dessert plate, and picked at the grapes. Everything had turned into a nightmare.

Finally she said, "I want to sing. Make more records, if I can ever write a song again."

"My dear, I promise you will write songs again."

She shook her head, slowly. "I don't know. So far all I have are bits of lyrics on matchbooks and napkins. I think I forgot how to do it."

"I'm sure it seems that way now, but in time, you'll see, it will be better."

She looked into his eyes and took a deep breath. "Can I . . . I mean, would it be possible for me to make records for Jacar?"

Marc beamed. "I thought you'd never ask. Of course, we'd be honored to have you."

She let out an audible sigh of relief. Marc laughed. "You didn't really think there was any doubt, did you?"

"Well . . ." She smiled. "I'm trying not to count on too much, anymore. But how would this all work? I mean, I'm still signed to his record company . . . and what about Dick Marsden? Where does that fit in?"

"Technically, the way the artist inducement letter that you signed is written, if he breaches your contract, then you record directly for us. And don't worry about Dick Marsden. Leave everything to me," Marc instructed. "The important thing is to get you back to work." He looked at her closely. "It has gone past the chance of reconciliation with Jeff, hasn't it?"

"Absolutely. I'm not a total lunatic."

"My dear," he chuckled, "I don't think you're a lunatic at all."

Marc pushed his chair back, away from the table.

"Let's go back into my office, shall we?"

They got up, and walked across the hall into the large, elegant corner suite. They both sat down on the leather couch against the wall. Lindel sipped at the red wine, and Marc lit a cigarette.

"Jeff thinks he's a power in this industry," he said. "Well, he hasn't been around long enough to realize that he started his rise with my support. I've helped a lot of careers in this industry. Look at Carl Willis. I invented him, I'm sorry to say. Know why? Because every time some manager would come to me with a tape, I would say, 'Talk to Carl Willis,' or 'I have to ask Carl Willis.' Eventually, they all got the idea that perhaps they should just tell Carl Willis. So, he became important. And I could stay out till five in the morning and come in to work at ten, knowing that Carl Willis was taking care of things."

Lindel laughed.

"Of course," Marc added, "then he went and took over a competitive company. But, to get back to Jeff, without my seal of approval, who do you think is going to take that . . . little putz, as he would put it, seriously?"

Marc continued. "Just remember, Jeff never had a hit record. You had the hit record. You can get anyone to make the phone calls or accept the offers, but he's not able to do the singing."

"I won't be either, if I don't cut down on this smoking." She ground out the cigarette in the large glass ashtray on the table in front of them.

Marc continued, his voice louder now. "I want you really to know that he didn't make you all that money, and he didn't make you a star. You did that, with your talent. Your songs, your voice, your work."

She began to feel a little bit better.

"I think you should take a few weeks off," said Marc.

Lindel made a face. "I've done nothing but take time off for the past six months."

"That's not what I mean," said Marc. "You've been feeling guilty about not doing the album. You haven't had a real vacation in some time."

"That's what I told Jeff."

"Why don't you get away? Somewhere completely out of context. Where no one is going to bother you about being Lindel

James. Have a real holiday. We'll pay for whatever it costs. I consider it an investment."

"Marc, that's kind of you, but I wouldn't even know where to go."

"Don't you have anyone you'd like to travel with?"

"No," she said, very softly. "Not really. I guess Marcia is my best friend, but technically she still works for Jeff, and it would look funny if she took a vacation with me."

"You're right. Besides, we need her around right now. She will, I suspect, prove very helpful to us. No one else?"

Lindel shook her head.

"Tim?"

"Not in such a large dose."

Wasn't it amazing, thought Marc, how this lovely girl, this star, who had thousands of fans, millions of fans, had so limited herself in her personal life. She didn't even have anyone special with whom she could go on a vacation.

"I have an idea," he suddenly said. "My wife is going to Paris for some dress collections," he smiled, "and then was thinking of spending a week in Italy."

Italy, she thought. Where she had wanted to go with Brian.

"Maybe you'd like to accompany her," said Marc.

Lindel looked at him with surprise. To go with Alexis Garnier to Europe? But why? Surely she, a rock and roll singer, would be hopelessly out of place in Alexis' world.

"Oh, no," she said, "I couldn't do that. But it's very sweet of you to suggest it."

"I'll tell you the truth," he twinkled, "this was Alexis' suggestion. She wanted to call you herself, but thought it might seem strange." He leaned back against the couch. "I think it will take us at least several weeks to even begin to straighten any of this out with Jeff. I don't think you should be here during that time. You'd just be checking in with Marcia every day and it wouldn't have a good . . . effect on you. A change of scene is needed. In fact," he smiled, "a change of scene is ordered."

Lindel didn't know what to say.

"Why don't you think about it?" Marc said. "I don't think it would just be you two girls alone. I think some other friends of Alexis' will be there, and it might be fun. I assure you, you haven't seen Paris or Rome until you've seen them with my wife."

It certainly was a peculiar idea. But then, thought Lindel, why not? Maybe it would be amusing. And it would make Jeff furious; Alexis' obvious lack of interest in him had always been a source of embarrassment to his ego.

"I have some money in the bank," she said slowly, "but I don't think I could possibly afford to go in the manner to which your wife is accustomed."

"I can't even afford to go in the manner to which my wife is accustomed." He laughed. "But you're not to worry about it. The trip would be a bonus. It's the least we can do. After all, we have to keep you happy."

"I couldn't accept that," Lindel said, "really, I'd insist on paying you back."

"Well, let's not worry about that now," said Marc, standing up. "As I said, think about it for a day or two. I could have Alexis call you with the details, and then you could make up your mind."

Lindel impulsively leaned over and gave Marc a kiss. "I really want you to know that I appreciate all of this."

"Lindel," he said, looking directly into her eyes, "without you, without the talented musicians who make the music, none of us would be here. I don't ever forget that, and I don't want you to, either."

He walked her to the elevator, took her downstairs where his car and driver waited to take her home. Then he turned, slowly, and walked back into the building, ready to wage war.

Lindel had almost drifted off to sleep when the phone rang.

"Did you hear?" It was Tim.

"Mmmm, what?"

"As my mother used to say, I hope you're sitting."

"I'm half asleep, what is it?"

"Well, I thought you would want to be among the first to know . . ."

"Tim . . ."

"Well . . . Lucy died two days ago."

"What?" Lindel sat up.

"I said Lucy . . ."

"What happened?" she broke in.

"I'm not sure. I was in the Grotto, and everyone was talking about it. I rushed right home to call you. I guess it was an old-fashioned O.D."

"Pills?"

"No. I think she thought she was snorting coke and someone gave her heroin. Cut with something. I'm not really sure, but her heart stopped, and by the time they got her to the hospital it was too late . . ."

"Who's 'they'?"

"These really low-rent drug trash she's been hanging out with lately. It's a good thing Hank wasn't mixed up in it."

"Hank? Why would he be?"

"She'd been trying to hang out with him and he was too nice to say no. But I knew this was going to happen. I even said that I hadn't seen her in the Grotto for three nights, and if she missed three nights in the Grotto, she must be dead. Now I'll never get that two hundred dollars she owed me."

Lindel hung up. She automatically dialed Marcia's number.

"Marcia, did you hear about Lucy?"

"I just heard. Tim's on my other line."

"That harbinger of doom. Get him off. I need you."

Marcia put her on hold for two seconds, and returned to the line.

"I feel so awful, Marsh."

"Lindel, it's not your fault."

"I know, but it's so creepy. I don't know, somehow I feel guilty. . ."

"Lindel, stop it. I hate to sound so cold-blooded, but she did this to herself. You had nothing to do with it."

Lindel reached around behind her and propped another pillow in back of her head.

"Do you know if there's some kind of a service, or something for her? Shouldn't I do something?"

"Tim told me that he had been trying to tell you but that you hung up on him—good for you—that her parents apparently just whisked her body out of the city. I think she was cremated. They didn't want to have anything to do with her New York rock and roll friends."

"I can't believe it," Lindel said. "I mean, we hadn't really spoken in awhile but I guess I just sort of assumed that she'd always be around. I feel awful. She used to be so sweet, she really had been interested in me. I feel like I let her down . . ."

"*Stop it.* Just because she's dead is no reason to turn her into a saint. Lindel, she's another rock casualty. Live fast, die young. She'd been on the fringe for a long time, and hooking up with you had been her only big score. You legitimized her, then what did she do with that? She had nothing, really, to offer, except a parasitic groupie personality. Every favor she did for you was designed not only to further her own standing, but to increase your dependency on her. I'm sorry that she died, but she was a very self-destructive girl. Life is really too precious to screw around with drugs like that. You have nothing to feel guilty about. You didn't stick those drugs into her system."

After Lindel had hung up the phone, she thought about what Marcia had said. Marcia was tough, but perhaps she was right. Still, Lindel felt awful. She couldn't be cavalier about it. Even though drug casualties and accidental, even purposeful deaths were a fact of life in rock and roll, they had always been something that happened to other people, not to anyone close to her.

It was as if she had started out, just those few years ago, with a big, beautiful crystal ball. And she had held it in her hands and looked into it and saw a glorious future. And then, suddenly, the glass exploded and shattered into tiny pieces. She didn't know how she was going to make life fit back together again. She needed to try and make some sense of all of this. Marc Garnier was right; she needed to get away.

22

The limousine arrived in the morning and the minute Lindel got in the car, Alexis handed her a glass of freshly squeezed orange juice, laced with champagne.

"Medicine." Alexis smiled.

Instantly, Lindel felt herself begin to relax. She smiled at Alexis, and for one second she felt the way she used to—it seemed like ages ago—on her first tour. As if she was starting out on an adventure. That drive to the airport always represented some kind of beginning. Lately she had been so bogged down with problems, she had forgotten what freedom even a plane ride could bring.

At JFK, the two of them were quickly ushered into the Concorde lounge, where the public relations man for the airlines gave them more champagne, and offered a silver tray filled with tiny sandwiches.

"I never eat before, or on the plane," Alexis murmured to Lindel, who had also declined the food. "It's so bad for the skin. Of course, you'll find that they try to dress it up a bit on this flight," said Alexis. "But don't be fooled. The caviar isn't Iranian, and the paté is usually a mousse." She wrinkled her nose in distaste.

Lindel had to force herself to keep a straight face. So, this was the way it was going to be. It certainly was a far cry from traveling with Jeff.

The Concorde was smaller than Lindel had expected; the seats were cramped, almost like the tourist section of a regular 707. But that was where the comparison ended.

The large digital clock at the front of the cabin was a constant reminder of how fast they were going. It was scary, but thrilling, too. The stewardesses brought little gifts: slippers, satin eyeshades, perfume, tiny bottles of brandy, and cigarettes. Would there ever be a time, Lindel wondered, when French cigarettes did not remind her of Brian?

She drank champagne, and closed her eyes. Next to her, Alexis thumbed through an issue of French *Vogue*. Lindel was glad that she didn't seem required to talk much. The worst thing was to travel with someone who wanted to talk all the time, like Jeff.

It was just twilight when they arrived in Paris, and the street lamps were starting to make pink spotlights on the boulevards as they drove in from the airport, up the Champs Elysees, to the Hotel Georges Cinq.

Alexis' two-bedroom suite was filled with flowers, with several buckets of iced champagne, baskets of fruit, and all the newest French fashion magazines carefully laid out on a large coffee table. It was impossible for Lindel not to compare: for the past two years her public stance had been defensive, rock and roll demanded a certain swagger. But now, in these opulent surroundings with Alexis, she felt hesitant, almost shy.

"Do you want to go out," Alexis asked, "or just have a quiet supper here, unpack, and start fresh in the morning?"

"Oh, I'd much rather stay in." Lindel was grateful. "Unless you have plans. I always sort of like to get organized first."

"Good," said Alexis, "me too. I'll order a supper for us, unless there's something special that you want . . .?"

"Whatever you get will be fine."

Lindel walked into her own room. The bed was large, with an ornate wooden headboard. A glass chandelier hung from the ceiling. There was an antique writing desk, two heavily carved chests of drawers, and a blue Oriental carpet on the floor. Lindel began to unpack. First she took out her portable tape recorder and cassettes: a few blank cassettes in case she got an inspiration for a song in the middle of the night, her favorite Rolling Stones, Otis Redding, and Velvet Underground tapes. The tape of her live album, the one with Brian on it, the one she wasn't sure if she should bring. But having it with her made her feel in touch with the familiar obsession that had taken over her life the past year. She wasn't able to totally let go. Not yet. The tape machine and cassettes looked startlingly out of place in this room.

She opened the huge closet. There were rows of blue quilted satin hangers, dozens of polished wood drawers inside the closet, and a separate small closet just for shoes. She had been unsure of what to bring, so had ended up with almost her entire wardrobe, which still wouldn't fill half this closet space.

After changing into T-shirt and jeans, she walked back into the living room and found Alexis instructing the room service waiter to set up the table. Alexis wore heavily embroidered purple and gold satin pajamas.

"Oh," Lindel stopped, "I should change . . ."

"Don't be silly, darling," said Alexis. "You look fine. It's just us, after all. This sort of thing happens to be what I'm most comfortable in."

"I've never seen you with your hair like that," Lindel said. "It looks nice."

Alexis smoothed her straight blonde hair which fell to her shoulders. She looked admiringly at Lindel and walked over to her. Putting her arm casually around Lindel's waist, she gently turned her so that the two of them faced the large mirror above the fireplace. "Did you realize that we're both just about the same height?," Alexis said. "And with my fair coloring and your dark beauty, we make a marvelous looking pair, don't we?"

She moved away and went over to the coffee table to light a cigarette. "Anyway," she said, "I wish I could wear jeans, but I'm afraid I would look hopelessly ancient and foolish."

"That's ridiculous," said Lindel, smiling, "your figure is better than mine."

"Well, it's not, although I must say I do work hard at it. But you're still in your twenties. It makes a big difference, believe me, when you're in your . . . ah, late thirties."

So, Alexis had a thing about her age. Lindel knew that the woman was surely in her late forties, perhaps even older. But she wore it well. I hope I look that good at her age, thought Lindel, and they sat down to eat.

Supper was beautiful, cold boneless breasts of chicken on leaves of pale green lettuce. There was an endive salad, with a vinaigrette sauce, and a chilled bottle of Taittinger champagne. Small french breads were in pink linen-lined silver bowls. The waiter poured the champagne, then left the room, and Alexis chatted about Paris, and her friends. After just one drink, Lindel felt slightly giddy. It was surreal; sitting in this large room with a stranger, drinking champagne . . .

" . . . or maybe you'd like to hear some music," said Alexis.

"I'm sorry, I was drifting . . ."

"I said, maybe you'd like to hear some music. I have no idea what's on, but we could call Jacar's office here and they could find out. Perhaps they could take you around?"

"Oh no," Lindel said quickly. "I don't even want to see those people if we can help it. No work. Please?"

Alexis smiled. "I have no intention of making you work. Please, let's just forget that I'm the wife of the record company president, okay? Really Lindel, I want you to think of me as your friend."

"Why, I do . . ." Lindel stammered.

"No, really." Alexis' gaze was penetrating, direct. "I know what you must think. That I'm one of those bored jet set types and a rock star is a new kick."

Lindel was embarrassed. "Well," she said, recovering, "frankly, I did wonder what it was you saw in me."

Alexis chuckled. "My dear, of course I'm bored. Most of my friends talk about furniture, or clothes, and while those are among my interests, a steady diet of that can be a bit taxing."

She got up and walked over to the large blue silk sofa, and lit a cigarette. "I'm not a rock and roll fan," Alexis continued, "but I have liked your music ever since Marc first brought your record home. I sensed a . . . kindred spirit. We're both strong women, we tend to be loners, and we need privacy. I don't have that many close women friends, Marc is really my best friend. And when I heard about you being at such . . . loose ends at the moment, I thought it would be a marvelous idea for you to come on this trip. I'd like to know you better. And I think we'll have fun."

"I certainly appreciate it," said Lindel. "I guess I've been kind of a basket case lately." She tried to laugh.

"Oh, please," said Alexis. "I don't believe that. You need a rest, that's all. And some good times."

They sat in silence for a moment, the smoke from Alexis' cigarette curling above her head in little cloudlike patterns. Suddenly she said, "Do you know how all those other wives look at me at those awful music business dinners? They're jealous because I get my name in *Women's Wear,* or some such foolish thing. I don't have their problems: we chose not to have children, so I'm not stashed away on Long Island while my husband sleeps with his secretary on the upper West Side. The . . . society women I know make fun of Marc and me behind our backs because we entertain rock stars; yet they're all dying to meet some."

Lindel was surprised at Alexis' bitter tone. Sitting there, cool and imperious on that blue silk couch, her face framed by icy blonde hair, her mouth accentuated by a slash of bright red lipstick, she looked unapproachable. Yet, she sounded quite human, even tender. Lindel felt a rush of sympathy for the woman, and a sudden impulse to confide.

"I know what you mean," said Lindel. "When I had my hit, so many things changed. Everyone started acting differently toward me. I got so tired of people tiptoeing around. The only one who didn't was Brian. But he just . . . disappeared."

"Well," said Alexis, "from what I gather about Brian Davis, he must be a frustrating person to become involved with. Somehow, even though he doesn't do it in a mean way, he seems to be the type of man who does exactly what he wants to do. Some people just have a way of wriggling out of things when they feel others closing in on them."

"I tried not to," said Lindel. "I just got so completely . . . carried away . . . I never made any real demands on him."

"Well," Alexis smiled, "I know I probably sound like an old, wise woman, but I promise, you will have your revenge."

Lindel looked thoughtful. "I don't want revenge," she said.

"Mmm," Alexis lit another cigarette, "we'll see."

The air was heavy with the smell of Alexis' perfume, and the cigarette smoke. The champagne and the trip had made Lindel sleepy. She tried to hold back a yawn, but Alexis was quick to notice.

"Time for sleep," she said, walking over to Lindel and leaning over to kiss her on the cheek. "We'll have a splendid day tomorrow." And she turned to walk into her room, closing the door behind her.

Hours later, Alexis lay in bed, staring at the ceiling. She had watched the end of a movie on television, read several magazines, and she still couldn't sleep. She got up, put on a white silk robe and walked out into the living room. The room service tables had been taken away, and the door to Lindel's bedroom was closed. Alexis stood there for quite some time, and then turned slowly to walk back into her own room.

Paris, with Alexis Garnier, was not like the Paris Lindel had seen the time she'd been there with Jeff and the band to do a concert. Early the next morning the black Citroen limousine was waiting for them in front of the hotel, and after a breakfast of croissants and hot chocolate at the Cafe de la Paix, Alexis instructed the driver to take them to the Bois de Boulogne. They spent a few hours in the beautiful private gardens, then went to L'Orangerie, where the linen and the roses were white and Alexis told Lindel wonderful stories of her travels with Marc. After lunch, the car dropped them off in the Rue Faubourg St. Honore, and Lindel watched in fascination as Alexis went through each shop looking at signature silk scarves, alligator handbags, and suede shoes, arranging for things to be delivered to the hotel. She had an impeccable eye; and Lindel thought with amusement that watching Alexis shop was like watching a great lead guitarist onstage.

They went to the bar at the Hotel Ritz for a late afternoon cocktail.

"Champagne?" Alexis looked at Lindel.

"This is all a bit rich for my blood," Lindel protested, as the waiter brought the bottle. "How will I ever get used to Ramada Inns and greasy spareribs again after this?"

"Well, you don't have to worry about that for awhile," smiled Alexis. "You know, I always fast for a week before I come here. It's the only way. What would you like to do tonight?"

"I don't care," said Lindel, stirring the swizzle stick in her drink, making the bubbles rise. "Whatever you like."

"These friends of ours are here, and they want us to join them for dinner. They're dying to meet you. Or, we could escape, and do something silly—like go to the Crazy Horse, or one of those big, touristy drag shows. Then we could meet up with these people later, at Castel's, or New Jimmy's."

"I've never been to any of those places, so whatever you want to do sounds fabulous. I just want to take a nap before dinner. I . . . haven't been sleeping too well."

"Neither have I," said Alexis, with a peculiar little smile. She looked closely at Lindel. "Do you want some Valium?"

"No, thanks. It makes me depressed the next day."

"Well, I have some if you change your mind. But a nap is a good idea. I could use one myself."

That night they went to a tiny, cavelike restaurant where Lindel ate the best food she had ever tasted. Alexis took her to Le Crazy Horse where gorgeous girls who looked like sex changes performed a cabaret show. The next stop was El Alcazar for a drag show; and while Lindel thought that it wasn't as good as some Tim had taken her to, she wouldn't have dared say so and spoil Alexis' obvious pleasure. At Castel's they met some of Alexis' friends, and by three in the morning Lindel was flushed, exhausted, and had a splitting headache from too much champagne. She signaled to Alexis, who was on the dance floor with a tall young man whose name Lindel forgot.

"It's been fabulous, but I'm really tired. Maybe it's delayed jet lag. Can I take the car back to the hotel?"

"Nonsense," said Alexis, "we'll go together. I've about had it here, too." She turned and gave the young man two kisses in the air, and maneuvered Lindel out of the club.

At two A.M. they stood in the middle of the living room of the suite, and Lindel felt strangely hesitant. Alexis looked Lindel straight in the eye, leaned over and kissed her on the mouth. "Goodnight," she whispered, and walked into her own room as she had the night before, slowly shutting the door behind her.

Lindel was stunned. Why had she done that?

No . . . she was tired, Alexis was tired. They both had had far too much to drink. It was Paris. It didn't mean anything.

Alexis could not sleep. She had been lying in bed for a half hour, and her eyes were still wide open and her heart was racing. This wouldn't do at all.

Slowly, she got out of bed and put on a pair of black tailored pants and a severely cut white silk blouse. She picked up a pair of dark glasses, put on low-heeled shoes and threw her sable coat over her shoulders. She opened the door that led directly from her bedroom to the hallway, and waited for the elevator to take her down to the lobby. The taxi drove up to the Rue Vieux Colombier, and Alexis recognized the brightly lit sign.

When the eyes that peered through the peephole at the Club Katmandou saw that she was female, and alone, the door opened and she walked inside, down the stairs and into the dark club. She sat at a small round table and ordered a brandy from the blonde waitress. As her eyes grew accustomed to the light, she saw women together, talking, dancing, kissing.

She saw the girl almost immediately. She had huge dark eyes and was dressed all in black. She looked almost waiflike, frightened, but she stared at Alexis, and when Alexis returned the look, she came right over to the table.

She looked at Alexis questioningly, indicated a chair, and Alexis nodded yes, sit down.

"Do you want a drink?" Alexis said, in perfect French.

"Yes," said the girl. Alexis looked around for a waitress, and they sat in silence for a few minutes, watching the women on the dance floor.

"Would you like to dance?" said the girl.

Alexis shook her head no.

"What's your name?" Alexis asked.

"Annette," she said. "What's yours?"

"Marguerite," she said. It still amused her to use different names, but it was protection, too.

"You're from New York?" said Annette.

"It's that obvious?"

"You look like you're from New York."

Alexis smiled and looked at Annette, who now watched the dance floor. She really was quite pretty. Probably wasn't older than twenty-five. Shiny black caplet of hair, those big, wide eyes. It would be so nice just to hold someone tonight, someone anonymous, someone sweet. She just couldn't be alone in that room. She didn't want to think about Lindel.

Marvin Gaye's "What's Goin' On" was playing on the sound system. Alexis drank her second glass of brandy, Annette drank a gin fizz. After a few minutes, Alexis said, "Do you want to come with me? I'm going back to my hotel."

Annette nodded.

The area around St. Germain des Pres was quiet, empty. A motorcycle sped by, there were a few people in the streets as Alexis and Annette walked up the Rue de Rennes to St. Germain des Pres to get a taxi.

Back at the hotel, Alexis avoided the door to the main part of the suite and opened the door to her bedroom. Fortunately, she had thought in advance to leave a chilled bottle of champagne and two glasses next to the bed. Of course, she had hoped that she would not be sharing it with a stranger.

Alexis left on only one small light, and she opened the champagne and poured a glass for Annette, who sat on the edge of the bed.

Annette smiled, and started to undress. Slowly she removed her jeans, and sweater, and started to unclasp a small strand of pearls around her neck.

"No," whispered Alexis, "leave them on."

Annette smiled, and stood in front of Alexis, wearing only black lace bikini underpants. It made a startling contrast to her pale skin. She looked at Alexis, and whispered something Alexis didn't hear, and then Alexis undressed and moved over to Annette and gently pulled her down onto the bed.

"You're so pretty," she whispered in French to Annette, "so pretty . . ." Annette returned her kisses; soft, warm gentle kisses, then more urgent, more demanding. Annette was soft, all curves, and Alexis felt the heat rise in her body. Alexis expertly moved her hand down Annette's smooth stomach, down further to the damp, silky hair, and Annette moaned.

They made love slowly, Alexis wanting to make the girl cry out, to want more. Teasing her—stopping—then talking quietly, then touching, petting, kissing. For this moment completely in control of this adorable child; wondering if her cries could be heard across the suite. Lindel . . . Her face, the long, lustrous black hair . . . Lindel's eyes, looking into hers, Lindel's lips on her lips . . .

If she could just get . . . through . . . to that other side where relief and sleep would come all at once, she would be all right. She held Annette tightly in her arms, kissing her eyes, her mouth, her hair . . . holding her hard, as a shield against the night.

23

"Well goddammit!" Jeff shouted into the phone. "You're the fucking lawyer! Don't tell *me* I've got to figure it out."

Jeff held the phone in his hand, and paced back and forth in front of the desk in his den. He leaned down and snorted two lines of cocaine and continued to listen to the voice on the other end of the phone.

"Alan," he said, "Alan, *listen* to me for a minute. Stop shouting and just *fucking listen* to me! Okay. One. Garnier comes to me and says he wants to buy me out. Have Jacar buy Valhalla— including Lindel, he says—and offers to give me money. Just like that. Get rid of me quietly, have her to himself—also, the Electric Toys, but you know he'll do *gornischt* for them, it's the cunt he cares about. And you tell me that I should consider his offer? Are you out of your fucking mind? I thought you were a smart Jewish lawyer. Who the hell are you representing, anyway?"

He stopped talking, and walked around the chair behind his desk and sat down. As he listened he looked out the window and thought, it's taken me so long to get here, it's so sunny and gorgeous outside. He could see the palm trees lining his driveway and the bright blue swimming pool in the backyard, and he had to be screaming on the phone to a lawyer in New York. He couldn't even enjoy this house. It was all so crazy.

"Alan, stop. I'm going to tell you once more how I feel, and what I want to do, and that's that." As he said it, he thought of Ronnie Marren. Ronnie Marren, who had given Lindel her first gig because he, Jeff, had begged for it. Ronnie Marren, who always said, "That's *that.*" Jesus, he hadn't even seen Ronnie in almost a year.

"Okay," said Jeff. "First of all, I made the fucking bitch happen. I was the one who went on my goddamn hands and knees to Marty Paretta, to Marren, to Tim Johns, to . . ." and he nearly spat out the name, "to Garnier. I sweat my balls off for two fucking years and now *she* wants to kick *me* out? Let's get a few things straight, here. *She's* pissed off because I sold my management interest in her to Marsden. *Why* did I do that? For her, goddammit. You know the kind of expenses she was running up on the road, screwing that fuckup Brian Davis, staying in fancy hotels, ordering staggering amounts of liquor. You know how those limeys drink. The clothes I bought her . . . I furnished her goddamn apartment, I went three weeks over schedule recording the album because *she* wanted to do things over, to record extra songs."

He stopped for a second, and took a few deep breaths. He was starting to feel slightly dizzy. He continued, "I don't have to tell you what a sacrifice I've made for the past seven months while she's been in bed, jerking off over this . . . doomed romance or whatever the fuck she thinks it is. I've lost hundreds of thousands of dollars by her not working, but do I push her? No. I understand her *artistic temperament.* Hah! She's another broad who thinks with her pussy and I'm the shmuck who stands by, trying to encourage her and see her through a bad time. I even worked as her manager when technically I didn't have to, and as the head of her record company I should want to know where's the record, but even *that* I let ride. I suggest releasing a dynamite live album so people don't think she's washed up, so they don't think she's a one shot, and does she thank me? No, she spits in my face. When I got the money from Marsden so she could continue to live the way she wanted to even while doing *nothing,* and I still continued to work on her behalf—she finds out and she throws me out. Well, *fuck her.*"

Jeff twirled a strand of hair around his forefinger. He wanted to get off the phone, to go outside, to feel the hot sun. He needed to relax or he was going to go nuts. But this had to be taken care of, and right away.

"So this is what I want you to do. First, I'm suing her. . . . No, I don't know the legal term, you tell me. I'm suing her for damages. To my reputation, for not working, the money I would have made. You figure it out. Second, I want her served with an injunction. That fucking little cunt isn't going *near* a recording studio if I can help it. It's a conflict of interest for Garnier to step in like this on her behalf and he is *not* waltzing off with *my* artist."

He leaned back in his chair and suddenly felt exhausted. He listened for a few minutes and then said, very quietly, "Alan, that's what I want done and if you won't handle it, I'll find someone who will. I am sick and tired of being pushed around by her. I mean it. You know what? She's a singer, baby, that's all. Just another singer. I could walk out on the Strip tonight or go to half a dozen clubs in New York and find ten chicks who could sing. Maybe not the same, maybe not as good—but I *invented* what the world knows as Lindel James. And I'm not letting her spit in my face anymore."

And, he thought as he hung up, that's that.

Marcia called Sculls, and while she waited on the phone for them to tell her when the cab would arrive, she cleared off her desk. Into her burgundy leather briefcase went her address book, the copy of the new *Billboard,* and some papers she had to look over that night. She checked off the phone calls she had returned that day, and marked with a red pen the people to call back tomorrow. Everything was in order.

The cab would be here in five minutes, just enough time to close the office, go downstairs, and battle the rush hour traffic. She was glad she had no plans tonight. Marc Garnier's phone call had been a surprise, and she needed time to think.

Forty minutes later she was home, in the cozy little nest she had made for herself. She walked into the living room and kicked off her high heels, sank back into the lime-colored linen sofa, and closed her eyes. She loved her new apartment, but it was definitely a woman's environment. The colors were pinks and greens and pale blue, there were dark green Rigaud candles on the glass coffee table, and vases were filled with flowers. Marcia had learned quickly about flowers as a business expense; these things helped the spirit. She wondered if a man could ever share this apartment with her. Probably not; it was too frilly, too immaculate. She hardly even had time for much of a social life these days. Now that Jeff was out of the picture, most of the details of Lindel's business had been left to her.

In the past two months she had slept with three men; two of whom were irritated that her work always came first, and the third was a musician with whom she wouldn't be involved in real life. Somehow, she didn't feel that her parents had struggled to give her a good education so she could wake up in the morning next to a bleary-eyed drummer whose breakfast was an orange methadone tablet dissolved in a glass of water.

This year she would be thirty, and she was afraid that she was getting set in her ways. She looked around her apartment now and wondered if this was the apartment of an old maid. Not that thirty was so old . . . but it had been a very long time since she'd had a real boyfriend. Everyone said she was a workaholic, driven, ambitious, devoted to the business. But there was always the problem of coming home to an empty apartment. Each time she had that thought, she quickly reminded herself of the hundreds of secretaries out there who would trade places with her in a second. The expense account, the travel, the accounts at the liquor store and the cab company and the florist might not make up for a warm body lying next to her at night, but she wasn't at all sure that that was the choice. She had always thought that she would deal with all of that later. The trouble was, later was quite possibly here right now, and she was still alone.

Since she was meeting Marc for lunch, Marcia figured that she'd treat herself to a few extra hours of sleep and skip the office. She needed to be at her best for this lunch. Marc's driver picked her up at twelve-thirty, and as the black Mercedes limousine drove the few blocks to Le Cirque, Marcia smiled. He's really laying it on, she thought. Well, why not?

Marc was already seated at one of the banquettes along the side wall of the restaurant. Marcia had never been here before, and she instantly thought it was one of the most beautiful restaurants she had ever seen. Art nouveau tulip-shaped light fixtures lined the walls like little umbrellas above the dark gray banquettes. The large room was filled with bright coral-colored chairs and white linen-covered tables, each with its own vase of exotic fresh flowers. The room looked like a box of candy. Marcia saw Irving Mansfield seated at the table next to Marc's. Barbara Walters walked in, accompanied by a tall, handsome man. Ahmet Ertegun was with his wife, Mica, and Earl McGrath, at a corner table. My mother should see me now, Marcia thought. Maybe it would make up, just a little bit, for my not being married.

After a few minutes of small talk Marc said, "Why don't we order now? You really should try the pasta primavera. It's excellent here."

They spent some time with the menu, Marc gave exact instructions to the waiter, and after the captain had poured two glasses of champagne from the silver bucket placed next to the table Marcia said, "Okay. You said you wanted to talk to me?"

"That's what I like about you," Marc smiled. "You're direct."

"Not really." Marcia smiled back. "It's just that I know I won't be able to eat a thing unless you tell me what's on your mind right this minute. And I have a feeling that that would be a terrible waste of very good food."

Marc laughed out loud. He took out a cigarette, but didn't light it. "You've heard, of course," he started, "about Jeff?"

"Well," said Marcia. "I know he served her with an injunction, and the lawsuit and all. But he doesn't have a leg to stand on, does he?"

"Well my dear, and partly thanks to you, no, he doesn't."

Marcia blushed. "Well, I couldn't continue to work for him. I really only did what I thought was right."

"Yes, yes you did." He regarded her warmly. "You've been a very good friend to Lindel. But don't be so modest. You're a very shrewd girl. It's not everyone who would have kept those kinds of records, or discovered the things you did when you sensed trouble. And it was all quite useful in the settlement."

"Settlement?" She was confused.

"Let me backtrack a bit. He sued her, and named me as well. You know all that. Well, with the evidence of mismanagement I was able to ... ah ... discuss with his lawyer, I made it clear that we had grounds, on Lindel's behalf, of course, for a countersuit."

"You know," Marcia said slowly, "when I first started to realize how he was ripping her off—charging all those things to her that had to do with other acts, and himself—and how he got a fifteen percent royalty from you and was giving her five and keeping ten, and how he really *stole* her publishing—well, I never really believed it would come to this. I kept thinking he'd stop, that he'd do something to make it right. I guess almost to the end, I couldn't believe he was so awful." She didn't add, *I didn't want to believe he was so awful.*

The waiter brought the cold tomato bisque, and endive salad. Marcia ignored her food, and, as Marc began to pick up his soup spoon, she said, "Please, I can't stand it. You have to tell me what you did."

He smiled, and put the spoon down. "Well, after our lawyers threatened the countersuit, his lawyer called and we worked out the settlement quickly. I have a feeling that Jeff wanted to fight, but he was convinced to do otherwise."

"What was the settlement?" Marcia said.

"Oh," Marc waved his hand, "the usual override. We'll pay royalty points to him on her continued record sales. He'll get a lump sum for the publishing—he'll continue to receive a small royalty on that too—but now we can co-own the songs with Lindel. And, of course, she'll record directly for us."

"Three albums?" Marcia said. "Was that what you agreed with her?"

"Yes. Three firm albums. Before she left for Europe we signed the papers. We agreed to represent her with all of this and to pay the costs of possible litigation, and she made the commitment to us."

"You gave him a lot," muttered Marcia. "He doesn't deserve it."

Marc sighed. "Well, perhaps not. But even though I don't think the contract he had with her would stand up in court, it would have been a very messy lawsuit. It could have taken years had it gone to court. And I think it's worth paying him off to get her back to work sooner and get him out of the way. I still, however, wish him the worst of luck."

"But you're forgetting one thing," Marcia said. "What about the management situation? What about Dick Marsden?"

Marc smiled. "That's not a problem. Dick will relinquish that at the proper time. We'll see that he gets recompensed for his investment. After all," Marc's eyes twinkled, "it was Alexis' idea in the first place to get Dick together with Jeff. Dick just did it for me."

"What?" Marcia stared at him, stunned.

"Yes, my dear." Marc's eyes turned cold. "I've wanted Jeff Stein out of the way for quite some time. I figured that this would help it along."

Marcia didn't know what to say. So many thoughts were racing around inside her head. If Alexis had introduced Jeff to Dick Marsden, and if the Garniers had engineered the management switch . . . She wasn't sure she understood.

"But Marc," she said, "why didn't you just sign her to Jacar when he first came to you? Why did you give him Valhalla?"

"Well, I wasn't sure. I thought he might be useful to us. And also, I appealed to his greed. I gave him enough rope to see if he'd hang himself. And he did. You'll have to forgive me," he picked up his soup spoon again, "I'm very hungry."

"Oh, I'm sorry," she said. "Of course, go ahead."

She couldn't eat a thing. She was trying to comprehend what he had just told her. Alexis had been involved. And now she was in Europe with Lindel. Marcia certainly had underestimated the Garniers' control.

"Tell me one more thing," Marcia said. "Why are you telling me all this?"

"Why Marcia," Marc looked at her with surprise. "I would imagine it would be obvious. You're Lindel's closest friend. You're a very smart girl. We're all tremendously impressed with the work you've done."

Marcia didn't say anything. She picked at the salad and thought about how she played the game. She was controllable, safe. Everyone liked her. When it came down to it, being a woman meant that you knew how to maneuver things your way. At least most of the time. All it took was the flirtatious look, the self-deprecating remark, the modesty, the bat of an eye, the threat of tears. She supposed she was quite good at it. It all made her feel slightly sad.

"Anyway," Marc continued, "it's going to work out fine for all of us. And you, my dear, should think very seriously about what you want to do. After all," he smiled, "we're going to have to find Lindel a manager we can work with."

And with that, the waiter brought their lunch and they both began to eat.

24

Alexis and Lindel had been in Rome for two days when Alexis asked, "What's wrong?"

They were sitting on the terrace outside their suite in the Hassler Hotel. To her left, Lindel saw the gorgeous colors of the Villa Borghese; to her right were the Spanish Steps, and beyond that, the elegant Via Condotti. The rooftops of Rome were pink, brick, burnt sienna. Alexis and Lindel had just finished a breakfast of hot chocolate, a dark red colored fresh orange juice, and pastry. Lindel didn't answer Alexis right away.

Then she said, "What do you mean?"

"Darling, I know something's wrong. You haven't been talking. Something's changed since Paris. What is it? Tell me. Maybe I can help."

Lindel lit a cigarette. "I don't know," she said, "something about all of this seems peculiar to me. I've been having all these dreams . . ."

"What about?"

"About being onstage. The audience gets smaller, and I get bigger. Or the audience gets bigger and I get smaller. They keep moving farther and farther away from me. I know it sounds so Lewis Carroll, but it's bothering me."

Alexis smiled. "Oh, I get those too, sometimes. It's anxiety. Well," she said, obviously relieved, "I thought it was something important."

Lindel gave her a cynical smile. "No, just my singing, that's all."

"I didn't mean to downgrade your work," Alexis said quickly, "it's just that of course you feel some anxiety about performing again. You haven't been onstage for awhile, and you feel guilty about not having done the record. We've talked about all of this. Maybe it's all a good sign. Your subconscious is thinking about going back to work."

Later that day Lindel begged off from one of Alexis' shopping expeditions, and said she'd rather be alone. After Alexis left the hotel, Lindel went downstairs to the lobby and outside, down the Viale della Trinita and into the Borghese Gardens. She sat on a bench in the park for a very long time. She bought a *gelati* from a vendor. There were groups of children in the park; flying kites, playing soccer. The late autumn sun felt warm, reassuring. The leaves were starting to turn beautiful colors.

Once—it seemed like a long time ago—she had wanted to go to Italy with Brian. He had told her about the night train from Paris to Rome, and she had imagined them together in a first-class compartment, huddled under the covers, making love all night as the train sped through the dark Swiss Alps. She used to have day-dreams about Brian with her in Venice, in a gondola in the black velvet waters of the Grand Canal, at the Piazza San Marco, listening to the violinists, drinking wine. Fast, Polaroid, tourist-type snapshots in her mind of Brian with her on the Via Veneto, at the Coliseum, wandering around Trastevere. Now that she was here, and alone, it was all so different and Brian seemed so very far away.

After an hour, Lindel got up from the bench and continued to walk down through the park to the Via Veneto. It was three o'clock, that lazy time in Rome when everyone was finishing the afternoon meal, or taking a nap, and the streets were strangely quiet. She was in front of the American Embassy, next door to the Excelsior Hotel, when she felt someone behind her tap her shoulder. She jumped, turned around and saw the boy.

He couldn't have been more than sixteen, and was obviously an American. A student, perhaps, or one of those perennial European travelers. His sandy colored hair was almost down to his shoulders, a throwback to the sixties, and he had one of those orange nylon backpacks on his back. He wore faded blue jeans, a white T-shirt covered by a loden green parka, and carried a camera around his neck. He was staring at her with a stunned look of recognition on his face.

"Aren't you Lindel James?" he said.

"Yes," she said.

"Wow! I can't believe it!" he shouted, beaming. "I mean, like, you won't believe this, but really, I'm your biggest fan. I mean it, you're my absolute favorite. What are you doing here in Rome? A concert?"

Normally, Lindel would have made the appropriate replies, and would have continued on her way. But for the past week and a half she had been in a cocoon, all wrapped up in gauzy, unreal pink cotton candy with Alexis and clothes and restaurants and Alexis' friends. This boy, with his backpack and obvious adoration, was so real to her, so welcome, that she didn't want him to go away just yet.

"No," she said, "I'm not here doing a concert. I'm just here on a holiday."

"I can't believe it's really you," he said. "I have to tell you, I wore out *two* copies of your record."

"What are you doing here? Going to school?"

"Nah. I'm just bumming around. I got fed up with everything over there, so I just took off."

"What's your name?" said Lindel.

"Paul Jenner. Mind if I walk with you a little bit?"

She hesitated, then said, "Sure, come on. I'm just on my way back to my hotel."

"Where are you staying?"

Some old instinctive force of habit caused her to stop before she spoke. Then she figured, what was the difference? "The Hassler," she said.

He let out a whistle. "Pretty fancy. I'm trying to find some cheap *pensione*. I just got here from Florence today, I've never been here before. Incredible, don't you think?"

Lindel didn't know what to say. No, she thought, I think I want to get the hell out of here. I've been bought and paid for as an amusing companion for a rich woman and I'm beginning to feel like an expensive pet. But all she said was, "Well, I've only been here two days. It's a beautiful city, of course. But, I should get back to New York soon . . ."

"Yeah, you have an album to do, right?"

"Mmmmm."

"Boy, I can't wait," he said as they walked back along the Via Veneto on the way to the hotel. "I thought it was going to come out last spring, and I kept calling *Rolling Stone,* asking them if they knew whether or not you were recording or what. But there was all this secrecy about it. What do you think it's going to be like? Like the last one? I'll bet it'll be fantastic. I went to all of your New York shows, you know, the ones where Brian Davis did 'White Bird' with you for the encore. God, that was *fantastic.* I know this is going to sound corny, but I have to tell you, maybe I'll never get the chance again."

He stopped walking and turned to look in her eyes. "I don't have that many friends," he continued, "and my girlfriend broke up with me last year, and, well, I've been pretty bummed out. But your music . . . well, it just helps me get . . . *through,* you know? It helped me get through some pretty bad times. I absolutely cannot believe I ran into you here. It must be fate. I mean, something good must be going to happen. It's like an omen, you know?"

As they walked and Paul talked on, seemingly ecstatic just to be with her, telling her more about himself, about his life, Lindel felt as if she might burst into tears. It had been so long since she had had this kind of close contact with a fan. And hearing this sweet, wonderful boy tell her what her music meant to him, how it made him feel, made her feel . . . clean.

She stopped, and turned to face him.

"Thank you," she said softly. Then she threw her arms around him and hugged him. "Thank you, Paul Jenner," she said, smiling, tears welling up in her eyes. "You can't possibly know what you've done for me."

And she started running. Running to the hotel. It was time to go home. Time to leave this hotel and this trip and this woman whose first reflex action every morning was to order a bottle of champagne for breakfast. This wasn't her life, this wasn't what she was supposed to do. She missed that energy, that surge of joy when she heard the music begin, the celebration she shared with the audience. She needed to get back. She wanted to sing again.

She rushed into the suite and went straight to Alexis' room. Alexis was sitting at the dressing table, staring into the mirror, applying makeup to her face.

"I was beginning to wonder where you were," Alexis said, continuing to curl her eyelashes.

"Alexis, I want to talk to you."

"Oh dear." Alexis smiled. "This sounds serious." She turned to face Lindel, who sat on the bed.

"I met this fan of mine today," Lindel began, "and he was talking about my album, and concerts . . . and well, I don't know how to explain it, but I've been thinking, and . . ."

"You want to go home."

Lindel was surprised. "What? I just started thinking about it, really, today. It came on me quickly . . ."

"Darling, you don't have to explain. I'm an old, wise woman, remember?"

Lindel burst out laughing. "Wise, maybe. Old? Come on, you have twice the stamina I do."

Alexis turned and looked herself in the mirror as if she was seeing herself for the first time and was pleased to find everything in order. "Well," she said, turning to face Lindel, "I suppose I've managed not to totally fall apart. Anyway, that's not the point."

She got up and walked over to Lindel, and sat down next to her on the bed. "Obviously, my life isn't really suited to you," said Alexis.

"You know," said Lindel, quickly, eager to explain, "I haven't heard any music for so long, I haven't wanted to. I haven't called New York. I have no idea how my band is, what Marc arranged with Jeff, and I appreciate how you've tried to shield me from everything, and just have fun, but it's all been kind of out of context."

Lindel got up and walked to the window. "It's truly gorgeous here, and you've been amazing. You've done everything for me, and don't think I haven't appreciated it." She turned and faced Alexis, who still sat on the bed, an impassive look on her face while she smoked a cigarette.

"It's just that I'm not used to this," Lindel continued, talking faster. "Even on my tours, when everything was done for me, around me, I had something to do. Each night I knew I was going to get up on a stage and sing." She stopped, and stared straight into Alexis' eyes. "I hadn't realized how much I've missed it."

Alexis walked over to the dressing table. She stubbed her cigarette out in the ashtray and walked to the small loveseat next to the window. She sat down and looked at Lindel.

"You know," said Alexis, "people often don't understand me. There is something to be said, after all, for a certain kind of life. A style of entertaining, of travel, of living. It takes talent, I feel, to be able to live this way in a world that is so . . . mediocre. You know, before I married Marc, I had no money. Oh, I came from a 'good' family, but basically I was broke. Still, even then, it was important to me to do things in a certain way."

Her eyes seemed distant, as if she were trying to remember. "I remember when I had a small beach house in Sag Harbor that I shared with a friend of mine. It was nothing like the house Marc and I have now, but it was a sweet little house. And that house had a guest room. There was just a tiny single bed in that guest room, but it was a . . . project of mine to get that guest room done right. I found some beautiful flowered sheets and I made a bedspread, and curtains, and cover for the pillow on the small wicker chair, all from those sheets. And I took my money and bought a stack of all the latest best sellers and put them in that guest room, next to the bed on the night table. And, of course, all the magazines. There were always fresh flowers in that room, and several different kinds of cigarettes. Large, fluffy cotton towels, a small TV set, a radio, and an extension telephone also next to the bed. I wanted that room to be . . . right."

Alexis stopped talking, and looked uncomfortable. She reached for a cigarette, lit it with a flick of the gold lighter, and said, with a small, embarrassed laugh, "I don't know what possessed me to go into all that. I was just trying to explain . . . Anyway, I do understand how you feel, Lindel, but I can't say I'm not disappointed. I thought we were becoming good friends, and I thought you were having a happy time."

"Well, I have been," said Lindel. "I guess I just need to do what I'm supposed to be doing again, that's all."

Alexis looked at her for a long minute. "Well," she said, cheerfully, "then there's no problem, darling. Marc will be thrilled that you're ready to go back to work. We'll call him right now and we'll get us on a plane to New York in the morning. How's that?"

Lindel leaned over to her and hugged her. "Oh, Alexis, I knew you would understand. And, how can I thank you? You've been . . . well, just so great."

"Don't be silly, darling," said Alexis, avoiding Lindel's eyes. "You don't need to thank me. I've had the best time. Sometimes, when something is over, it's over. No sense trying to drag out a trip when it's already done its work, yes? We'll be the best of friends in New York. Now let me go call Marc, to let him know we're coming." She leaned over and gave Lindel one of those kisses in the air, and then went to place the transatlantic call.

Lindel quickly began to plan. She could be in New York by tomorrow, maybe late afternoon, and call Hank. Maybe in a few weeks they'd have enough songs to go into the studio and begin the album. They could write the rest of them in the studio . . . She'd have to call Marcia and let her know she was on her way back. She had so much to tell her . . .

"Oh, no!" Alexis exclaimed into the telephone.

"What's the matter?" Lindel said.

Alexis held the telephone, shook her head, and put her finger to her lips. She listened some more, and then said, "Oh, dear. Yes, she's right here, I'll tell her . . ."

"What happened?" Lindel was alarmed.

"We'll be on the first possible flight out. With any luck, TWA. Yes, I'll call back when I get the confirmation."

Alexis put the phone down, slowly. She turned and looked at Lindel and said, very quietly, "Hank was performing with some band at a benefit concert in Tampa. He accidentally fell from the stage. He's in a hospital in Florida, and they're planning to move him to New York as soon as possible."

"What?" Lindel screamed.

Alexis rushed over to her, and put her arms around Lindel's shoulders. "There isn't anything we can do now, there isn't even anything we can find out until we get back to New York . . ."

Lindel started to cry. "I can't stand it," she sobbed. "Hank . . . is he going to be all right?"

"Well, apparently the stage was high, and he fell onto concrete. He suffered a severe concussion and I think he may have needed several stitches in his head. The problem is his neck."

"And what did they say about his chances . . .?"

"Well," said Alexis, "good, I think. It depends on how much damage was done to the nervous system. He might be paralyzed. I don't know whether or not it will affect his walking . . ."

" . . . or playing the guitar," said Lindel. "Which to Hank is more important than walking."

"Darling," Alexis' voice grew stern, "let's get him walking again before you start to worry about whether or not he can play the guitar."

"I assure you, playing the guitar is more important to Hank than walking." Lindel nearly spat out the words.

"Lindel, you're upset, I understand. But these dramatic statements won't make anything better."

"I don't think you understand," Lindel said in a calm, deadly voice. "The guitar, the music, is his *life*." And, she thought to herself, it's going to be mine again, too.

Alexis talked, soothing, quiet, stalling words, but Lindel heard nothing. All she could think of was Hank, her guitarist, her friend, the only one in the whole band she could really count on. Oh my god . . . this was her fault. If she hadn't wasted the last seven months, they would have been in the studio, they would have been together. He wouldn't have been in some benefit concert in Tampa on a high stage. How could he fall? That didn't sound like Hank. Hank had been waiting for her, she let him down, and now this happened. It was her fault; oh god, what was she going to do?

25

Marcia slowly turned the key in the door and walked inside the bare two-room office suite. Even with the windows open, the rooms still smelled of fresh paint, a smell she didn't mind at all. It was a new beginning; just those two coats of white paint seemed to make everything clean again.

She had been really lucky to find this space for the new office. Not only was it on Fifty-seventh Street—between Sixth and Seventh, right near Bendel's and the Tea Room—but it had the one amazing room with a double height ceiling. She loved the room, and had already made extensive plans for its decoration.

She wanted it to be the right setting for her, and of course for Lindel. Big, comfortable white couches and chairs. A sleek glass table, large, unusual plants, and that wonderful maroon Lucite art deco styled desk she was having built. One wall completely covered with mirrored paneling. Modest area rugs of bright colors on a highly lacquered blond wood floor. Tasteful, but nothing too expensive. Marc Garnier had offered them the offices at Jacar for as long as they wanted to stay there, but she and Lindel had agreed that it was better to establish themselves away from the record company and on their own.

She walked around the room, her high heels clicking against the wooden floor. The sun shone in through the huge French windows and the room was bright and Marcia was full of hope.

She took her orange wool poncho and spread it out in the middle of the floor. She sat down on it and looked around the large room, up at the ceiling, out the window. She felt small in this room, but she wasn't afraid. This time, things were going to be done right. Up to now, there had been so much manipulation. She had been taken advantage of by Jeff, Jeff had maneuvered things with Lindel, he in turn had been used by the Garniers, and of course Lindel had been the one who had suffered the most. But all of that was finished. This office was proof: a clean slate.

Marcia recalled how surprised and confused Lindel had been last month when she returned from Europe and Marcia had told her about Jeff and Dick Marsden and the Garniers. They were on the phone, Lindel hadn't even unpacked her bags yet, but this time Marcia was determined not to hold anything back, not for a minute.

"The *Garniers* were responsible for Jeff selling his management interest in me?" Lindel had said. "I don't understand."

"It's simple, really," Marcia had explained. "Very early on, Marc realized that Jeff was going to be trouble. He knew how much Jeff was spending—these things are easily found out—and he was aware that Jeff was not going to be easy to control. He wanted you on the label, so he figured that if he set something up that would appeal to Jeff's greed and desperation, you two would split and then you'd go to Jacar."

"And Marc told you this?"

"Yes. Very matter of fact, too."

"But didn't he know you'd tell me?" Lindel had said.

"I don't think he cared," Marcia had replied. "I think he feels that in the end he did you a favor. And, to tell you the truth, he's not wrong."

"I guess so," said Lindel. "It's just the way it was all done . . . so underhanded. I can't believe it was all going on behind my back. Even though I suppose I wasn't really paying attention."

"Don't start blaming yourself," Marcia had said. "The point was, you trusted Jeff, and he was a creep. Of course, I suspected it. I should have told you . . ."

Lindel had laughed. "Let's not all start blaming ourselves," she had said. "Just promise me something."

"Anything."

"You will manage me, won't you?"

"I thought you'd never ask. Seriously, yes, it would be an honor."

"And Garnier will approve, I'm sure."

"Oh, I think he already thinks it was his idea," Marcia had said. "I think he knows he can work with me."

"One thing—you did say Alexis introduced Jeff to Dick Marsden?"

"Yes, but you know how she and Marc are. They're just opposite sides of the same coin. I don't think she had any real ulterior motive other than to help Marc. By the way, I haven't even asked you, how was the trip? Did you have fun?"

Lindel hadn't answered for a few seconds, then she said slowly, "I'll tell you about it when I see you. I need to digest all this. Marcia, promise me one more thing?"

"Of course. What?"

"Let's always tell each other the truth, okay? No matter how awful, I really want to know *exactly* what's going on. I don't believe anymore that what I don't know won't hurt me. Okay?"

"Promise. And you do the same with me."

Lindel had sighed. "Well, it's nice to know that I have a manager—and a friend—whom I can trust."

Now Marcia got up from the floor, and throwing the poncho around her shoulders, she went to leave notes instructing the telephone men where to install the new phones. That done, she closed the door behind her but left it unlocked so that the movers and the telephone men would be able to get inside.

On Fifty-seventh Street she automatically began to walk toward Bendel's. She looked at her watch. It was twelve-thirty. If she still worked for Jeff, what would she be doing right now? She wasn't sure what he was doing right now. He was in Los Angeles, that much she knew, but she hadn't heard anything about him since Marc had made the settlement. Funny, she didn't miss him at all. She didn't have the stomach for his kind of hustle.

Walking into Bendel's, she took the elevator up to the second floor, to the fur department. There it was, hanging on a quilted pink hanger: the silver fox coat. There was no way she could afford to buy it, but still, this was the third time she'd been back to try it on. She hoped the salesgirl who was there when she tried it on last week wouldn't be there today. She was sure that the second she got off the elevator that salesgirl would spot her, roll her eyes, and mutter something perfectly hideous and embarrassing to the other salesgirls.

"No . . . I'm just looking, thank you," Marcia practically whispered to the—thank god—new salesgirl who offered help. Then she thought, the hell with them, I'm sure they're used to it. And they don't know I can't afford it.

As she put the coat on, feeling the soft, silky fur and admiring how the large collar framed her face, Marcia thought how nice it would be to just be a woman for awhile. To shop for a man who came home to her each evening. To buy out-of-season fruits and the best cuts of meat. To organize a linen closet of different colored silk embroidered sheets. To travel to Paris, first class, with a husband who adored her. To have fittings with a dressmaker who would make her gorgeous taffeta evening gowns. To have a man of her very own, who would buy her this beautiful coat.

And, as quickly as she had these thoughts, she remembered that she forgot to call the rehearsal studio to book time for Lindel's auditions for a new guitarist. And then there was the meeting with Marc Garnier at three to discuss the recording budget. She still had to interview receptionists, and then she told Lindel she'd go to her apartment to hear her new song. She'd better hurry; there was so much to do.

She put the coat back on the hanger and waited for the elevator to take her downstairs. She realized that she was actually looking forward to the afternoon's work. For the first time in nearly ten years, she was truly on her own. She was in a partnership with a friend whose talent she believed in, and she was secure about her own ability to make it all work. It wasn't a bad deal at all.

And, she thought as she walked outside, onto Fifty-seventh Street, it was better this way. She didn't want to be dependent on anyone but herself for that silver fox coat.

"Marcia, it's so good to see you." Marc Garnier came around from behind his desk to embrace her.

"I hope I'm not late," she said, as he led her over to the couch. "This moving, and arranging everything for the new office, has been madness. I think it's easier to die than to move."

"Can I get you something? Coffee? A drink?"

"Coffee, please. Black. Thanks."

Marc sat down in the chair across from the couch and picked up the phone. He pressed the intercom button and said, "Please bring coffee for Miss Weissman. No cream, no sugar."

He hung up and smiled at Marcia. "Well, you're a busy young lady, so let's get right to the point. I've seen the budget you've proposed, and it appears to be reasonable. I'd just like business affairs to look it over and then I think you can proceed and book the time in the studio."

"Great," Marcia smiled. "I'm hoping to have her in there in about two months, at the latest. She's got to find a new guitarist first."

"Whatever happened to ... what was his name, her first guitarist?"

"Tony Valeska. He stayed with Eyeteeth."

Marc raised his eyebrow. "Well, nothing's happening with them, surely she could get him back."

"No . . ." Marcia said. "I think she wants to try someone new. Tony's been too closely associated with Jeff lately."

The door opened and Marc's secretary brought in a steaming hot mug of coffee on a white lacquer tray.

As Marcia gratefully reached for the coffee, she looked at Marc. "Aren't you having anything?"

"No. I never drink coffee after noon. It prevents me from sleeping at night. Anyway, how is Hank?"

"He'll be okay. It'll take almost a year before he's fully recovered, but we won't be on tour until then anyway. He'll be able to play on the record. The therapy he's had at the Sports Training Institute is fantastic. And of course Lindel sees him every day. They've already written two songs together."

"Well, that is good news," Marc beamed. "I did know that Lindel had been working hard. Alexis told me that she tried to make a lunch date with her but that Lindel's been holed up like a little mouse, just writing songs."

Marcia started to say something, then changed her mind. She had seen Lindel four times for lunch in the past three weeks. If Lindel didn't want to see Alexis Garnier, that was her business.

Marc was talking about the Jacar Records Convention. Something about how they were thinking of canceling it this year.

Marcia looked alarmed. "Cancel the convention? Why? Is business that bad?"

"Not at all," Marc chuckled, "although the last quarter wasn't what I had hoped. Of course, all our biggest albums have just been released for Christmas. What do you think the chances are of getting her done by the spring?"

"I wouldn't count on it," Marcia said, slipping off her high-heeled shoes and curling her red-stockinged feet under her on the couch. "I'm not even asking her when she thinks it will be done. Let's get her in there first."

"Well, naturally . . ." Marc interrupted smoothly. "But I'm sure you're aware that we like to have a sense of when to schedule things."

"Marc, I honestly can't say. I'm sure you understand that she's quite nervous about this album. It's not just having to top the last one, it's that there have been so many rumors about her. She wants to prove that she's back, as strong as before. I can't rush her."

"Of course not," Marc said, smiling. "Well, you just let me know."

He got up and walked to his desk. He reached into a silver box and took out a cigarette.

"You know," Marcia said, "I do have another idea."

Marc turned to look at her.

"We really don't have to worry about this album at all right now," she said.

"What do you mean?" Marc lit the cigarette and returned to the chair facing her.

"Well," she said, haltingly, then, her words coming faster, "she can take as long as she likes with this record and we could still have an album out in time for the spring."

Marc raised an eyebrow. "How is that possible?"

Marcia took a deep breath. She had rehearsed this over and over in her head so many times. Still, she was nervous. "We have practically an entire album done already," she said, her heart pounding so loud she was sure Marc would hear it. "All the outtakes from the first album. I've kept the tapes in a safe place for over a year. I'm not even sure Jeff remembers about them."

"Why, that's marvelous," Marc beamed. "And it doesn't even matter if Jeff remembers them or not. He's waived rights to royalties on any previously recorded, unreleased material. It was part of the settlement. I assume the material is good?"

"It's wonderful," Marcia said.

"Well, I always said you were a smart girl. When do you think I can hear it? Not that I don't trust your judgment," he added quickly.

"Oh, you can hear it anytime," she said. "But there is one thing."

"Yes?"

"Well, I'm sure you realize that Lindel was under a great deal of pressure when she came to you for help. She was operating without a manager at that time, and I'm not sure that the papers she signed were really fair."

Marc stared at her, not saying a word.

"She signed for three firm albums," Marcia continued, "and technically we've got one done already. Now, I could give you that album and begin negotiations with another company to take effect after her third album is done for you. You know that it's quite normal to negotiate with two albums left on the deal. And frankly, Marc, even I am surprised at the offers I'm getting already for Lindel. It's extremely . . . reassuring."

"After the way I helped her," Marc said softly, "get rid of Jeff, take care of the legal problems, sent her on a vacation, encouraged you to manage her . . . and you're telling me that you're going to take her to another company? Now?"

She looked directly into his eyes. "Marc, this is business. You did all that because you stood to gain from it. I'm not saying that we're not deeply grateful, but you're not running a charity here. Now, I didn't say I was going to negotiate with another company. I said I could, technically, do that. I don't want to do that. Lindel wants to stay here and I want her here. But, as I said, I'm not sure that the deal she signed was completely fair to her. What I'd really like to do is just fix up the deal a little bit. So it's fair to both of us, of course."

"You want more money," Marc said. He was no longer smiling.

"Well, yes, more money. But there are a few other points as well. Nothing that I think we have to discuss now. In fact, I'm sure it can even be handled through business affairs once you inform them of my . . . intentions."

Marc just stared at her. His eyes were cold, but Marcia thought she detected in them a faint glimmer of new respect.

"As I said," she repeated, "I want to work this out with Jacar. I don't think you'll find me unreasonable, Marc. I really just want what's right for Lindel."

And, as she put her shoes on and got up to leave, her heart pounding even more wildly than before, she watched him out of the corner of her eye. He still didn't smile, but she was sure of it now, he was looking at her in a totally new way. It was a way she knew she could get used to very quickly. In fact, she had never felt better in her life.

26

SPRING 1977

The last eight months had been difficult for Jeff Stein. After the split with Lindel, Jeff found that he couldn't muster up any of his original enthusiasm for the music business. So, he tried other things. But the New Hollywood did not like Jeff Stein. A big success in the music business meant nothing when it came to movies, or television. If anything, those people were more corporate, more frightened, than anyone at Jacar Records. The TV industry made the record companies look like a gang of wild outlaws. Even his attempts to suggest big name rock stars—proven, given successes—for movies, or television specials, proved fruitless. Jeff was convinced that the future of aging rock and rollers ultimately lay in Hollywood, but for now he couldn't get any projects off the ground.

His name was by no means a welcome household word in this world of Malibu beachhouses, Laurel Canyon hideaways, in Roy's Restaurant or upstairs at the Roxy; with these people who drank cinnamon tea when they weren't snorting cocaine, who talked about making righteous movies about the Vietnam War. Jeff didn't want to make movies about the goddamned Vietnam War; he wanted to *entertain*.

He made the occasional trip back to New York to meet with his lawyer, to try to get something going, to look busy. He was still involved with the Electric Toys and Eyeteeth, but their albums hadn't taken off as he'd hoped, and the Marquis remained unsigned. And, even though he was still good for a decent table at the Tea Room or Elaine's, and had no trouble getting a backstage pass at a big concert at the Garden, he worried that his name was dead on the street.

Perhaps he'd gotten out just in time. The returns on albums were increasing, the industry was beginning to worry. Jeff was sure that if he wanted to, he could easily sniff out what was in the air, what the kids would buy. He didn't know much about this new punk stuff—"new wave," as the industry called it in order to make it more palatable—but he was sure he could learn. How different could it be from what had come before? There were only so many chord changes. He wasn't even sure that it would last. The stars— the Elton Johns, the Paul McCartneys, the ones who were played on Album Oriented Radio—those were the ones who would always be up there, on top.

So he bided his time. He rented a house in the Malibu colony, equipped with a swimming pool and electronic front door gate. He found an EST trainer/decorator who convinced him to redo the interiors in a style she called "Mediterranean funk." He bought a Magritte oil painting because it reminded him of one of the paintings in the Garniers' East Hampton house. He learned about expensive French wines, began to collect art nouveau, installed Advent video projectors in two rooms, and hung Lindel's platinum album in the master bathroom.

It should have been everything he ever wanted. But now, after eight months, he was bored with it; bored with Hollywood. Fed up with the batty religions and exercise nuts and the Jacuzzis and the TV movies of the week and the endless "pilots," with their development money and treatments, and projects that never, ever got off the ground. Even with his excessive tastes, he couldn't believe the town. How many cars could one person drive?

He knew he had to do something major. Something big, like getting The Beatles back together. Or stealing a superstar away from another label. He couldn't just stick his nose back into the music business after nearly a year of inactivity with a "Hi, I'm back." He had to do something really heavy. In that business, you were only as good as your last two minutes and fifty-five seconds, and he hadn't had that in over a year.

Even though he didn't want to take the call, Marc Garnier picked up the phone.

"Did you hear what that little cocksucker did now?" the voice screamed in his ear.

Marc sighed. "No, Marty, what did Jeff do now?"

"Listen, I don't know about you, but I am not going to sit back and let him influence the artists this way," said Marty Paretta. "I thought that when you made that settlement with him that he was getting the hell out of the business. Going into movies, cable TV. Instead of sniveling around here again, stirring up trouble."

"What did he do?"

"Well," said Marty, "he goes to Josh Turner, who's due to record his first solo album, right?"

"Yes, yes," Marc was impatient, "Josh is doing it for us. So?"

"He goes to Josh and he says, 'I have a great idea for you, Josh,' he says, 'instead of just doing a boring album like everyone else, why don't you do something creative, something different.' " Marty paused.

Marc waited.

Marty went on, " 'Get other artists,' he tells him, 'from different labels, and get them to give you songs they never recorded themselves. And maybe sing with you on the record,' he says. Are you getting my drift?"

"Who did he talk to?" Marc sounded unruffled.

"Sandra Lewis. Carl Willis is hopping mad. Jeff even tried to call *Lindel,* can you believe, but Marcia had her new assistant call back and ask what it was in reference to." Marty chuckled.

Marc was impatient. "I'm not sure what you see as the problem, here."

"Don't you see?" Marty exploded. "First of all, the little *shnorrer* is encouraging this . . . *folk singer* to get songs from a bunch of people, some of whom are supposed to be busy getting ready for tours I have arranged, and get them into the studio. Which would totally fuck up the projected tours. Now I, for one, don't care if an act I book wants to go in and record the goddamned 'Send in the

Clowns' with U Thant if they choose, but no one is going to mess with my tours. And also, who the hell is Josh Turner to get to the likes of my superstars . . .?"

"Marty, calm down. First of all, Josh is one of our artists."

"Yeah, yeah, sure. You don't know what to do with him, either. This solo album is a joke and everyone knows it. The point is, the band might get back together one day, and then you'll want him happy."

"Well, obviously," Marc said, "Jeff Stein has figured that out as well."

"The point is, he's giving the kid fancy ideas. Making him think that he can do this special kind of an album . . ."

"Who else has he approached about it?" Marc broke in.

"Neil Diamond. Streisand. Jackson Browne. Want me to go on?"

Marc whistled. "You're kidding. He's really got nerve."

"Balls, I call it. I say he's dangerous. First, he meddles with tour schedules and recording schedules. And he's filling the head of one of the most selfish artists in the business with these ideas. Why should anyone give a song to Josh Turner? Where was he when they were in trouble? I said to Sandra, 'For god's sake, Sandra, when you were cleaning toilets, or whatever it was you were doing from 1968 to 1976, where was *he?*' Where was Josh Turner then? To say nothing of Jeff Stein. Were they helping *her?*"

"Go on."

"Okay. So, also, we've got a problem because the managers are pissed off. No one wants Jeff Stein near any one of their artists. Neither, might I add, do any of the other record company presidents."

"I couldn't agree with you more," said Marc. "He should be stopped. But what can I do?"

"Is it true you're giving him a label?"

Marc laughed. "Are you mad? After what we just went through with him? Where on earth did you hear that?"

"He's been telling everyone in sight that he's tight again with you. That you two had lunch."

"Lunch?" Marc said.

"Marc," said Marty, with a sigh, "people saw him in the building."

"Can I control who comes into the building?" Marc sounded

annoyed. "We don't have security downstairs, this isn't CBS. And the man does still have some business here, after all."

"But you're not giving him a label? He says it was part of the deal, the settlement with Lindel."

"The settlement with Lindel, which I'm sure is a matter of public record by now, involves paying him a percentage of the royalties on Lindel's albums. We gave him a certain sum of money in advance against those royalties, plus the money he got for selling Valhalla back to us, and stock. A sum of money for the publishing. Period. He waived his rights on commissions for performance and publishing in return for Lindel not pressing any charges regarding his . . . ah . . . mismanagement. I have no plans to give him a label. You have my word."

"Well, that's good to hear. But maybe you could talk to Josh. You know, warn him about Jeff. After all, you certainly can speak from experience. And I'm sure you have some influence with Josh. He *is* on your label."

"I'll see what I can do."

"I would really appreciate it," said Marty. "I want that creep to stay the hell away from my acts."

Marty was quiet for a few seconds. Marc could hear noise in the background through the phone. It sounded like bells; probably was one of those gadgets, or pinball machines, that Marty had in his office. Finally Marty said, "I'll tell you Marc, I know Jeff, we go way back together. I'll never trust him, never. It may have been over a year since he's had to do any business with a musician, but I'll bet he remembers how. I think you'd be smart to bring some pressure on Josh. I just think Jeff Stein is a threat to the . . . *order* of the industry."

Marc laughed. "Order? With this bunch of cutthroats and thieves? Please. Personally, I think Jeff Stein fits right in." Marc hesitated for a minute, then said, "I'll see what I can do. But I think you're overreacting just a bit to all of this. After all, Marty," he chuckled, "this is the music business. It's not a cure for cancer."

Jeff paced the living room of his giant suite in the Sherry Netherland. He was waiting for Tim to arrive, to take him to one of those clubs that had opened since he'd last been in New York. It seemed as though two new ones opened every week. The limo was waiting downstairs, and Tim was, as usual, late. Jeff looked at his watch, and went over to the bar to pour himself a glass of Perrier. Everything in New York started so late. None of the clubs even opened until midnight, and by the time the band got on the stage it could be two in the morning. He was scheduled to fly back to L.A. on the nine A.M. flight; he'd be lucky if he got any sleep at all tonight. He probably should have canceled with Tim tonight, but he couldn't risk Tim gossiping that Jeff wasn't interested in checking out new bands.

He glanced at the TV set, and then rushed over to turn up the sound. " . . . called the King of Bubblegum," said Merv Griffin to Neil Bogart, who had settled comfortably into an orange naugahyde sofa, "but more recently, you really have been responsible for the upsurge of disco in the record industry, isn't that true?"

Jesus, thought Jeff, Neil Bogart on the Merv Griffin show. It seemed as though everything Neil did made news. As he sat and watched the rest of the interview, Jeff was determined that this time he'd get some attention. Enough of always having to watch out for the artists' egos. This time, he might even get his own press agent.

He felt a familiar rush flow through his veins. It was starting. It would happen again. He was getting something going. He would soon be back in business.

He was talking to Carl Willis about finally making a deal for the Marquis. He might even get Phil Spector to come out of semi-retirement to produce the album. Spector hadn't done anything since John Lennon's *Rock and Roll* album; he would really be a coup.

Jeff signed Marcy Danton, a backup singer who had had a hit TV show a few years ago, to a management contract. He wasn't even going to bother with the record business for her, she was going straight to Vegas, Broadway. He had Josh Turner's ear, he was getting friendly with superstars who, he was sure, would want to be associated with him when their current deals were up.

It was all happening again, and despite all he knew, all he'd been through, he had to admit to himself that he was excited about being in the middle of the action again. But he still needed one thing. He needed a star.

The bell to the suite rang, and Jeff went to the door. Tim stood there with a boy who couldn't have been more than seventeen.

"Jeff," said Tim, "this is my friend Duncan."

"Nice to meet you, Duncan," said Jeff, shaking the kid's hand, thinking *this is going to be one of those nights,* and leading them both into the suite. How does he ever remember their names, Jeff wondered.

"Well," said Jeff, "where should we go first?"

"Oh," Tim whined, "it's way too *early.* We shouldn't get anywhere for at least an hour, maybe longer."

Jeff tried not to show his annoyance. "Tim, it's almost ten, and some of us have to get up and catch early planes tomorrow."

Tim ignored this, and said, "Do you have anything to drink?"

"Sure. What do you want?"

"Do you have a beer?" said Duncan.

"Beer . . . no, I don't think so. Want some wine?"

"I'd love some," said Duncan in a soft voice. While Jeff went to the bar to pour a drink, Tim pulled out the glass vial and the rest of the cocaine paraphernalia. *I've got to cut down,* Jeff thought. On the other hand, I've got to stay awake. He brought the glass of wine to Duncan, leaned down and did a line, and sat down on the couch. He really wasn't up for this evening at all.

"You know, Duncan is in a *wonderful* new band," said Tim.

"Ummmm-hmmmm," said Jeff. He had heard it all before.

"They're called the Video Children and they're playing tomorrow night at Trax."

"Maybe you could come and see us," said Duncan.

"I would love to," said Jeff, "but I've got to get back to L.A." He appraised the kid differently now, as if he was looking at a cut of meat he was considering buying for his dinner. The kid was cute, in that New York street way: black leather jacket, jeans and sneakers, and very short hair which was now the punk style. He would probably photograph well. Maybe the band was good.

Actually, he shouldn't have said he was going back to L.A. He learned a long time ago that you could always tell them you were planning to come to the show. They'd never know the difference.

"Where else have you played?" Jeff said.

"Oh, the usual places. You know . . ."

"I don't," said Jeff. "That's why I'm asking."

Tim laughed. "Jeff doesn't know much about music."

"Thank god I don't have to," Jeff snapped.

"Jeff used to be a New Yorker," Tim said to Duncan.

"And I'm in the process of trying to move back here, if I could find an apartment I like. Where do you live, Duncan?"

"On the Bowery, with the rest of the band," he said.

"You should stay over another night," said Tim, "just to see them. They're fabulous."

"Hmmm," Jeff said.

"Well, we're playing CBGB's again in two weeks," said Duncan.

"Perhaps I can see you then," said Jeff. What if this kid, sitting right here in the living room of his suite, was the next big thing? Stranger things had happened. Look at that singer, that Patti Smith, who was recently in *The New York Times Magazine* section. Tim had tried to get him to go see her two years ago at some poetry reading.

Jeff tried again. "What kind of music does the band play?" Terrible name, he thought, Video Children. They'd have to get rid of the name.

"Oh, well, we have this girl singer," said Duncan, "and she's really a knockout. Real blond, pretty, and she has a voice that's like . . . oh, the old Shangri-Las, Ronettes, you know, like that. And then, there's us five guys. We all have kind of different tastes, but the music the band makes is . . . kind of a cross between electronic pop and punk."

You should have brought the girl, Jeff thought, that's who I should see. The rest don't matter. Turning to Tim, he said, "Shouldn't we be getting down there soon? Will there be seats left?"

"Seats?" said Tim. "You're lucky to find a spot to stand at the bar. Ever since *New York* magazine wrote about the place it's on the rock slumming map. But they usually save me a table. We can go in a little while."

Tim got up, walked to the television set and turned the channel to a station that was showing an old pirate movie. He turned the sound down.

"Duncan has a cassette of the band, don't you, Duncan?" said Tim.

Duncan pulled a cassette out of his pocket.

"Oh, my machines are all in L.A.," said Jeff, silently relieved that he'd packed earlier. "I don't really like listening to the tape in front of the artist, anyway. I'd be happy to take it with me, unless it's the only copy you have."

"No, we have more," said Duncan, handing it over. "But it's just a rough mix, we did it with a cheap two-track Teac."

"Don't worry," Jeff assured him. "I can imagine what it would sound like done in a good studio." Then, to Tim, he said, "Who are we going to see?"

"The Ramones are at CBGB's," said Tim, "and even though they're signed to Sire, I think you should see them. It'll give you an idea of what's happening. And Wayne County is at Max's. Of course, you should have come with us two years ago, it's all pretty predictable now."

Jeff just shook his head. Was this necessary? It was a long way from Malibu and On The Rox, Lou Adler and The Eagles—the music business he had come to observe over the past year. But Tim had picked up on Lindel, and Jeff couldn't afford to take chances. He needed a crash course. Then he'd make his move.

The limo pulled up to CBGB's, on Bleecker and the Bowery. Jeff had avoided coming here, even though it had been the rage for the past two years. He didn't know what he had been expecting, but surely this couldn't be it. Once inside, it was an unimpressive long, railroad-like room with large neon beer signs hanging above the crowded bar, and waitresses carrying trays of drinks. At the end of the room, a band was onstage, playing very loud music.

"Are these The Ramones?" Jeff shouted to Tim.

"No," Tim yelled back. "They're Primo, another Talking Heads ripoff. The singer's great, don't you think?"

Jeff shrugged his shoulders. To tell the truth, he wouldn't know the difference. To him, this wasn't singing. They sat down at a table, and all ordered beers. Jeff looked around. The crowd was young, many in their late teens, certainly younger than anything he had recently seen in a Los Angeles rock club. These really were the hardcore fans, and even though Jeff had heard that business types were filtering down here in alarming numbers, he didn't recognize anyone he knew. Tim leaned back in his chair, adjusted his sunglasses, and stared straight ahead. The minute the band stopped playing, Jeff leaned over to say something to Tim, but the jukebox right behind them blared out more music, and there was no possibility of conversation.

About twenty minutes later, The Ramones exploded onto the stage. "One-two-three-faw!" yelled one of them, and for the next half hour there was an unbelievable attack of sound. All four boys wore black leather jackets, jeans and sneakers, just like Duncan did, and every song sounded the same. The decibel level was inhuman. Jeff saw Tim take bits of a paper napkin, wet them in his mouth, and then stick them in his ears. Watching The Ramones, Jeff thought about the energy, and the charisma of the lead singer, who was kicking things around the stage. It made him think of others. And, as he sat there, with the sound blasting all around him, his thoughts were miles away from that hot, crowded little club on the Bowery. They were, to be exact, three thousand miles away. In London. With Brian Davis.

27

Lindel left Hank's apartment and hailed a taxi. On the way home she thought about what that doctor had just told her. Polyps. On her vocal chords. They could be serious; if she didn't stop smoking she might need an operation. Her voice didn't even sound any different to her, maybe a bit huskier than before, but nothing really noticeable. The coughing, however, was something entirely different. It had gotten progressively worse in the months since she'd been back from Europe, and had just been so bad in Hank's apartment that the doctor who had been giving Hank his weekly checkup had looked at her with concern and had insisted on examining her throat.

Back in her own apartment she went to lie down on her bed. She should call Marcia, and tell her about this. She got up from the bed; she was too restless to lie down. She reached for a cigarette from the pack on her dresser, and then she stopped. She felt scared. What if this really got worse? What if she needed an operation, and she had to go into a hospital and what if—she forced herself to face it—what if she couldn't sing anymore?

That doctor was probably just trying to scare her. She lit the cigarette and went into the living room. Some doctors just really had this . . . *thing* about smoking. Half of the blues singers whose music she loved had been smoking cigarettes for more years than she had been alive.

She took the small tape recorder off the shelf of the record cabinet, and rewound the cassette to the song she had worked on the night before. She pressed a button and her voice filled the room. It was just a cheap mono tape recorder, and her voice sounded tinny. But the song was good, and she thought she could finish it tonight.

Hank had been so amazing. Even in the midst of his recovery from that hideous fall, he seemed to want to work harder on the songs. He derived strength from their sessions together, and for Lindel he was an inspiration. For the first time in a long while, she felt good about waking up to each new day.

Lindel felt as though she could not be stopped. She was interested in everything again; she went with Marcia to the movies, she listened to the new records, and when Hank was well enough to go out, they went to see all the bands at the new clubs that had sprung up all over the city. But it was her own music that excited her the most. There never seemed to be enough hours in the day to do all she wanted to do.

She had songs to work on, arrangements to figure out with Hank. She had business details to go over with Marcia. This time around, everything was going to be done right, and carefully; she was going to pay attention. She and Marcia approached everything with a joyous spirit that had never existed with Jeff and his combat hustle.

For the first time in over a year, the world looked good to Lindel James. Now she looked at the cigarette, its smoke curling up from the ashtray. Maybe it was an unnecessary scare, but she really didn't want to take the chance. Something had snapped in her head when she saw that boy—Paul Jenner—on the street in Rome, and it had continued to New York, through the weeks and now the months of getting back to work. She couldn't lose it, not now. The doctor had said that if she stopped smoking the polyps might go away by themselves. She looked at the papers spread out on the floor, bits of songs, scribbled with the energy that came from somewhere—she didn't know how, or why—often in the middle of the night. And she knew that she had no choice. Nothing was going to come between her and her music again. And very slowly, deliberately, she ground the cigarette out in the ashtray.

If Jeff had still been her manager, she never would have been allowed to do this local television show. But the host of the show—who used to be a disc jockey on WBCN in Boston—had been one of Lindel's early supporters, and she felt she owed him the favor.

Still, she could hear what Jeff would have said: *"Make your first television appearance in over a year on a fucking local show? Are you out of your mind?"* She was sure that he would have wanted no less than the Carson show for her return. But this was the way she wanted to do it, low key. Start over, slowly.

She poured herself a small glass of white wine, just to give her some courage. She changed her mind six times about what to wear and finally decided on a pair of black corduroy jeans and a black silk blouse. She put on her makeup, and when she was through, she looked at the results in the mirror. She was surprised that she felt so nervous. At exactly eight o'clock, the buzzer rang, and she went downstairs to meet Marcia for the short drive to the studio.

"You look gorgeous," said Marcia, as Lindel got into the limousine.

"Thanks," said Lindel, smiling. "I was afraid I'd forgotten how to put on this face."

Hank was already at the studio, the cameras were set up, and the crew was waiting for her. She asked if she could brush her hair, accepted the glass of white wine offered to her by the host, and said, "Let's tape the first song, okay? Then Hank, sit in with me when we do the interview." She looked with affection at her bass guitarist. They had been through so much together. Her depression . . . she was never sure what to call the last year. Hank's accident. Looking at it from this end, having come through it and feeling stronger, she was glad it was over. And, over it was. She was lucky. She had some really good friends.

Lindel sat in a chair, with Hank alongside her, and they started to play so the engineer could fix the sound level. When the engineer signaled that he was ready, she turned, looked at Hank, and they began. For the first time in front of anyone other than themselves, they played one of Lindel's new songs, the still untitled one about Paul Jenner and that day in Rome. It felt so good to be singing in front of people again. She was operating on automatic. Once again, and she hadn't felt it for so long, when she began to sing, something else took over, and she knew she was doing exactly what she wanted to do, what she was supposed to do. She didn't even have to look at anyone for approval after she was finished, she felt it inside. It felt right.

Still, she was somewhat taken aback by the spontaneous applause from the crew. She smiled, and turned to face them as if she was coming out of a dream. It would take a few seconds to come back down to earth, but she made conversation, having no idea at all what she said, and took a big drink from the glass of wine.

After the interview, everyone thanked her for coming. The host was so grateful that Lindel was embarrassed. By now, she had finished the wine and felt slightly giddy. "I hope I was okay," she said, more times than she should have, knowing full well that it had been far better than okay, but wanting, needing to hear it again.

In the car with Marcia, Lindel asked her again how she thought it had gone. Marcia was effusive with praise. In the past, Lindel had always known when she'd done a good show, and nothing anyone said—except, perhaps, Brian—had ever made a difference. Now she needed to be sure that what she felt was right. She needed the reassurance, and she needed to hear it again and again.

Back in her apartment, alone, she still felt a sense of elation. It had only been a small local television show, but it was a job well done. She felt that she was truly home.

She went and lay on the bed. She thought perhaps she should eat something. Pizza was all she could think of, so she picked up the phone and called Ray's. Twenty minutes later, she still felt that sense of elation. An hour later, after she had finished half of the pizza and lay in bed watching the end of the Yankees game on TV, she realized that tonight had been her official re-entry into that part of her life that made her feel better than anything else possibly could. It had gone away, she had pushed it away, but here it was, it came back. She couldn't wait to get back into the recording studio. She felt like laughing out loud. How could she have denied herself this for so long?

Through the glass window that separated her from the engineer's room, Lindel saw Tim come into the studio. He looked tanned, but tired; older somehow. She waved at him, then finished singing the song.

"You sound fabulous," said Tim, kissing her when she went back into the control room.

"Well, it's just rough vocals," she said. "When did you get back?"

"Just now off the plane. Anyway, rough vocals or not, you sound great." And, eyeing her, he added, "You look great. I guess all the things I've heard about you the last month are true."

"What have you heard?" She couldn't resist asking.

"That you're working again, have all these great new songs, the new guitarist couldn't be cuter, that Garnier gave you a fortune to go back to the studio."

"That's not exactly true." She was annoyed. "I owe them so much money for getting me out of that mess with Jeff."

"Well, I'm just telling you what I hear . . ."

Same old Tim. And to think she'd been glad to see him. But all she said was, "Things couldn't be better. Want a drink?"

Tim shook his head and offered her a vial of coke.

"You know I don't do that," she said.

Tim raised his eyebrows. "It's good for you," he said. "Especially when you're working. You'll feel like you can conquer the world."

"Did you ever notice," said Lindel, "that all the people who think they can conquer the world with cocaine haven't conquered the world?"

The engineer put the song they'd worked on the night before through the big speakers in the control room. When it was through, Tim whistled.

"That's a hit," he said.

Despite herself, she said, "Do you really think so?" She still cared about his—that is—anyone's, opinion. "I don't care if it's a hit or not," she added quickly. "But I do want it to sound right. It's not right yet."

"What are you doing after the session?" Tim asked.

"Probably going home to sleep. It'll be about four in the morning when we get out of here," she said.

"Want to come to a party with me? Come on, I've been in L.A. for a month, you haven't seen me."

"I don't think so," she said. "I'm not ready for parties yet. I need sleep. I want this album done on time."

"I just thought you might want to come to this one. Brian's probably going to be there."

Her heart stopped.

Careful, she thought. "Oh?" she said, hoping her voice sounded as casual as his.

"Yeah. He's in town by himself. Just for a day or two. Something about trying to find another manager. They let Ian go."

She was surprised. "Why? What happened?"

"Well, it's all very hush-hush." Tim lowered his voice to a confidential tone. "But it seems that Ian was involved in some drug scandal. Something about selling pills with fake prescriptions to half of London. It was really sleazy, and even though he bought his way out of it, Brian was afraid that the group would get too hassled traveling, especially in Europe, where going across borders is such a performance anyway."

"There were other things, too," Tim went on. "After Ian got out of trouble, some dealer he ripped off dangled him upside down out of a window of a Manchester hotel. I don't know all the details, but their last tour was pretty notorious. One of their roadies got thrown into jail for assault. And then, of course, the scandal at the last concert when the lighting rig fell . . ."

"What?"

"You didn't hear about that? It was in all the papers."

"I haven't seen a paper since I started recording the album. What happened?"

"They did a concert in Germany, and they had a new lighting rig that they took with them, and the whole damn thing fell. One kid died, several others were hurt, and to make it worse, there was no insurance. It was a mess. The band was sued, Brian was so freaked he said he never wanted to perform again . . . I'm shocked that you didn't hear about it."

"Marcia didn't tell me . . . Hank didn't say anything . . . none of the other guys in the band . . . I don't see anyone else. If he's not going to perform, why is he looking for a manager?"

"I guess he wants someone to tell him what to do. I think he's had it with the cult bit, wants to figure out how to get his career off the ground in America."

Lindel's mind was racing. She remembered so many things Brian had said. How he never wanted to lose touch with his audience. How bored he was with the concept of "breaking America": how it was vital for him to stay where he was, how necessary it was for his music.

"Guess who's trying to get to him?" said Tim, smiling.

"I can't imagine." Lindel's mouth curled.

"Well, I think it's a fabulous idea," said Tim. "After all, Jeff is trying to make a comeback, and Brian needs help. I think they'd be perfect for each other."

Perfect, she thought. You have no idea. But she said nothing. Lindel turned to the engineer.

"Can we run that tape back, please? I want to hear it again."

Her mind was no longer on the song, but she would not let Tim see that. She had heard Marcia mention that Tim might be going to work for Jeff, and Lindel was certain that Jeff had sent him along to feel her out in some way about Brian. He might even be waiting downstairs in the godamned car, Lindel thought, just waiting for a signal that all was forgiven and he should rush right up. He was totally capable of thinking that. Lindel suppressed a hysterical giggle.

She blew a kiss to Tim, and went back into the studio, more determined than ever to work on the song. This was her only weapon. Only one hell of an album would really show Jeff that she didn't need him anymore. And it would show Brian that she didn't need him, either.

She was exhausted when she got home that morning. It was five A.M., but she couldn't fall asleep right away. So, Brian was in New York. How like him to be here and not call. For all she knew he could have been here other times too, and never called. But now, knowing that he was here—probably at the Navarro or the Gramercy Park, within such easy reach—had a highly unsettling effect. She could just pick up the phone and call him, and she was sure that if she asked him, he would be at her apartment in a matter of minutes. She sensed that the time they had been apart would mean nothing to Brian. She was sure that if he was low, and needed someone, if someone wasn't there already, he'd probably be happy to hear from her.

What would they be like together? Could they just melt into each other's arms again? Perhaps the whole awful year would just fade away if she saw his face. To see Brian again, to touch him, feel his lips on hers, his arms around her, to feel his touch. She lay there, thinking about him, trying to remember exactly what his face looked like. The image kept slipping away. She didn't even want to get out of bed and go inside to the record cabinet, take out his album and look at his picture to remember what he looked like. A year ago she would not have believed that she could stand it if Brian was in New York and didn't call her. But now, she didn't even mind being alone. If she was with Brian, she'd have to worry about his mood, what he wanted. She knew that in order to do what she had to do right now, she had to be alone.

For so long she had thought about Brian, wondered where he was, why he didn't call. She had been afraid he'd disappear, afraid, even, that she'd forget about him, that she'd let him go.

Now she realized that sometimes it was the thing you feared the most that ultimately, when it happened, set you free.

28

The phone woke Jeff at four-thirty. He had no idea how long he'd been asleep at the pool. Picking up the half-empty vial of cocaine, he pushed the mirrored sunglasses against his nose, and walked into the den to take the call.

Lindel's voice jarred him. He had been waiting and thinking of her call for weeks. Now he wasn't sure exactly what he should say. He needed something to get him through. Just one hit, he promised himself, as he took the tiny spoon and lifted the coke to his nostril.

"Lindel," he said, "thanks for returning my call."

"Calls," she said.

"Well," he laughed, nervously, "you would rub it in."

"What do you want, Jeff?"

"Ah, right to the point. You know, this makes me sad. Why do you think I want something? Maybe I just thought that after all this time we should talk. I miss you."

"Please, Jeff. I know you. You want something."

"I heard you were in town and I thought we could get together."

"Why?"

"Lindel, for god's sake. We used to be friends."

She was silent for a few seconds. With his finger, Jeff rubbed a grease spot off the white telephone. He reached for a silver ball-point pen on his desk and doodled on the back of an envelope.

Lindel sighed. "You know, you still have so much chutzpah. But I admit I'm curious to hear what you have to say to me after all this time. Okay, Jeff. I'll meet you for a drink."

"Drink? Don't be silly. I want to take you to dinner. Where do you want to go? Chasens? The Bistro?"

Lindel laughed. "Are you trying to impress me?"

"I just wanted to take you somewhere nice." He sounded hurt. "I don't care about food, we could get a cup of coffee for all I care . . ."

"I'm still paying for the last cup of coffee you bought me," she said.

He didn't answer. Clearly, this was going to be even more difficult than he had anticipated.

Then she said, "Look, I'm not much for the Hollywood social scene. I've been here for a week, and I hardly get out except to go to the Record Plant to mix the album. I don't know the difference between one restaurant and another. Someplace quiet would suit me fine."

"Fine. Tomorrow night okay for you?" He didn't want to seem too eager. "I've had a busy day." That's a laugh, he thought. I've done nothing for weeks except sit at this pool, with occasional breaks to line up the cocaine.

"Can't. Has to be tonight. I might be leaving tomorrow."

"Okay, tonight then. Shall I pick you up at seven?"

"If you're eating dinner that early you've been out here much too long," she laughed.

He kept the edge off his voice. "Whatever. Let's make it nine. I'll see you then."

Lindel put down the phone and leaned back in bed. Jeff sounded really down. Well, no wonder. Marcia had told her that he hadn't done a damn thing in months. Once this might have given her reason to gloat, but now it just didn't seem to matter.

Yet she was curious to see him. He was a part of her life that seemed, somehow, unresolved. All communication between them since the split had been handled through lawyers, or through Marcia. She wondered if she should call Marcia and tell her she was having dinner with Jeff. No, she'd wait until after she saw him.

Marcia might try to talk her out of it, and she didn't want that. She wanted to see this through.

There were so many questions she wanted to ask him. Not that his answers would make a difference, she was sure he probably wouldn't tell her the truth anyway, not even now. And she knew him well enough to know that he must want something. She also knew that despite everything, despite the last year and all of his dishonesty before that, she would listen to Jeff. She couldn't help it. The bigger person, she thought, and then she smiled. Not so big that she wouldn't make him really ask for whatever it was that he wanted.

Jeff had grown a beard, and Lindel immediately noticed the small gold earring he wore in one ear. She had forgotten how uncomfortable he always looked, how even all the "right" clothes managed to look all wrong on him.

He walked with her out of the hotel and opened the door to the silver Mercedes convertible parked on the street.

"Where are we going?" she asked.

"I thought we'd go to Chow's. I remembered that you liked it in London."

She looked at him sharply, started to say something, and then changed her mind. Trust Jeff to forget that they had been at Mr. Chow's the first night she had been with Brian. Or maybe he hadn't forgotten at all. But all she said was, "It won't be too private."

Jeff just smiled.

Driving up Sunset Strip into Beverly Hills, they passed the Hyatt House, the Roxy . . . How odd to be sitting with Jeff again, watching places from their past roll by as if she were watching a movie. Jeff had turned the radio up loud and Lindel was relieved not to have to talk. It was some consolation to her that Jeff seemed far more nervous than she was, but still Lindel felt as though she could use a drink.

Jeff pulled up to the sleek modern restaurant on North Camden Drive. After leaving the car with the parking attendant, Jeff and Lindel walked inside, where the hostess greeted Jeff and took them through the large dining room to the stairs in the back. People turned and stared at Lindel as she walked by, and Jeff beamed with pride.

"What's this?" said Lindel, as they walked into a small room on the second floor with a large round table set for two.

"A private room," smiled Jeff. "I still have some pull in this town."

Lindel stared at him. She shook her head. "Still with the grand gestures," she said.

"Hey, it's business," he said. "We'll be in three columns tomorrow. Hank Grant will put in his Hollywood Reporter column that we were "table for two-ing it at Mr. Chow's."

They sat down, ordered drinks, and looked at each other. Jeff seemed tired, she thought. But he still had that look in his eye. Even with all the money he must have from their settlement, he still looks hungry. What surprised her the most, however, was the way she felt, seeing him again after so long a time. No anger, no sadness . . . just nothing. Like seeing someone she used to know.

"You look gorgeous," he said.

"Thanks," she said, looking at him, waiting.

When he didn't say anything right away, she said, "You look strange without that little notebook."

"Oh," he looked embarrassed. "I guess I got out of the habit. I'll have to get a new one."

He played with the small yellow box of wooden matches, he folded and unfolded his napkin, he seemed even more fidgety than she had remembered. She sipped her glass of water, and still said nothing, staring at him with her eyes purposely wide above the rim of the oversized wine glass.

"Lindel, I really think we should patch things up," he blurted out.

"Patch . . . things . . . up?"

"You know what I mean," he said quickly. "Look, we both made mistakes. I was in too much of a hurry, I overlooked some of the details . . ."

"Details? Like my not owning my songs? Not getting my fair share of my own royalties? Details?"

He tried to take her hand but she pulled it away. "Lindel, baby, you have to understand, I was new to all of this. I was so enthusiastic and excited and had such hopes."

"I had hopes too," she said in a low voice. "And you lied to me.

Tell me, Jeff, why did you lie? Why couldn't you have just done it honestly? Why did you have to . . . steal?"

He looked as if she had struck him in the face. He averted his eyes, and then said, "I didn't steal, Lindel, no matter what they told you. I had to protect myself. I'd heard so many stories about artists who split once they made it, about managers who went broke busting their balls for ungrateful musicians . . ."

"I wasn't ungrateful," she interrupted.

"But, baby, how could I know what would happen? This was the deal that was recommended to me. I really want you to understand."

There was a knock on the door and the waiter came in with drinks, set them down and left again. Jeff pulled out a pack of cigarettes and offered one to Lindel. She shook her head no and said, "I don't smoke anymore. But since when did you start?"

"Oh, I don't really smoke. Just once in awhile." His voice trailed off and he looked at her.

"Lindel, do you really hate me so much?"

She didn't answer right away. Then she said, "I'm not so sure this is good dinner conversation, Jeff. Maybe we should change the subject."

He drank some of his ginger ale, and stubbed his cigarette out in the ashtray.

"Well, to be honest with you, Lindel, I did kind of want to clear all that up first. Because I could really use your help."

Lindel looked at him, thinking, *here it comes*. What on earth would he have the nerve to ask her?

"It's Brian," he said simply.

"Brian?"

"Yes, yes," he was impatient. "Brian Davis. Surely you remember him?" He tried to laugh and stopped immediately when he saw the look on her face.

I don't believe it, she thought. Tim had mentioned that Jeff was after Brian a month ago, but she'd heard nothing since, and what did it have to do with her?

"Well, you know his bass player?" said Jeff. "What's his name . . ."

"Brad."

"Yeah, him. Well, he's been busted so many times that they can't move around from country to country without a big hassle, and there was some trouble with Ian, and it won't be any better when they tour here next time. If they can get visas. Plus, everyone's asking Brian all the time when the band is breaking up, *if* the band is breaking up, if he's making a movie, when is he doing a solo album. I think the pressure is getting to him."

Lindel continued to stare and still said nothing.

"Look," Jeff said, "I know you're not too wild about Brian after all you went through, but you're much stronger than he is, really. And I think he could use your help."

The waiter came to take their order. Jeff looked at her and asked, "Do you want a spring roll to start?"

"Do I have to give you fifty percent of it?" she said.

"Lindel . . ."

She turned to the waiter, and started to order for herself, dragging it out for as long as she could. Yes, she'd like a spring roll and spicy beef with vegetables and some rice. She knew she wouldn't touch a thing.

Jeff drank the rest of his ginger ale, some of the water in her glass, and he started to twirl a strand of his hair around one finger. She'd almost forgotten that old habit. Jeff quickly ordered the same food as she had, and then when the waiter left, he said, "Look, I know how you feel about Brian. You were hurt. And angry. And justifiably so. However, that was so long ago, and things are so different now."

"How?" she said. "How are they different?"

"Well, I mean . . . you're okay now," he faltered.

"Just like that," she practically whispered. "You have the nerve to say that to me." She stared at him; stared at him with a combined look of amusement and rage.

"Well, listen, I know it's not that simple . . ."

"It sure as hell isn't," she raised her voice. "Now, you listen to me. I agreed to meet you for this little dinner because I was curious, I admit it. I've been hearing all kinds of stories about you, and I wanted to check them out. That's one reason. The second is, I was curious to know what you wanted from me."

"Lindel," Jeff interrupted, "lower your voice." He looked nervously at the door.

"I had an idea," she said, "and I wasn't far wrong, but somehow in person you're always more of a handful than in my mind. With you, Jeff Stein, the myth is never greater than the reality." She stopped for a minute, took a sip of her margarita, and tried to calm down.

"I think you misunderstand me," he said.

"Oh no, I don't," she said. "First of all, how dare you sit there and blithely say I'm okay now? You don't have the slightest clue as to what I went through this past year."

Jeff got up and closed the door.

"Please," he said, sitting down again, "honey, calm down. I made some mistakes, I admit it, but we all did. It was just such a crazy, hysterical time. I did my best for you, Lindel, I really did. I suppose I had this coming to me, but please, can't you just calm down?"

"You just better hear me through," she said. "I've waited a long time to say this."

She took another sip of her drink and, then, more in control, she said, "Marcia helped me, Marc helped me. But you? And Brian? I thought he cared for me, and that son of a bitch went merrily back to England and I never heard from him again. Now," she stopped and smiled sweetly, "what was it you wanted, Jeff?"

He just stared at her. "Jesus," he said, "I forgot about how tough you can be sometimes."

Neither of them said anything for a few minutes. The waiter knocked on the door, and then entered with the appetizers. He quickly arranged the food on their plates as they both watched silently, then he left.

Lindel sighed. "I'm not so tough, Jeff."

Jeff looked relieved, smiled at her, and picked up a fork and started to eat. How amazing, thought Lindel, no matter how tense the situation, Jeff could always pack away a full meal. He'd probably start in on hers in a minute, as soon as he noticed that she wasn't eating a thing.

She just sat there. He looked at her and, with a guilty expression, he put down his fork. "I'm too upset to eat," he said. "Look, I know how you feel. I know what you've been through, and I'm sorry, deeply sorry. But did it ever occur to you that maybe I, too, had a bad time? After all, I ended up losing my company, my baby, the thing we started together."

She stared at him. "You know, I honestly think you believe that. It's amazing the way you've rewritten history."

He ignored her and went on. "Look, it hasn't been a day at the beach for me out here. They're all a pack of shmucks, of course, and don't have a clue as to where the entertainment industry is headed. It's been pretty rough. I want to get back into the music business, yes, of course I do. Why shouldn't I? It's what I know, and I still think I can do a better job than any of these assholes who think they know what's happening. There hasn't been another, younger guy to come up and do any better than me, and I've been watching. Who is there? Irv Azoff? With two acts? I've had two acts working while I've been *out* of the business. Geffen's retired, enjoying his money, and Bogart wants to go into films. But me, Lindel, what's left for me?"

She was so tempted to say *frankly, my dear, I don't give a damn,* but she stopped herself, and giggled instead.

"I don't think it's funny," he said, clearly hurt.

"Oh, all right Jeff, stop the violins. Cut to the chase."

"Well," he said, getting excited, "it's this. I have an incredible idea. For Brian. But for you, too. I think I can swing a solo deal for him. But why should he just do any old solo album? Anyone can do that, and he'd end up using The Vipers on it, so big deal. But ..." And she saw his eyes begin to take on an old, familiar sparkle, a look she did not remember with affection.

"What if you and he ... now wait a minute," he held up his hand, "don't say a word until you hear me out. What if *you,* and *he,* did a duet album together ... you know, like the finales you two did on the tour. Kind of like Marvin Gaye and Tammi Terrell type duets? Hah? You and him together, like those Motown songs, only your own songs, brought up to date stuff. Jesus, what an album *that* would be."

Lindel stared at him.

He held up a hand. "I know, I know what you're thinking. But just for a minute, think about it from an *artistic* point of view."

"You never thought about anything from an artistic point of view in your life," she hissed. She stood up and said, "I don't have to think about it. Not for one second. Is that all?"

He pushed her back down into her chair. "Now you listen to me, goddammit. You may not want to work with him again, or me, for that matter, but I've got it all figured out. You can go in and do your part, and he can do his, and then it all can be mixed together in the studio. You can even send in any producer or engineer you want to oversee your part."

Lindel just looked at him for a minute. Then she started to laugh. "You really don't get it, do you?"

"What?"

"All right. I do not want to work with you again. Two, I don't want to work with Brian. I think he's an incredible singer but I have no desire to have anything to do with him again. Why on earth would you think I would want to do this?"

"I thought you'd be excited," he said. "I thought it would be just the kind of thing you'd get into, musically, I mean."

She looked at him suddenly. "You haven't mentioned this to him, have you?"

"Of course not." Jeff looked offended. "Why would I, before talking to you?"

"Well, I wouldn't put it past you. He knew about the live album before I did," she said. "Anyway, forget it, Jeff. It's completely out of the question. I think, if that's all, that we should go."

"Well," Jeff said, "that isn't all, actually."

Lindel smiled a wry smile and shook her head slowly, unbelievingly. "Of course. What else do you want?"

"Oh, Lindel," he cried, "why does it have to be this way? I know we went through some bad times together but you know that I love you. And I can't believe that somewhere, deep down in your heart, that you still don't have some feeling for me. Lindel, don't you remember Brandy's, that first night in the rain . . . and all those Sunday afternoons with the bagels and the newspapers when we mapped out everything that was going to happen? And then it did, didn't it, baby? It happened just like we dreamed it. We had some good times, Lindel, you can't deny that."

She didn't say anything.

"I guess we should go," said Jeff, with a sigh of resignation. "I'm sorry, I really thought this was a good idea. I thought there might still be some affection. And now, since you're really more in the power position, I thought maybe you would be able to help."

"Help do what?"

"Talk to Brian for me," he said, looking at her straight in the eye.

"What?"

"Just talk to him," he pleaded.

She grabbed the edge of the table. "And say what? That he should sign with you? After all we went through? Are you mad? He'd never fall for it. More to the point, why should I?"

"Because you still care about us both." Jeff's words came faster now. He put his hand on her hand and held it so she couldn't pull away. "You know you still have some feelings. You can't help it. And you don't need either of us anymore, but he and I need each other. I need Brian to get a label deal. And he needs me, I can help him . . ."

"What would you do for him?" Lindel said.

"Are you kidding? You, of all people, know what I can do. Get that look off your face, you know what I mean. I could get him together. Get big stories in the press—lots of those people still owe me favors. Get him a movie. A solo album. I thought the idea of the two of you was dynamite, but you don't want to do it, okay, so you don't do it. Maybe I'll get another girl to do it with me . . ."

She smiled. "That won't work, Jeff, not with me, not anymore."

"Anyway, I can convince him to tour again. I know I can, especially if it's done the right way. The possibilities are endless. He needs a manager. He's never understood America, and I think he can trust me. Especially if you put in a good word for me."

"Lindel," Jeff added, looking for all the world like a scared little boy, "I need you."

"Marcia, are you asleep?" Lindel said into the phone. "Marcia, please wake up, I've got to talk to you."

"What time is it? Where are you? You sound like you're under water."

"The L.A. phone connections are awful. It's late, I'm sorry, it's about four your time, but I really need to talk to you."

"What's the matter?"

"I saw Jeff."

"Uh-oh. What happened? Where did you run into him?"

"I didn't run into him," Lindel said. "I had dinner with him."

"What?" Marcia was instantly awake.

"Oh, I know it sounds crazy, but I was so damn curious." Lindel was talking faster now. "He's been calling all week, leaving messages at the hotel and the studio, and I really wanted to hear what he had to say."

"Why didn't you ask him on the phone?"

"I knew you'd say that. I don't know. I just had this real curiosity about seeing him. He has a beard."

"Charming," muttered Marcia. "He must look divine. So? What happened? How is the little prince?"

"The same. Honestly, he's the same. Oh, a bit more pathetic but basically the same rap. He wanted to make up, to let bygones be bygones . . ."

"Amazing," Marcia said.

"Wait. You haven't heard the best. He wants to manage Brian."

"We heard that, didn't we?"

"Yes. Well, it seems that Brian's here in town, and Jeff wants me to see him."

"I'm not hearing this."

"I know. But I have a feeling that he and Brian have already discussed this. I think Brian might want to see me too, aside from the Jeff business, and somehow Jeff was feeling me out. What do you think?"

"This is all a bit too complicated for me at this hour," said Marcia. "Hang on a second, okay? I want to get some water."

Lindel waited for Marcia to get back on the phone. She stared across the room at the blank TV screen. The room was neat, clean; there was a bunch of pale green grapes on a white china plate next to the bed. She felt as if her life was in order again. She couldn't permit anyone to ever threaten that order.

Marcia was back on the phone. "Okay. Now. How do you feel?"

"About Brian? I don't know. Nervous. Kind of curious. What do you think?"

"Has he called?"

"No. But I think he will."

"You're not going to call him, are you?" Marcia said.

"No. But I can't swear that if he calls me I won't see him."

"Well, what's the worst that could happen?"

Lindel gave a short laugh. "That I'd fall in love with him all over again."

"Do you really think you could?"

"I don't know, I don't trust myself. No . . . I suppose not, not after all this time. I was just too hurt. And I feel too good about myself now to ever be back in that place again. Still . . ."

" . . . you want to see him," Marcia said.

"Well, you must admit, it is a temptation to ask him whatever happened to him."

"He might not give you a satisfactory answer. What can he say? That he's had amnesia for the last year?"

[380]

"So, you think I shouldn't see him?"

"Right. That's what I think."

"Well, he hasn't called yet."

"If he does, though . . . promise me you'll be careful, and let me know the minute anything happens."

"Okay. Thanks, Marsh. Go back to sleep. I'll talk to you tomorrow."

And they both hung up.

It was one in the morning when Lindel knocked on Brian's hotel room door. She waited almost a minute before she knocked again.

"Hang on," he yelled, "coming."

Brian answered the door wearing only a striped silk bathrobe. They looked at each other for a full ten seconds. He looked exactly the same as she had remembered.

"Pardon my appearance," he grinned. "I was just getting into the bath." He made a small, mock bow, and ushered her into the room. Funny, he seemed nervous too.

Lindel's eyes darted around the suite.

"It's just me and the usual clutter," he said. "Make yourself at home. I'll be back in two seconds, and we can have our meeting."

Did she imagine it, or was the word "meeting" delivered with a note of sarcasm? As he grabbed the bottle of Jack Daniels to take with him into the bathroom, she couldn't help but glance to see if he had anything on underneath his bathrobe. He didn't.

Brian had called in the middle of the night last night, after she'd talked to Marcia. He had sounded casual, as if she had spoken to him only minutes ago. He said he had a lot to tell her. Strange, she realized, she didn't have all that much she wanted to tell him.

She looked around the room. It wasn't as bad as she expected; he must have allowed a maid in to clean up. At least the usual room service tables weren't littering up the place. She lowered the stereo, which had been blasting an Otis Redding tape, only to have Brian shout from inside, "Hey, turn that up, will you? I can't hear it."

She turned the volume up, turned the TV set off, and walked over to the desk. There was some opened mail bearing English postmarks, some fan mail forwarded from his London office, and a copy of *Rolling Stone,* which he'd always loudly proclaimed he never read.

She almost laughed out loud. She hadn't seen him in over a year, and, as if driven by some old habit, she was snooping around his things. It was with a tremendous relief that she realized that she didn't need to do this anymore.

She walked over to the couch, sat down, and looked at the room service menu. Here she was, at one in the morning, waiting for Brian to make the next move. She had purposely chosen to come to his hotel, rather than invite him to hers. In a peculiar way, it made her feel more in control. She didn't want him in her room. This way, she was free to leave when she chose.

She noticed that he still covered the lamps with scarves, as he had always done in the old days. A Pignose amp was on the floor next to his Gibson guitar. Stacks of records and cassettes were piled next to the elaborate stereo system. Clothes overflowed from opened suitcases.

She checked her watch. He'd been in the bath for five minutes. How like him to take a bath while she waited. It was, somehow, part of a performance. She went to the door of the bathroom and shouted, "Mind if I take that record off and turn on the TV?"

"Suit yourself," he said. "Of course, if you're really bored, you can join me."

"No, thanks." She kept her tone light. "Let's keep this strictly business."

She wondered if his invitation had been serious. How many girls could he have had with him in hotel rooms this past year? He had only done a short tour of Europe, but still, she was sure she would need a pocket calculator to figure it out. Never again did she want to be with someone who was with so many women. Nor did she ever again want to worry about where someone was, what he was doing, whom he was with.

She walked over to the mirror above the fake fireplace. Ego had motivated her to look her best. Her hair fell in long ringlets down past her shoulders. She was tanned; a thin black dress clung to her body; and she wore the same high-heeled sandals that she had worn with him in London and in New Orleans. She wondered if he'd remember.

A few minutes later, he came out of the bathroom, still wearing only the silk bathrobe. He turned the TV sound down, dialed room service, and ordered some vanilla ice cream for himself and a bottle of wine. He looked at her questioningly.

"The wine is fine for me," she said.

"Make that two bottles of wine," he said into the phone. "Right. Pouilly-Fuissé."

She wanted to tell him that they wouldn't need two bottles, but she said nothing.

He sat down next to her, a bit too close, she thought, but she didn't move. Even without touching, she immediately felt his presence. All she had to do was turn her head the slightest bit, just lean toward him, and he would be kissing her. She knew it, she could have done it, and yet she felt that they couldn't be farther apart. Somehow he looked so . . . less larger than life than she had once thought. She tried to conjure up the vision of what he had looked like onstage. How awesome he'd been. It was hard to remember.

"So," he said. "What do you think I should do?"

She burst out laughing. "Typical. I haven't seen you for a year and here we go, talking about you."

He looked sheepish. "Sorry. It's just, well, I'm not really sure what I should say to you."

"Well, for a start," she said, "you might ask me how I've been."

"I know how you've been. Jeff told me. You're in terrific shape—I can see that—finishing your record, big plans for a tour coming up." He chuckled. "Madison Square Garden . . . I think that got to Jeff more than anything."

"Brian," she said softly, "that's not what I mean."

He didn't answer. He leaned over to the table and took a cigarette out of the rumpled pack.

She continued to look at him until he could no longer avoid her eyes. "Brian, why did you just disappear? Why didn't you ever call me? And when I called you, why didn't you call me back?"

He stretched his legs out in front of him, and stared straight ahead. He didn't say anything for a long while, then finally said, "It was just too much. I couldn't handle it. I knew I had to go back and do the record, and I honestly didn't know how to deal with you."

He stopped and looked at her. "I'm not very good at that sort of thing. At first I guess I thought that we could sort of just go in and out of each other's lives. Then it seemed . . . more, somehow, and I just had to split. I do that sometimes. But I've thought about you a lot, you know."

Oh Brian, she thought, if only you knew what I went through. If I'd known you were thinking about me just for one second I would have called you again and made sure we talked and maybe things would have been different. She felt sad, but said nothing.

He reached for her hand, and she let him hold it. Neither of them said anything for a few minutes. Then he said, "The music isn't even there for me anymore."

"What?"

"It just seems like it's all over . . ."

"I can't believe I'm hearing you say that."

"Well, I don't know," he said. "So many awful things have gone down. We had this riot in Germany . . ."

"Oh, I heard about that," she said. "The lighting rig?"

"No," he said. He seemed unusually eager to talk. "That was later on. This was an outdoor gig in Munich. We kind of had it hushed up a bit."

He talked in a low, serious voice. "The rain started coming down fifteen minutes into the concert. Sixty-five thousand kids were seated, festival style, and they were immediately drenched, but we were protected onstage by the overhead canopy. Then the wind started to blow the rain onto the stage, and Bernie had to go to the mike and say we'd take a fifteen-minute break. We all went backstage to the dressing room and figured that we'd wait until the rain stopped. Then the pandemonium started. The next thing we knew, all the security people were pushing and shoving us into limos. It was bizarre, I had no idea of what was happening. We just left. We figured that we'd have to go back the next night to do the rain date."

He stopped, looked at her, and then continued talking. "It wasn't until we got back to the hotel that we heard about the police, and the two killings. We didn't know that the tickets had said rain or shine. I saw those tickets afterwards and I couldn't believe it. They were so expensive—four color on silver stock. Anyway, at the next concert we got a bomb threat. And then that lighting rig. I just don't know." He stopped, then continued, "Why bother anymore?"

He went on. "Yet, Jeff promises me the moon. I can't believe that I'm still in a position to want to believe this stuff."

"I think Jeff can do it for you."

He looked at her with narrowed eyes. "How can you say that? I heard about what happened with you two."

"I think, maybe, he's learned. He's scared, and he needs you. And you can watch him more closely than I did. I was . . . ah . . . caught up in other things. You'll be good for each other."

He laughed. "Deserve each other, you mean."

"Well," she smiled, "that too."

"What about you?" he said. "Who takes care of your business now?"

"Marcia is my manager."

He raised an eyebrow. "Marcia? Really?"

"It's working out just fine," she said. "Marcia is a really close friend. She's smart. And I trust her completely. You know," she said quietly, "the last year was a bad time for me. There's nothing to say about it, not really, and I suppose that now we've had some distance from each other, we can realize all our mistakes. It's funny, I had a couple of thousand questions I wanted to ask you, but none of them seem to matter anymore."

There was a knock on the door, and Brian jumped up to answer it. It was the room service waiter with the wine and the ice cream. Brian signed the check, poured a glass of wine for Lindel, one for himself, and sat down. Only this time, he sat down in a chair, facing her.

So many images raced through her mind: seeing Brian backstage in Philadelphia, Brian singing "White Bird" with her for the first time, Brian leaving without a word.

Now he stared at her. "How's your new record? Are you making good music? So much of it is just music to dance to now."

She leaned forward, looking at him. "Rock and roll has always been music to dance to. That's what's so great about it. Of course, there's lots of predictable stuff these days. But every so often, something, someone, comes along who refuses to give in. And I don't feel my music is complacent. Dammit, Brian, neither is yours."

She clasped her hands around her knees and said, "How can you say that you don't care? Just look at some of those faces in the front row when they're looking at you onstage. Or imagine what it all means to a boy in Kansas City who doesn't want to work in a hardware store and his guitar is the only way out. You know we get more from them than we could possibly give back."

He just looked at her.

"I mean it," she said. "When you talk to someone who thinks your music is the most important thing in the world, how can that not make you feel strong? It breaks down all the barriers. It's . . . magic. That one hour on the stage might not be worth the twenty-three-hour wait all day to get there, but I've never found anything else for me that felt as honest. Or as good. Have you?"

He sat perfectly still for what seemed like a very long time. Finally, he mumbled, "I guess not."

"And besides," she joked, "I still don't really want to *work*."

They sat and drank in silence. Suddenly, Lindel wanted to be alone. She didn't want to talk to Brian anymore, not tonight. She felt trapped. She wanted to get out of there right now—and walk for awhile. Of course, this was Los Angeles and she couldn't walk, but she wanted to leave. She wished that planes went all night long. The pink umbrellas would be up on the terrace of the Tavern on the Green. She missed Madison Avenue at three in the morning. She wanted to go home. After all those months of being alone, frightened of the solitude, she now found that she relished it. Perhaps solitude came only at the wrong times.

Brian sensed her change of mood. "Do you want to go out somewhere?" he asked. He seemed lonely. But that was no longer her problem. She was sure that with one phone call he could take care of that.

"No," she said gently. "I think I'll go back to my hotel."

"Well, I see I'm as devastating as ever."

She looked him straight in the eye. She owed him no explanation. He had left her alone many nights without a word. But she said, "Brian, we just have different things to do right now. I'll always remember what we had. I cared for you very much."

"I care too," he said. "I hope you know that."

She realized that she had said "cared," while he talked in the present tense. She let it pass. She knew he didn't want her to go, and she knew that she didn't even have to make up her mind. In two minutes she'd be out of there, alone again, as if the slate had been wiped clean. The thought of it made her almost giddy.

She stood up to leave. He quickly got up, and moved in front of her. He put his arms around her, and looked into her eyes. After a very long minute, he saw whatever it was he was looking for, and let her go.

"Listen," he said, almost too casually, "we should stay in touch, you know. Jeff told me you don't want to do that duet album, but still, it's good to see you."

So, Jeff had lied about talking to Brian about the album. Some things never changed. "Oh, I don't know," she said, "maybe we will be able to do that album one day, who knows?" And she gave him a quick kiss and was out the door.

Downstairs, she got into the back seat of the waiting limousine. She pressed the button that lowered the glass partition, and asked the driver, "Do you have any tapes?"

"Sure. What do you want to hear?"

"Do you have any Vipers' albums?"

The driver opened the glove compartment, fumbled around, and said, "Only the last one."

"That's fine," said Lindel and as he took out a cassette, and inserted it into the tape deck, Brian's voice instantly hit her from all sides.

This was the album he had made after their tour. She knew the lyrics to all the songs, what each one was about, when they had been written, under what circumstances. He had sung many of them to her in their hotel rooms on tour. When this album first came out, she couldn't bear to hear it. Now she wanted to listen, carefully. Brian still had things to teach her.

She wondered if she was really safe. For the past few years she really had lived like someone trying to walk on glass.

She had started out full of hope, taking tentative steps. Walking slowly, then with more confidence, on a beautiful sheet of smooth, clear glass. One that could, without any warning at all, shatter into dozens of sharp, jagged pieces.

Being involved with rock and roll was like that; being in love was like that, too. But she never wanted to stop taking chances, to stop trying to walk on glass. Maybe one day there would be someone special with whom she could share her life. But for now, there was her music. It was the most honest thing she knew.

And somehow, just hearing the music made her feel strong, and she smiled as the car continued its way down Sunset.